Recipes from the Root Cellar

RECIPES *from the* ROOT CELLAR

250 Fresh Ways to Enjoy Winter Vegetables

Andrea Chesman

Storey Publishing

To the farmers who keep us well stocked with
wonderful vegetables all through the year.

The mission of Storey Publishing is to serve our customers by
publishing practical information that encourages
personal independence in harmony with the environment.

Edited by Margaret Sutherland and Nancy Ringer
Art direction and book design by Mary Winkelman Velgos
Text production by Vicky Vaughn Shea/Ponderosa Pine Design
   and Jennifer Jepson Smith

Illustration by © Susy Pilgrim Waters
Indexed by the author

Storey Publishing
210 MASS MoCA Way
North Adams, MA 01247
www.storey.com

Printed in the United States by Versa Press
10 9 8 7 6 5 4 3 2 1

LIBRARY OF CONGRESS CATALOGING-IN-PUBLICATION DATA
Chesman, Andrea.
  Recipes from the root cellar / by Andrea Chesman.
    p. cm.
  Includes index.
  ISBN 978-1-60342-545-2 (pbk. : alk. paper)
  1. Cookery, American. 2. Cookery (Vegetables) I. Title.
TX715.C52456 2010
641.5973—dc22
                          2010009608

Preface.............................vi

1 An Introduction to Winter Vegetables....1

2 Salads and Pickled Vegetables....41

3 Soups....91

4 Simple Vegetable Dishes....129

5 Beans, Rice, and Grains....201

6 Vegetarian Main Dishes....227

7 Main Dishes with Fish and Seafood....267

8 Main Dishes with Poultry....289

9 Main Dishes with Meat....319

10 Baked Goods and Desserts....349

Appendixes....364

Index....366

Preface

It all started when I fell in love with salsify, a root vegetable that once graced the tables of many a colonial American kitchen but has since fallen out of favor. Salsify, also known as oyster plant, is said to taste a bit like oysters. Being a major fan of oysters, I thought: What could be better than a root vegetable that lasts and lasts in a root cellar and tastes like oysters even though it grew in my landlocked garden?

I planted my first crop of salsify about 30 years ago. It is a stubborn vegetable to grow. As it emerges from the soil, it looks a lot like grass, so it is easy to weed away the entire crop. And so went the first harvest. After learning from that mistake, I planted again, only to be defeated by clay soil. Salsify likes a deep, loose loam and will produce only the skinniest, gnarliest, and most miserable roots if it isn't given the loose soil it likes. A vigorous and early thinning also is absolutely necessary to give the roots sufficient space. Did I mention that this plant is fussy about its growing conditions?

But the flavor! Even a meager harvest is worth the labor. Sautéed in butter, salsify has none of the cabbagey nuance of turnips and rutabagas, nor the (sometimes) overwhelming sweetness of carrots and beets. It tastes like, well, a cross between globe artichokes and Jerusalem artichokes. I think it is a terrific vegetable, but so demanding of my care as a gardener that I decided to form an organization called the National Association of Growers of Salsify (NAGS). As the founder of NAGS, my mission was to try and convince vegetable growers to tackle this challenging vegetable.

I wrote an open letter to the newsletter of the Middlebury Natural Foods Co-op, where I shop, entreating members to join NAGS. I promised no dues, no meetings, no t-shirts, no newsletter, no tote bags — just the satisfaction of promoting the spread of this worthy vegetable.

Have you even ever heard of salsify? No? Well, then you know how successful NAGS has been . . . .

By now most adventurous eaters have tasted their way around the globe. On demand, our supermarkets have stocked exotic fruits and vegetables from all over the planet, and the distinct flavors of Southeast Asia, Mexico, and Italy have profoundly changed the way we cook. We have dined on asparagus in January and come to regard the tomato as a year-round vegetable instead of the seasonal treat it truly is.

"Eat locally, spice globally" are the watchwords that have recently begun to inform tables across America. Best-selling works by Michael Pollen (*The Omnivore's Dilemma*) and Barbara Kingsolver (*Animal, Vegetable, Miracle*) have strongly influenced people to think about the choices they make when shopping for food and to buy locally grown foods that have not been shipped over long distances, accumulating many "food miles." This in turn means eating seasonal foods, at their peak, and fits in nicely with a growing aesthetic that celebrates fresh foods in their seasons. Eating locally means continuing the practice of enjoying the flavors of all the great cuisines of the world, while focusing the bulk of our choices on the foods that grow close to home.

The United States is blessed with a variety of different climates, but almost all locales experience some sort of winter, when few, if any, crops can be grown. Fortunately a variety of vegetables store well and can be enjoyed fresh instead of frozen or canned. These include root vegetables, hard-shelled winter squashes, and hardy greens that hold up well in the cold. Dried beans are another vegetable that keeps through the winter; heart-healthy, full of fiber, inexpensive, easily stored, and delicious, they make a lot of sense in the modern diet.

In recent years, I have grown to have a greater appreciation of turnips and rutabagas. I have served Brussels sprouts to a friend who said it was the first time she had enjoyed them, because I roasted them. I have made peace with parsnips, particularly if they are roasted. Kale is such a favored vegetable in my household that we actually miss it in the summer.

The hardy greens, winter squashes, and root vegetables have been largely ignored in recent years as people have been tempted by the unfamiliar and exotic. But a number of factors have converged to make eating long-keeping winter vegetables a good choice. Between an awareness that processed and exotic foods bring with them a significant carbon footprint and a shortfall in many household economies in the grip of a global recession, eating more humble vegetables makes sense. A lot of sense.

It is time for a rediscovery and celebration of the humble vegetables that have sustained so many people for so long before the advent of transcontinental shipping and overnight transoceanic flights. And if this includes a rediscovery of an unfamiliar root vegetable like salsify, then so much the better.

Eat More Vegetables

While dietary wisdom changes seasonally, the one piece of advice that never alters is "eat more vegetables." It turns out that a diet filled with winter vegetables isn't boring at all. The variety of dishes one can enjoy is infinite, and this collection of more than 250 recipes is only a beginning.

One theme that emerged in my experiments with using only winter vegetables in the winter is that favorite dishes are easily adapted. We love California nori rolls, a vegetarian sushi roll usually made with avocado, carrot, and scallions. Well, my experiments revealed that nori rolls made with carrots, turnips, and red cabbage are even more beautiful to behold and equally tasty. Love New England clam chowder? Try a scallop-and-salsify chowder. Love beef stew? Choose roots for the vegetables. This isn't about applying some abstract "locavore" discipline. This is just good eating.

Many people think that salads start with lettuce. And in the summer, this is often true in my house. For winter salads, napa cabbage, the tenderest of the cabbages, does nicely as a substitute for lettuce and other greens. Belgian endive is also a fine "green." We are all familiar with shredded-carrot salads. It turns out that shredded beets and turnips also make interesting salads. Shredding is a wonderful way to tame a winter vegetable; the act of shredding transforms a tough root or cabbage into a tender mouthful. There is no limit to the number of salads you can enjoy in the winter, without lettuce and without tomatoes.

Time for Experimenting and Slow Cooking

I think of summer as time for salad suppers, quick sautés and stir-fries, and grazing meals of fresh-picked corn, sliced tomatoes, and other raw vegetables, perhaps accompanied by breads and cheeses. Winter meals, on the other hand, are often slow-simmered soups and stews, braised meats, and bean pots. It doesn't seem unreasonable to tackle a new recipe or cooking technique, or to put something in the oven that will cook for hours. The extra heat provided by the active oven is welcome in the winter kitchen.

Slow cooking is sometimes needed to bring out the best in winter vegetables. Winter squashes, potatoes, and rutabagas aren't really edible raw. Turnips harvested young are delicious sliced raw and added to a salad instead of radishes. Turnips pulled up from the root cellar may be bitter or starchy raw, but delicious cooked. Likewise, a freshly harvested carrot is so sweet and juicy it is a shame to cook it. By late winter, however, much of the sugar has been converted to starch, and carrots may taste best cooked.

But don't avoid winter vegetables because they seem too time-consuming to prepare. Shredded root vegetables and winter squash, as well as hearty greens, cook quickly and are terrific in sautés and stir-fries. That's where some of the experimentation comes in. Trying out new flavorings and sauces keeps the sautés and stir-fries fresh tasting and interesting.

About the Recipes

I try to use what is known as "market measures" in my recipes. I don't call for "2 cups shredded carrots" when I can avoid it. Instead I call for "2 carrots, shredded." I don't want you stuck with half of a peeled carrot. (Okay, the peeled carrot will get eaten pretty quickly if left on the cutting board, but half of a celery root is just going to sit there.) You can figure that I am talking about an average-size carrot, so if you have only tiny carrots, use two or three. If you have only large carrots, don't hesitate to use the whole thing. If it makes a difference, I will let you know.

The same goes for shallots. Have you noticed how variable the size of a shallot has become? When I first started cooking, I found shallots sold as two small bulbs to a pack in the supermarket. Now I buy shallots at a natural foods store, and they are usually quite large and often contain two or more small bulbs within one skin. Don't fret about sizes. Just use whatever comes to hand — the recipe will work out regardless.

Market measures for greens are a little tricky. I have found that a "bunch" of kale from the farmers' market in the fall is more generous than a bunch of kale at a store later in the season. I could call for a certain number of stems, but the outer stems may contain double the volume of leaves of an inner stem, and a slightly wilted stem has less volume than a freshly harvested stem. In many recipes you can use the entire bunch, regardless of the measure called for in the recipe, but greens require a lot of space, and the volume of the entire bunch may be more than your pot can hold with the other ingredients. Where it matters, I have called for a cup measure. If you should harvest too much of a

Canned Tomatoes

Canned tomatoes are an integral part of the winter kitchen. It's no surprise that people can more tomatoes than any other vegetable. Tomatoes and tomato products can be processed safely in a boiling-water bath, while other vegetables require a pressure canner. Some years I can, but other years I don't find the time or my tomato harvest is too meager.

My recipes are designed to use either a 28-ounce can or a quart of home-canned tomatoes. They aren't precisely equivalent; there are about 3 cups of tomatoes in a 28-ounce can and anywhere from 3½ to 4 cups in a home-canned quart. Don't worry about the difference; just use whichever you have on hand.

green, or even strip too many leaves off the stems, keep the extra greens in a well-sealed bag for a few days in the refrigerator. They should survive nicely. When you measure the greens, lightly pack them into the measuring cup.

My mother never cooked a dish that didn't begin with "First, sauté an onion." My recipes are more varied than her home-style Jewish cooking, but when I write up my recipes, I find I am in a similar rut with garlic. I rarely make a dish that doesn't include garlic. If you don't like garlic, simply omit it, or substitute a tablespoon or two of minced onion or shallot. I prefer the subtle flavor of shallots over onions in most dishes. If you don't have a shallot on hand, substitute one-quarter of an onion.

I encourage you to substitute freely with ingredients you have on hand or ones you prefer. Collard greens and kale are often interchangeable, though I tend to use only kale

Bum Rap for Root Vegetables

The very dependability and nutritional value of root vegetables has led to their decidedly uncherished status. Take the rutabaga, for example. This relatively large root vegetable was the result of a chance hybridization between a turnip and cabbage, first appearing in eastern Europe in the seventeenth century. One of the few vegetables to last through long, cold Scandinavian winters, the rutabaga was the food of the poor, valued as an important source of nutrition. From Sweden, it reached Scotland, and from there it spread to the rest of Great Britain and to North America.

In continental Europe, it acquired a bad reputation during World War I, when it became a food of last resort. In the German Steckrübenwinter (rutabaga winter) of 1916–17, large parts of the population were kept alive on a diet consisting of rutabagas and little else; grain and potato crop failures combined with the disruptions of war had resulted in severe food shortages. After the war, most people were so tired of "famine food" that they turned against the dependable rutabagas that had sustained them. The fact that the rutabaga was also fed to livestock in winter didn't help its image.

Salsify, for its part, is associated with "gray meat" stews served in school lunches in France and Germany. These stews have done nothing to enhance the image of salsify and other root vegetables in Europe.

It is time for root vegetables to come out of the cellar and be fully appreciated for the nutritional and flavor powerhouses that they are. Roast a rutabaga today!

in recipes that originated in Italy, where kale is preferred. Collards may take some extra cooking to become tender, so judge doneness by the tooth, not the clock. Turnips and rutabagas are quite similar in flavor and texture and can be used interchangeably.

Many of my dishes call for mixed root vegetables. I prefer using a mixture for color and flavor, but you can certainly use just one type of vegetable, if that is what you have. Beware of using only carrots or parsnips, which can add too much sweetness to a dish. I recommend using golden beets in mixes of root vegetables; you can substitute red beets, but they will stain the entire dish a garish red that isn't always appealing.

I have identified those recipes that are vegetarian with a 🌀, and they make up the bulk of the book. Some of these recipes are vegetarian only if you so choose — either I have given a choice of broths that include a vegetable broth, or a vegetarian variation follows the main recipe. In my definition, vegetarian recipes may include dairy products and eggs.

About the Book

The first chapter is devoted to the vegetables: how to buy and store them, how to prepare them, and cooking tips that will ensure success with every recipe. I've suggested ways to cook the vegetables without following specific recipes. I've done the math to help you figure out how much a typical vegetable will yield if it is sliced or shredded. The rest of the book contains recipes. The recipes represent many winters of good eating in my household. I hope they lead to many delicious winters in yours.

An Introduction to Winter Vegetables

I love winter! The garden has been put to bed, and there are few outdoor chores that demand my attention. There is time for quilting and skiing. And plenty of time for cooking and having fun in the kitchen. What could be better?

The fresh vegetables that are available for cooking at this time of the year are the hearty greens, the members of the onion family, white potatoes and sweet potatoes, root vegetables, and winter squashes. Dried beans are also readily available. With the exception of beans, all of these vegetables can be stored in a root cellar with no time-consuming processing. Many are vegetables that have been neglected in winters of recent years in favor of frozen or imported summer vegetables. If you need information on how to choose, store, or prepare these vegetables, read on.

A QUICK GUIDE TO THE
VEGETABLES

I've organized the vegetables by family — all the greens together, all the root vegetables together, and so on. Here's an alphabetical listing of the vegetables to help you find specific ones along with the page number.

Beans (dried), 38

Beets, 24

Brussels sprouts, 4

Cabbage, 5

Carrots, 26

Celery root, 27

Collard greens, 8

Garlic, 12

Jerusalem artichokes, 18

Kale, 9

Leeks, 14

Mustard greens, 11

Onions, 16

Parsnips, 28

Potatoes, 20

Rutabagas, 29

Salsify, 31

Shallots, 17

Sweet potatoes, 21

Turnips, 34

Winter squashes, 35

Hearty Greens and Cabbages

HEARTY GREENS, as opposed to salad greens, stand up to cooking, though cabbage is delicious raw in a well-dressed salad. Hearty greens include Brussels sprouts, cabbage, collard greens, kale, and mustard greens. (Spinach, Swiss chard, turnip greens, and beet greens are tender greens that are mostly unavailable in the winter.) Most of the hearty greens belong to the Cabbage family, all descendants of the wild cabbage, *Brassica oleracea* var. *oleracea*.

These vegetables stand up to some pretty cold growing conditions in the garden and can be counted on to store reasonably well in a refrigerator or root cellar. Best of all, they are all very nutritious, ranking high as sources of vitamins A, C, and E and calcium and well regarded for their sulfur-containing phytochemicals, which are thought to provide significant protection against several different types of cancer. One of the best things you can do for the long-term health of your eyes is to enjoy a serving of greens a few times a week.

You could also call these greens *strongly flavored* or *assertive* greens, because their flavors are strong — even bitter sometimes. There are plenty of people who think they don't like the hearty greens. Usually these are people who are particularly sensitive to the bitterness of certain strongly flavored greens, such as mustard greens. You can tame the bitterness by blanching the vegetables for 5 to 7 minutes in plenty of boiling salted water, which will leach out some of the flavor compounds and give the greens a silken texture. Then prepare the recipe, sautéing or braising as the recipe directs. In my family, we love the bitterness, so I don't usually bother blanching.

When preparing leafy greens, you'll want to wash the leaves carefully; the more crinkled the leaves, the more likely they harbor grit or insects. The tough stems should be removed before cooking: Working one stem at a time, hold the stem in one hand and use the thumb and index finger of your other hand to strip the leaf off the stem. Discard the stem. Stack the leaves together, roll them into a cigarlike shape as best as you can, and chop into ribbons. Especially tough greens, such as collards, will cook more quickly if the ribbons are thinly cut.

It is challenging to measure greens accurately. If the greens are fresh out of the garden, the leaves stripped off the stems will be resistant to being packed in a cup, producing more volume. A wilted bunch, on the other hand, compresses into a cup easily, resulting in less volume. At the beginning of the harvest season, greens have lighter stems, yielding a greater volume of leaves per pound. At the end of the season, though, the stems are woody and heavy, yielding a lesser volume of leaves per pound. The solution to this problem? Use more or less greens, depending on what you have on hand. Use your judgment, and don't worry about getting the measurements exactly right.

You can use kale, collards, and mustard greens interchangeably in most recipes. Collards seem to require a little extra cooking, in my opinion, so adjust the timing as needed when swapping greens in a recipe.

Brussels Sprouts

Brussels sprouts are gaining popularity. A good indication of this trend is that they are becoming available almost year-round in the supermarket, whereas not so long ago the supply ended around the first of the year. Their rise in appeal may have something to do with the fact that many people have discovered that their unruly flavor can be tamed by roasting.

Unruliness can be avoided entirely if you harvest your own Brussels sprouts or buy fresh ones (since the strong flavors develop in storage) and do not overcook them. The flavor also benefits from a light frost; red- or purple-tinged leaves are a good sign that the sprouts have experienced weather cold enough to improve their flavor.

Brussels sprouts do come from Brussels, or at least Belgium, where the plant was developed as a dwarf cultivar of savoy cabbage. The "sprouts," which emerge from the tall stalk, are made up of tightly packed leaves, each resembling a miniature cabbage head.

Availability

Freshly harvested Brussels sprouts appear in eastern markets in the fall and generally last through the end of December. The harvest season in coastal California is year-round, with both spring and fall crops.

Storage

Since Brussels sprouts withstand the cold well, there is no reason to harvest them until the ground begins to freeze. Sprouts will keep in perforated plastic bags in the refrigerator or root cellar for 3 to 5 weeks; they keep longest in damp, cool conditions (near 32°F, with 90 to 95 percent humidity). An excellent, low-fuss way to store the Brussels sprouts you grow yourself is to lift the whole stalk out of the garden, strip off the leaves, and hang the stalk from the rafters of your root cellar.

How to Buy

Brussels sprouts grown in warmer climates tend to be sweetest when picked small. In cold climates, Brussels sprouts taste best after a few frosts, when the leaves are tinged purple or red. Select compact heads with no hint of yellow. The cut end should be dry, not slimy, and green, not dark brown. If you are picking the sprouts individually from a bin, select ones that are uniform in size so they will cook evenly.

Preparation

Trim away the ends of each sprout. Remove any damaged or yellowed leaves. Cut in halves or quarters as needed to make them uniform in size. If you're going to add them raw to salads or use them in a stir-fry or sauté, you can slice the sprouts into thin ribbons (chiffonade).

Cooking Ideas

The cabbagey flavor of Brussels sprouts is most easily tamed by roasting. But don't stop there. Stir-fries with garlic, ginger, and sesame oil do wonders for the flavor. Brussels sprouts are also excellent sautéed, particularly when paired with strong flavors, such as smoked bacon or sausage. They are lovely braised and can be finished with a touch of cream or mustard.

Brussels Sprouts Math

1 pound Brussels sprouts = 3 to 3½ cups whole sprouts = 3 cups halves

Cabbage: Green, Red, Savoy, and Chinese

I regard green cabbage as the workhorse of the winter kitchen. It is the backbone of winter salads and stir-fries. It melts into sweet tenderness when cooked slowly in braises or soups. It is easily pickled as sauerkraut. If I had to choose just one vegetable to get me through the winter, I would probably choose cabbage.

Long-keeping cabbage comes in four basic forms. Green cabbage, which has a white center, is the most common. Red cabbage looks like green cabbage, except for its vibrant maroon color; it tends to be tougher in texture than green cabbage and turns a blue-purple when cooked. As a color accent in a salad, red cabbage is exceptional. Savoy cabbage has tender, crinkled leaves with a mild flavor. Savoy cabbage is increasingly rare in U.S. markets but worth seeking out. When cooked, it holds its green color well, making it an attractive choice for a stir-fry or sauté. It is the cabbage of choice for cabbage rolls. Chinese cabbages fall into two groups: *Brassica rapa chinensis* and *Brassica rapa pekinensis* (sometimes you just have to resort to Latin to keep it all straight). The chinensis group includes bok choy (also called pac choi) and has juicy white stems with dark greens attached. The pekinensis group includes napa cabbage, which is a mild-flavored cabbage with long, oval-shaped bunches of pale green leaves. Both types of cabbage are excellent in stir-fries, and napa cabbage makes excellent salads. Baby bok choy is a treat that should be lightly steamed and enjoyed with a drizzle of soy sauce and sesame oil.

Availability

Cabbage of every type is available in supermarkets all year long; it is grown and harvested year-round in California. Savoy cabbage is not commonly stocked in supermarkets, so you are much more likely to see it in the fall at farmers' markets.

Storage

Solid, firm heads keep well in a root cellar at 32° to 40°F and 90 percent humidity (the same conditions root vegetables require). Place the heads on shelves, several inches apart, with the root ends up, or suspend them from rafters by the root. You might consider wrapping the heads in newspaper, which will help them retain moisture. If your root cellar is in your basement and not well ventilated to the

outdoors, you may find that green cabbage releases an unpleasant odor that creeps into the house (Chinese cabbages do not).

Green and red cabbages keep better and longer than savoy cabbage and Chinese cabbage. If you've grown Chinese cabbages, simply pull up the plants, roots and all, and replant them in boxes of dirt in your root cellar for long-term storage. Or refrigerate in a perforated plastic bag for a week or two.

The conventional wisdom is that unwashed, firm heads will keep up to 2 weeks in the refrigerator. In reality, cabbage keeps for at least a month. As cabbage ages, it loses its vitamin C content. It also toughens and is best suited to being cooked rather than used in salads.

How to Buy

Buy whole heads when possible. Choose unblemished, compact heads that are heavy for their size, which means they have not lost their moisture.

Preparation

Remove the outer leaves of the cabbage, then rinse the head under cold water. Slice the cabbage into quarters and cut out the core, then slice, grate, or shred as the recipe requires. Specialized cabbage slicers are available, but a food processor or a sharp knife works just fine.

If a cabbage you want to use raw is tough, sprinkle it with salt and let it drain in a colander for at least 30 minutes. Then taste for saltiness. If it is too salty, rinse under cold running water. If it isn't too salty, just use it as is, but adjust the salt the recipe requires and season with more salt only if needed. Salting and draining cabbage in this manner before dressing it softens the cabbage and prevents the dressing from becoming watery.

Cabbage loses volume when cooked, so don't worry when a dish calls for 8 to 12 cups of sliced cabbage; it will quickly cook down.

Cooking Ideas

Above all, do not overcook cabbage, which results in a mushy texture and a strong flavor. Cabbage can be delicious boiled (think corned beef and cabbage), but overcooked boiled cabbage is what has given cooked cabbage a bad name. It can also be steamed. It really shines when briefly cooked in a stir-fry. Both green and Chinese cabbage can be stir-fried with every kind of meat or tofu and are compatible with any Asian sauce or seasoning. They are used as the filling for spring rolls, egg rolls, and all manner of dumplings.

Slow cooking renders cabbage meltingly tender and sweet. Try slowly sautéing a mixture of cabbage and onion over low heat for 10 to 20 minutes. Combine it with freshly cooked egg noodles and sour cream to make a delicious eastern European dish known as haluska.

There are plenty of really terrific "peasant-style" cabbage dishes that should not be ignored, beginning with bubble-and-squeak, which takes its name from the sound cabbage is supposed to make as it cooks: Sauté shredded cabbage in butter, then add leftover mashed potatoes and press down to make a pancake. Brown on both sides. Or braise cabbage in beer with sausages: Brown sausages in a large skillet, add beer, and simmer until the sausage is almost cooked through. Add sliced or shredded cabbage, cover, and continue to simmer until the cabbage is tender crisp and the sausage is fully cooked. Chlopski is a similar dish made with bacon and braised in water, wine, or broth. Caldo gallego (Spanish) and garbure (French) are rib-sticking soups made with white beans, cabbage, and an accent meat, such as bacon, salt pork, or ham, for flavor.

Of course, cabbage does not need to be cooked at all to be delicious. Coleslaw is an all-American standard, and it can be made in dozens of different ways (see pages 50 to 56).

Cabbage Math

1 small head green cabbage = about
    2 pounds, trimmed

1 medium head green cabbage = about
    3 pounds, trimmed

1 medium head bok choy = about
    2 pounds

1 pound cabbage = 4 cups shredded =
    2 cups cooked

Collard Greens

I once met a grower who spends half the year in Florida and half the year in Vermont. When in Vermont, he can't grow enough beet greens to meet demand; in Florida, the beet greens don't move but the collards fly out of the market. Collard greens just aren't that well-liked in New England, but they are deliciously popular in the South.

This member of the Cabbage family has flat, round, blue-green leaves on tough, fibrous stems. Collards and kale are genetically quite similar and both are ancient plants, much like the original nonheading cabbage from which all the Cabbage family plants evolved. Like kale, you can harvest the outer stems of the collards (roughly one-quarter of the plant at a time) to keep the plant producing more leaves.

Collards probably came to the New World from Africa via slaves who brought them into plantation kitchens. The tradition of long-simmering collards and drinking the juices from the greens (known as "pot likker") is of African origin. Traditionally, collards are eaten on New Year's Day, along with black-eyed peas or field peas and cornbread, to ensure wealth in the coming year, perhaps in reference to the leaves' resemblance to folded bills.

If you enjoy eating kale, you are likely to enjoy eating collard greens, and the two can be used interchangeably in most recipes. Collard greens do not have to be cooked until they are a soft, Southern-style mess o' greens if a more toothsome dish is desired. But I highly recommend trying Southern-style greens (simmered with salt pork, bacon, or a ham bone, and doused with apple cider vinegar) before making any judgments on what you *think* you like.

Collards, like kale and other greens, cook down to one-quarter to one-eighth of their original volume. A brown-paper grocery bag filled with unpacked leaves is just about the right amount for serving collards to a family of four as a main course.

Availability

Collard greens are available from September through June and are considered best after a few light frosts.

Storage

Where winters are mild, keep the collard greens in the garden. Where winters are harsh, leave them in the garden until a killing frost or heavy snow threatens. Then harvest the leaves and store them in perforated plastic bags in a cold, damp root cellar (32° to 40°F, 90 to 95 percent humidity) for a week or two, or in the refrigerator for about a week. Blanched or cooked collard greens can be frozen.

How to Buy

Avoid yellow or limp leaves. You'll need about 2 pounds to feed four people as a side dish.

Preparation

Wash the leaves carefully to get rid of any grit and insects. Stories abound of people washing large quantities of greens in a washing machine, but I can't verify that it is a good idea. Remove the tough stems before cooking: Grasp the end of the stem with one hand. Run the thumb and index finger of your other hand right along the stem, ripping off the leaf.

Cooking Ideas

You can use collards anywhere you would use kale, but slightly increase the cooking time. Collards can also replace cabbage in soups and stews.

Collards are good as a sauté: Blanch for 10 to 15 minutes, then drain. Sauté with olive oil and garlic or butter and pine nuts and finish with a dusting of Parmesan. You can also cook blanched collards with rice or grits, or you can combine them with canned or cooked beans, seasoned with hot sauce or vinegar.

For traditional Southern-style collards, cook the greens slowly in water with a ham bone or piece of salt pork until meltingly tender. Serve over cornbread, and pass hot sauce and vinegar on the side.

Collard Math

2 pounds collards = 1 pound collard leaves (with stems removed and discarded) = about 12 cups lightly packed = 2 cups cooked

Kale

Like collard greens, kale is a nonheading cabbage. It has been grown extensively in Europe, where it is more common than collards. It is more tender than collards, but the two are often used interchangeably in recipes.

There are several varieties of kale, and each variety has its fans. Blue-green curly kale, the type most common in the United States, is known simply as kale or curly kale. Lacinato kale goes by many names, including Tuscan kale, dinosaur kale, black kale, and *cavalo nero*. Its leaves are a dark, dark green and more ridged than curly. Red kale, also known as Russian kale or Siberian kale, has red-veined, greenish purple leaves that are frilly and shaped somewhat like oak leaves. The varieties can be used interchangeably, though curly kale is the best choice for roasting.

Availability

Kale is available pretty much all year long, but the best-tasting kale is a cold-weather crop.

Storage

Kale is very hearty in the garden and will easily withstand many frosts and even snow if kept under a blanket of mulch. Like collards, the larger, outer leaves can be harvested (as much as one-quarter of the plant), allowing the plant to continue producing leaves. Keep store-bought kale in perforated plastic bags in the refrigerator for about 4 days. Kale will yellow and become limp and bitter if stored too long.

How to Buy

Kale is sold in bunches, and the bunches vary in weight. Figure you will need to buy about ½ pound per serving. Choose Lacinato, if possible, for Italian-style dishes. Avoid leaves that are limp or yellowed.

Preparation

Wash well. The curly leaves, in particular, may harbor grit and insects. Remove the tough stems before cooking: Grasp the end of the stem with one hand. Run the thumb and index finger of your other hand right along the stem, ripping off the leaf.

Cooking Ideas

You can enjoy kale steamed, blanched, sautéed, stir-fried, even roasted (see page 158). It is a versatile green, much less bitter in flavor than other greens. It can be used interchangeably in recipes calling for cabbage, collards, or mustard greens.

Although cabbage is more typically called for in Chinese recipes, kale does just fine in stir-fries and paired with Chinese seasonings. It holds its color well and, when sliced thinly, doesn't require much cooking time in a stir-fry or sauté. It is best matched with assertive flavors, such as soy sauce, garlic, and bacon. There are many delicious rustic soups that are based upon kale, including caldo verde (Portuguese kale soup; see page 108).

Kale Math

1 pound kale = about 12 cups lightly packed = 1¼ to 1½ cups cooked

Mustard Greens

Mustard greens are the leaves of the mustard plant, *Brassica juncea.* While the seeds are used to make yellow ballpark mustard, the peppery greens are a delicious addition to the winter table. The greens are rich in vitamins A and C and a good source of calcium and iron.

In the United States, mustard greens are consumed mainly in the South, where they grow well in the mild winters. Some people find mustard greens a little too assertive in flavor, but they are a favorite in my household.

Mustard greens are available in a number of different varieties. They range in color from emerald green to deep purple, and the leaves may be crumpled or flat, with toothed, scalloped, frilled, or lacy edges.

The flavor of mustard greens is best when the crop is grown in cool weather; hot, dry weather enhances the peppery bite. As the plant grows, you can snap off individual leaves, leaving the growing tip to produce replacements. Leaves of 3 to 4 inches in length are tender enough to use in salads. The plant will continue to grow even when exposed to light frosts.

Availablity

Mustard greens are found in the fall and early spring in northern climates. They are found from January through April in the South.

Storage

The best storage for mustard until the first heavy frost is in the garden. Once harvested, mustard greens should be stored in a plastic bag in the refrigerator. They should keep fresh for 3 to 4 days.

How to Buy

Like other greens, mustard greens are sold in bunches, and the bunches vary in weight. Figure you will need to buy about ½ pound per serving. Avoid leaves that are limp, yellowed, or browned.

Preparation

Wash well. The curly leaves may harbor grit and insects. Remove the tough stems before cooking: Grasp the end of the stem with one hand. Run the thumb and index finger of your other hand right along the stem, ripping off the leaf.

Cooking Ideas

You can enjoy mustard greens steamed, blanched, sautéed, stir-fried, and even roasted. They can be used interchangeably in recipes calling for kale or collards. They are best matched with assertive flavors, such as soy sauce, garlic, and bacon.

Mustard Greens Math

1 pound mustard greens = about 12 cups
  lightly packed = 1¼ to 1½ cups cooked

The Onion Family

UNLESS YOU HAVE A WINDOW BOX providing you with year-round fresh herbs, chances are that once the garden has been put to bed and the farmers' markets are shuttered, the vegetables in the Onion family — garlic, leeks, onions, and shallots — provide the flavor underpinnings for most of the dishes you cook.

Garlic and onions are pretty heady vegetables, but you can get a whisper of their flavors by cooking with shallots or leeks instead. The onion family, then, provides a range of intensity from mild to strong. And, with the exception of leeks, these vegetables can be stored in a cool, dry spot. How convenient!

Garlic

Garlic is thought to have originated in central Asia, and its cultivation dates back at least as far as the Egyptians, who believed that the bulb strengthened the body and prevented disease. Nicholas Culpeper's *The Complete Herbal,* published in England in 1652, credited garlic with healing the bites of mad dogs and venomous snakes, ridding children of worms, and curing ulcers.

Scientific research has since substantiated some of these claims. For example, in 1858 French chemist Louis Pasteur described garlic's antibacterial properties after observing that bacteria he exposed to the bulb died. Subsequent research has also shown that garlic can guard against blood clots and high blood pressure and may have a role in cancer prevention.

It may be the cure for whatever ails you, but it does cause a strong odor on the breath, which explains why garlic was shunned by cooks in the United States in the nineteenth century. It was only with the popularity of French and Italian cooking in this country, that the variously called "truffle of Provence," "stinking rose," and "Bronx vanilla" gained complete acceptance.

There are more than 600 cultivars of garlic representing a range of flavor from mild to hot. When you find a type of garlic you like, grow some. Although there are cultivars for different climates, if you can grow your own seed garlic, it will adapt to conditions in your garden over time. That said, growing conditions also affect the flavor of garlic, so the same variety in the same garden varies in flavor from year to year, depending on the amount of heat, sunlight, and water the garden receives. Furthermore, garlic is usually milder soon after it is pulled from the ground, developing more flavor in storage.

Garlic grows as a bulb underground, with each bulb composed of some 10 to 20 cloves. It adds tremendous flavor to a dish, with the pungency of its flavor directly related to how you prepare it. In general, the finer the chop, the stronger the flavor; however, the longer it is cooked, the mellower the flavor. Garlic added at the end of cooking will result in a stronger flavor than garlic prepared the same way but added earlier. Raw garlic is much stronger in flavor than garlic that is sautéed in oil or roasted.

Availability

Garlic is available year-round because it stores well.

Storage

How well garlic keeps depends on how well it is handled from harvest on. The bulbs should be harvested when the tops begin to die back, before the individual cloves burst through their papery sheaths. Remove all loose dirt and let the garlic cure for a week or two in a sheltered, well-ventilated spot. Then snip off the roots close to the bulb and either braid the tops or snip them off. Store in a cool dry place, such as an unheated closet. When you bring garlic into the kitchen, store in a basket or open container out of direct light.

How to Buy

Look for large, firm heads with plenty of dry, papery covering and no soft spots or signs of shriveling. Heads showing signs of sprouting are past their prime and were probably not dried properly. Garlic that is too old will crumble under gentle pressure from the fingers. Avoid little boxes of supermarket garlic; these are sure to be improperly stored and old.

Preparation

Strip off some of the papery covering from the bulb, then break off as many cloves as required. Garlic cloves come in a wide variety of sizes, so the numbers given in a recipe should be treated as a rough guide. Feel free to increase or decrease the number of cloves according to your preference.

The easiest way to peel garlic is to smash the whole unpeeled clove with the side of a cleaver or wide chef's knife, causing the skin to separate from the clove. And then the clove is well on its way to being minced. You can peel them one by one with a paring knife, but it is quite a tedious process. You can also cover the cloves with boiling water for 1 minute, which separates the skins from the cloves and makes it easier to peel.

Toward spring, a greenish sprout may emerge from the cloves, signaling a break in dormancy. The sprouts are somewhat bitter, but not so much that you will notice it in most dishes. It can be removed or left, as you prefer.

Garlic cloves are usually minced or crushed. Some people prefer mincing with a chef's knife (which has already been dirtied when you smashed the clove to peel it). Others prefer using a garlic press, which crushes the cloves and forces out a tiny purée of garlic.

Cooking Ideas

To roast garlic, cut off the top of the bulb so that some of the cloves are exposed. Drizzle with olive oil and cover (or wrap the bulb in aluminum foil) and roast for about 20 minutes at 350°F. You should be able to squeeze the roasted cloves from their papery linings. Roasted garlic makes a tasty addition to many dishes, from soups to sauces to salad dressings.

Dishes that taste just of garlic are rare but wonderful to the garlic lover. Aioli, homemade mayonnaise flavored with garlic, is the ultimate expression of raw garlic flavor. Find a lemony version on page 181 and use it to top everything from roasted vegetable salads to roasted fish. The cream of garlic soup on page 106 is an expression of how slow cooking can coax a gentler, kinder garlic to full expression. And in between, just about every dish from stir-fries to panfries starts with sautéing garlic in olive oil. Just don't let the garlic scorch or turn black; this will impart a bitter flavor to the dish. If the garlic does burn, it is best to discard the oil and garlic and start over.

Garlic Math

1 clove garlic = ½ teaspoon minced

Leeks

Leeks in most gardens will usually last well into December, making them a choice vegetable to grow. They offer the "green" of a fresh summer vegetable, suitable for serving as a side dish, but impart a delicate oniony flavor when cooked in a soup, stew, or casserole.

That the leek has been called "the poor man's asparagus" comes as no surprise to anyone who has cooked with them. Basically, any recipe that

uses asparagus can be made with leeks with surprisingly good results, though the flavor is quite different. The irony, however, is that leeks in the United States are neither particularly plentiful nor inexpensive; the nickname arose in France, where leeks are both.

Availability

Leeks are available year-round, but they are more plentiful in fall and winter.

Where the temperature remains above freezing, leeks may be harvested all through the winter, as in market gardens in Europe. If you grow your own leeks, you will find that they can be harvested any time up to a killing freeze.

Storage

Leeks do quite well in the garden, surviving frosts and even a few snowfalls, especially if protected with a good layer of mulch. Alternatively, you can dig them up and replant them in a box in the root cellar, where they will keep for several months. Dug up, they will keep in a perforated plastic bag in the refrigerator for a couple of weeks.

How to Buy

Choose leeks that are straight, firm, and intact. The green part should not be dry, yellow, or blemished. The greater the proportion of white to green, the greater the amount of usable vegetable.

Preparation

Leeks often harbor quite a bit of dirt between their leaves. To prepare leeks, first cut away the tough dark green tops and peel off any tough outer leaves. (Save these for making broth.) Trim off the root end, leaving you with the white and tender pale green parts. Make a long vertical slit through the center of the leek or slice it in half vertically. Wash under cold running water, flipping through the leaves to expose the inner surfaces to the water. Pat dry.

If you are slicing the leeks anyway, you can cut them into slices before washing. To wash, immerse the slices in a bowl of water. Swish the slices, then let the water settle. The grit will all fall to the bottom of the bowl. Lift out the clean slices and drain well in a colander.

Cooking Ideas

Thin leeks are a delicacy; blanch them briefly, toss with a vinaigrette, and garnish with crumbled hard-cooked egg. Bigger, thicker leeks are more fibrous but still delicious and never strong in flavor. They are excellent in most soups and can usually replace onions with good results.

Cook sliced leeks slowly in butter and serve them as a bed for baked or sautéed fish. Or slice them and blanch in salted boiling water until tender, about 5 minutes. Drain and transfer to a shallow baking dish and sprinkle them with freshly grated cheddar or Parmesan. Pop into a 300°F oven and bake for about 10 minutes, until the cheese melts.

Sauté sliced leeks in olive oil or with bacon and use to top pizza or pasta. Take advantage of leek's affinity for potatoes and add to chowders, cream of potato soup, mashed potatoes, scalloped potatoes, and gratins.

Leeks Math

1 large leek = ½ to ¾ pound

1 pound leeks = 6 cups sliced

Onions

Despite the popularity of onion rings at hamburger joints and "blooming onions" at certain steakhouses, in most cases onions are used as flavoring rather than served as side dishes. Although there are many types of onions, onions grown specifically for storage are essential in the winter kitchen. They may have white, red, or yellow skins, but they can be used interchangeably. Storage onions are distinguished from green onions, sometimes called spring onions, which require refrigeration and are mild in flavor.

As a flavoring agent, the onion appears in many different types of dishes. In Cajun cooking, it is part of the trinity of flavors that includes celery and peppers. Quintessential eastern European Jewish cooking combines chicken fat with onions, while Hungarian cooking typically includes onions, lard, and paprika. Many French dishes begin with a mirepoix — a mixture of diced onion, carrots, and celery — perhaps sautéed in butter with herbs. A similar mixture in Italy, sautéed in olive oil, is called a soffrito.

Availability

Because they store so well, onions are available year-round.

Storage

Onions will keep best if they are properly cured, and this means that they must be allowed to fully mature in the ground. When more than half the tops in a row have browned and bent over, drag a rake over the row (teeth-side up) and knock down the remaining tops. Leave the plants for another week to fully die back, then spread them on screens to cure in the sun for 3 to 7 days. Cut off the tops, leaving a 1-inch stub, and dry in the shade for another 2 to 3 weeks. Then store them in a cool, dry spot with plenty of ventilation. Moisture will cause rot. Well-cured onions will keep at room temperature for about a month. Sweet onions, such as Vidalias, do not store as well as regular onions.

How to Buy

Look for dry onions, well covered with crackling, papery skins. Avoid any that show green sprouts emerging from the stems. I choose my onions by size. I prefer smaller ones because I am unlikely to put a huge onion in a single dish for fear it will overwhelm other flavors.

Preparation

Peel onions before using unless you are making broth and want the skins to impart color. To peel small pearl onions, put the onions in a bowl and cover with boiling water. When the water has cooled, drain. The skins will slip off easily.

If you aren't going to use a whole onion, remove slices from the stem end, but leave the root end in place; this will prevent the onion from falling apart.

Cooking Ideas

Cooking sweetens onions and tames their heat. The longer the cooking, the sweeter the onion becomes. Many recipes call for sautéing the onion until softened, about 3 minutes. At this point the flavor of the onion is fairly sharp and the texture still crisp. If you continue to sauté for 10 minutes or more, the onion will sweeten and become golden in color. If you continue to cook for about 30 minutes, the onions will brown and the sugars will caramelize. Caramelized onion is a traditional topping for hamburgers and steaks. Add stock to caramelized onions and you have an instant onion soup.

Onions can also be baked or roasted whole to serve as an accompaniment to roasted or grilled meats. Peel the onions, slice a little off the bottoms so they will sit flat in a pan, drizzle them with olive oil, and bake at 425°F for 1 hour.

Onion Math

1 pound = 4 medium onions = 4 cups diced

Shallots

Shallots are prized for their delicate flavor, which is less aggressive than that of either garlic or onion. They grow somewhat like garlic, with a head composed of multiple cloves, but they arrive at the market usually broken into individual cloves. The skin color can vary from pale brown to pale gray to rose, and the off-white flesh is usually tinged with green or purple. They are used both raw and cooked.

Availability

Shallots are dried and cured much like onions and are available year-round.

Storage

Store shallots as you would onions.

How to Buy

Look for plump, dry shallots with no sign of sprouting.

Preparation

Shallots are peeled before they are minced or chopped, like onions.

Cooking Ideas

Shallots are classically used to flavor vinaigrettes. They are often sautéed in butter or olive oil and used to flavor sauces.

Shallot Math

1 pound shallots = 4 cups chopped
1 medium shallot = 2 tablespoons minced

Tubers

OF ALL THE FOODS that originated in the New World, potatoes may be the most significant — or at least the most densely caloric. Both regular potatoes and sweet potatoes had their origins in South America, and both are tubers, though the similarities pretty much end there.

When distinguishing regular potatoes from sweet potatoes, we might say "white potatoes," but that is certainly misleading, since potatoes come in many colors, including blue, red, pink, and yellow, as well as the familiar brown with white flesh. Sweet potatoes are even more confusing, because sweet potatoes are sometimes called yams, which they most certainly are not. (Yams are starchy, not sweet. They grow in tropical climates, where they can reach 7 feet in length, with flesh ranging in color from off-white to yellow to pink to purple and skins from off-white to a dark brown.)

Potatoes are America's most popular vegetable according to the U.S. Department of Agriculture's Economic Research Service; the typical American consumes more than 140 pounds of them every year (compared with 50 pounds per year for tomatoes, the next most popular vegetable). On the other hand, sweet potatoes are considered the most nutritious vegetable. Nutritionists at the Center for Science in the Public Interest (CSPI) ranked the sweet potato number one in nutrition of all vegetables. Clearly potatoes are prizewinners in the vegetable family.

Like potatoes, Jerusalem artichokes originated in the New World. Their roots sustained Native Americans but have not been widely adopted by modern cooks. The slightly sweet roots taste like a cross between potatoes and globe artichokes, if you can imagine that.

Jerusalem Artichokes

The Jerusalem artichoke, a member of the Sunflower family, is an edible tuber sometimes called the Canadian potato or sunchoke. A native of the Americas, it was first described by Samuel de Champlain, who discovered it in his explorations of Lake Champlain in the 1600s.

The tubers grow underground like potatoes, but they are harder to harvest because they cling to their roots and become entwined. Any tubers left in the ground will reseed themselves, which can result in the plants spreading like weeds. The plants grow from 3 to 12 feet high and have large leaves and bright yellow flowers that are 1½ to 3 inches in diameter. They grow well in almost any soil but do best when it's alkaline. They are a common sight growing wild along fencerows in New England.

Jerusalem artichokes are starchy, like potatoes, but the starch is in the form of inulin, a polysaccharide from which fructose can be produced. Not everyone can digest inulin easily, and some people find that it causes a great deal of gastric distress. For this reason, sample the root carefully when first eating it to avoid what John Goodyer, an early English adapter, wrote in the 1600s: "But in my judgement, which way soever they be drest and eaten they stir up and cause a filthie loathesome stinking winde with the bodie, thereby causing the belly to bee much pained and tormented, and are a meat more fit for swine, than men."

Availability

Jerusalem artichokes are harvested beginning in the fall, after a few frosts have sweetened them, through early winter, for as long as the soil can be worked. They may be harvested again in early spring.

Storage

Although you can store Jerusalem artichokes for a few weeks buried in sand in a cold root cellar, they overwinter nicely and are best stored in the ground. Once harvested, they should be stored in a perforated bag in the refrigerator, where they will keep for 1 to 2 weeks.

How to Buy

Choose firm, unwrinkled tubers with a minimum of knobs.

Preparation

To peel or not to peel is the question. If the tuber has a minimum of knobs, it isn't difficult to peel, and it looks better that way. But if you do peel the tubers, drop them into acidulated water (1 tablespoon vinegar or lemon juice added to 4 cups water) to keep them from discoloring. If you don't want to peel, then give the tubers a good scrubbing with a vegetable brush. They can be cooked whole or sliced.

Cooking Ideas

Jerusalem artichokes can be thinly sliced and added to salads, much like water chestnuts. Their flavor is more developed when cooked, and they are best roasted (see page 159). They can be cooked alone or with potatoes and mashed. They are also quite good pickled — just adapt your favorite dilly bean or bread-and-butter recipe.

Jerusalem Artichoke Math

1 pound Jerusalem artichokes = 6 cups whole = 3 cups sliced

Potatoes

"All that meat and no potatoes," sings Louis Armstrong in a famous song. "It just ain't right, like green tomatoes." I couldn't have put it better myself. Potatoes turn a slab of meat into a meal. Add a vegetable and you have the definition of classic American cuisine.

Potatoes are enjoying the same revival as tomatoes, with new varieties and heirlooms popping up all the time. And, by all means, I encourage you to get excited over the differently colored potatoes (red, blue, yellow) and to discern flavor nuances among them (buttery, creamy). Basically, though, potatoes fall into three categories: baking (also known as "floury," "mealy," or "russet"), waxy (also known as "low-starch"), and all-purpose (also known as "medium starch"). The important thing to know is that baking potatoes are best for baking, mashing, and deep-frying. Waxy and all-purpose potatoes, which are thin skinned, are best for holding their shape in salads, soups, and stews.

Availability

Because they store well, potatoes are available year-round.

Storage

Homegrown potatoes should be cured before storing to toughen their skins. One to two weeks spread out in a protected area at 60° to 75°F is ideal. Then store them in a cold, damp, dark spot. Under ideal conditions, potatoes will keep for 4 to 6 months.

How to Buy

Look for firm, dry potatoes that show no sign of sprouting and a minimum of bruises, healed or otherwise.

Preparation

Potatoes are either peeled with a vegetable peeler or scrubbed well with a stiff vegetable brush, depending on whether the recipe calls for a peeled potato. Brown, black, or green spots should be cut away. Once peeled, the flesh of the potato will darken on exposure to air. To prevent this, drop potatoes into a bowl of water as soon as they are peeled.

Cooking Ideas

There are so many wonderful ways to prepare potatoes that the mind boggles at the thought of coming up with a few cooking ideas. Quite simply, potatoes can be cooked by almost any method (baking, boiling, braising, pan-frying, roasting, sautéing, steaming). When in doubt, though, bake or mash and be lavish with the butter. And when baking potatoes, do prick the potatoes in several places with a fork to release the steam that builds up; cleaning up after an exploded potato is a miserable chore.

Mashed potatoes can be combined with other winter vegetables to make a number of classic northern European dishes. Colcannon (Irish) and kailkenny (Scottish) are made from mashed potatoes and sautéed cabbage. Clapshot and neeps and tatties are both combinations of mashed potatoes and turnips from Scotland. Rumbledethumps is that same dish plus cheese, also from Scotland. These are rib-sticking dishes that can sustain you over a long, cold winter.

Potato Math

1 pound potatoes = 2 to 3 large potatoes = 3½ cups chopped or sliced = 3 cups shredded = 2 cups cooked and mashed

Sweet Potatoes

Like regular potatoes, there are different types of sweet potatoes, expressed as "dry-fleshed" or "moist-fleshed." The terminology refers to the mouthfeel, not the actual moisture present in the sweet potato. Moist-fleshed types tend to convert more of their starch to sugar during cooking, becoming softer and sweeter than the dry-fleshed types. The moist-fleshed types are often called yams.

The confusion over yams versus sweet potatoes began several decades ago, when orange-fleshed sweet potatoes were introduced in the southern United States. Producers and shippers wanted to distinguish these sweet potatoes from the more traditional, yellow-fleshed types and adopted the term "yams," never guessing that in just a few decades, the global supermarket and immigration patterns would bring the true yam into the United States, causing endless bewilderment.

Different sweet potato cultivars have markedly different flesh colors and flavors. The cultivars with the paler skin are generally preferred by northerners. They are said to have nuttier, more nuanced flavors, and often a more stringy texture; this allows them to hold their shape better when cooked diced or sliced. The darker-skinned, orange types are said to be sweeter and more creamy in texture, best for mashing. The differences, however, are not so great that you can't use these sweet potatoes interchangeably.

Sweet potatoes are more popular in the southern United States than in the North, where supersweet dishes are also less well received. But the popularity of sweet-potato fries and the promotion of sweet potatoes as supernutritious are changing all that.

Availability

Because they store well, sweet potatoes are available year-round.

Storage

Homegrown sweet potatoes should be cured before storing to heal wounds and improve flavor; during the curing process starches are converted to sugar. Cure sweet potatoes by holding them for about 10 days at 80° to 85°F and high relative humidity (85 to 90 percent). Packing the sweet potatoes in perforated plastic bags will keep the humidity high. If you can't provide the necessary heat, the curing period should be extended.

Once the sweet potatoes are cured, move them to a dark location where a temperature of about 55° to 60°F can be maintained. (An unheated closet may be ideal.) Under ideal conditions, sweet potatoes will last 4 to 6 months.

How to Buy

Choose unblemished, unwrinkled sweet potatoes with tips that are intact.

Preparation

Sweet potatoes may be baked whole, just as with regular potatoes. To peel sweet potatoes, use a vegetable peeler. The flesh will darken on exposure to air, so drop potatoes into a bowl of water if you are not going to cook them immediately.

Cooking Ideas

The easiest way to prepare sweet potatoes is to cut them into chunks and boil or steam until tender, 25 to 30 minutes, then mash with butter. You can add a small amount of orange juice, maple syrup, brown sugar, cinnamon, and/or nutmeg for extra flavor.

Julienne-cut sweet potatoes can be deep-fried to make fries or tossed with oil and roasted at 500°F for about 20 minutes to make oven fries.

To bake sweet potatoes, pierce the skin of each one in several places with a fork, place on a baking sheet, and bake at 400°F for 40 to 60 minutes, depending on the size. The baking sheet is to keep your oven clean; the sweet potatoes will ooze a sticky syrup while baking. Sweet-potato slices also can be layered with slices of apple and then topped with brown sugar or maple syrup and butter and baked in a covered casserole dish at 375°F for about 30 minutes.

Good flavors for seasoning sweet potatoes include orange, pineapple, apples, pecans, cinnamon, nutmeg, brown sugar, maple syrup, chile peppers, cilantro, lemon, lime, and curry.

Sweet Potato Math

1 pound sweet potatoes = 3 cups sliced = 2⅓ cups diced
1 large sweet potato = 1 cup cooked and mashed

Root Vegetables

ROOT VEGETABLES have a bum rap. They are sometimes considered boring and limited. Nothing could be further from the truth.

Root vegetables — beets, carrots, celery root (celeriac), parsnips, rutabagas, salsify, turnips — have many culinary virtues. First and foremost, they are all terrific roasted. Alone or in groups, there isn't a root vegetable that doesn't taste wonderful when roasted. And here's the secret to roasting: use a hot oven (425° to 450°F) and a large enough pan for the vegetables to barely touch each other. If the vegetables are crowded, they will steam rather than roast, and you won't get the delicious caramelized sugars that give roasted vegetables their distinctive flavor. Half sheet pans, at 13 inches by 18 inches, won't crowd vegetables, and they fit into standard-size ovens.

Cut the vegetables to a uniform size (my favorite is a ½-inch to ¾-inch dice) so they will cook evenly and fairly quickly, toss them with a little olive oil, and spread them out on an oiled half sheet pan. If they won't fit in a single layer, use two pans. Roast for 20 to 35 minutes, shaking the pan once or twice. If you have the option of using convection, they will roast better (faster, with less risk of steaming). They are done when the vegetables have shrunk considerably in size and are lightly browned and tender. Season with salt and pepper and serve. Or drizzle with balsamic vinegar or pomegranate molasses, season with salt and pepper, and serve.

Many classic French recipes begin with a mirepoix, a flavoring combination of diced carrots, onions, and celery. Celery root can replace celery stalks. For a white mirepoix, parsnips replace the carrots. The Italian soffrito is similar, usually including garlic. So root vegetables plus onions and garlic can flavor soups, sauces, and stews throughout the winter — with no limit to the types of different dishes you can make.

Purées or mashes of individual root vegetables are less popular than they used to be, perhaps because we have developed a fear of butter. But as the occasional treat, a butter-laced mash of turnips or rutabagas, well seasoned with salt and pepper, is a delicious dish.

Peeling and then shredding root vegetables on the coarse side of a box grater or in a food processor prepares root vegetables for quick cooking. They can then be quickly sautéed in a skillet with butter or olive oil, thus eliminating the complaint that root vegetables take a long time to cook.

There are just a few things to be careful about when it comes to root vegetables. Some root vegetables, especially carrots, beets, and parsnips, are quite sweet. So add them sparingly when sweetness is inappropriate — in soup stock, for example. As root vegetables age, they use up their sugars. In the case of turnips and rutabagas, sulfurous flavors can become stronger.

Root vegetables store well in a root cellar, given cold temperatures (32° to 40°F) and sufficient humidity (90 to 95 percent). Layering the vegetables in damp sawdust, moss, or sand in bins or boxes helps maintain the proper humidity. If you don't have a root cellar, you may have another spot in your home that provides the right conditions, such as a staircase leading from an outdoor entrance to the basement. The steps can be used as shelves, with the top shelves holding vegetables that should be kept coolest (potatoes) and the bottom steps holding vegetables more tolerant of heat (winter squashes). You may also be able to leave the root vegetables in the ground under a heavy layer of mulch and harvest as needed, provided the soil drains well.

Finally, like most other vegetables, root vegetables are low in calories, with about 10 to 60 calories per half-cup serving. They are good sources of fiber, providing 1 to 4 grams per half cup. Several root vegetables are good sources of potassium, vitamin C, vitamin A, and folic acid. In addition, root vegetables, especially those deeper in color, contain health-promoting antioxidants known as phytochemicals.

Beets

The beet is an embarrassing vegetable. Add it to any dish and it will stain all the ingredients (and the hands that peeled them) an outlandish pink color. Who can work with such an outrageous vegetable?

Beets don't have to be red! Golden beets have won my heart. Their mild flavor and golden color make them easy to include in recipes where the dye of the red beet is unwelcome but the flavor is an asset. In addition to the golden beet, there is the Chioggia beet, which is striped red and white, and there are pure white versions as well. So if there are those you know who don't think they like beets, you might try slipping them some golden or white beets and see if you don't win converts.

Beets originated from the same wild species in the Mediterranean that gave rise to Swiss chard, and the two plants share the Latin name of *Beta vulgaris*. Both the Greeks and early Romans ate chard, but the root, which was hard and fibrous, was used medicinally only. Sometime during the third and fourth centuries AD, beets began to be cultivated for their roots.

Beets can taste strongly of the earth in which they were grown, a reason many people shun them. A good way to tame that earthy flavor is to combine beets with cream.

Availability

You can start harvesting in midsummer when the roots are about 2 inches in diameter; they will grow to about 4 inches in diameter. Supplies generally last through the winter.

How to Buy

Look for firm, not spongy, roots, and avoid any with bruises and soft spots. If the greens are attached, they should be vibrant, not yellowed or wilted. Smaller beets are less likely to be woody in texture.

Storage

For short-term storage, trim off any green tops. Store greens and roots separately in plastic bags in the refrigerator in a plastic bag; the greens will keep for 3 to 4 days, the roots for a couple of weeks. For long-term storage, store in a root cellar.

Preparation

Wash well. Do not peel beets before boiling or roasting. Just scrub well, trim off the tops, leaving 1 inch of stems, and trim off the dangling roots within 1 inch of the bottom of the beet. If you are grating to sauté or serve raw in a salad, peel with a paring knife.

Cooking Ideas

Raw beets are a delicious, unexpected addition to salads. Peel and grate, shred, or julienne very finely. Red beets will stain every vegetable they touch, but golden beets will not. I prefer to taste the beet before using raw; sometimes they have a strong mineral flavor that needs taming with cooking. Generally, the younger the beet, the better it tastes raw, which means that beets lend themselves to raw preparations in the fall but as winter progresses, plan to cook them.

When cooking is required, the recipes generally call for boiling or roasting them. Either method is fine, but roasting preserves their flavor better.

To roast, preheat the oven to 350°F. Wrap the beets individually in aluminum foil and roast for 50 to 60 minutes, depending on the size, until fork-tender. The skin may be removed after roasting, but it isn't always necessary.

To boil beets, put them in a large pot and cover with cold water. Bring the water to a boil, then reduce the heat and simmer until fork-tender, 30 to 60 minutes, depending on size. Peel after boiling; the skins will just slip off.

Beet Math

1 small beet = 2 ounces

1 medium beet = 3 to 5 ounces

1 large beet = 8 to 10 ounces

1 pound = 4 to 5 medium beets = 3 cups
    cubed beets = 4 cups shredded beets

Carrots

Carrots are such perfect vegetables when freshly harvested that it is hard to imagine improving upon them by cooking. But, alas, sugars convert to starches as the winter progresses, and cooking may be the best option. If the very idea of cooked carrots makes you shudder, you have probably been subjected to boiled carrots at some point in your life. There are better ways to cook carrots, with roasting topping the list.

Carrots have been reverting to their roots lately and appearing in many different colors. In Egyptian times, the carrot was purple. The Romans enjoyed white and purple carrots. Purple, white, and yellow carrots were imported to southern Europe in the fourteenth century. Black, red, and white carrots were also grown.

Carrot consumption in the United States increased sharply in the 1990s, from about 10 pounds per person per year to 14 pounds. This is probably due to the appearance of bagged "baby" carrots in the supermarkets. These "babies" are actually carved from large carrots grown in California, washed in chlorinated water, and packed for a long shelf-life. It's hard to see how this is actually an improvement over market-grown or homegrown local carrots.

Among the nutrients that make carrots such a healthful option are the carotenoids, which are converted to vitamin A in the liver and are essential for the body's maintenance of vision, skin, teeth, and the immune system. Carrots are also a good source of vitamins C and K, fiber, and potassium.

Availability

Carrots are available year-round, but freshly harvested carrots are superior in flavor.

Storage

For short-term storage, trim off any green tops. Store the carrots in perforated plastic bags in the refrigerator, where they will keep for several weeks. For long-term storage, store in a root cellar.

How to Buy

Carrot roots should be firm, smooth, and bright in color. A deeper orange color indicates more beta-carotene in the carrot. Avoid carrots that are excessively cracked or are limp or rubbery. If the green tops are attached, they should be brightly colored and feathery.

Preparation

Carrots should be peeled or well scrubbed before eating or cooking.

Cooking Ideas

I freely toss shredded carrots into many dishes when I want to boost the nutritional content of the food, or when I just want to get rid of some of the carrots in the vegetable bin. Macaroni and cheese? Delicious with a shredded carrot. Quiche? A shredded carrot adds color and texture. Salad? Well, that's rather obvious, but it's worth remembering that a recipe doesn't have to call for a carrot to work well with one.

Roasted carrots are superior in flavor to boiled or steamed carrots, in my opinion. A drizzle of balsamic vinegar perfectly complements the sweet vegetable.

Carrot Math
1 pound carrots = 4 to 6 large carrots =
　　3 cups sliced or diced = 4 cups shredded

Celery Root

Also called celeriac (its French name) or knob celery, celery root just hasn't been embraced by American cooks, probably because fresh celery is such a convenient supermarket staple. The appearance of celery root hasn't won it any friends, either. It is brown and knobby and looks difficult to prepare. But slice away the knobby skin and you have a vegetable with the flavor of celery and the handling properties of a root vegetable, meaning it stores well in a root cellar and tastes delicious roasted or braised.

Celery root can be used instead of celery in any cooked dish, maintaining its texture in situations that would reduce a stalk of celery to a mass of strings. The classic French dish *céleri rémoulade* is made with shredded raw celery root tossed with a mayonnaise dressing. I find the flavor of raw celery root too strong, sort of a cross between overgrown parsley

and celery, and prefer to blanch it rather than using it raw. This opinion is not shared by everyone; some food writers prefer celery root raw and don't like it cooked. To each his own.

Storage
For short-term storage, trim off any green tops and rootlets. Store the celery root in perforated plastic bags in the refrigerator, where they will keep for several weeks. For long-term storage, store in a root cellar.

How to Buy
Choose small, firm celery roots that are heavy for their size. Avoid those with soft spots and a lot of rootlets. Large and old celery roots may be woody inside. Avoid celery root out of season; no matter how well it has been stored, it will be unpleasant in both texture and flavor.

Preparation

To prepare celery root, scrub it well, then remove the skin with a good sharp knife. You will end up with quite a bit of waste. The flesh darkens on exposure to air, so either cook it immediately or drop it into a bowl of acidulated water (1 tablespoon vinegar or lemon juice added to 4 cups water).

Cooking Ideas

Celery root is often used as a celery substitute to flavor soups and stews. It can also be used on its own, braised, roasted, or baked. It makes a very velvety purée. Celery root can also be eaten raw in thin slices; it has a zesty crunch. Celery root is delicious in a mix of root vegetables, mashed with potatoes, or roasted with chicken.

Celery Root Math

1 pound celery root = ½ pound usable flesh = 2 cups cubes = 1 cup purée

Parsnips

Parsnip has been eclipsed by potato as a go-to vegetable, but there is no reason to disdain it. Like the carrot, it is a root with a tendency to taste sweet; unlike the carrot, it is never eaten raw. Like most root vegetables, parsnips store well, which is both a blessing and a curse. It is a blessing because you can count on it not spoiling whether you store yours in a root cellar, in the ground under mulch, or in a refrigerator. It is a curse because supermarkets sell really, really old parsnips that have lost their flavor and don't suggest the nutty depth of flavor a homegrown or freshly harvested parsnip can show.

In Europe, before the potato became popular, parsnips were a very popular vegetable and even enjoyed in desserts. Clearly, there is plenty to explore here.

Availability

Parsnips are available year-round, but the best flavor comes from newly harvested parsnips after a few frosts, in late fall or early spring.

Storage

For short-term storage, trim off any green tops. Store the parsnips in perforated plastic bags in the refrigerator, where they will keep for several weeks. For long-term storage, store in a root cellar. Parsnips also do well left in the garden under a bed of mulch.

How to Buy

Look for firm, unblemished roots. Avoid ones in plastic bags where you can't judge their age or soundness. Although we tend to think that parsnips look like white carrots, in fact they tend to vary widely in diameter, from wide near the stem end to very narrow at the end. Look for uniformity in size, as best you can.

Preparation

Parsnips, like carrots, should be peeled or well scrubbed before using.

Cooking Ideas

The best way to prepare parsnips is to roast them, which brings out flavors of nutmeg, honey, and nuts. Just cut into chunks or slices, slick with oil, and roast for 20 to 30 minutes at 425°F. Parsnips can also be steamed and left whole or puréed, sautéed, or fried. Basically you can cook them in any way that you would cook carrots. Be careful when throwing parsnips into a soup; it may contribute too much sweetness.

Parsnip Math

1 pound parsnips = 4 to 8 medium
   parsnips = 3 cups sliced or diced

Rutabagas

What's not to love about a rutabaga? First, there's the name. The Swedes named it, and it means "thick root," which isn't half so euphonious as "rutabaga." (In the 1800s, Americans called it "turnip-rooted cabbage," which really isn't a pretty name!) Then there are the legends associated with it. In the British Isles it was the original jack-o'-lantern, a tradition based on the legend of a blacksmith named Jack who mortgaged his soul to the demons of the underworld. Jack found his way through the netherworld guided by a large hollowed-out rutabaga containing a glowing coal. Then there is the rutabaga's willingness to grow in the most marginal climates and soils, including places like Scandinavia, Finland, and Ireland. Until the potato arrived from the New World in the mid-sixteenth century, entire populations on the fringes of Europe were sustained by the rutabaga. Yet I never even tasted a rutabaga until I was in my thirties, and I don't think that is unusual in the United States.

The rutabaga developed as a cross between cabbage and turnip, but it more closely expresses its turnip ancestry. In fact, you can use rutabagas interchangeably in recipes that call for turnips, though they are generally milder, sweeter, and larger than turnips. Rutabagas are sometimes called Swedes or yellow turnips; their flesh is yellow, whereas the turnip's flesh is white.

Availability

Rutabagas are harvested in the fall and generally are available all through the winter. Many supermarkets dip rutabagas in wax, a protective measure that makes them available year-round, but freshly harvested rutabagas have better flavor. As they age, rutabagas develop a cabbagey, bitter flavor.

Storage

For short-term storage, trim off any green tops. Rutabaga greens are very tasty and should be enjoyed like turnip greens. Store unwaxed rutabagas in perforated plastic bags in the refrigerator for a week or two. Waxed rutabagas can sit on the counter for a week or two. If your rutabaga is too large to use in one dish, you can wrap the remainder in plastic and keep it for up to 1 week. For long-term storage, store in a root cellar.

How to Buy

Look for firm, not limp, unblemished roots. Smaller is generally better, but rutabagas do not have the same tendency to become woody as large turnips do.

Preparation

Rutabagas have a tough, inedible skin that should be sliced away with a knife before using. Rutabagas should be cooked before eating.

Cooking Ideas

Like all root vegetables, rutabagas are terrific roasted. They are also delicious steamed or boiled, and then mashed with butter or olive oil, salt, pepper, and nutmeg to taste. In Scotland, a classic dish is neeps and tatties (see page 163), a mash of potatoes and rutabagas, while in Sweden the mix would also include carrots. Another classic Scottish dish is clapshot, which is mashed potatoes and rutabaga with chives, butter, onions, and salt and pepper. I throw rutabagas into chicken pot pie, beef stew, and lamb stew. I also throw cubes of rutabagas, and other root vegetables, into the roasting pan whenever I roast chicken.

Rutabaga greens are delicious, though not as commonly served as turnip greens.

Rutabaga Math

1 pound rutabaga = 3 cups sliced or diced = 4 cups shredded = 2 cups steamed and puréed

Salsify

Salsify is a difficult and fussy vegetable to grow. The reward for growing it, however, is a great-tasting vegetable that is very easy to store in a root cellar. It was popular in colonial America and is commonly found in Europe. Unfortunately for Europeans, salsify is most often cooked out of a can and served in a school cafeteria stew; this is no way to treat a delicious vegetable!

There is some confusion about the name. It used to be called oyster plant or vegetable oyster, because of a slight resemblance to oysters in flavor (very slight). There are two types of salsify: white and black. The black type, commonly known as scorzonera, grows thicker than white salsify and is less likely to fork, so I think it is far preferable to white salsify. Both have white flesh when peeled.

No Place for Cold Storage?

Even if you don't have a storage area for root vegetables, you can preserve them by blanching and freezing. Or you can sauté slices or cubes in butter or oil until they are softened and then freeze them. Beets, carrots, and Jerusalem artichokes are excellent pickled.

The soft white flesh has a slightly sweet, earthy taste and a wonderful, almost creamy texture. I think the flavor is a cross between globe artichokes and Jerusalem artichokes. It contains the carbohydrate inulin (as does Jerusalem artichoke), which makes it desirable for diabetics.

Availability

This root is theoretically available from fall to early spring, though hard to find in most markets. Its flavor is best after a few frosts.

Storage

If you grow your own salsify, you can overwinter it in the ground as you do parsnips, or store it in a root cellar. For short-term storage, trim off any green tops. Store salsify in the refrigerator in a perforated plastic bag, where it will keep for several weeks.

How to Buy

Look for medium to large roots, with a minimum of forking. I generally have to special-order it. For many years I have special-ordered a case, which I keep in a box on my basement stairs, and they last through the winter.

White salsify is sometimes sold in bunches with leaves still attached. Black salsify is usually sold without leaves, in plastic bags.

Preparation

Prepare salsify by peeling, removing the skin, rootlets, and all dark spots. Trim the tops and bottoms and slice as you would a carrot or leave whole. Its flesh will darken on exposure to air, so unless you are cooking immediately, drop the salsify into acidulated water (1 tablespoon lemon juice or white vinegar added to 4 cups water). Salsify oozes a sticky substance that blackens on exposure to air, so some people advise wearing gloves when peeling it. (Some people scrub salsify but do not peel; I think the peel is bitter and the vegetable tastes better without it.)

Cooking Ideas

The taste of salsify is delicate, so simple preparations are best to coax out its flavor. It can be sautéed in butter or oil, roasted, or steamed and mashed with butter. I like to sauté it in butter for a few minutes, then cover the pan and let the salsify steam a few minutes until tender. Delicious. In Belgium, salsify fritters (see page 189) are popular bar snacks.

Salsify Math

1 pound salsify = 4 to 8 roots = 3 cups sliced or diced = 4 cups shredded = 2 cups steamed and puréed

Kohlrabi: The Mysterious Vegetable in the Cabbage Family

Kohlrabi looks like no other vegetable. A leafy aboveground bulb, it resembles a flying saucer more than either the cabbage or turnip from which it developed. It goes by many names, including cabbage turnip and stem cabbage. The bulb can be pale green, in which case it is called white kohlrabi, or purplish, in which case it is called violet kohlrabi. Either way, the skin is peeled away, revealing a white bulb that is close to a turnip in flavor, but sweeter and more delicately flavored. It can be eaten raw or cooked. Choose or harvest small ones, ideally about the size of tennis balls, and peel before using. Figure that each bulb will yield about 1 cup when cut into 1-inch cubes.

You can substitute kohlrabi for turnips in most recipes. The leaves can be cooked and enjoyed like turnip greens.

Vermont Roots: Gilfeather Turnips

In the late 1800s, the Gilfeather turnip was either developed or discovered by John Gilfeather (1865–1944) of Wardsboro, Vermont. A secretive, crusty old bachelor, he cut off the tops and bottoms of the plants before taking them to market so no one could reproduce them. Turnips — and rutabagas — are biennials. If you buy a turnip with the roots and tops intact and store it properly in a root cellar, the vegetable likely will survive the winter dormancy; replant it in the spring and it will quickly produce seeds, enough to allow you to produce a new crop. John Gilfeather had no intention of letting this happen.

Fortunately, after John Gilfeather died, a number of Wardsboro residents acquired the seed somehow and continued to plant the turnip. Seeds passed from friend to friend. Eventually, the name was trademarked, and the vegetable was registered as an heirloom variety with the Vermont Agency of Agriculture. Today the seeds are available through the Fedco Seed Company in Waterville, Maine.

To taste the Gilfeather turnip is to become a fan. It has none of the bitter cabbagey flavor a turnip will develop in storage. Harvests of 3- and 4-pound roots with perfect texture and flavor are not unusual. The Gilfeather turnip's mild-tasting flesh is terrific in chicken pot pie or paired with potatoes in a mash-up. It is absolutely delicious roasted, especially with chicken or duck, and bathed in drippings. Surprisingly, it is also terrific raw, with a pleasingly crisp texture and mild flavor. And the greens are arguably the best-tasting turnip greens ever, mild and sweet compared to the usual turnip greens.

An heirloom vegetable, the Gilfeather turnip is included in Slow Food's Ark of Taste, an international catalog of great-tasting foods that are threatened by industrial standardization, the regulations of large-scale distribution, or environmental damage. The Gilfeather is the only turnip to have made it to the Ark of Taste, and it is a great-tasting vegetable.

The Gilfeather is unique among turnips. Although it is white-fleshed and white-skinned, its mild, sweet flavor closely resembles that of a rutabaga. Furthermore, its shape is like that of a rutabaga, with a wide taproot tapering from the bottom of the bulb, rather than one that emerges off the rounded bottom. As the Fedco Seed folks write in their catalog description, "This heirloom has come down in folklore as a turnip but is really a rutabaga, big-knobbed and bulky."

I love the idea that the most celebrated turnip in America may well be a Vermont rutabaga in disguise.

Turnips

The turnip goes far back in history, dating back to the prehistoric development of agriculture. Its culture spread widely, from the Mediterranean across Asia to the Pacific, probably because it is so easy to grow and so easy to store. The turnip was brought to the Americas by Jacques Cartier, who planted it in Canada in 1541. It was also planted in Virginia by the colonists in 1609 and in Massachusetts in the 1620s; Native Americans adopted it from the colonists. Since colonial times, the turnip has been one of the most common garden vegetables in America. But like many root vegetables, it has been neglected in recent years.

A young turnip is different from a fully mature turnip. A freshly harvested turnip, particularly one harvested small, is often milder in flavor than radishes and well suited to enjoying raw. At this point it is interchangeable with a daikon radish and is delicious in Asian-style salads or as an addition to a crudités plate. An older turnip has stronger flavor and is best cooked. At this point it is interchangeable with a rutabaga, though it may not be as sweet and mild.

Availability

Turnips are available from fall to early summer.

Storage

For short-term storage, trim off any green tops and enjoy them cooked separately. Store turnips in perforated plastic bags in the refrigerator for up to 1 week. For long-term storage, store in a root cellar.

How to Buy

The smaller the turnip, the sweeter the flesh and the less likely the texture will be woody. Choose firm, not limp, unblemished roots.

Salad Turnips

In recent years, salad turnips have been showing up at farmers' markets and in seed catalogs. Grown as a spring or autumn crop, these turnips are small, sweet, and juicy, sometimes even fruity. They are milder in flavor than traditional turnips, even milder than radishes. They are best peeled and eaten raw or very quickly cooked, as in a stir-fry.

Salad turnips are not good keepers for the root cellar, but don't let that stop you from trying them. They are delicious, and the greens are a tasty bonus.

Preparation

Peel turnips before cooking and trim off the stem and root ends.

Cooking Ideas

Roast 'em, bake 'em, mash 'em, fry 'em. You can employ any cooking method you like with turnips. They marry well with butter, cream, and bacon. If you find that your turnips have become strongly flavored with storage, consider boiling them with a peeled potato. Discard the potato and then mash the turnips with butter and season with salt and pepper and a pinch of nutmeg. The flavor you objected to will be absorbed by the potato. Of course, you could also boil them with potatoes and keep the potatoes for a delicious mash (see pages 20 and 21).

Turnip Math

1 pound turnips = 4 to 8 roots = 3 cups sliced or diced = 4 cups shredded = 2 cups steamed and puréed

Winter Squashes

IMAGINE YOU ARE AN EXPLORER and encounter a vegetable you have never seen before. Would you accept the native name for it? Or would you somehow relate it to the vegetable back home? Such was the quandary of the New World explorers. For the most part, the explorers chose to sow confusion by conflating new vegetables to known ones back home in Europe. Thus, while New World natives had been enjoying squashes and pumpkins for at least seven thousand years, the first European explorers who visited the Americas reported that the natives were cultivating a new type of melon. Nonetheless, squashes were adopted readily by the first European settlers, who couldn't be too choosy, given their near-starvation circumstances.

Native Americans showed the settlers how to bake whole pumpkins buried in the ashes of a fire, then cut them open and flavor them with animal fat and maple syrup or honey. The Pilgrims modified the recipe, adding milk, sweetener, and spices. A recipe for "Pompkin Pie" appeared in Amelia Simmon's 1796 cookbook. From then on, pumpkin pie lit up our culinary horizon, and winter squash remained a staple in New England.

Botanists do not distinguish between pumpkins and winter squashes — or between winter and summer squashes, for that matter. There are three basic types of edible squashes. *Cucurbita pepo* is noted for its pentagonal stems with prickly spines. This group includes pumpkins and acorn squash as well as all the summer squashes, spaghetti squash, and numerous gourds. Butternut squash, which is one of the best replacements for pumpkin in any recipe, is in another grouping entirely (*C. moshata,* which has pentagonal stems without spines). *C. maxima* (round stems) includes buttercup, Hubbard, and turban squashes. In other words, pumpkins and winter squashes are pretty much interchangeable.

Choosing and Using Winter Squashes

There are many different types of winter squashes, and which to grow or buy pretty much depends on your taste preferences. I prefer butternut squash above all others because it is the easiest to peel and therefore the most versatile in the kitchen. Delicata is also a favorite because the skin is edible.

Availability

Winter squash is generally available year-round, but the greatest variety is available in the late fall.

Storage

Winter squash should be harvested when fully mature (when its skin has hardened) and then cured in the sun or in a warm (55° to 65°F), dry place. Store in an unheated, dry space. A temperature of about 50°F is ideal. For short-term stor-age, store for up to 1 week in a paper bag in the refrigerator. If your squash is too large to use at one time, wrap the unused portion in plastic and store in the refrigerator for 4 to 5 days.

How to Buy

Look for firm, heavy squash with no soft spots. The stem should be intact.

Preparation

Butternut squash may be peeled. Others should be cut in half or into pieces. Scrape out and discard any seeds and fibers.

Cooking Ideas

Winter squash must be fully cooked; a fork inserted into the squash should meet no resistance. Baking is a good way to become acquainted with the flavor of squash. Place the halved squash in a baking dish, skin side up. Add about an inch of water. Bake at 350°F for 45 to 90 minutes, depending on the size of the squash, until fork-tender. Then serve pieces of squash with a pat of butter and sprinkling of brown sugar. Or scrape the flesh into a bowl and mash with butter. Slices of winter squash can be dipped in batter and deep-fried. Roasting cubes of oil-slicked winter squash at 425°F for 20 to 30 minutes is another excellent preparation.

Winter squash or pumpkin, flavored with sage, is a traditional filling for ravioli in Italy. Winter squash pairs well with cream sauces and can be used as a filling for a "white" lasagna (see page 254). Winter squash pairs well with brown sugar, maple syrup, honey, apples, cinnamon, and nutmeg.

Winter squashes and pumpkin are interchangeable in desserts, but a moist type, like butternut or Hubbard, is best.

Winter Squash Math

1 pound winter squash or pumpkin =
    4 cups cubed = 3 cups diced =
    1¾ cups puréed

Winter Squash Varieties

Acorn. Shaped like an acorn, this squash comes in three colors: green, orange, and white. The flesh is somewhat drier and stringier than other varieties, but it is a convenient size for stuffing and for serving in roasted wedges.

Banana. A prizewinner of a squash, these can grow up to 100 pounds with mild, sweet, very creamy pink flesh. Banana squash is more commonly found in the West than in the East. When it does show up in the supermarket, it is usually sold in pieces wrapped in plastic.

Buttercup. Fans of the buttercup claim that this squash is so sweet, it doesn't need a sweet glaze. It is dark green and round in shape, with a pale green cap.

Butternut. The one winter squash that is easily peeled, butternut has moist, rich, smooth flesh. It makes a delicious purée, and its cubes and slices also can be grilled or roasted. Butternut squash can be shredded raw and used as a stand-in for shredded carrots in baked dishes. This is a very good, all-purpose squash that is usually available year-round.

Calabaza. Caribbean recipes calling for "pumpkin" are inevitably referring to the calabaza. It is rounded or pear-shaped and fairly large. Its mottled skin may be green, orange, amber, or cream. It is the one "winter squash" that is grown year-round in warm climates.

Delicata. Also known as sweet-potato squash, this squash is shaped like a long, ridged tube, with cream, orange, and green stripes. Delicata should be sliced in half lengthwise and seeded; it can then be cut into crescent-shaped pieces if you like. The peel is edible.

Hubbard. Hubbards present a grand challenge in the kitchen. They can weigh anywhere from 8 to 40 pounds, and their skins are extremely hard to cut through (an ax is sometimes required). Once wrestled into manageable-size pieces, the light orange flesh is sweet and moist and makes an exceptionally smooth purée.

Pumpkin. Pie pumpkins, also known as sweet pumpkins or cheese pumpkins, are smaller than those cultivated for jack-o'-lanterns.

Red Kuri. The skin is a brilliant orange and the bland flesh is a brilliant deep orange flesh, making this squash something of a beauty queen.

Spaghetti. Yellow and football-shaped, spaghetti squash has turned the distressing tendency of winter squash to be stringy into a virtue. When cooked, the flesh of this squash turns into long spaghetti-like strands. Although many suggest serving spaghetti squash as a pasta substitute, it is probably better to acknowledge its sweet flavor and work with it as a winter squash.

Sweet Dumpling. Small and pumpkin-shaped, sweet dumplings are cream-colored with dark green stripes. Like delicata squash, the skin of the sweet dumpling squash is edible. The flesh is smooth, sweet, and moist.

Turban. As much prized for its decorative appearance as its flavor, the turban is indeed shaped like a turban. It can be used like any other winter squash. The skin is tough and difficult to cut into.

Dried Beans

A WELL-STOCKED WINTER KITCHEN contains plenty of dried beans, lentils, and split peas. These legumes add variety to the diet and are an extremely economical and healthful alternative to meat. Beans keep indefinitely, though age will toughen the skins and increase the cooking time.

Beans may have been the inspiration for the development of the art of cooking, since all beans, peas, and lentils, whether fresh or dried, will cause digestive distress if eaten raw. Boiling for 2 to 3 minutes destroys the toxic lectins that cause all the problems.

Beans should be salted *after* cooking. The reason is not, as it's often said, that salt in the cooking liquid toughens the skins, but that you are reducing the liquid so much that the beans may end up too salty — especially if you are cooking them with a ham bone or a piece of salt pork or bacon. Acids do toughen the skins, so never add acidic ingredients, including tomatoes, until the beans are fully cooked.

Choosing and Using Dried Beans

Beans grow in an incredibly wide range of climates, from the cold mountain plateaus of Peru (where lima beans originated) to the hot, humid tropics (where pigeon peas were first cultivated). More than 70 varieties of beans are currently enjoyed worldwide.

Availability

Dried beans, lentils, and split peas are available year-round.

Storage

They require no special storage conditions, just an airtight container at room temperature.

How to Buy

Never buy more than the amount of beans you will consume in a couple of months. Beans aren't really old until they have sat around for a year, but you don't know how old the beans are when you purchase them. It is a good idea to buy beans at a natural-foods store where stock turns over regularly.

Preparation

First, pick over and rinse the beans, discarding any foreign debris and shriveled beans. Then put the beans in a bowl, cover with water so there is at least 3 inches of water above the level of the beans, and leave to soak for 8 hours or overnight. You can skip this step, but your cooking time will lengthen by at least an hour, and you will have to just about double the amount of cooking liquid required in the recipes. If you forgot to soak overnight, you can use the "quick-soak method." Put the rinsed and sorted beans in a pot and cover them with cold tap water by at least 3 inches. Cover and bring to a boil. Remove from the heat, and let stand, covered, for 1 to 2 hours. Lentils and split peas do not require presoaking.

Cooking Ideas

Canned beans are very, very convenient, but beans that you cook yourself have more flavor. Combine 2 cups soaked beans with 8 cups water, a chopped onion, and bay leaves, and cook until tender. Then use the beans as a basis for any bean dish that calls for canned beans, including chili, soups, and stews. Your home-cooked beans will have much more flavor than canned ones.

Dried Bean Math

1 pound beans = about 2½ cups uncooked beans = 5½ to 6½ cups cooked

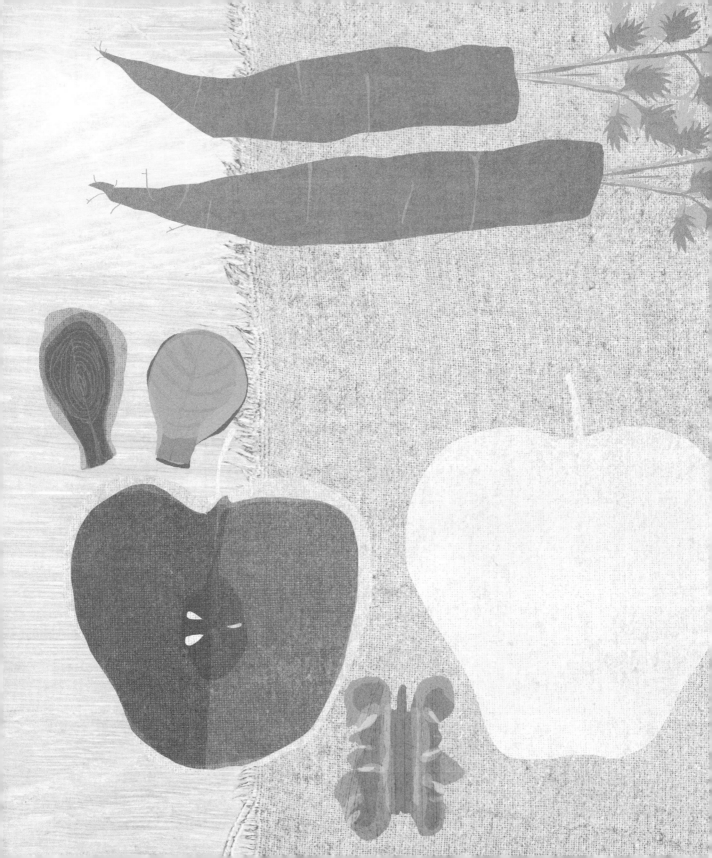

2
Salads and Pickled Vegetables

Many people think the ultimate challenge for those who want to eat solely fresh, long-keeping winter vegetables is coming up with salads. This chapter, with more than 40 recipes, proves otherwise. I think I could come up with 365 cabbage-salad recipes alone — a different coleslaw for every day of the week — and I wouldn't get tired of eating it. Cabbage is also a great replacement for lettuce and tomatoes on sandwiches, if you happen to have leftovers.

Coleslaw is just for starters. Potato salads? Carrot salads? Obviously. Beet salads? On the menu of every bistro in the country. Shredded celery-root salad? Ditto. But wilted kale? Roasted root vegetables? Shredded daikon radishes? Now it starts to get interesting. And don't forget pickled vegetables. They offered variety to our ancestors who lacked supermarkets to rely upon, and they offer variety to us today.

This chapter starts with a basic roasted-vegetable salad. It is followed by salads arranged by vegetable, then by hearty, could-be-main-dish salads made with noodles, grains, or, in one case, chicken. It ends with a few pickles that can be served in lieu of a more traditional salad and a few salad dressings that go particularly well with winter vegetables.

Balsamic Vinegar

RECILE LIST FOR
SALADS AND PICKLED VEGETABLES

Roasted Vegetable Salad

Beets in Sour Cream

Beet and Napa Cabbage Salad with
    Goat Cheese

Wilted Cabbage Salad, Italian Style

Roasted Beet and Potato Salad

Wilted Brussels Sprouts Salad

Brussels Sprouts and Citrus Salad

Classic American Coleslaw

Creamy Mustard Coleslaw

Creamy Coleslaw

Crunchy Dilled Coleslaw

Sweet-Pickle Coleslaw

Festive Fruity Coleslaw

Zesty Lemon Coleslaw

Carrot-Mustard Slaw

Chipotle-Cabbage Salad

Lahanosalata

Soy-Sesame Cabbage Salad

Thai Cabbage Salad

Thai Sweet-Spicy Cabbage Salad

Copper Coins

Carrots in Citrus Vinaigrette

Thai Vegetable Salad

Lentil Salad with Carrots and Goat
    Cheese

Celery Root, Apple, and Walnut Salad

Endive and Apple Salad with Candied
    Nuts and Blue Cheese

Wilted Kale Salad

Dilled Potato and Egg Salad

Roasted Sweet-Potato Salad with
    Sesame-Ginger Vinaigrette

North African Turnip Salad

Soba Noodle Salad

Sesame Noodle Salad

Couscous Salad with Kale and Feta

Wild Rice Salad with Roasted Squash
    and Fennel

Curried Rice Salad with Mango
    Chutney Dressing

Winter Pasta Salad with Red Cabbage
    and Carrot

Chinese-Style Chicken Salad

Chinese Vegetable Pickles

Quick Ginger-Pickled Beets

Sauerkraut

Walnut Vinaigrette

Orange Vinaigrette

Sesame-Ginger Vinaigrette

Molasses-Mustard Vinaigrette

Maple-Balsamic Vinaigrette

Maple-Soy Vinaigrette

Vegetarian dishes are marked with this symbol:

Roasted Vegetable Salad

Serves 4

Locavores living in northern climates sometimes have to prove that it is possible to have delicious salads all winter long without resorting to mushy frozen or canned vegetables. This salad is proof that wonderful salads can start with root vegetables. Vary the vegetables if you like, but be sure to have some colorful ones in the mix. The vegetables can be added to the salad warm, or at room temperature if you'd prefer to roast them ahead of time.

> 1 large beet, peeled and diced
> 2 carrots, peeled and diced
> 1 parsnip, peeled and diced
> 1 rutabaga, peeled and diced
> 1 whole garlic head, cloves separated and peeled
> 2 tablespoons extra-virgin olive oil
> 4–6 cups thinly sliced mixed tender winter greens (Belgian endive, napa cabbage, or Chinese cabbage)
> Maple-Soy Vinaigrette (page 89) or Molasses-Mustard Vinaigrette (page 88)
> Salt and freshly ground black pepper

1 Preheat the oven to 450°F. Lightly oil a half sheet pan (preferred) or large shallow roasting pan.

2 Combine the beet, carrots, parsnip, rutabaga, and garlic in a large bowl. Add the oil and toss well. Transfer to the pan and arrange in a shallow (preferably single) layer.

3 Roast the vegetables for 35 to 40 minutes, stirring or shaking the pan occasionally for even cooking, until they are tender and lightly browned.

4 Just before serving, toss the greens with about ¼ cup of the vinaigrette in a large salad bowl. Add the roasted vegetables and another ¼ cup of the dressing and toss again. Season with salt and pepper. Serve at once, passing the remaining vinaigrette at the table.

Kitchen Note: *When roasting root vegetables, it is important to cut all the vegetables to the same size. I prefer ½-inch cubes.*

Beets in Sour Cream

Serves 4

Four ingredients, plus salt and pepper. Nothing could be simpler. If you don't have a shallot on hand, substitute a few tablespoons of finely chopped red onion.

1½   pounds beets
1   shallot, minced
1   tablespoon apple cider vinegar, or more to taste
1   cup sour cream
    Salt and freshly ground black pepper

1   Preheat the oven to 350°F.

2   Wrap the beets individually in aluminum foil. Roast for 50 to 60 minutes, until fork-tender. Unwrap and let them cool.

3   Peel the beets and cut into small cubes. Transfer to a bowl with the shallot. Mix in the vinegar and sour cream. Season generously with salt and pepper.

4   Serve immediately or refrigerate for up to 8 hours before serving.

Kitchen Note: *If you prefer, you can boil the beets instead of roasting them. Put the beets in a medium saucepan and cover with water. Cover the pot, bring to a boil, and boil gently until the beets are fork-tender, about 40 minutes. Drain, let cool, and peel. (Boiled beets must be peeled. Roasted beets do not require peeling.)*

Vegetable Art

In the winter, there is time for wasting time. In ancient times, our ancestors practically hibernated, spending long days in bed, getting up occasionally to stoke the stove, consume a little bread, and then return to bed. How do we spend the winter? Many people troll the Internet. If you go to YouTube and look for videos of vegetable art, you will see some amazing work. Better than hibernating.

Beet and Napa Cabbage Salad with Goat Cheese

Serves 6-8

Napa cabbage is more tender than green cabbage, so it makes an excellent ingredient for a fresh salad. In this case, the cabbage provides a bed for the roasted beets, a role that might be played by spinach or lettuce in warmer months. The salad is dressed with a vinaigrette flavored by orange juice and zest and topped with goat cheese, resulting in flavors that are greater than the sum of its parts.

4	medium beets
¼–½	head napa or Chinese cabbage, thinly sliced (6-8 cups)
	Salt and freshly ground black pepper
	Orange Vinaigrette (page 87)
4	ounces soft fresh goat cheese (chèvre), crumbled

1 Preheat the oven to 400°F.

2 Wrap the beets individually in aluminum foil. Roast for 50 to 60 minutes, until fork-tender. Remove them from the oven and let cool. When the beets are cool enough to handle, peel and slice into matchsticks.

3 Transfer the cabbage to a large platter. Season generously with salt and pepper and toss to mix. Add about three-quarters of the dressing and toss to coat. Taste and season with salt, pepper, or vinegar as needed. Spread out the cabbage to form a bed for the beets.

4 Arrange the beets on top of the cabbage. Top with crumbled goat cheese. Drizzle the remaining dressing over the salad and serve.

Kitchen Note: *If you prefer, you can boil the beets instead of roasting them. Put the beets in a medium saucepan and cover with water. Cover the pot, bring to a boil, and boil gently until the beets are fork-tender, about 40 minutes. Drain, cool, and peel. (Boiled beets must be peeled. Roasted beets do not require peeling.)*

Wilted Cabbage Salad, Italian Style

Serves 6

A high-quality vinegar makes all the difference in a recipe this simple.

> 4 ounces pancetta, finely chopped
> 1 small head green or savoy cabbage, thinly sliced or shredded (6–8 cups)
> ¼ cup red wine vinegar
> 1 teaspoon sugar
>   Salt and freshly ground black pepper

1 Heat a Dutch oven over medium-high heat. Add the pancetta and cook until somewhat browned, 5 to 7 minutes. Add the cabbage and toss until well coated with fat. Add the vinegar and continue to cook, stirring occasionally, until the cabbage is wilted, 5 to 8 minutes.

2 Stir in the sugar. Season generously with salt and pepper. Let stand for about 30 minutes to allow the flavors to develop. Serve at room temperature.

Variation: Wilted Cabbage Salad, American Style

Substitute bacon for the pancetta. Substitute artisanal apple cider vinegar for the red wine vinegar.

> *You can't get too much winter in the winter.*
> — Robert Frost (1874–1963)

Roasted Beet and Potato Salad

Serves 6-8

If you take care with arranging the vegetables, this salad will be as beautiful to behold as it is delicious to eat. The lemon aioli is a perfect topping for roasted vegetables.

> 4 medium beets
> 1 pound thin-skinned potatoes, cut into 1-inch cubes
> 3 tablespoons extra-virgin olive oil
> Salt and freshly ground black pepper
> Lemon Aioli (page 181)

1 Preheat the oven to 425°F. Lightly oil a half sheet pan (preferred) or large shallow roasting pan.

2 Wrap the beets individually in aluminum foil and transfer to the oven to roast. Mound the potatoes on the half sheet pan. Drizzle with oil and sprinkle with salt and pepper. Toss to coat. Spread the potatoes on the prepared pan in a single layer and transfer to the oven.

3 Roast the potatoes for 35 to 40 minutes, turning occasionally for even cooking, until the potatoes are fork-tender and browned. Roast the beets for 50 to 60 minutes, until fork-tender. Remove the vegetables from the oven and let cool.

4 When the beets are cool enough to handle, peel and slice into thin rounds.

5 To serve, arrange the beets in a concentric circle on a serving platter or individual serving plates. Mound the potatoes in the center. Dollop the aioli on top and serve.

Kitchen Note: *If you prefer, you can boil the beets instead of roasting them. Put the beets in a medium saucepan and cover with water. Cover the pot, bring to a boil, and boil gently until the beets are fork-tender, about 40 minutes. Drain, let cool, and peel. (Boiled beets must be peeled. Roasted beets do not require peeling.)*

Wilted Brussels Sprouts Salad

Serves 4

Bacon is a famously good partner to Brussels sprouts. Here it adds great flavor to what is essentially a variation on the classic spinach salad. With so few ingredients, use only the best. If you can, choose high-quality, artisanal bacon, which is often thick-cut, and unfiltered artisanal apple cider vinegar.

- 4 ounces bacon, diced
- 1 large shallot, diced
- 1¼ pounds Brussels sprouts, trimmed and halved, or quartered if large
- 3 tablespoons apple cider vinegar, or more to taste
- Salt and freshly ground black pepper
- 2 cups toasted croutons

1 Heat a large skillet over medium-high heat. Add the bacon and fry until the bacon starts to become crisp, about 3 minutes. Add the shallot, reduce the heat to medium, and sauté until the shallot is translucent, about 3 minutes. Stir in the Brussels sprouts and sauté until the sprouts are mostly tender, about 7 minutes.

2 Stir in the vinegar and cook until the Brussels sprouts are tender crisp, about 3 to 5 minutes longer. Season with salt and pepper and more vinegar, if desired.

3 Transfer the salad to a serving bowl. Add the croutons and toss to mix. Serve warm.

Kitchen Note: *To make your own croutons, cut enough stale bread into ¾-inch cubes to make about 3 cups. Heat 2 to 3 tablespoons extra-virgin olive oil in a large skillet over medium heat. Add the bread and season with salt, pepper, and ½ teaspoon dried herbs (your choice). Fry until crisp and golden, stirring frequently, 20 to 30 minutes.*

Brussels Sprouts and Citrus Salad

Serves 4–6

Roasting brings out the sweetness that lies dormant in Brussels sprouts. When the roasted sprouts are combined with oranges and a citrus dressing, they make a delicious winter salad. You can use any type of orange you have on hand, including navel or juice oranges, clementines, or tangerines.

3	tablespoons extra-virgin olive oil
1–1½	pounds Brussels sprouts, trimmed and halved, or quartered if large
1	shallot, diced
½	cup slivered almonds
1	large orange or two small tangerines or clementines, peeled, halved, and sliced
3	tablespoons lime juice
½	teaspoon finely minced orange zest
	Salt and freshly ground black pepper

1 Preheat the oven to 425°F. Lightly oil a large sheet pan (preferred) or shallow roasting pan.

2 Drizzle the oil over the Brussels sprouts and shallot in a large bowl and toss gently to coat. Transfer to the sheet pan and spread in a single, uncrowded layer.

3 Roast for 12 minutes. Shake the pan, stir the vegetables, and sprinkle with the almonds. Roast about 5 minutes longer, until the sprouts are tender and lightly browned.

4 Return the vegetable mixture to the bowl. Add the oranges, lime juice, and orange zest. Season with salt and pepper. Toss to coat. The salad can be served immediately or held at room temperature for 1 hour before serving.

Kitchen Note: *In a pinch, use canned mandarin oranges instead of fresh oranges.*

Classic American Coleslaw

Serves 8

Coleslaw is the perfect accompaniment to baked beans and cornbread for a wintry Sunday supper. This version is typical diner fare, but undoubtedly fresher. Add raisins for a classic school lunchroom twist.

1   small head green cabbage, thinly sliced or shredded (6–8 cups), or a mix of green and red cabbage
1   carrot, peeled and shredded
½   small onion, finely chopped
1   cup Miracle Whip salad dressing
3   tablespoons white vinegar
2   tablespoons sugar
    Salt and freshly ground black pepper

1   Combine the cabbage, carrot, and onion in a large mixing bowl. Add the Miracle Whip, vinegar, and sugar, and mix until well combined.

2   Season with salt and pepper; be generous with the pepper. Cover and refrigerate for at least 1 hour, and up to 8 hours, before serving.

Kitchen Note: *In old American cookbooks, you will find recipes for "boiled salad dressing," which is what cooks used to whip up before they had Miracle Whip close at hand. It is both sweeter and tarter than mayonnaise. You can substitute mayonnaise for Miracle Whip in any recipe, but the flavor will definitely suffer.*

Creamy Mustard Coleslaw

Serves 4-6

For an interesting variation on the standard American coleslaw, try this family recipe. It is tasty on a grilled cheese sandwich and makes the perfect accompaniment to hot dogs or cold cuts. It may not impress you on first bite, so be sure to let it stand for an hour before serving.

4	cups thinly sliced or shredded green or savoy cabbage, or a mix of green and red cabbage
2	carrots, peeled and shredded
¼	cup minced onion
1	cup mayonnaise
3	tablespoons yellow ballpark mustard
	Salt and freshly ground black pepper

1 Combine the cabbage, carrots, and onion in a large bowl. Mix well.

2 Combine the mayonnaise and mustard in a small bowl and mix until well combined. Spoon the mayonnaise mixture over the cabbage mixture, tossing to coat. Season with salt and pepper.

3 Cover and refrigerate for at least 1 hour, and up to 8 hours, before serving.

Kitchen Note: *In any salad recipe that calls for mayonnaise, a "light" mayonnaise or vegan mayonnaise can be substituted, though you do lose some creamy goodness.*

I will not move my army without onions.

— Ulysses S. Grant (1822–1885)

Creamy Coleslaw

Serves 8

Looking for a low-fat coleslaw? Look no further. Buttermilk replaces most of the mayonnaise in this slightly sweet version.

1	small head green or savoy cabbage, thinly sliced or shredded (6-8 cups), or a mix of green and red cabbage
3	carrots, peeled and shredded
¼	Vidalia or other sweet onion, finely chopped
1½	cups buttermilk
3	tablespoons sugar
3	tablespoons mayonnaise
3	tablespoons apple cider vinegar
½	teaspoon celery seed
	Salt and freshly ground black pepper

1   Combine the cabbage, carrots, and onion in a large mixing bowl.

2   In a smaller bowl, stir together the buttermilk, sugar, mayonnaise, vinegar, and celery seed until well blended. Pour the buttermilk mixture over the cabbage mixture and toss to combine. Season with salt and pepper. The salad will be dry, but the longer it stands, the wetter it will become.

3   Cover and refrigerate for at least 1 hour, and up to 8 hours, before serving.

Kitchen Note: *If you don't have a sweet onion on hand, substitute half of a small yellow onion or a shallot. Don't use so much onion that it overwhelms the other flavors.*

> *In the night the cabbages catch at the moon, the leaves drip silver, the rows of cabbages are a series of little silver waterfalls in the moon.*
> — Carl Sandburg (1878–1967)

Crunchy Dilled Coleslaw

Serves 6-8

One of the great mysteries of life is why people leave the last pickle in a jar to languish in the back of the refrigerator for months. The rest of the jar was consumed in a matter of days, sometimes hours. Why does that last pickle remain? This recipe addresses the problem by using up that last pickle. The sunflower seeds combined with the pickle add great crunch to this salad, which is particularly good on sandwiches.

6 cups thinly sliced or shredded green or savoy cabbage, or a mix of green and red cabbage
2 carrots, peeled and shredded
⅔ cup chopped dill pickles
¾ cup mayonnaise
¼ cup brine from the dill-pickle jar
1 tablespoon yellow ballpark mustard
½ cup sunflower seeds, toasted
Salt and freshly ground black pepper

1 Combine the cabbage, carrots, and pickles in a large bowl.

2 Combine the mayonnaise, pickle brine, and mustard in a small bowl and blend well.

3 Add the mayonnaise mixture to the vegetables. Mix in the sunflower seeds. Taste and add salt, if needed, and pepper; it may not need any salt, depending on the saltiness of the brine.

4 Let stand for about 30 minutes before serving, or refrigerate for up to 8 hours and mix well before serving.

Kitchen Note: *To toast sunflower seeds, place them in a small, dry skillet over medium heat. Toast, stirring frequently, until the seeds begin to change color, about 5 minutes. Do not let the seeds scorch or they will become bitter.*

Sweet-Pickle Coleslaw

Serves 6–8

If your pickle-making tends toward the sweet rather than the sour, you may want to try this coleslaw, which uses bread-and-butter pickles.

> 6   cups thinly sliced or shredded green or savoy cabbage, or a mix of green and red cabbage
> 1   carrot, peeled and shredded
> ½   onion, minced
> 1   cup bread-and-butter pickles, chopped
> ¼   cup brine from the pickle jar
> ¼   cup buttermilk
> ¼   cup extra-virgin olive oil
>   Salt and freshly ground black pepper
> 1–2 tablespoons sugar

1   Combine the cabbage, carrot, onion, and pickles in a large bowl.

2   Combine the pickle brine, buttermilk, and oil in a small bowl. Blend well and add to the cabbage mixture, stirring until well blended. Season with salt and pepper and add sugar to taste; it may not need much sugar.

3   Let stand for at least 30 minutes before serving, or refrigerate for up to 8 hours and mix well before serving.

Kitchen Note: *Because red cabbage is somewhat coarser in texture than green cabbage, I rarely use it as a base for coleslaw. But using about one-quarter red cabbage and three-quarters green cabbage makes a beautiful salad with perfect texture.*

Festive Fruity Coleslaw

Serves 4–6

If ever a coleslaw deserved a place on a holiday table, it is this one.
The salad is colorful, delicious, and full of surprise flavors.

6	cups thinly sliced or shredded green or savoy cabbage
2	cups thinly sliced or shredded red cabbage
¼	red onion or other mild, sweet onion, thinly sliced
¼	cup sugar
¾	cup buttermilk
½	cup mayonnaise
¼	cup lemon juice
½	cup dried cranberries
½	cup pistachio nuts, chopped
2	clementines or tangerines, peeled, divided into segments, and chopped
	Salt and freshly ground black pepper

1   Combine the cabbages and onion in a large bowl.

2   Mix the sugar, buttermilk, mayonnaise, and lemon juice in a small bowl until smooth. Pour the buttermilk mixture over the vegetable mixture and toss to coat thoroughly.

3   Fold in the cranberries, pistachios, and clementines. Season with salt and pepper.

4   Let stand for at least 1 hour, or refrigerate for up to 8 hours, before serving. Taste and adjust the salt and pepper just before serving.

Kitchen Note: *Red cranberries and green pistachios give this salad great color, but other dried fruits and nuts will work just as well.*

It's no use boiling your cabbage twice.
— Irish proverb

Zesty Lemon Coleslaw

Serves 4–6

Simplicity is the hallmark of this salad. Lemon tastes like sunshine on a cold wintry day.

6	cups thinly sliced or shredded green or savoy cabbage, or a mix of green and red cabbage
1	carrot, peeled and shredded
1	(1-inch) slice onion, finely chopped
3	tablespoons extra-virgin olive oil
	Finely grated zest and juice of 1 lemon
1	teaspoon dried dill
1	teaspoon sugar
	Salt and freshly ground black pepper

1　Combine the cabbage, carrot, and onion in a large mixing bowl and toss to mix.

2　Add the oil and toss to coat. Add the lemon zest, lemon juice, dill, and sugar, and season with salt and pepper. Toss well to mix. Let stand for 30 minutes.

3　Taste and adjust the seasoning before serving.

Carrot-Mustard Slaw

Serves 4

The typical carrot slaw is sweet. Here's a savory version to defy expectations.

1	pound carrots (6 medium), peeled and shredded
1	cup finely shredded red cabbage
¼	cup finely chopped red onion
¾	cup mayonnaise
2	tablespoons yellow ballpark mustard, or to taste
	Salt and freshly ground black pepper

1　Combine the carrots, cabbage, and onion in a medium salad bowl. Add the mayonnaise and mustard and mix until well blended. Season with salt and pepper.

2　Cover and let stand for at least 30 minutes, or refrigerate for up to 2 hours, to allow the flavors to develop.

3　Stir well and adjust the seasoning before serving.

Chipotle-Cabbage Salad

Serves 4-6

Designed to replace the lettuce, tomato, and sour cream topping on tacos, this cabbage salad is creamy and mildly spiced to act as a foil for a spicy meat or bean topping. But don't restrict this delicious salad to a single role; it is delicious on its own or topping a turkey or roast beef sandwich. If you're not using this salad to mitigate the heat of another dish, ramp up the chipotle and lime juice for additional flavor.

¾ cup mayonnaise

¾ cup sour cream

3 tablespoons lime juice, or more to taste

2 teaspoons minced chipotle canned in adobo sauce, or more to taste

Salt and freshly ground black pepper

1 small head green or savoy cabbage, thinly sliced or shredded (6-8 cups)

1 carrot, peeled and shredded

⅛-¼ red onion, thinly sliced

1 Mix the mayonnaise, sour cream, lime juice, and chipotle in a small bowl. Season with salt and pepper and additional lime juice and chipotle, if desired.

2 Combine the cabbage, carrot, and onion in a large salad bowl. Add the dressing and toss to coat. Taste and adjust the seasoning.

3 Let stand for at least 30 minutes before serving. The salad holds up well in the refrigerator for at least 8 hours.

Kitchen Note: *Chipotles in adobo sauce are smoke-dried jalapeños in a vinegar sauce, usually found in cans wherever Mexican food is sold. A single can will hold more than this recipe needs, but you can store the leftovers in a glass or plastic container in the refrigerator, where they will keep for months.*

Lahanosalata

Serves 4-6

Greek salad has only one interpretation in this country: a delicious summery base of lettuce, tomato, and cucumber, topped with olives and feta cheese. But that same combination can also be made with cabbage. The revelation of this iteration is how well it holds up on a buffet table or even on a picnic — no dreaded wilted lettuce or water-logged tomatoes. As a winter salad made with cabbage, it is just about perfect.

	Juice of 1 lemon (3-4 tablespoons)
3	tablespoons extra-virgin olive oil
1	small head green or savoy cabbage, thinly sliced or shredded (6-8 cups)
½	red onion, thinly sliced
½	cup Kalamata olives
2-3	ounces feta cheese, crumbled
	Salt and freshly ground black pepper
1	teaspoon dried dill weed

1   Whisk the lemon juice and oil in a large mixing bowl until blended.

2   Add the cabbage and onion and toss to coat. Add the olives and feta and toss gently. Let stand for 30 minutes.

3   Season with salt and pepper. Serve garnished with the dill.

If we had no winter, the spring would not be so pleasant: if we did not sometimes taste of adversity, prosperity would not be so welcome.

— Anne Bradstreet (1612–1672)

Soy-Sesame Cabbage Salad

Serves 4–6

When making a stir-fry, it is sometimes nice to have one dish that has been prepared ahead. This fits the bill nicely.

1 small head green or savoy cabbage, thinly
   sliced or shredded (6–8 cups)
1 carrot, peeled and shredded
1 garlic clove, minced
1 (½-inch) piece fresh ginger, peeled and minced
3 tablespoons rice vinegar
3 tablespoons Asian sesame oil
1 tablespoon soy sauce
1 tablespoon sugar
  Salt and freshly ground black pepper
1 cup slivered almonds, toasted
2 tablespoons sesame seeds, toasted

1 Combine the cabbage, carrot, garlic, and ginger in a large bowl. Add the vinegar, sesame oil, soy sauce, and sugar, and toss to coat. Season with salt and pepper.

2 Let stand for 30 minutes. Add the almonds and sesame seeds and toss to combine. Taste and adjust the seasoning before serving.

Kitchen Note: *To toast the almonds and sesame seeds, combine them in a small, dry skillet over medium heat. Cook, stirring, until slightly colored, about 5 minutes. Do not let them scorch or they will become bitter.*

Thai Cabbage Salad

Serves 6–8

With nothing but napa cabbage and carrots, you can make a delightful salad to accompany any Asian-style meal. If you happen to have scallions, cilantro, and/or mint on hand as well, add a handful of each. Either way, this light salad is filled with fresh, unexpected flavors. Try it in a wrap with a grilled chicken breast.

⅓   cup Asian fish sauce
¼   cup white vinegar
3   tablespoons sugar
2   garlic cloves, minced
    Pinch crushed red pepper flakes, or more to taste
1   small head napa or Chinese cabbage (about 1½ pounds), thinly sliced or shredded
1   large carrot, peeled and shredded
½   cup chopped, roasted peanuts, plus more for garnish

1   To make the dressing, combine the fish sauce, vinegar, sugar, and garlic, and heat gently until the sugar is completely dissolved. (Half a minute in the microwave should do the trick.) Add the red pepper flakes.

2   Combine the cabbage, carrot, and peanuts in a large bowl.

3   Pour the dressing over the salad and toss until completely coated.

4   Let stand for about 30 minutes. Transfer to a serving bowl and serve garnished with peanuts.

Kitchen Note: *Fish sauce is a pungent liquid made from the liquid that drains from salted, fermented fish. It is called* nam pla *in Thailand and* nuoc mam *in Vietnam, where its unique flavor is used much as soy sauce is used in China. Look for it wherever Asian foods are sold; there is no substitute for it, but a bottle will keep indefinitely.*

Thai Sweet-Spicy Cabbage Salad

Serves 6-8

This cabbage salad uses regular green cabbage, but napa cabbage could be substituted. It is simpler to prepare than the previous recipe, but equally wonderful. The secret ingredient is Thai sweet chili sauce, a condiment found in Asian markets. It is made of sugar, vinegar, and chiles and makes a wonderful dressing for salads or a dip for spring rolls. Like the previous salad, this salad combined with chicken makes a delicious wrap.

1	small head green cabbage, thinly sliced or shredded (6-8 cups)
2	teaspoons salt
1	carrot, peeled and shredded
½	cup Thai sweet chili sauce
½	cup chopped roasted peanuts

1 Combine the cabbage and salt in a colander and toss to mix. Let stand for about an hour to wilt the cabbage.

2 Taste the cabbage. If it is too salty, rinse with cold running water, and then drain. Combine the cabbage, carrot, and chili sauce in a large bowl and toss to mix. Add the peanuts and toss to mix.

3 Let stand for 30 minutes to allow the flavors to develop before serving.

Copper Coins

Serves 4–6

One of my early cooking jobs was at an assisted-living home, where I learned to cook many old-fashioned American classics. Why the three-bean salad remains in the average American repertoire but this tasty salad rarely gets made any more is a mystery to me. It was a favorite among my ladies.

6	carrots, peeled and sliced	1	shallot, chopped
¼	cup ketchup	2	garlic cloves, chopped
⅓	cup water	1	teaspoon soy sauce
2	tablespoons extra-virgin olive oil	1	teaspoon ground ginger
2	tablespoons apple cider vinegar		Salt and freshly ground black pepper
1	tablespoon brown sugar		

1 Bring a pot of salted water to a boil. Add the carrots and blanch until tender crisp, about 3 minutes. Plunge into ice water to stop the cooking, then drain.

2 Combine the ketchup, water, oil, vinegar, sugar, shallot, garlic, soy sauce, and ginger in a blender and process until smooth. Season with salt and pepper.

3 Transfer the carrots to a large bowl. Add the dressing and toss. Taste and adjust the seasoning as needed.

The World Carrot Museum

Thanks to the Internet, museums don't have to be brick-and-mortar affairs that one visits on vacation or on a school field trip. The World Carrot Museum, a virtual museum curated by John Stolarczyk, has dozens of pages of photos of carrot-abilia from collectors all over the world, including plates, teapots, pitchers, carrot scrapers, key rings, refrigerator magnets, corkscrews, knives, badges, Christmas ornaments, jewelry, and more. Carrot history, recipes, nutrition, festivals, trivia, science experiments, jokes, cultivation tips, and so much more are found in this engaging "museum." This is possibly the single best vegetable site ever. Visit it for yourself at www.carrotmuseum.co.uk.

🌿 Carrots in Citrus Vinaigrette

Serves 4-6

Freshly harvested carrots are so perfect in flavor and texture it is a shame to do anything more to them than peel and eat. But, as carrots are stored over the winter, the sugars that made the carrots so sweet when freshly harvested, are slowly turned into starch. Then it is time to play with the flavor and try a recipe like this one.

1	shallot, chopped
½	teaspoon finely grated lemon zest
3	tablespoons lemon juice
3	tablespoons orange juice
¼	teaspoon Dijon mustard
½	teaspoon ground ginger
	Salt and freshly ground black pepper
6	carrots, peeled and cut into matchsticks

1 Combine the shallot, lemon zest, lemon juice, orange juice, mustard, and ginger in a blender and process until smooth. Season with salt and pepper. Pour into a bowl.

2 Bring a pot of salted water to a boil. Add the carrots and blanch until tender crisp, about 3 minutes. Drain.

3 Transfer the carrots to the bowl with the dressing. Toss to coat. Taste and adjust the seasoning.

4 Let stand for at least 30 minutes before serving.

Thai Vegetable Salad

Serves 4

"Eat locally, spice globally" is one of the rallying calls for people who are concerned about the carbon footprint of their foods. They are talking about a dish like this one, simply made with locally grown root vegetables but transformed into an exotic dish with the addition of Thai sweet chili sauce. This traditional Thai condiment, found wherever Asian foods are sold, is also wonderful as a dipping sauce for spring rolls and grilled chicken. I also use it in a cabbage salad (page 61).

1	pound daikon radish or 1 large turnip, peeled and cut into matchsticks
½	pound carrots, peeled and cut into matchsticks
1	tablespoon salt
¼	cup Thai sweet chili sauce

1   Combine the daikon, carrots, and salt in a colander. Toss to mix. Let drain for 1 hour. Rinse well.

2   Transfer the vegetables to a bowl. Add the chili sauce and toss to coat. Let stand for at least 30 minutes before serving.

Kitchen Note: *Early in the fall, turnips are crisp and sweet enough to be used interchangeably with daikon radish. Later in winter, turnips are best in recipes where they are cooked.*

There's no getting blood out of a turnip.
— Frederick Marryat (1792–1848)

My Asian Pantry

My first cooking job was in a tiny upstate New York Chinese restaurant. I had taken the waitressing job as an opportunity to eat Chinese food; I was moved into the kitchen after I proved to be a lousy waitress. In the kitchen I was exposed to a world of Chinese ingredients, and that has made all the difference in my cooking. Here's what I always have on hand.

Chinese Chili Paste with Garlic. Made with ground chilis, vinegar, and salt, it adds great flavor and heat to dishes. An opened jar will keep forever in the refrigerator but will lose its punch after a while.

Hoisin Sauce. Called the Chinese barbecue sauce, hoisin is a thick, sweet sauce that can be used as a barbeque sauce. It is the condiment that is served with moo shu dishes and Peking duck at Chinese restaurants in this country.

Mirin. A sweetened Japanese rice wine. If you don't have any on hand, substitute Chinese rice wine.

Oyster Sauce. Oyster sauce is a Cantonese cooking staple, originally made with oysters, salt, and water, but now likely to contain caramel coloring and cornstarch as well. Store open bottles in the refrigerator. Mock oyster sauce and stir-fry sauce are vegetarian equivalents.

Rice Wine. Chinese rice wine is a clear, light wine. Shaoshing rice wine is of high quality and has the flavor and color of sherry, which makes a good substitute.

Sesame Oil. Asian sesame oil is made from toasted seeds, so its color is a dark amber. It is used more for flavoring than as a cooking medium.

Soy Sauce. Kikkoman is a good brand that is nationally distributed.

Lentil Salad with Carrots and Goat Cheese

Serves 4-6

French green lentils, or *lentiles du Puy*, are the lentil of choice for this simple combination because they hold their shape so well. The carrots and red onions provide a vivid color and texture contrast, and the goat cheese applied to the warm lentils gives the dressing both flavor and a creamy consistency. Serve as either a side dish or main dish salad.

1½	cups dried French green lentils, rinsed and picked over
2	carrots, peeled and finely diced
½	red onion, finely diced
4	ounces soft fresh goat cheese (chèvre), crumbled
¼	cup extra-virgin olive oil
¼	cup red wine vinegar
1	teaspoon sugar
	Salt and freshly ground black pepper

1 Combine the lentils with about 8 cups salted water. Bring to a boil and boil gently until the lentils are tender but not mushy, 15 to 20 minutes. Begin tasting at 15 minutes and be sure to remove the lentils from the heat when they are fully tender but still hold their shape; do not overcook. Drain and transfer to a large mixing bowl.

2 While the lentils are still warm, use a rubber spatula to gently mix the carrots, onion, and goat cheese into the lentils. Add the oil, vinegar, and sugar, and mix carefully but thoroughly. Season with salt and pepper and mix gently.

3 Let stand for at least 15 minutes before serving. Taste and adjust the seasoning just before serving.

Kitchen Note: *Tossing a salad with one or two rubber spatulas is a good way to mix fragile ingredients, such as lentils or roasted sweet potatoes.*

Celery Root, Apple, and Walnut Salad

Serves 6-8

This dish has the same blend of flavors as a Waldorf salad, with the advantage of being made with a root vegetable that stores well. The apples for this salad can be whatever you have on hand, although Cortlands do particularly well in salads because they are slow to brown. The blanching step is optional, but I prefer it; I think it improves the flavor and mouthfeel of celery root.

1	celery root, peeled and shredded
2-3	large apples, quartered, cored, and thinly sliced
1	cup walnuts, toasted
1	tablespoon lemon juice, or more to taste
1	teaspoon sugar, or more to taste
⅓	cup mayonnaise
	Salt and freshly ground black pepper

1   Bring a pot of salted water to a boil. Add the celery root and cook for 1 minute. Drain well and rinse under cold running water until cool.

2   Combine the celery root, apples, and walnuts in a medium bowl. Sprinkle with the lemon juice and sugar. Add the mayonnaise and mix well. Season to taste with salt and pepper.

3   Let stand for at least 30 minutes to allow the flavors to develop. Taste and add more lemon juice, sugar, salt, and pepper as needed, and serve. You can hold the salad in an airtight container in the refrigerator for up to 4 hours before serving.

Kitchen Note: *To toast walnuts, heat a large dry skillet over medium heat. Add the walnuts and toast, stirring frequently, until fragrant and lightly colored, about 5 minutes.*

Endive and Apple Salad with Candied Nuts and Blue Cheese

Serves 4

This salad is a study in contrasts: the sweet-and-sour dressing, the crunchy apples and nuts, the slightly bitter endive, and the earthy, soft cheese.

CANDIED NUTS

- 2   tablespoons sunflower or canola oil
- 1   cup walnuts, pecans, or almonds
- 2   tablespoons balsamic vinegar
- 1   tablespoon sugar
-     Pinch of ground cinnamon

ENDIVE SALAD

- 6   Belgian endives, trimmed and sliced
- 2   apples, cored and diced
-     Maple-Balsamic Vinaigrette (page 89)
- ½   cup crumbled blue cheese

1   To prepare the candied nuts, heat the oil in a medium skillet over medium heat. Add the nuts and sauté until fragrant and lightly toasted, 2 to 3 minutes. Add the vinegar, sugar, and cinnamon, and toss with a spoon until the sugar caramelizes. Continue until the sugar sticks to the nuts and is no longer grainy. Spoon the nuts onto a plate and let cool; the nuts will crisp as they cool.

2   To assemble the salad, toss the endive, apples, and candied nuts in a large bowl. Drizzle the vinaigrette over the salad and toss gently. Taste and adjust the seasoning. Top with the blue cheese and serve immediately.

Extend Your Harvest Season with Belgian Endive

If you have a root cellar or cool basement, consider growing Belgian endives. It is a two-part process: first you grow the roots in the garden, then you force a new plant in the darkness of a cool basement.

Begin in the garden in early spring. Sow the seeds for Belgian endive (also known as witloof chicory) in loose soil, thinning to space the plants about 9 inches apart. Keep well watered and well weeded.

In the fall, carefully dig up the roots. Cut off any side roots. Then cut off the leafy tops to within 1 inch of the crowns, and shorten each root to a manageable length of about 8 inches. Store the roots in a perforated plastic bag in the refrigerator (just as you would store carrots), and remove a few at a time for forcing. Forcing will take 3 to 4 weeks, so plan accordingly.

To force the Belgian endive, pack the roots upright in a deep flowerpot or wooden box filled with well-drained garden soil, sand, or potting soil. Water thoroughly. Then cover the crowns of the plants with about 8 inches of dry sand, soil, or sawdust to keep the growing leaves blanched.

Leave the box in the basement or some other dark spot where the temperature is cool, preferably in the low 60s. Check every few days to make sure the mix around the roots is moist. In three or four weeks, depending on the temperature, tips of leafy heads will begin to peek through the top layer. Cut the bullet-shaped head from the roots and compost the roots. There's only one harvest (of a "chicon") from a root.

Belgian endive has a bracing bitterness and a juicy texture. Sliced raw, it makes a fine replacement for lettuce, and it goes particularly well with earthy goat cheese. Fill the spear-shaped leaves with a dab of goat cheese or boursin cheese, and arrange them in a sunburst pattern on a platter to make a very attractive-looking appetizer.

Cooking mellows the bitterness. Halved Belgian endives are terrific braised (25 to 40 minutes), grilled (8 to 14 minutes), or roasted (20 to 25 minutes at 450°F).

Wilted Kale Salad

Serves 4

The kale in this recipe is lightly cooked and then dressed in a Japanese-style dressing. The salad includes carrot for color and arame, a type of seaweed, for flavor. You can find arame at most natural-foods stores and wherever Japanese foods are sold.

½ cup dried arame (sea vegetable)
2 tablespoons Asian sesame oil
3 garlic cloves, minced
1 (1½-inch) piece fresh ginger, peeled and minced
1 bunch kale, thinly sliced (6–8 cups; remove and discard tough stems)
1 carrot, peeled and shredded
2 tablespoons tamari or soy sauce, or to taste
1 tablespoon rice vinegar, or to taste
1 tablespoon sesame seeds, toasted

1 Put the arame in a bowl, cover with boiling water, and let soak until tender, about 10 minutes. Drain well.

2 Heat the sesame oil in a large wok or skillet over medium heat. Add the garlic and ginger and stir-fry until fragrant, about 30 seconds. Add the arame, kale, and carrot, and sauté until the kale is limp, about 1 minute. Add the tamari and vinegar, cover, and cook until the kale is tender, 3 to 5 minutes; do not overcook.

3 Transfer the kale mixture and cooking liquid to a serving bowl and let cool. Taste and adjust seasoning if needed. Garnish with toasted sesame seeds and serve.

Kitchen Note: *To toast sesame seeds, heat a small saucepan over medium heat. Add the sesame seeds and cook, stirring, until the seeds are fragrant and lightly colored, 3 to 5 minutes.*

Let food be your medicine and medicine be your food.
— Hippocrates (460–377 B.C.)

Dilled Potato and Egg Salad

Serves 6–8

Potato salad needs little bits of crunchy vegetables to play against the soft potato-egg-mayonnaise mixture. Instead of out-of-season celery and red bell peppers, how about shredded carrots and crunchy bits of dill pickle? Delicious!

2½	pounds waxy potatoes
3	hard-cooked eggs, peeled and chopped
1	carrot, peeled and shredded
½	small onion, finely chopped or shredded
1	cup diced dill pickles
1	cup mayonnaise
1	tablespoon yellow ballpark mustard
	Salt and freshly ground black pepper
	Paprika or dried dill, for garnish

1 Cover the potatoes by 1 inch with cold salted water in a large saucepan. Bring to a simmer over medium-high heat and simmer until the potatoes are tender, 15 to 30 minutes, depending on the size of the potatoes. Drain well and let cool.

2 When the potatoes are cool enough to handle, peel and slice them into ½-inch cubes.

3 Combine the potatoes, eggs, carrot, onion, and pickles in a large mixing bowl. Add the mayonnaise and mustard and season with salt and pepper. Mix well. Chill for at least 4 hours and up to 8 hours. (The flavor of the salad improves after several hours.)

4 Just before serving, taste and adjust the seasoning. Sprinkle with paprika to garnish.

Kitchen Note: *We often say "hard-boiled" egg, but the reality is that eggs shouldn't boil unless you want an egg with a rubbery texture. Put the eggs in a small saucepan, cover with cold water, and bring to a boil. When the water boils, cover the pot and remove it from the heat. Let stand for 10 minutes, then drain off the hot water and replace it with cold water, letting the water run from the tap until the water in the pan is truly cold. The faster you chill the egg, the less likely the shell will stick to it.*

Roasted Sweet-Potato Salad with Sesame-Ginger Vinaigrette

Serves 6

Healthful, colorful, delicious — you couldn't ask for a better salad.

3	sweet potatoes (about 3 pounds), peeled and diced
2	shallots, diced
3	tablespoons sunflower or canola oil
	Salt and freshly ground black pepper
1	cup dried cranberries
1	cup flaked or sliced almonds
	Sesame-Ginger Vinaigrette (page 88)

1   Preheat the oven to 500°F, with the rack in the lower third of the oven. Lightly oil a half sheet pan (preferred) or large shallow roasting pan.

2   Mound the sweet potatoes and shallots on the prepared pan. Drizzle with the oil and season with salt and pepper. Toss to coat. Arrange in a single layer on the pan. Do not crowd the potatoes or the final texture will be soft and mushy.

3   Roast in the lower third of the oven for 20 to 25 minutes, stirring or shaking the pan once for even cooking, until the potatoes are tender.

4   Combine the roasted vegetables, cranberries, and almonds in a large salad bowl. Toss to mix. Pour in the dressing and toss until fully coated. Taste and adjust the seasoning. Serve warm or at room temperature.

Kitchen Note: *Some varieties of sweet potato are better for roasting, others for mashing. Garnets are a good choice for roasting because they hold their shape well.*

North African Turnip Salad

Serves 4–6

Freshly dug turnips are delightfully crisp and sweet. This salad combines turnips and carrots with some unusual flavors, including harissa, an aromatic North African chili paste.

6	turnips, peeled and shredded
2	carrots, peeled and shredded
¼	cup minced red onion
2	clementines or small tangerines, peeled, seeded, and chopped
¼	cup extra-virgin olive oil
3	tablespoons lime juice
½–2	teaspoons harissa
	Salt and freshly ground black pepper

1   Combine the turnips, carrots, onion, and clementines in a large mixing bowl. Sprinkle with salt and mix well. Set aside for 30 minutes.

2   Combine the oil, lime juice, and ½ teaspoon harissa, and mix well. Season with salt and pepper and additional harissa, as desired.

3   Pour the dressing over the vegetables and toss to coat.

4   Let stand for at least 30 minutes before serving. (The salad can be made up to 1 day in advance and kept in the refrigerator.)

Kitchen Notes: *One large lime typically yields about 3 tablespoons of juice. You may want to buy two limes, just in case. Also, the heat levels of various harissa brands vary, so add cautiously until you determine the heat level you prefer. If you can't find harissa, substitute another hot sauce or chili paste.*

Soba Noodle Salad

Serves 4

Seaweed and other ingredients typical in Japanese cooking can be found in natural-foods stores, Asian markets, and many supermarkets. Adding cubes of tofu makes this a one-dish meal.

2 cups arame (sea vegetable)	2 tablespoons Asian sesame oil
3 tablespoons rice vinegar	1 cup peeled and julienned carrots
¼ cup tamari or soy sauce	1 cup peeled and julienned daikon radish or turnip
3 tablespoons mirin (Japanese sweet rice wine)	12 ounces soba noodles
2 garlic cloves, minced	2 tablespoons sesame seeds
1 tablespoon chopped pickled ginger	

1. Combine the arame with hot water to cover in a nonreactive saucepan. Let soak for 15 minutes.

2. To make the dressing, combine the vinegar, tamari, mirin, garlic, ginger, and 1 tablespoon of the sesame oil in a jar with a tight-fitting lid. Shake vigorously and set aside.

3. Bring a large pot of salted water to a boil for the noodles.

4. While the water for the noodles is heating, drain the arame and return to the saucepan. Cover with fresh water and bring to a boil over high heat. Add the carrots and daikon and cook until the vegetables are just tender, 3 to 4 minutes. Drain immediately and transfer to a bowl.

5. Boil the soba noodles until al dente, 5 to 7 minutes. Drain, rinse in cold water, and drain again. Toss with the remaining 1 tablespoon sesame oil. Add to the bowl with the vegetables.

6. Shake the dressing and pour over the salad. Toss well to coat. Garnish with the sesame seeds and serve immediately.

Kitchen Note: *Soba is a Japanese noodle made from buckwheat and wheat flour. It is the perfect noodle for this salad, but whole-wheat or regular wheat noodles can be substituted.*

🍃 Sesame Noodle Salad

Serves 4–6

An arsenal of Chinese condiments combines to make the spicy dressing for these noodles. Serve as soon as you combine the noodles and dressing. If you want to make the components ahead, cook the noodles and toss with sesame oil, assemble the vegetables, and make the dressing. Refrigerate separately and combine just before serving.

1	pound dried vermicelli	1	tablespoon Chinese black vinegar
1	leek, trimmed and very thinly sliced	1	tablespoon rice vinegar, or to taste
3	tablespoons Asian sesame oil	1	tablespoon Chinese rice wine or dry sherry
2	garlic cloves, chopped	1	teaspoon Chinese chili paste with garlic, or more to taste
1	(½-inch) piece fresh ginger, peeled and chopped	2	tablespoons sugar, or more to taste
¼	cup tahini	1	carrot, peeled and finely julienned
¼	cup water	1	(6-inch) piece daikon radish or 2 turnips, peeled and finely julienned
3	tablespoons soy sauce, or more to taste		

1. Bring a large pot of salted water to a boil. Cook the noodles in boiling water according to the package directions, until al dente. Reserve 1 cup of the cooking water.

2. Place the leeks in a colander. Drain the noodles in the same colander; the hot water will cook the leeks. Rinse with cold water. Transfer the noodles and leeks into a large bowl and toss with 2 tablespoons of the sesame oil.

3. Combine the garlic and ginger in a blender and process until finely chopped. Add the remaining 1 tablespoon sesame oil, tahini, water, soy sauce, black vinegar, rice vinegar, rice wine, chili paste, and sugar. Blend well. Dip a noodle into the sauce and adjust the seasoning.

4. Toss the noodles with the carrot and daikon and serve immediately. If you can't serve immediately, cover and refrigerate the noodle mixture. Hold the dressing at room temperature for up to 4 hours. Just before serving, add the dressing to the noodles and toss well. Taste and adjust the seasoning as needed.

Kitchen Note: *Chinese black vinegar is the ingredient you are least likely to have in your pantry, and buying it may require a trip to an Asian market. You can come reasonably close to it with a mixture of 1 part soy sauce, 1 part Worestershire sauce, and 1 part rice vinegar.*

Couscous Salad with Kale and Feta

Serves 6

Kale chopped into bite-size pieces works surprisingly well as a salad ingredient. The kale adds the green, and the lemon and feta contribute bold flavor.

1½   cups couscous
½   teaspoon salt, plus more as needed
2¼   cups boiling water
6   cups lightly packed chopped kale, in bite-size pieces (remove and discard tough stems)
     Finely grated zest of 1 lemon
     Juice of 1½–2 lemons (about 5 tablespoons)
¼   teaspoon Dijon mustard
⅓   cup extra-virgin olive oil
3   ounces feta cheese, crumbled
1   cup pitted Kalamata olives
     Salt and freshly ground black pepper

1   Combine the couscous, salt, and boiling water in a large bowl. Cover and let stand until the couscous is tender and the water is absorbed, about 10 minutes. Fluff with a fork and let cool.

2   Bring a large pot of salted water to a boil. Add the kale and cook until tender, about 5 minutes. Drain and immediately plunge into ice water to stop the cooking and preserve the bright color. When cooled, drain well again.

3   Combine the lemon zest, juice of 1 lemon, and mustard in a small bowl. Slowly pour in the oil, whisking constantly, until the oil is completely blended. Pour over the couscous and mix well.

4   Add the kale, feta, and olives to the couscous. Mix well. Season with salt, if needed, and pepper. Let stand for 30 minutes before serving to allow the flavors to develop. Taste again and add more salt, pepper, and lemon juice as needed.

Wild Rice Salad with Roasted Squash and Fennel

Serves 6–8

With its triple dose of native North American ingredients (wild rice, winter squash, and cranberries), this delicious salad makes a wonderful addition to the Thanksgiving meal. It is easily made in advance and holds up well on a buffet table.

1½ cups wild rice	1 onion, halved and slivered (sliced vertically)
4½ cups water	Walnut Vinaigrette (page 86)
1 teaspoon salt	½ cup pecan or walnut pieces
1 medium fennel bulb, stalks discarded and bulb cut into matchsticks	1 cup dried sweetened cranberries
1 small butternut squash, peeled, seeded, and diced	Salt and freshly ground black pepper

1 Rinse the rice in a sieve under cold running water. Drain. In a saucepan, combine the rice, water, and salt. Bring to a boil, then reduce the heat and simmer, covered, until the rice is tender and most of the grains have burst open, 40 to 60 minutes. Drain off any excess water. Transfer to a large bowl to cool.

2 Preheat the oven to 425°F. Lightly oil a half sheet pan (preferred) or large shallow roasting pan.

3 Combine the fennel, squash, and onion in a medium bowl. Add 2 tablespoons of the dressing and toss to coat. Transfer the vegetables to the pan and arrange in a single layer. Roast the vegetables for 20 to 30 minutes, stirring or shaking the pan occasionally for even cooking, until barely browned.

4 Meanwhile, spread out the nuts on a baking sheet. Roast for about 5 minutes, until fragrant. Check after a few minutes and remove the nuts from the oven as soon as they begin to color; do not allow the nuts to scorch.

5 Add the roasted vegetables, nuts, and cranberries to the rice. Pour the remaining dressing over the salad and toss to coat. Season with salt and pepper.

6 Let the salad stand for about 30 minutes to allow the flavors to blend, or cover and refrigerate for up to 3 hours. Warm to room temperature before serving.

Curried Rice Salad with Mango Chutney Dressing

Serves 6–8

Rice and beans are always perfect together. Here the combination includes not only rice and beans but also apples, carrots, and almonds. Mango chutney forms a light and flavorful base for the salad dressing. If you happen to have any fresh cilantro or mint, toss in a handful for extra color and flavor.

SALAD

- 2 cups basmati or long-grain white rice
- 2 tablespoons sunflower or canola oil
- 1 shallot, minced
- 1 (1-inch) piece fresh ginger, peeled and minced
- 2 garlic cloves, minced
- 4 teaspoons curry powder
- 1 teaspoon garam masala
- 1 teaspoon salt, or more to taste
- 3½ cups water
- 2 red-skinned apples
- 2 tablespoons lime juice
- 3 carrots, peeled and shredded
- 1½ cups cooked chickpeas, or 1 (15-ounce) can, rinsed and drained
- 1 cup whole roasted almonds

DRESSING

- ⅔ cup mango or peach chutney
- ¼ cup lime juice
- 3 tablespoons sunflower or canola oil
- 1 teaspoon Tabasco or other hot pepper sauce

Salt and freshly ground black pepper

1 Wash the rice in several changes of water until the water runs clear. Drain well. (This keeps the rice from clumping together, but it is an optional step.)

2 Heat the oil over medium heat in a large saucepan. Add the shallot, ginger, garlic, curry powder, garam masala, and rice. Sauté until the rice appears dry, about 4 minutes. Add the salt and water, then reduce the heat and cook at a gentle boil, covered, until the rice is tender and the water is absorbed, about 15 minutes. Fluff with a fork and let cool.

3 Grate the unpeeled apple into a large salad bowl and toss with the lime juice. Add the cooled rice, carrots, chickpeas, and almonds, and toss to mix.

4   To make the dressing, combine the chutney, lime juice, oil, and Tabasco in a blender or food processor and process until smooth. Season with salt and pepper. Pour the dressing over the salad, toss to coat, and serve.

Kitchen Note: *Major Grey's, made by Crosse & Blackwell, is the most popular brand of chutney in the United States. It is a lovely, well-balanced, light-colored chutney made with mangoes. Feel free to substitute another chutney, preferably one made with light-colored fruit.*

Sunflower Oil

A recent addition to the locavore's pantry is organic cold-pressed sunflower oil. This light oil is slightly nutty in flavor and has a combination of monounsaturated and polyunsaturated fats with low saturated-fat levels, which makes it a healthful oil for cooking. When I need a neutral-tasting oil, I turn to sunflower oil where I used to turn to canola oil, in part because I love the idea of fields of sunflowers waving in the wind. There is one such field near me, and it never fails to bring me delight.

Sunflower was a common crop among American Indian tribes throughout North America. It may even have been domesticated before corn. The seed was cracked and eaten as a snack or ground or pounded into flour.

Spanish explorers brought this exotic North American plant to Europe in the 1500s, and it was widely planted, mainly as an ornamental. Then, in 1716, an English inventor was granted a patent for squeezing oil from sunflower seed. By 1830, the manufacture of sunflower oil was done on a commercial scale. Its popularity was greatly boosted when the Russian Orthodox Church failed to list sunflower oil as a forbidden oil during Lent. By the early nineteenth century, Russian farmers were growing more than 2 million acres of sunflower.

In the United States, sunflower seeds were commercially grown for poultry feed in the eighteenth and nineteenth centuries. In 1926, the Missouri Sunflower Growers' Association participated in what is likely the first processing of sunflower seed into oil. Since then, with modern technology and improved seed, acreage devoted to sunflowers has steadily increased.

The newest development in the history of the age-old crop has been the growing of organic seeds for small-scale cold-pressed oil production. Look for some at your local farmers' market.

Winter Pasta Salad with Red Cabbage and Carrot

Serves 6–8

Like most main-course salads, we think of pasta salads as summer dishes. But made with hearty tortellini and colorful red cabbage and carrots, this salad fits the bill for a lovely winter dish. Tortellini is a child-friendly ingredient — I like to bring this dish to potlucks where I suspect the kids won't find other foods they will like.

1 (20-ounce) package fresh or frozen (not dried) tortellini
3 tablespoons extra-virgin olive oil
¼ head red cabbage, shredded
1–2 carrots, peeled and shredded
1 large shallot or ¼ red onion, finely diced
1 cup pitted Kalamata or Niçoise olives
Finely grated zest and juice of 1 lemon
Salt and freshly ground black pepper

1 Bring a large pot of salted water to a boil. Cook the tortellini in the boiling water until tender throughout. Drain. Rinse briefly under cool running water. Drain well. Transfer to a large bowl and toss with the oil.

2 Add the cabbage, carrots, shallot, olives, and lemon zest, and toss well. Add the lemon juice and season with salt and pepper. Toss again. Taste and adjust the seasoning.

3 Let the salad stand for about 15 minutes before serving to allow the flavors to develop.

Chinese-Style Chicken Salad

Serves 6

My favorite way to serve this salad is as a filling for a wrap that has been brushed with hoisin sauce. It can also be served as a filling for lettuce cups, or set out on a table with an array of other salads or Chinese-inspired dishes. Incidentally, it is also a good way to use leftover chicken, something I find myself with whenever I make chicken broth.

NOODLES
- 2 ounces cellophane noodles
- 1 tablespoon Asian sesame oil
- ¼ teaspoon salt

DRESSING
- 3 tablespoons soy sauce
- 2 tablespoons Asian sesame oil
- 2 tablespoons hoisin sauce
- 1 tablespoon rice vinegar
- 1 teaspoon Chinese chili paste with garlic
- 1 (1½-inch) piece fresh ginger, peeled and minced
- 1 garlic clove, finely minced

SALAD
- 2 cups shredded cooked chicken
- 3 cups finely chopped napa or Chinese cabbage
- 1 large carrot, peeled and shredded
- 1 (4-inch) piece daikon radish or 1 small turnip, peeled and shredded
- ¼ cup chopped fresh cilantro (optional)
- 2 scallions or 1 shallot, finely chopped
- 1 tablespoon sesame seeds

1 Soak the noodles in hot water to cover for 10 minutes while you bring a small pot of water to a boil. When the water boils, add the noodles and boil until tender, 3 to 5 minutes. Drain and run under cold water to stop the cooking. Toss with the sesame oil and salt and set aside.

2 To make the dressing, whisk the soy sauce, sesame oil, hoisin sauce, vinegar, chili paste, ginger, and garlic until well blended.

3 Combine the chicken, cabbage, carrot, daikon, cilantro, if using, and scallions in a large bowl. Add the dressing and toss to coat.

4 Arrange the cellophane noodles on a platter. Mound the chicken salad on top. Sprinkle with the sesame seeds and serve.

Kitchen Note: *Cellophane noodles, also called glass noodles or bean threads, are made from mung-bean starch. They are found wherever Asian foods are sold. If you can't find them, use rice noodles instead, or omit altogether.*

Chinese Vegetable Pickles

Serves 4–6

This makes a great side dish to add to any meal, but particularly one with an Asian theme. The pickle eaters in my household make short work of this one, but it will keep for up to 2 weeks in the refrigerator.

1	(8-inch) piece daikon radish or 1 turnip, peeled and cut into matchsticks
2	carrots, peeled and cut into matchsticks
6	leaves napa or Chinese cabbage, thinly sliced (about 2 cups)
1	tablespoon salt
¾	cup rice vinegar
¾	cup sugar
2	garlic cloves, minced
2	thin slices fresh ginger
1	teaspoon crushed red pepper flakes

1   Combine the daikon, carrot, and cabbage in a large mixing bowl. Sprinkle with salt and mix well. Let stand for 30 minutes.

2   Meanwhile, combine the vinegar, sugar, garlic, ginger, and red pepper flakes in a non-reactive saucepan. Bring to a boil, stirring to dissolve the sugar, then reduce the heat and simmer for 5 minutes. Let cool completely.

3   Transfer the vegetables to a colander, rinse under cold running water, and drain well. Return the vegetables to the bowl, add the vinegar solution to the vegetables, and toss to coat.

4   Let stand for 30 minutes before serving.

Quick Ginger-Pickled Beets

Serves 6–8

If you love the occasional pickled beet but don't want to fuss with a boiling-water bath for long-term storage, this recipe should work for you.

4–6	medium beets, tops and roots trimmed to 1 inch
1	cup apple cider vinegar
1	cup water
½	cup sugar
2	tablespoons chopped crystallized ginger
1	onion, thinly sliced
1	teaspoon salt

1 To cook the beets, preheat the oven to 350°F. Wash the beets, but do not peel. Wrap individually in aluminum foil. Roast for 50 to 60 minutes, until the beets are tender and can be pierced easily with a fork. Remove from the oven, cover, and let cool. Alternatively, place the beets in a large pot of water, bring to a boil, and boil gently until the beets are tender and can be pierced easily with a fork, 50 to 60 minutes. Let cool in the cooking liquid.

2 Meanwhile, combine the vinegar, water, sugar, ginger, onion, and salt in a small non-reactive saucepan. Simmer over low heat until syrupy, about 10 minutes. Pour the syrup into a large bowl and let cool.

3 Peel the beets if desired and cut into thin wedges or slices. Add the beets to the syrup and stir gently to coat. Cover and marinate overnight in the refrigerator.

4 Bring to room temperature before serving.

Sauerkraut

Makes about 2 quarts

Sauerkraut is so much easier to make than you may think, particularly if you make it in small batches. I have a batch or two going all through the winter; that way I can enjoy my sauerkraut without the complication of making it in large batches. Do use sterilized quart jars (use the sanitizing cycle in your dishwasher or boil for 10 minutes) and make sure you bruise your cabbage aggressively to create enough brine to keep the cabbage covered. Using a mix of red and green cabbage makes a beautiful pink sauerkraut. You can add a couple of tablespoons of chopped garlic, dill seed, or juniper berries to the cabbage to vary the flavor.

5	pounds trimmed green or red cabbage
3	tablespoons pickling salt

1   Quarter and core the cabbage. Thinly shred using a food processor (use a slicing blade, not a grating one), a kraut-cutting board, or a knife.

2   In a large bowl or crock, mix the cabbage and salt thoroughly. Let stand at least 2 hours, until the cabbage has softened and begun to release liquid. With a potato masher or meat pounder, pound the cabbage until it releases enough liquid to cover itself when pressed.

3   Pack the sauerkraut into two sterilized quart canning jars, tamping down on the cabbage very firmly. Cover with the lid and screwband. Place in a container to catch juices that may overflow once the fermentation gets going. Store where the temperature remains fairly steady, between 60 and 70°F.

4   Check the sauerkraut after 24 hours. The cabbage should be completely covered in brine. If necessary, make up more brine by dissolving 1½ tablespoons pickling salt in 1 quart water. Pour in enough brine to keep the cabbage submerged.

5   Check the sauerkraut every few days and remove any scum that appears on the surface. If air is fully excluded, no scum will form. You should see little bubbles rising to the surface, indicating that fermentation is taking place. Start tasting the sauerkraut in 2 weeks. It will be fully fermented in 2 to 6 weeks, depending on the temperature. The flavor should change from salty to pickled.

6   Store fermented sauerkraut in the refrigerator for several months. For long-term storage at room temperature, process sauerkraut in pint jars for 20 minutes in a boiling-water bath (see the box on page 355). (Unprocessed sauerkraut has a pleasing crunch, which is lost when heat is applied.)

Kitchen Note: *Some people think they don't like sauerkraut. If their dislike is based on sampling canned sauerkraut, it is akin to disliking peas because you've tasted them only out of a can. Homemade sauerkraut or refrigerated store-bought sauerkraut is vastly different in flavor and texture from canned sauerkraut. Whether it's homemade or store-bought, taste sauerkraut before serving or adding to a dish. If it is too salty, rinse with warm water before serving. Do not rinse more than you will serve and consume at a single sitting.*

The first gatherings of the garden in May of salads, radishes and herbs made me feel like a mother about her baby — how could anything so beautiful be mine. And this emotion of wonder filled me for each vegetable as it was gathered every year. There is nothing that is comparable to it, as satisfactory or as thrilling, as gathering the vegetables one has grown.
— Alice B. Toklas (1877–1967)

Walnut Vinaigrette

Makes about ⅔ cup

Walnut oil at its best is fragrant with walnuts. Look for walnut oil in natural-foods stores. Like all nut oils, it should be stored in the refrigerator and used within 2 months. But if you don't have walnut oil on hand or don't want to buy it for just occasional use, use olive oil. Although lacking the punch of walnut, the dressing will still be flavorful and well balanced.

3 **tablespoons sherry vinegar**
1 **small shallot, minced**
1 **teaspoon sugar**
6 **tablespoons walnut or extra-virgin olive oil**
   Salt and freshly ground black pepper

▶ Combine the vinegar, shallot, and sugar in a small bowl. Whisk in the oil until completely blended. Season with salt and pepper.

Kitchen Note: *This is a lovely dressing for a beet salad, topped with blue cheese or goat cheese and garnished with walnuts.*

Orange Vinaigrette

Makes about ¾ cup

Oranges have an affinity for beets, a fact that suggests the orange flavor will marry with other root vegetables as well. Try this dressing on any roasted-vegetable salad.

3	tablespoons orange juice
3	tablespoons rice vinegar
1	tablespoon minced shallot
1	teaspoon finely grated orange zest
1	teaspoon sugar
¼	cup extra-virgin olive oil
	Salt and freshly ground black pepper

▶ Whisk the orange juice, vinegar, shallot, orange zest, and sugar in a small bowl. Whisk in the oil until it is fully incorporated. Season with salt and pepper.

Kitchen Note: *A Microplane is the ideal tool for grating citrus zest.*

Microplane Grater: A Wonderful Kitchen Gadget

Very rarely do I get a new kitchen tool that makes me wonder how I ever cooked successfully without it, but the Microplane grater is just that sort of gadget. Developed by the Microplane Company, the Microplane grater hit the market in the 1990s. It is very similar to a woodworking rasp: a long metal shaft covered with small, sharp metal teeth. Don't know what it looks like? Check the Internet or see the movie Ratatouille *and watch the little rat chef grate Parmesan with a Microplane! (It's also a great movie.) Because the teeth are small, they are perfect for removing just the zest from citrus fruit without cutting into the bitter white membrane. The shreds they create are very fine: just what you want for citrus zest. I also use my Microplane for grating nutmeg, ginger, and hard cheeses like Parmesan.*

Sesame-Ginger Vinaigrette

Makes ½ cup

This dressing is perfect on roasted sweet potatoes and other roasted vegetables. It also makes a lovely dressing for Asian-style noodle salads.

1 (2-inch) piece fresh ginger, peeled and sliced
1 shallot, quartered
1 garlic clove
3 tablespoons sunflower or canola oil
3 tablespoons lemon juice
1 tablespoon Asian sesame oil
1 tablespoon sugar
Salt and freshly ground black pepper

▶ Combine the ginger, shallot, and garlic in a blender and finely chop. Add the sunflower oil, lemon juice, sesame oil, and sugar, and process until blended. Season with salt and pepper.

Molasses-Mustard Vinaigrette

Makes about 1 cup

The molasses-mustard combination is fairly common in Southern barbecues. I was reminded of the combination at a tapas restaurant in Worcester, Massachusetts, where they served it as a dipping sauce for "Mediterranean egg rolls" (go figure). As soon as I tasted it, I knew it would be perfect with roasted vegetables.

½ cup dark unsulfured molasses
⅓ cup Dijon mustard
1 tablespoon whole-grain mustard
2 tablespoons apple cider vinegar
2 tablespoons extra-virgin olive oil

▶ Whisk together the molasses, both mustards, vinegar, and oil. Serve immediately, or store in the refrigerator in an airtight container for up to 1 month.

Maple-Balsamic Vinaigrette

Makes ⅓ cup

This is my house dressing, the one I make most often throughout all the seasons. It is terrific on summer greens and is easily scaled up.

1   shallot, minced
2   tablespoons white balsamic vinegar
1   teaspoon maple syrup
3   tablespoons extra-virgin olive oil
    Salt and freshly ground black pepper

▸ Combine the shallot, vinegar, and maple syrup in a small bowl. Whisk in the oil until completely blended. Season with salt and pepper.

Maple-Soy Vinaigrette

Makes about ⅔ cup

There's a wonderful restaurant in Morrisville, Vermont, known as The Bee's Knees. It is part of a growing movement (at least in Vermont) of community-supported restaurants, wherein patrons lend money to the restaurant (for start-up money, capital improvements, whatever) in exchange for coupons exchanged for meals at the restaurant. As soon as I tasted Chef Jeff Eagan's maple-soy vinaigrette on top of a roasted vegetable salad, I knew I had to be able to re-create it at home (or drive the two hours to the restaurant on a regular basis). This dressing is as good on a summer salad of mixed greens as it is on a wintry salad of roasted root vegetables.

2   tablespoons balsamic vinegar
2   tablespoons pure maple syrup
2   tablespoons soy sauce
2   garlic cloves, minced
1   (½-inch) piece fresh ginger, peeled and minced
3   tablespoons extra-virgin olive oil

▸ Whisk together the vinegar, maple syrup, soy sauce, garlic, and ginger until combined. Whisking constantly, drizzle in the oil until completely blended. Serve immediately, or store in the refrigerator in an airtight container for up to 1 week.

miso

3

Soups

At the end of this chapter you'll find
recipes for different types of broth. When you are making soup, it is always preferable to start with homemade broth. But realistically, sometimes you will use commercial broths, and there are some fine ones out there, especially chicken and beef broths packed in aseptic boxes. I haven't yet found a vegetable broth I really like. Taste several before settling on a brand; some taste strongly of carrot or tomato and are extremely sweet, while others are really mushroom broths. The Better-Than-Bouillon brand makes an acceptable base for beef, chicken, and vegetable broth, and I stock this brand for times when I don't have homemade broth on hand. It is sold as a paste in jars and is reconstituted with boiling water.

Many of the soups in this chapter are equally good when made with either chicken broth or a neutral-tasting vegetable broth. I am calling these soups "vegetarian"; it is up to you whether to make them so or not.

The chapter begins with some hearty soups that feature a mix of vegetables. Following are soups organized alphabetically by the main vegetable and then some bean soups. There are some 30 soups here, plus recipes for variations and for making broth from scratch. But there are many, many more soups that could be made with winter vegetables. Really, I feel like I have just begun to explore the possibilities.

RECITE LIST FOR
SOUPS

Winter Minestrone
Pasta e Fagioli
Barley-Vegetable Soup
Lentil-Vegetable Soup
Chicken Noodle Soup
Chicken Soup with Rice
Borscht
Hot-and-Sour Soup
Udon with Bok Choy and Tofu
Cabbage and Tomato Soup
White Bean and Cabbage Soup
Creamed Celery Root Soup
Cream of Garlic Soup
Italian Wedding Soup
Portuguese Kale Soup
Tuscan White Bean and Kale Soup
Caldo Gallego
Leek Soup with Carrots and
    Parsnips
Miso Noodle Bowl
Onion-Miso Soup
Curried Potato-Carrot Soup

Potato-Garlic Soup
Creamy Potato-Leek Soup
Scallop and Salsify Chowder
Apple-Squash Bisque
Spaghetti Squash Chowder
Coconut Curried Winter Squash Soup I
Coconut Curried Winter Squash Soup II
Smoky Black Bean Soup
Tomato-Leek Soup
Mushroom Broth
Beef Broth
Vegetable Broth
Turkey Broth
Chicken Broth

Vegetarian dishes are marked with this symbol:

❧ Winter Minestrone

Serves 6–8

I know it is a cliché, but this soup really can be made in less than an hour and tastes like it simmered all day. Minestrone lends itself to variations, so improvise with the ingredients that you have on hand. If you were wise enough to freeze pesto at the end of the summer, you can turn this soup into Minestrone alla Genovese by stirring about ¼ cup of pesto into the pot just before serving.

2 tablespoons extra-virgin olive oil	1½ cups cooked white beans (cannellini, navy, pea), or 1 (15-ounce) can, rinsed and drained
1 onion, diced	1 teaspoon dried rosemary
1 celery root, peeled and diced	1 teaspoon dried thyme
1 carrot, peeled and diced	1 cup small pasta (rings, ditalini, alphabets, bowties)
4 garlic cloves, minced	Salt and freshly ground black pepper
6 cups vegetable broth, chicken broth, or turkey broth (pages 126–27)	
1 quart crushed tomatoes or tomato purée, or 1 (28-ounce) can	
3 cups thinly sliced green or savoy cabbage, or kale (remove and discard tough stems from kale)	

1 Heat the oil in a large soup pot over medium heat. Add the onion, celery root, carrot, and garlic, and sauté until the vegetables are slightly tender, about 3 minutes. Add the broth, tomatoes, cabbage, beans, rosemary, and thyme. Bring to a boil, then reduce the heat and simmer until the vegetables are tender, about 30 minutes.

2 Return the soup to a boil. Add the pasta and boil gently until the pasta is tender, about 10 minutes. Season with salt and pepper. Serve hot.

Kitchen Note: *Like all soups that contain pasta, this will thicken on standing. Thin with additional broth or water if needed.*

Pasta e Fagioli

Serves 6

I love feeding teenagers — they are so *hungry* and appreciative. A friend of my son called this soup "rib-sticking goodness." It is a minimalist version of the classic Italian soup of pasta and beans.

2	tablespoons extra-virgin olive oil
1	onion, diced
4	garlic cloves, minced
8	cups water
1	cup dried borlotti, pinto, red or white kidney beans, or great Northern beans, soaked overnight and drained
2	bay leaves
1	quart crushed tomatoes or tomato purée, or 1 (28-ounce) can
1	tablespoon mixed dried Italian seasoning, or to taste
1–2	cups vegetable broth, chicken broth, turkey broth, or beef broth (pages 125–27)
1½	cups small pasta (rings, ditalini, alphabets, bowties)
	Salt and freshly ground black pepper

1 Heat the oil in a large saucepan over medium heat. Add the onion and garlic and sauté until limp, about 3 minutes. Add the water, beans, and bay leaves. Bring to a boil, then reduce the heat and simmer, partially covered, until the beans are completely tender, 1½ to 2 hours. (The beans will not continue to soften once the tomatoes are added, so be sure they are fully cooked before continuing.)

2 Add the tomatoes and Italian seasoning. Return to a boil, then reduce the heat and simmer for 15 minutes.

3 Add enough broth to achieve a soupy consistency (the pasta will thicken the soup). Remove the bay leaves. Return to a boil, add the pasta, and boil gently until the pasta is tender, 10 to 20 minutes. Season with salt, pepper, and more Italian seasoning if desired. Serve hot.

Kitchen Note: *The soup will thicken on standing. Thin with additional water or broth if needed.*

Barley-Vegetable Soup

Serves 4–6

The rich flavor of this soup is thanks to the dried porcini mushrooms, which contrast beautifully with the nutty-sweet barley and root vegetables. This soup makes a very satisfying meal with a whole-grain bread. It is another rich-tasting soup that takes only about 1 hour to make.

1   cup sliced dried porcini mushrooms (about 1 ounce)
2   cups boiling water
2   tablespoons extra-virgin olive oil
1   onion, diced
1   large carrot, peeled and diced
1   large celery root, peeled and diced
8   cups vegetable broth, mushroom broth, chicken broth, turkey broth, or beef broth (pages 124–27)
⅔   cup pearl or hulled barley
1   teaspoon dried thyme
    Salt and freshly ground black pepper

1   Place the dried porcini mushrooms in a small bowl. Pour the boiling water over the mushrooms and set aside to soak.

2   Heat the oil in a large soup pot over medium heat. Add the onion, carrot, and celery root, and sauté until the vegetables are softened, about 5 minutes. Add the broth, barley, and thyme. Add the soaked mushrooms with their liquid, avoiding any grit that has settled in the bottom of the bowl. Bring to a boil, then reduce the heat and simmer until the barley and vegetables are tender, 40 to 60 minutes. Taste and add salt and plenty of pepper. Serve hot.

Worries go better with soup than without.
— Yiddish proverb

Lentil-Vegetable Soup

Serves 6-8

The only trick to making lentil soup is to be sure to cook the lentils until they are completely soft, even mushy. In the case of this soup, it is better to overcook than undercook the lentils. This hearty soup has rib-sticking power and is simply delicious.

2	tablespoons extra-virgin olive, sunflower, or canola oil
1	onion, chopped
1	celery root, peeled and chopped
4	garlic cloves, peeled and halved
2	cups dried red, green, or brown lentils, rinsed
6	cups vegetable broth, chicken broth, turkey broth, or beef broth (pages 125–27), or water, plus more as needed
1½	tablespoons dried oregano or mixed Italian herbs
1½	cups diced tomatoes with juice, or 1 (15-ounce) can
1	carrot, peeled and diced
1	rutabaga, peeled and diced
	Salt and freshly ground black pepper

1   Heat the oil in a large soup pot over medium-low heat. Add the onion, celery root, and garlic, and sauté until the celery root is softened, about 5 minutes. Add the lentils, broth, and oregano. Bring to a boil, then skim off any foam that rises to the top. Reduce the heat and simmer, covered, until the lentils are mushy, 45 to 60 minutes, depending on the variety and age of the lentils.

2   Let cool slightly, then purée in a blender. You may have to do this in batches. Return to the pot and thin with additional broth, if desired. Add the tomatoes, carrot, and rutabaga. Bring back to a boil, then reduce the heat and simmer until the vegetables are tender but still just slightly crunchy, about 30 minutes.

3   Season generously with salt and pepper. Serve hot.

Chicken Noodle Soup

Serves 6

Chicken noodle soup is one of the greatest of all comfort dishes. The vegetables add much in the way of nutrition and heartiness. This soup is a meal in a bowl. If you start by making broth from scratch, you will have just enough broth and more than enough chicken, which can be frozen for another dish.

12	cups chicken broth (page 127)
2	cups peeled and finely diced mixed celery root and carrots
2	cups chopped or shredded cooked chicken
6	ounces egg noodles (about 4 cups)
2	cups very thinly sliced kale (remove and discard tough stems)
	Salt and freshly ground black pepper

1   Bring the broth to a boil in a large soup pot. Add the celery root and carrots and simmer until tender, about 20 minutes.

2   Add the chicken, noodles, and kale. Stir well and simmer until the noodles are tender, 15 to 20 minutes.

3   Season with salt and pepper. Serve hot.

Kitchen Note: *Kale in soup gets less and less delightful each time it is reheated. If I expect to have leftovers, I cook the kale in a little broth and add it to the individual servings. I save any leftover soup, but I don't save leftover kale — either because I reduced the amount of kale I prepared or I served extra in each bowl (we love kale at my house).*

Winter is the time for comfort, for good food and warmth, for the touch of a friendly hand and for a talk beside the fire: it is the time for home.

— Edith Sitwell (1887–1964)

Chicken Soup with Rice

Serves 6

In his wonderful book *Chicken Soup with Rice: A Book of Months*, Maurice Sendak wrote, "In January it's so nice, / while slipping on the sliding ice, / To sip hot chicken soup with rice. / Sipping once, sipping twice, sipping chicken soup with rice."

Carole King put the words to music. Here's the soup to make while singing the song.

12	cups chicken broth (page 127)
½	cup wild rice
2	cups peeled and finely diced mixed celery root, carrots, and/or parsnips
2	cups chopped or shredded cooked chicken
1	cup long-grain white rice
	Salt and freshly ground black pepper

1 Bring the broth to a boil in a large soup pot. Add the wild rice and simmer for 40 minutes.

2 Add the vegetables and simmer until tender, about 20 minutes.

3 Add the chicken and white rice. Stir well and simmer until both kinds of rice are tender, about 30 minutes.

4 Season with salt and pepper. Serve hot.

Kitchen Notes: *If you make the broth from scratch, you will have more than enough chicken for the soup. Also, the soup will thicken on standing. Thin with additional broth or water if needed.*

Winter is not a season, it's an occupation.

— Sinclair Lewis (1885–1951)

Borscht

Serves 4

There are hundreds of different ways to prepare borscht, but if you order a bowl of borscht at a Jewish deli, this is basically the soup you will be served. It may be served hot or cold and with or without the potato. In the summer, I prefer it cold and without the potato, but in the winter, it is perfect served hot over a freshly boiled potato. Add a nice loaf of Jewish rye bread and butter to make a meal that is unparalleled in its simplicity and goodness.

4	medium-to-large beets (1½–2 pounds)
1	onion
4	cups vegetable broth or beef broth (pages 125–26) or water
4	thin-skinned potatoes
	Juice of ½ lemon
	Salt and freshly ground black pepper
	Sour cream
	Dried dill, for garnish

1 Peel and shred the beets and onion. A food processor makes lovely uniform pieces, which greatly enhances the soup.

2 Combine the beets, onion, and broth in a saucepan. The broth should just barely cover the vegetables. Add additional broth or water if needed. Bring to a boil, then reduce the heat and simmer, covered, for 30 minutes.

3 Meanwhile, cover the potatoes with water in a saucepan. Bring to a boil and boil gently until the potatoes are tender, 15 to 20 minutes. Drain and keep warm.

4 When the beets have simmered for 30 minutes, add the lemon juice and season with salt and pepper. Simmer until the beets are fully tender and the flavors have blended, about 5 minutes longer.

5 To serve, put a potato in each bowl. Break up the potato with a fork or potato masher, but do not mash. Ladle the hot soup over the potato in each bowl and top with a dollop of sour cream. Sprinkle dill over the sour cream and serve at once.

Kitchen Note: *To make a chilled borscht, refrigerate the cooked borscht and omit the potato when serving.*

Hot-and-Sour Soup

Serves 6

Hot-and-sour soup is a popular item on many Chinese-restaurant menus. At its best, the unique blend of heat from ground pepper and sour from vinegar is a warming, and winning, combination.

DRIED VEGETABLES

- 6 dried shiitake mushrooms
- 6 dried wood ear mushrooms (optional)
- 10 dried lily buds (optional)

PORK AND MARINADE

- 8 ounces boneless pork, cut into matchsticks
- 2 tablespoons Chinese rice wine
- 1 teaspoon soy sauce
- 1 teaspoon Asian sesame oil
- 1 teaspoon salt
- 1 teaspoon cornstarch
- ½ teaspoon sugar

SOUP

- 2 tablespoons peanut, sunflower, or canola oil
- 1 leek, trimmed and thinly sliced
- 1 carrot, peeled and cut into matchsticks
- 1 (4-inch) piece daikon radish or 1 turnip, peeled and cut into matchsticks
- 2 garlic cloves, minced
- 1 (½-inch) piece fresh ginger, peeled and minced
- 6 button mushrooms, sliced
- 6 cups chicken broth (page 127)
- 1 (7-ounce) can baby corn, drained (optional)
- 3 tablespoons soy sauce, plus more as needed
- 5 tablespoons rice vinegar, plus more as needed
- 1½ teaspoons Asian sesame oil
- 2 teaspoons freshly ground black pepper, plus more as needed
- 1 pound firm or silken tofu, cut into 1-inch cubes
- ¼ cup cornstarch
- 2 eggs, lightly beaten

1 Cover the shiitakes with cold water and set aside to hydrate for at least 4 hours, and up to 8 hours. Put the wood ears and lily buds in a separate bowl, if using, cover with hot water, and let soak for 20 minutes.

2 To marinate the pork, combine the pork, rice wine, soy sauce, sesame oil, salt, cornstarch, and sugar; set aside.

3 To prepare the soup, heat the oil in a large saucepan over medium-high heat. Add the leek, carrot, daikon, garlic, and ginger, and sauté until the leek is wilted, about 3 minutes. Add the pork with its marinade and the button mushrooms and sauté for 3 minutes. Add the broth, baby corn, if using, soy sauce, vinegar, sesame oil, and black pepper.

4 Drain the shiitake mushrooms, reserving the soaking water. Slice and add to the soup. Drain the lily buds and wood ears, if using, and add to the soup. Add the tofu.

5 Bring the soup to a boil. Mix the cornstarch with the reserved shiitake soaking liquid. Slowly add the cornstarch mixture to the soup, stirring to prevent lumps. Taste for seasoning and add more soy sauce, vinegar, or pepper as needed.

6 Remove the soup from the heat. Add the eggs, pouring in a slow, thin stream. Stir the soup once in a circular motion, just until the eggs appear as ribbons. Serve at once.

Kitchen Note: *The long soaking of the shiitakes in cold water gives them a silken texture. If you forget to start them early enough, use boiling water instead of cold water and soak for at least 10 minutes.*

Do you have a kinder, more adaptable friend in the food world than soup? Who soothes you when you are ill? Who refuses to leave you when you are impoverished and stretches its resources to give a hearty sustenance and cheer? Who warms you in the winter and cools you in the summer? Yet who also is capable of doing honor to your richest table and impressing your most demanding guests? Soup does its loyal best, no matter what undignified conditions are imposed upon it. You don't catch steak hanging around when you're poor and sick, do you?

— Judith Martin (Miss Manners)

Udon with Bok Choy and Tofu

Serves 4

Noodle soups are comfort food, whatever their origins. This Japanese version is prepared with a traditional broth called dashi, made from kombu (kelp) and katsuobushi (dried bonito flakes), both readily available wherever Asian foods are sold. The broth has a mysterious, almost smoky flavor that makes it a perfect match for the udon noodles, bok choy, tofu, and shiitake mushrooms.

DASHI

- 8 cups water
- 1 (6-inch) piece kombu (kelp)
- ⅓ cup katsuobushi (dried bonito flakes)
- ¼ cup tamari, plus more to taste
- 2 tablespoons mirin or dry sherry
- 1 teaspoon sugar

SOUP

- 3 shiitake mushrooms, sliced (remove and discard the stems)
- 12 ounces dried udon noodles
- 1 head bok choy, trimmed and sliced
- 1 leek, trimmed and very thinly sliced
- 1 pound silken tofu, cut into 1-inch cubes

1 To make the dashi, combine the water and kelp in a saucepan and let soak for 1 to 2 hours. Add the katsuobushi and bring to a boil. Boil for 4 minutes, then strain and discard the solids. This is the dashi. Flavor the dashi with the tamari, mirin, and sugar. Add the mushrooms and let simmer while you prepare the noodles.

2 Bring a large pot of salted water to a boil. Add the noodles and cook according to the package directions. Drain well and rinse with hot water.

3 Add the bok choy, leek, and tofu to the dashi. Heat until the bok choy is wilted but still crisp and the leek is tender, about 5 minutes.

4 Divide the noodles among four large bowls. Ladle the broth, vegetables, and tofu over the noodles, and serve immediately.

Kitchen Note: *If you can't find udon, substitute vermicelli pasta.*

Variation: Vegetarian Udon with Bok Choy and Tofu

Substitute miso broth for the dashi.

Cabbage and Tomato Soup

Serves 4-6

Over the years I have come up with several variations of this soup. This version is the simplest and quickest, and perhaps my favorite. It is ready to enjoy in less than an hour and makes a delicious and filling supper.

2 tablespoons extra-virgin olive, sunflower, or canola oil
1 small head green or savoy cabbage, quartered and thinly sliced (6-8 cups)
1 onion, halved and thinly sliced
1 quart tomato purée, or 1 (28-ounce) can
6 cups chicken broth, turkey broth, or beef broth (pages 125-27)
4 ounces Spanish chorizo (or any dry-cured sausage), thinly sliced
   Salt and freshly ground black pepper

1 Heat the oil in a large soup pot over medium heat. Add the cabbage and onion and sauté until they begin to color, 8 to 10 minutes. Add the tomato purée, broth, and sausage. Bring to a boil, then reduce the heat and simmer until the cabbage is meltingly tender and the broth very flavorful, about 30 minutes.

2 Season with salt and pepper. Serve hot.

Variation: Vegetarian Cabbage and Tomato Soup

Substitute vegetable broth (page 126) for the chicken broth. Substitute 1 tablespoon cumin seeds for the sausage. Be very generous with the pepper.

Miso: A Vegetarian Broth

Miso is the original vegetarian concentrate for making broths, and it should not be forgotten. Once miso has been added to a soup, do not allow it to come to a boil.

Boiling will destroy the aroma of the soup as well as beneficial enzymes that are said to promote health.

White Bean and Cabbage Soup

Serves 6-8

When you make a soup out of a simple combination of ingredients, every ingredient must pull its weight. The broth must be full-flavored, and so must be the sausage. Don't expect a low-fat sausage — say one of those gourmet chicken sausages that one finds in a supermarket — to do the job. This soup is rustic, hearty, and, with the right ingredients, sublime.

2 tablespoons extra-virgin olive oil

1 small head green or savoy cabbage, thinly sliced (6-8 cups)

1 onion, halved and thinly sliced

6 cups chicken broth or vegetable broth (pages 126-27)

½ pound thin-skinned potatoes (do not peel), cut into 1-inch cubes

8 ounces Spanish chorizo, andouille, or other full-flavored, fully cooked sausage

1½ cups cooked white beans, or 1 (15-ounce) can, rinsed and drained

Salt and freshly ground black pepper

1 Heat the oil in a large saucepan over medium heat. Add the cabbage and onion and sauté until beginning to color, about 10 minutes.

2 Add the broth, potatoes, and sausage. Bring to a boil, then reduce the heat and simmer until the potatoes are tender, about 30 minutes.

3 Stir in the beans and simmer until heated through, about 10 minutes. Season with salt and pepper, and serve hot.

There is in every cook's opinion
No savoury dish without an onion:
But lest your kissing should be spoiled
The onion must be thoroughly boiled.

— Jonathan Swift (1667–1745)

Creamed Celery Root Soup

Serves 4-6

There's very little milk in this cream soup, because a purée of celery root is creamy by itself. If you prefer, you can omit the milk altogether, although it does add richness.

> 2 large celery roots (about 3 pounds), peeled and coarsely chopped
>
> 1 russet (baking) potato, peeled and coarsely chopped
>
> 4 garlic cloves, peeled
>
> 5 cups chicken broth (page 127), plus more as needed
>
> ¼ pound bacon, diced
>
> 2 large leeks, trimmed and sliced
>
> ¼ cup whole milk, plus more as needed
>
> Salt and freshly ground black pepper

1 Combine the celery root, potato, garlic, and broth in a saucepan. The broth should cover the vegetables. If not, add a little more broth or water. Bring to a boil, then reduce the heat and simmer, covered, until the vegetables are completely tender, about 35 minutes. Set aside to cool slightly.

2 Sauté the bacon in a large saucepan over medium heat until crisp, about 6 minutes. Using a slotted spoon, transfer the bacon to paper towels to drain and set the bacon aside. Pour off all but 2 tablespoons of the bacon grease. Add the leeks and sauté until wilted, about 4 minutes.

3 Using a blender and working in batches, purée the celery root mixture until smooth; pour into the saucepan with the leeks. Stir in the milk. If you would prefer a thinner soup, add more milk or broth. Season with salt and pepper. Reheat as necessary to serve hot, garnished with the reserved bacon.

 ## Variation: Vegetarian Creamed Celery Root Soup

Substitute vegetable broth (page 126) for the chicken broth, omit the bacon, and sauté the leeks in 2 tablespoons extra-virgin olive oil. Garnish with something crunchy — either crispy fried onions or croutons. Crumbled potato chips will do in a pinch.

Cream of Garlic Soup

Serves 4–6

Slow cooking gently infuses this soup with the goodness of garlic. The soup is velvety in texture and deeply satisfying on a cold wintry night. It is a cure for whatever ails you.

2 tablespoons butter

2 tablespoons extra-virgin olive oil

2 whole garlic heads, cloves separated, peeled, and chopped

2 cups vegetable broth or chicken broth (pages 126–27)

¼ cup dry sherry or white wine

2 cups milk

1 medium russet (baking) potato, peeled and cut into 1-inch cubes

1 cup heavy whipping cream

Salt

1 Melt the butter in the oil in a large saucepan over low heat. Add the garlic and cook until softened and fragrant, about 10 minutes. Do not let the garlic color. Stir in the broth and sherry. Bring the mixture to a boil, then reduce the heat and simmer for 30 minutes.

2 Stir in the milk and potato and adjust the heat as needed so the soup continues to simmer until the potato is completely tender, 30 to 45 minutes longer. Purée the soup in a blender. If you are looking for an absolutely smooth, velvety texture, strain through a fine-mesh sieve back into the saucepan.

3 Add the cream and simmer until heated through. Season with salt. Serve at once or hold overnight in the refrigerator to allow the flavor to develop even more. Reheat gently before serving.

Kitchen Note: *If you are using a vegetable broth, make sure it has good, well-rounded flavor. A broth that tastes strongly of tomato or carrot will not work well in this delicately flavored soup.*

Italian Wedding Soup

Serves 6

Minestra maritata, a "marriage" of greens and soup, is not a traditional dish to serving at weddings, but it is a marriage made in soup heaven, with tiny meatballs and pasta. This a deliciously healthful, filling bowl of comfort.

12	cups chicken broth or turkey broth (pages 126–27)
1	pound ground turkey, or ½ pound ground pork and ½ pound ground beef
2	eggs
1	cup fresh breadcrumbs
½	cup freshly grated Parmesan cheese
2	garlic cloves, minced
	Salt and freshly ground black pepper
½	cup acini de pepe, pastina, or orzo (or other small pasta shapes)
1½	pounds Lacinato kale, cut into ribbons (about 18 cups lightly packed; remove and discard tough stems)

1 Bring the broth to a simmer in a large saucepan.

2 To make the meatballs, combine the meat, eggs, breadcrumbs, Parmesan, garlic, 1 teaspoon salt, and ½ teaspoon pepper in a food processor. Process until well mixed. Alternatively, mix by hand in a large bowl. With wet hands (to prevent the meat from sticking), form the meat mixture into ½-inch balls (the size of marbles) and add to the simmering soup. Simmer until the meatballs are cooked through, about 20 minutes.

3 Increase the heat slightly, add the pasta, and boil gently until cooked al dente, about 10 minutes. Add the greens and continue to boil gently until tender, 8 to 10 minutes longer. Taste and adjust the seasoning, remove from the heat, and serve.

Kitchen Note: *The greens can be altered with the season, using curly kale, mustard greens, turnip greens, escarole, chard, spinach, broccoli di rabe, chicory, and cabbage, so feel free to substitute.*

Portuguese Kale Soup

Serves 4 as a main dish

Some combinations are so perfect that nothing can be done to improve them. Such is the case with *caldo verde* ("green soup"), considered one of the national dishes of Portugal.

8	ounces linguiça or Spanish chorizo, thinly sliced
8	cups chicken broth or turkey broth (pages 126–27)
3–4	thin-skinned potatoes (about 1 pound)
12	ounces kale, chopped (about 8 cups lightly packed; remove and discard tough stems)
	Salt and freshly ground black pepper

1 Bring the sausage and broth to a boil in a large saucepan, then reduce the heat and simmer while you prepare the potatoes.

2 Peel and dice the potatoes. Cover with salted water in a medium saucepan. Bring to a boil and boil, covered, until the potatoes are tender, about 8 minutes. Drain and briefly mash with a potato masher for an uneven, lumpy texture. Add the potatoes to the broth along with the kale.

3 Simmer until the kale is quite tender, 10 to 15 minutes. Season with salt and pepper and serve hot.

As the days grow short, some faces grow long. But not mine. Every autumn, when the wind turns cold and darkness comes early, I am suddenly happy. It's time to start making soup again.

— Leslie Newman

Tuscan White Bean and Kale Soup

Serves 4–6

With homemade chicken broth on hand and canned beans, this delicious soup takes about 30 minutes to make. Obviously, the Italians use Lacinato kale in this soup, but curly kale works just as well.

2 tablespoons extra-virgin olive oil

8 ounces Italian-style hot sausage, casings removed

4 cups chicken broth or turkey broth (pages 126–27)

2 cups cooked white beans, or 2 (19-ounce) cans cannellini beans, rinsed and drained

2 carrots, peeled and diced

4 garlic cloves, minced

1 teaspoon chopped fresh rosemary

4 cups lightly packed chopped kale (remove and discard tough stems)

Salt and freshly ground black pepper

1 Heat the oil in a large soup pot over medium heat. Add the sausage and brown, breaking it up with a spoon as it cooks, about 5 minutes.

2 Add the broth, beans, carrots, garlic, and rosemary. Bring to a boil, then reduce the heat and simmer, covered, until the carrots are tender and the flavors have blended, about 15 minutes. Stir in the kale.

3 Simmer until the kale is quite tender, 10 to 15 minutes. Season with salt and pepper and serve hot.

Caldo Gallego

Serves 6-8

White bean soups are found throughout the Mediterranean. This Spanish version also contains hearty greens and potatoes. It is a rib-sticking potage. A French version is known as *garbure*. Traditionally a slice of toasted bread is placed in the bottom of a wide soup plate, and the soup is ladled over.

2	cups dried white beans (cannellini, navy, Great Northern), soaked overnight and drained
10	cups water
1	pound Spanish chorizo, sliced
4	ounces pancetta or salt pork, diced
1	onion, finely diced
4	garlic cloves, minced
2	bay leaves
1	pound thin-skinned potatoes, peeled and thickly sliced
4	cups shredded hearty greens (green or savoy cabbage, collard greens, kale, or mustard greens; remove and discard any tough stems)
1	teaspoon pimenton (optional)
	Salt and freshly ground black pepper

1   Combine the beans, water, chorizo, pancetta, onion, garlic, and bay leaves in a large pot. Bring to a boil, then reduce the heat and simmer, uncovered, for 1 hour.

2   Add the potatoes and greens and simmer for 1 hour.

3   Remove about 2 cups of the soup and purée or mash. Stir back into the soup with the pimenton, if using. Season with salt and pepper.

4   Simmer for another 15 minutes and serve hot.

Kitchen Note: *Pimenton is made from the same peppers that are dried and ground to make paprika, but these peppers are smoked, which adds layers of flavor. There are many online sources for pimenton, and once it lands in your pantry, you will find many uses for it. If you don't want to use pimenton, you can substitute very fresh paprika (but avoid using paprika that has languished in your pantry or on the store shelves).*

Leek Soup with Carrots and Parsnips

Serves 4

This is a simple soup of few ingredients, so be sure to use the best-quality broth. If you use a vegetable broth, make sure it is neutrally flavored. The carrots and parsnips are cooked just long enough to soften them but not long enough to impart much sweetness to the broth. They should be very finely diced, so each piece is a tiny cube of color against the pale green soup.

> 1 tablespoon extra-virgin olive oil
> 2 leeks, trimmed and sliced
> 2 garlic cloves, minced
> 6 cups vegetable broth or chicken broth (pages 126–27)
> ½ cup dry white wine
> 2 tablespoons butter
> 1 carrot, peeled and very finely diced
> 1 parsnip, peeled and very finely diced
>   Salt and freshly ground black pepper

1 Heat the oil in a large saucepan over medium heat. Add the leeks and garlic and sauté until softened, about 3 minutes. Add the broth and wine. Bring to a boil, then reduce the heat and simmer until the leeks are completely tender, about 30 minutes. Let the soup cool slightly.

2 Process the soup in a blender until smooth; you will have to do this in batches. Return the soup to the saucepan and heat gently.

3 Melt the butter in a medium skillet over medium-low heat. Add the carrot and parsnip and simmer in the butter until softened, about 10 minutes.

4 Transfer the carrot mixture to the soup. Season with salt and pepper and serve hot.

Miso Noodle Bowl

Serves 4

Miso and kombu combine to make a delicious broth for this vegetarian soup that is both comforting and filling. Kombu is a dark brown to gray-ish black seaweed that is dried and folded into sheets. It may be covered with a white powder, which should be wiped, but not washed, off. You can find both the seaweed and the miso in natural-foods stores and wherever Japanese foods are sold.

¼	ounce kombu (two 6-inch pieces)
4	cups water
12	ounces udon noodles
2	tablespoons canola, sunflower, or other vegetable oil
1	onion, thinly sliced
2	garlic cloves, thinly sliced
2	large carrots, peeled and julienned
1	(½-inch) piece fresh ginger, peeled and minced
3	cups vegetable broth (page 126)
4	cups lightly packed finely chopped kale (remove and discard tough stems)
1	pound silken tofu, cut into 1-inch cubes
⅓	cup light or dark miso
1	tablespoon soy sauce, or more to taste

1   Bring the kombu and water to a boil in a saucepan, then reduce the heat and simmer, covered, for 15 minutes. Remove the kombu, reserving the broth.

2   Meanwhile, bring a large pot of salted water to a boil. Add the udon noodles and simmer, covered, until al dente, 7 to 10 minutes. Drain and rinse the noodles with cold water to remove excess starch. Set aside.

3   Heat the oil in a large saucepan over medium-high heat. Add the onion and garlic and sauté until limp, about 3 minutes. Add the carrots and ginger and sauté until the carrot is tender, about 5 minutes.

4   Add the broth, cover, and bring to a boil. Add the greens and tofu and simmer for 3 minutes.

5   Meanwhile, whisk the miso into the reserved kombu broth until it is free of lumps and mostly dissolved. Stir in the soy sauce, and then stir the kombu broth into the soup. Gently reheat, if necessary, but don't allow the soup to boil.

6 To serve, evenly divide the noodles among the soup bowls and top with the hot
soup.

Kitchen Note: *You can use any miso you have on hand, but if you are buying miso for the first time, you might want to start with light (shiro) miso, which is quite mild in flavor. Darker miso has been fermented longer and is saltier. Store miso in its container in the refrigerator for up to 1 year.*

Onion-Miso Soup

Serves 4–6

A cross between a French onion soup and a simple miso broth, this vegetarian soup contains delicious caramelized onions, silken tofu, and crispy napa cabbage.

2 tablespoons peanut, sunflower, or canola oil
2 onions, halved and thinly sliced
1 cup sliced shiitake mushroom caps (remove and
   discard the stems)
6 cups water
3 tablespoons tamari, plus more to taste
12 ounces firm silken tofu, cut into 1-inch cubes
2 cups thinly sliced napa or Chinese cabbage
¼ cup light or dark miso, dissolved in ½ cup hot water

1 Heat the oil in a large saucepan over medium heat. Add the onions and mushrooms
and sauté until the onions are golden, about 10 minutes.

2 Add the water and bring to a simmer. Simmer, covered, for 10 minutes.

3 Add the tamari, tofu, and cabbage, and simmer just until the cabbage wilts, about
3 minutes.

4 Remove from the heat and stir in the miso broth. Taste and add more tamari if
desired. Serve at once.

Curried Potato-Carrot Soup

Serves 4

This scrumptious soup is ready in less than an hour. Choose baking potatoes for the best texture, but any potato will work. The fenugreek, found wherever Indian foods are sold, adds a flavor reminiscent of toasted cumin, but sweeter. Milk is added just before serving to give the soup a creamy texture and smooth out any rough flavor edges.

2	tablespoons sunflower or canola oil
1	onion, diced
1	(1-inch) piece fresh ginger, peeled and minced
4	garlic cloves, minced
1	tablespoon curry powder
1	teaspoon fenugreek seeds (optional)
3	cups vegetable broth, chicken broth, or turkey broth (pages 126–27)
1½	pounds potatoes, peeled and diced
2	carrots, peeled and diced
1	cup milk
	Salt and freshly ground black pepper

1   Heat the oil in a large heavy saucepan over medium-high heat. Add the onion, ginger, garlic, curry, and fenugreek, if using, and sauté until the onion is translucent, about 3 minutes. Add the broth, potatoes, and carrots. Bring to a boil, then reduce the heat and simmer until the potatoes and carrots are completely tender, about 30 minutes.

2   Stir the soup, smashing some of the potatoes against the side of the pot to mash them and thicken the soup. Stir in the milk and season with salt and pepper. Reheat until hot enough to serve; do not bring to a boil once the milk has been added.

Potato-Garlic Soup

Serves 4-6

There's a whole head of garlic in the soup, but its bite is quite tamed by slow cooking. This can be made as a vegetarian soup with vegetable broth, but my preference is to use a high-quality chicken broth. Pimenton is a smoked paprika from Spain. Substituting plain paprika will give lovely color to the soup, but the flavor won't be the same.

2 tablespoons extra-virgin olive oil

1 shallot, chopped

4 cups chicken broth, turkey broth, or vegetable broth (pages 126-27)

2½ pounds potatoes, peeled and cut into ½-inch pieces

1 whole garlic head, cloves separated, peeled, and chopped

½ teaspoon dried thyme

1 bay leaf

Pimenton, for serving

1 Heat the oil in a large saucepan over medium heat. Add the shallot and sauté until translucent, about 3 minutes. Add the broth, potatoes, garlic, thyme, and bay leaf. Bring to a boil, then reduce the heat and simmer, covered, until the potatoes are very tender, about 30 minutes. Cool slightly. Discard the bay leaf.

2 Briefly purée the soup in a blender 1 cup at a time, about 20 seconds per batch (do not overprocess). Return the soup to the saucepan. Season with salt and pepper. Simmer until heated through.

3 Ladle soup into bowls. Sprinkle with pimenton and serve.

Creamy Potato-Leek Soup

Serves 6

"Rich and satisfying" is the only way to describe this hearty soup. If you want to turn this soup into vichyssoise to serve cold, purée the entire batch of soup and thin with a little more broth or cream.

2 tablespoons butter
2 tablespoons extra-virgin olive oil
4 large leeks, trimmed, split lengthwise, and chopped
2 garlic cloves, chopped
Salt and freshly ground black pepper
3 cups chicken broth or vegetable broth (pages 126–27)
½ cup white wine
2 pounds potatoes, peeled and diced
1 cup light cream, half-and-half, or whole milk

1 Melt the butter with the oil in a large heavy saucepan over medium-low heat. Add the leeks and garlic, season with salt and pepper, cover, and cook over low heat, stirring occasionally, until the leeks are very tender but not browned, 15 to 20 minutes. Add the broth, wine, and potatoes, and simmer until the potatoes are tender, about 30 minutes. Let cool briefly.

2 Ladle about half the soup into a blender and purée until smooth. Return the purée to the pot. Add the cream. Taste and adjust the seasoning, then reheat until hot enough to serve.

Kitchen Note: *Baking potatoes yield the best texture in this soup, but any potato can be used.*

Chowder breathes reassurance. It steams consolation.
— Clementine Paddleford

Scallop and Salsify Chowder

Serves 6–8

Select thin salsify roots for this chowder and slice them to the size of the scallops. Each spoonful will contain some salsify and some scallops, and the two blend perfectly in flavor. This is a wonderful, rich New England–style chowder.

1 pound salsify	½ cup dry white wine
8 strips thick-cut bacon, chopped	2 potatoes, peeled and diced
2 onions, diced	1 cup whipping cream
1 celery root, peeled and diced	1½ pounds bay scallops
1½ teaspoons dried thyme	Salt and freshly ground black pepper
4 cups bottled clam juice	

1 Peel the salsify and cut into ½-inch pieces. Drop into acidulated water (1 tablespoon vinegar or lemon juice added to 4 cups water).

2 Sauté the bacon in a large heavy saucepan over medium heat until crisp, about 10 minutes. Using a slotted spoon, transfer the bacon to paper towels to drain and set the bacon aside. Drain all but 2 tablespoons of the bacon fat from the saucepan. Add the onions, celery root, and thyme to the saucepan and sauté over medium-high heat until the onions are light golden, about 5 minutes. Add the clam juice, wine, and potatoes. Bring to a boil, then reduce the heat and simmer until the potatoes are tender, about 30 minutes.

3 With a potato masher or an immersion blender, partially purée the soup to thicken. There should still be chunks of vegetable.

4 Add the salsify and half the bacon to the soup and simmer until the salsify is tender crisp, 12 to 15 minutes.

5 Add the cream and scallops to the chowder. Simmer until the scallops are cooked through, about 5 minutes. Season with salt and pepper.

6 Ladle the chowder into bowls. Sprinkle with the remaining bacon and serve immediately.

Apple-Squash Bisque

Serves 4-6

This soup is all about balance: the sweet squash and apples contrasted with the earthy leek and garlic. Although almost any squash will work in this soup, butternut is the squash of choice because it is easily peeled.

4	tablespoons butter
3	pounds butternut squash, peeled, seeded, and cut into 1-inch cubes
1	leek, trimmed and sliced
4	garlic cloves, peeled
2	cups apple cider
1	(½-inch) piece fresh ginger, peeled and minced
3	cups chicken broth or vegetable broth (pages 126–27)
	Salt and freshly ground black pepper
	Freshly grated nutmeg

1   Melt the butter in a large saucepan over medium heat. Add the squash, leek, and garlic, and sauté until the leek is softened and fragrant, about 5 minutes.

2   Add the cider and ginger. Bring to a boil, then reduce the heat and simmer, covered, until the squash is tender, about 1 hour.

3   Divide the vegetables into three batches and purée in a blender or food processor, adding 1 cup of the broth to each batch.

4   Combine the batches in the saucepan. Bring the soup to a simmer. Season with salt and pepper. Serve hot, topping each bowl of soup with a sprinkle of nutmeg.

Kitchen Note: *Freshly grated nutmeg is far superior in flavor to preground nutmeg. Nutmegs are easily ground on a Microplane, the same tool that is handy for finely grating citrus zest and Parmesan.*

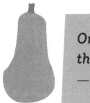

One kind word can warm
three winter months.
— Japanese proverb

Spaghetti Squash Chowder

Serves 6-8

The slightly sweet spaghetti squash plays off brilliantly against the velvety, garlic-infused cream base. This is an amazing soup, easily my favorite way to enjoy spaghetti squash.

1　medium spaghetti squash
2　tablespoons butter
2　tablespoons extra-virgin olive oil
1　whole garlic head, cloves separated, peeled, and chopped
2　cups chicken broth or vegetable broth (pages 126–27)
¼　cup dry sherry or white wine
2　cups milk
1　medium russet (baking) potato, peeled and cut into 1-inch cubes
1　cup heavy whipping cream
　　Salt and freshly ground black pepper

1　Halve the squash, remove the seeds and fibers, and cut into quarters or sixths. Steam over boiling water until tender when pierced with a fork, about 30 minutes.

2　Meanwhile, melt the butter in the oil in a large saucepan over low heat. Add the garlic and cook until softened and fragrant, about 10 minutes. Do not let the garlic color. Stir in the broth and sherry. Bring the mixture to a boil, then reduce the heat and simmer for 30 minutes.

3　Stir in the milk and potato and adjust the heat as needed so the soup continues to simmer until the potato is completely tender, 30 to 45 minutes longer. Purée the soup in a blender. Return the mixture to the saucepan.

4　Using a fork, scrape the squash into a bowl and separate the strands with the fork to create "spaghetti." Add to the saucepan along with the cream. Season to taste with salt and pepper. Simmer until heated through. Serve at once or hold overnight in the refrigerator to allow the flavor to develop even more. Reheat gently before serving.

Kitchen Note: *Spaghetti squash is named for its fibrous texture, not for its affinity for tomato sauce. In fact, I think spaghetti squash is best with all the traditional winter squash seasonings, but especially cream and garlic.*

Coconut Curried Winter Squash Soup I

Serves 6

A taste of the tropics is wonderfully warming on a cold night. The heat of the curry is counteracted by the sweet squash and creamy coconut milk. Any squash will work here, but the preferred squash has a creamy, not stringy, texture when puréed.

1 medium buttercup, butternut, or red kuri squash, or 1 small baby blue Hubbard squash (3–4 pounds), halved and seeded	1 tablespoon curry powder
	1½ cups chicken broth or vegetable broth (pages 126–27)
2 tablespoons peanut, sunflower, or canola oil	1 (14-ounce) can coconut milk
	Juice of 1 lime (about 2 tablespoons), or to taste
4 garlic cloves, minced	Salt and freshly ground black pepper
1 jalapeño pepper, seeded and finely minced	¼ cup chopped fresh cilantro
1 (1-inch) piece fresh ginger, peeled and minced	

1 Preheat the oven to 400°F.

2 Place the squash skin-side up in a baking dish. Add 1 inch of water to the baking pan. Bake for about 1 hour, until the squash is completely tender when pierced with a fork. Let cool slightly.

3 While the squash cools, heat the oil in a small skillet over medium-low heat. Add the garlic, jalapeño, ginger, and curry. Simmer until the spices are fragrant and the garlic just begins to color, about 5 minutes. Do not let the spices scorch or they will become bitter. Remove from the heat.

4 Scoop the flesh from the squash skin. Combine half the squash in a blender with half the spices and half the broth. Purée until smooth. Transfer to a saucepan. Repeat with the remaining squash, broth, and spices.

5 Add the coconut milk and lime juice to the soup. Taste and adjust the seasoning, adding salt, pepper, and lime juice as needed.

6 Reheat over medium heat, stirring frequently. Stir in the cilantro and serve hot.

Coconut Curried Winter Squash Soup II

Serves 6-8

Fish sauce works its magic to bring the flavors together in this version of curried squash soup. Also, the squash is steamed rather than baked, a method that could be employed in the previous recipe.

1	medium to large buttercup, butternut, or red kuri squash, or 1 small baby blue Hubbard squash (3–4 pounds), cut into large pieces and seeded	2	teaspoons curry powder
		1½	cups chicken broth or vegetable broth (pages 126–27)
		1	(14-ounce) can coconut milk
2	tablespoons peanut, sunflower, or canola oil	2–3	tablespoons lime juice
		2	tablespoons Asian fish sauce
1	onion, diced	2–3	tablespoons brown sugar
4	garlic cloves, minced		Salt and white pepper
1	(1-inch) piece fresh ginger, peeled and minced	¼	cup chopped fresh cilantro (optional)

1 Steam the squash over boiling water until completely tender, 20 to 40 minutes, depending on the size of the pieces. Let cool slightly.

2 Meanwhile, heat the oil in a large saucepan over medium heat. Add the onion, garlic, ginger, and curry. Simmer until the spices are fragrant and the garlic just begins to color, about 5 minutes. Do not let the spices scorch or they will become bitter. Remove from the heat.

3 Scoop the flesh from the squash skin. Combine half the squash with the onion mixture in a blender. Add the broth. Purée until smooth and return to the saucepan. Repeat with the remaining squash and coconut milk.

4 Bring the soup to a gentle simmer, stirring frequently; watch carefully because the soup will scorch easily. Add the lime juice, fish sauce, and sugar to taste. Season with salt and white pepper. Taste and add additional salt, white pepper, lime juice, and fish sauce as needed.

5 Just before serving, stir in the cilantro, if using. Serve hot.

Kitchen Note: *If you prefer, the squash can be baked as it is in the previous recipe, instead of steamed.*

Smoky Black Bean Soup

Serves 6–8

The smoky flavor comes from the chipotle, a smoked and dried jalapeño. It is a terrific soup when made for vegetarians, and it is a terrific soup when made with sausage (see the variation below) — your choice.

2   cups dried black beans, soaked overnight and drained

8   cups water

2   garlic cloves, minced

2   onions, chopped

2   dried chipotles

2   cups tomato purée, or 1 (15-ounce) can unseasoned tomato sauce

1   quart diced tomatoes with juice, or 1 (28-ounce) can

Salt and freshly ground black pepper

Sour cream, for garnish (optional)

1   Combine the beans with the water, garlic, onions, and chipotles in a large soup pot. Bring to a boil, then skim off any foam that rises to the top. Reduce the heat and simmer, covered, until the beans are very tender, about 2 hours.

2   Remove the chilis from the pot. Discard the seeds and finely chop the flesh; return to the pot. Let the beans cool briefly. Purée in a blender and return to the pot.

3   Add the tomato purée and diced tomatoes along with the juice from the can. Season with salt and pepper. Simmer for about 30 minutes to blend the flavors. Serve hot, garnished with a dollop of sour cream, if using.

Variation: Smoky Black Bean Soup with Sausage

Dice 8 ounces andouille or other smoked, fully cooked sausage. Add to the soup along with the tomato sauce.

Tomato-Leek Soup

Serves 6

Sometimes it is best to let the vegetables just speak for themselves. This soup couldn't be simpler to make. Together leeks and tomatoes make a perfect flavor combination that needs no embellishment. However, meat lovers may prefer it with the addition of sausage. I love it either way.

2	tablespoons sunflower or canola oil
3	large leeks, trimmed and thinly sliced
2	garlic cloves, minced
1	quart tomato purée, or 1 (28-ounce) can
6	cups chicken broth or vegetable broth (pages 126–27)
	Salt and freshly ground black pepper

1 Heat the oil in a large soup pot over medium heat. Add the leeks and garlic and sauté until the leeks are limp, about 5 minutes. Add the tomato purée and broth. Bring to a boil, then reduce the heat and simmer for about 15 minutes.

2 Season with salt and pepper. Serve hot.

Variation: Tomato-Leek Soup with Sausage

Remove the casings from 1 pound sweet or hot Italian sausage. Sauté in the oil, breaking it up with a spoon, until cooked through, about 8 minutes. Add the leeks and garlic and proceed with the recipe above.

It breathes reassurance, it offers consolation; after a weary day it promotes sociability. . . . There is nothing like a bowl of hot soup, its wisp of aromatic steam teasing the nostrils into quivering anticipation.

— Louis P. DeGouy

Mushroom Broth

Makes about 3 quarts

One option for a vegetarian broth is a mushroom broth. It has a more pronounced flavor than the vegetable broth and should be used mainly in soups that are enhanced by a mushroom flavor, such as Barley-Vegetable Soup (page 95).

2	tablespoons sunflower or canola oil
1½	pounds mushrooms (any kind), chopped
1	leek, trimmed and chopped
1	celery root, peeled and chopped
2	garlic cloves, coarsely chopped
4	quarts water
1	cup dry white wine
¼	cup soy sauce, plus more as needed
1	cup dried mushrooms, such as porcini or shiitake (about 1 ounce)
	Salt

1 Heat the oil in a large saucepan over medium-high heat. Add the fresh mushrooms, leek, celery root, and garlic, and cook, stirring, until the mushrooms release their liquid, about 5 minutes.

2 Add the water, wine, soy sauce, and dried mushrooms. Bring to a boil, then reduce the heat and simmer, uncovered, for 1 hour.

3 Strain the broth through a sieve, pressing on the solids to extract as much liquid as possible. Strain again, leaving any particles at the bottom of the bowl. Taste and add salt and additional soy sauce as needed, or leave unsalted to use as a base for soup and grain dishes.

4 Use immediately, or cool and refrigerate. The broth will keep for about 5 days in the refrigerator or 4 to 6 months in the freezer.

Beef Broth

Makes 2–3 quarts

Beef broth is made from bones, which can often be found at the super-market. If you don't see any, ask the butcher for help.

4 pounds cracked beef marrow, shin, and/or shank bones, with meat on them
4 quarts water, plus more as needed
1 large onion, chopped
1 carrot, chopped
1 celery root, peeled and chopped
1 leek, trimmed and chopped
1 bay leaf
10 black peppercorns
   Salt (optional) and freshly ground black pepper

1 Preheat the oven to 425°F.

2 Arrange the bones in a single layer in a large roasting pan. Roast for about 45 minutes, turning the bones occasionally, until well browned.

3 Drain the fat from the roasting pan and discard. Remove the bones and set aside. Place the roasting pan over two burners on top of the stove and add 1 cup of the water. Bring to a boil, stirring to scrape up the browned bits on the bottom of the pan.

4 Pour the boiling liquid into a large stockpot. Add the remaining 3¾ quarts water, the bones, and the onion, carrot, celery root, leek, bay leaf, and peppercorns. Bring to a boil, then reduce the heat to a simmer. Skim off any foam until no more appears. Simmer over very low heat, partially covered, until flavorful and deeply colored, 4 to 5 hours, adding more water if the bones become exposed.

5 Strain the broth and discard all the solids. Rinse the strainer clean and line it with cheesecloth or paper coffee filters. Pour the broth through the cheesecloth into another bowl or pot. Season with salt and pepper, or leave unsalted to use as a base for soup and grain dishes.

6 Refrigerate the broth for several hours, until a layer of fat congeals on the top and can be lifted off. Refrigerate and use within 4 days or freeze for up to 6 months.

Vegetable Broth

Makes about 4 quarts

The goal with vegetable broth is to make a good-tasting, well-balanced liquor with no one vegetable dominating the flavor.

2	carrots	1	tablespoon dried thyme
2	leeks, trimmed	1	cup dried porcini mushrooms
1	large onion	4	quarts water
¼	small head green cabbage	1	cup dry white wine
1	fennel bulb	1	tablespoon black peppercorns
4	garlic cloves		Salt (optional)

1   Quarter all the vegetables. Combine all the vegetables, herbs, and mushrooms in a large soup pot. Add the water. Bring to a boil, then reduce the heat and simmer, covered, for 30 minutes.

2   Add the wine and black pepper and continue to simmer, covered, for 10 minutes. Strain and discard all the solids.

3   Season with salt, or leave unsalted to use as a base for soup and grain dishes. Use immediately, or cool and refrigerate. The broth will keep for about 5 days in the refrigerator or 4 to 6 months in the freezer.

Turkey Broth

Makes about 2–3 quarts

The fall and winter bring festive meals where turkey takes center stage. Here's how to make broth from a leftover turkey carcass. Turkey broth can be used in place of chicken broth in any recipe.

1	carcass from a roasted turkey	1	celery root, peeled and cut into chunks
	Water		
1	carrot, cut into chunks	1	bay leaf
2	onions, cut into chunks		Salt (optional)

1   Break the carcass into four or five pieces. Cover with about 4 quarts of cold water in a large soup pot. Add the carrot, onions, celery root, and bay leaf. Bring to a boil, then reduce the heat and simmer for 1½ hours.

2   Remove the turkey pieces, and strain the liquid through a sieve, pressing on the solids to extract as much flavor as possible. Remove any meat from the bones and save for another use, such as other soups or turkey salad.

3   Chill the broth for several hours. Skim off the fat that rises to the top and hardens.

4   Season with salt, or leave unsalted to use as a base for soup and grain dishes. Use immediately, or refrigerate. The broth will keep for up to 3 days in the refrigerator or 4 to 5 months in the freezer.

Chicken Broth

Makes 2–3 quarts

I prefer to make chicken broth with dark meat chicken. I think it makes a richer broth.

3–4	pounds chicken parts	4	garlic cloves
1	large onion, chopped	4	quarts water
1	celery root, peeled and chopped		Salt (optional)

1   Combine the chicken, onion, celery root, and garlic in a large soup pot. Add the water. Bring almost to a boil, then immediately reduce the heat and simmer gently, partially covered, for 2 hours. Do not allow the broth to boil.

2   Strain and discard the vegetables. Remove the meat from the bones and save the meat for another use, such as chicken salad.

3   Chill the broth for several hours. Skim off the fat that rises to the top and hardens.

4   Season with salt, or leave unsalted to use as a base for soup and grain dishes. Use immediately, or refrigerate. The broth will keep for about 3 days in the refrigerator or 4 to 6 months in the freezer.

Kitchen Note: *Boiling doesn't ruin a broth — it just makes it cloudy.*

4
Simple Vegetable Dishes

Here it is: the heart of the book.
These are the everyday vegetable dishes that
you can enjoy again and again for as long as
your root cellar, in-garden storage, CSA share,
or natural-foods store allows.

The chapter begins with a collection of
recipes that feature a mix of root vegetables,
and I think all of them are wonderful. I was
pleased to discover that shredded root vegetables cook as quickly as summer vegetables
for those nights when I don't have time to
roast. I think, however, that roasting remains
the gold standard in terms of little fuss and
great flavor in root vegetables.

If you make only one dish from this
chapter, make the Crispy Kale Chips. It is a
favorite for everyone who has tried it.... But
what am I saying? This chapter contains some
70 delicious ways to enjoy hearty greens, root
vegetables, tubers, and winter squash. Why
stop with one recipe? Try them all!

RECIPE LIST FOR
SIMPLE VEGETABLE DISHES

Sautéed Shredded Vegetables

Maple-Balsamic Root Vegetables

Maple-Glazed Baked Winter Vegetables

Gingered Purée of Root Vegetables

Baked Beets in Béchamel

Harvard Beets

Basic Roasted Brussels Sprouts

Crunchy Roasted Brussels Sprouts

Cornmeal-Crisped Brussels Sprouts

Garlic-Crumbed Roasted Brussels
    Sprouts

Pan-Seared Brussels Sprouts

Cream-Braised Brussels Sprouts

Bacon-Sautéed Brussels Sprouts

Lemony Brussels Sprouts

Hot Slaw

Stir-Fried Cabbage in Brown Sauce

East-Meets-West Braised Red Cabbage

Baked Carrots and Fennel Béchamel

Sautéed Greens with Apple Cider
    Vinegar

Braised Celery Root Gratin

Garlic-Crumbed Greens

Parmesan Greens

Chinese Steamed Greens

Sichuan-Style Stir-Fried Greens

Sautéed Collard Greens

Crispy Kale Chips

Crisp Roasted Jerusalem Artichokes

Oven-Braised Leeks

Braised Balsamic-Glazed Parsnips and
    Pears

Honey-Balsamic Roasted Parsnips

Neeps and Tatties

Smashed Potatoes with Root Vegetables

Samosas

Potato Knishes

Buttermilk Mashed Potatoes

Potato-Stuffed Pierogi

Potato Galette

Mashed Potatoes with Greens

Rosemary Roasted Potatoes

Roasted Spiced Potatoes

Saffron Potatoes

Potatoes with Dill and Sour Cream

Hasselback Potatoes

Two-Potato Latkes

Potato-Carrot Tart

Twice-Baked Stuffed Potatoes

Hot German Potato Salad with
    Sauerkraut

Spicy Sweet-Potato Oven Fries

Lemon Aioli

Mashed Sweet Potatoes

Maple-Candied Sweet Potatoes

Cider-Braised Sweet Potatoes with
    Apples

Southern-Style Mashed Rutabagas
    or Turnips

Sautéed Turnips

Rutabaga Chips

Rutabaga Squares

Butter-Braised Salsify

Salsify Mash

Salsify Fritters

Gratin of Turnips and Rutabagas

Turnip Puff

Spicy Turnip Stir-Fry

Stuffed Sweet Dumplings

Apple-Braised Delicata Squash

Baked Winter Squash

Baked Spaghetti Squash

Whipped Winter Squash

Kathleen Pemble's Winter Squash

Winter Squash with Caramelized Apples

Vegetarian dishes are marked with this symbol:

Sautéed Shredded Vegetables

Serves 4-6

This sauté of root vegetables takes 10 minutes to cook and looks as beautiful on the plate as it is delicious to eat. Vary the seasonings if you like; the shredded vegetables are amenable to experimentation.

3 tablespoons sunflower or canola oil
4 cups peeled and shredded mixed root vegetables (beets, carrots, celery root, parsnips, rutabagas, salsify, and/or turnips)
1 leek, trimmed and thinly sliced
4 garlic cloves, minced
1 (½-inch) piece fresh ginger, peeled and minced
¼ cup dry white wine
   Salt and freshly ground black pepper
   Freshly grated nutmeg

1 Heat the oil in a large skillet over medium heat. Add the root vegetables, leek, garlic, and ginger, and sauté until the vegetables are limp, about 5 minutes. Add the wine, cover, and cook until the vegetables are tender, about 5 minutes longer.

2 Season with salt, pepper, and nutmeg. Serve hot.

Kitchen Note: *A food processor makes fast work of shredding root vegetables, but a box grater also can be used.*

Large, naked, raw carrots are acceptable as food only to those who live in hutches eagerly awaiting Easter.

— Fran Lebowitz

Maple-Balsamic Root Vegetables

Serves 4

There's no question that roasting is one of the best ways to prepare root vegetables, as this sweet-and-sour vegetable medley proves. Feel free to mix and match different vegetables — they are all terrific with the maple-balsamic glaze, though the inclusion of beets makes the combination particularly colorful.

2 carrots, peeled and cut into ¾-inch cubes	2 tablespoons extra-virgin olive oil
1 large rutabaga, peeled and cut into ¾-inch cubes	Salt and freshly ground pepper
	2 tablespoons balsamic vinegar
1 large beet, peeled and cut into ¾-inch cubes	¼ cup pure maple syrup
	2 tablespoons butter, melted
1 onion, halved and slivered (sliced vertically)	

1 Preheat the oven to 450°F. Lightly oil a large sheet pan (preferred) or shallow roasting pan.

2 Mound the carrots, rutabaga, beet, and onion on the sheet pan. Drizzle the oil over the vegetables and season with salt and pepper. Toss to coat. Spread in a single layer in the pan.

3 Roast for about 45 minutes, stirring or shaking the pan occasionally for even cooking, until the vegetables are lightly browned and mostly tender.

4 Meanwhile, stir together the vinegar, maple syrup, and melted butter in a small bowl; pour over the vegetables and roast about 10 minutes longer, until the vegetables are well browned and completely tender.

5 With a metal spatula, turn and toss the vegetables to make sure all the pieces are well coated. Taste and add more salt and pepper if needed. Serve hot.

Kitchen Note: *Make sure the vegetables are cut to roughly the same size for even cooking, and do not crowd the pan.*

Rutabagas: A Root by Any Other Name

The rutabaga undoubtedly has the oddest name of any vegetable. The word comes from the Swedish word rotbagge, meaning "round or baggy root." For some reason it isn't called a rotbagge in Sweden; its common name there is kålrot (cabbage root). Rutabaga is a mouthful, which may be why it has so many alternative names, including Swede or Swedish turnip (it didn't originate in Sweden, though it does grow well there), yellow turnip (it does look like a turnip but has yellow flesh), neep or tumshie (in Scotland), and even snadgie (in parts of northeast England).

The word rutabaga has been used by biologists to describe a specific mutation in fruit flies, resulting in impaired mental capacity. (Who knew fruit flies had enough mental capacity to show signs of impairment?) It is also an algorithm used in computer science. I'm not too sure what that means, but I'm pretty sure the computer scientist who named it was enthralled by the word rutabaga. The wonder is that more people aren't enthralled by the flavor of rutabaga. I know I am.

Maple-Glazed Baked Winter Vegetables

Serves 6

If you don't have a large sheet pan for spreading out vegetables for roasting, this is a fine alternative.

6	cups peeled and diced mixed root vegetables (beets, carrots, celery root, parsnips, rutabagas, salsify, and/or turnips), in ¾-inch cubes
2	cups peeled and diced butternut squash (about 1½ pounds), in ¾-inch cubes
1	onion, halved and slivered (sliced vertically)
5	tablespoons butter
¼	cup pure maple syrup
2	garlic cloves, minced
1½	teaspoons chopped dried rosemary or sage
1	teaspoon salt
½	teaspoon freshly ground black pepper

1   Preheat the oven to 375°F. Butter a 9- by 13-inch glass baking dish.

2   Combine the root vegetables, squash, and onion in a large bowl. Melt the butter in a small saucepan over medium heat. Whisk in the maple syrup, garlic, rosemary, salt, and pepper. Pour over the vegetable mixture and toss to coat. Transfer to the prepared baking dish and cover with aluminum foil.

3   Bake for 40 minutes. Uncover and continue baking for about 20 minutes longer, until all the vegetables are tender. Serve hot.

Gingered Purée of Root Vegetables

Serves 6

Consider this a method as much as a recipe. The carrot and rutabaga give the purée a light orange color, the ginger and nutmeg add a touch of sweetness, and the cream makes it luxuriously rich. This blend of root vegetables is particularly pleasing, but other root vegetables could be used instead.

1	large carrot, peeled and cut into 1-inch slices
1	large parsnip, peeled and cut into 2-inch slices
1	large rutabaga, peeled and cut into 1-inch pieces
1	large turnip, peeled and cut into 2-inch pieces
1	onion, peeled and quartered
2	garlic cloves, peeled
3	tablespoons butter
½	cup heavy whipping cream
1	(½-inch) piece fresh ginger, peeled and minced
¼	teaspoon freshly grated nutmeg, plus more for garnish
	Salt and freshly ground black pepper

1 Combine the carrot, parsnip, rutabaga, turnip, onion, and garlic in a medium sauce-pan and cover with salted cold water. Bring to a boil and boil until very tender, about 20 minutes. Drain well.

2 Transfer the vegetables to a food processor and add the butter, cream, and ginger. Process until smooth. Season with the nutmeg and salt and pepper.

3 Transfer to a serving dish and garnish with a light sprinkling of additional nutmeg.

Kitchen Note: *If you are making this for a holiday meal, you can make it in advance and keep it in the refrigerator for a day. Reheat in a 350°F oven, covered, for about 45 minutes.*

Baked Beets in Béchamel

Serves 4

If this beet dish isn't the perfect dish for Valentine's Day, I don't know what is. The creamy sauce, tinted pink by the beets, is a delicious change from the usual sweet-and-sour preparations you might associate with beets.

> 4   medium beets, peeled and cut into ¼-inch slices
> ½   cup water
> 3   tablespoons butter
> 1   shallot, minced
> 3   tablespoons all-purpose flour
> 1   cup milk
> ¼   cup dry white wine
>   Salt and freshly ground black pepper
>   Pinch of freshly grated nutmeg

1   Preheat the oven to 425°F. Lightly oil a 9- by 13-inch baking dish.

2   Arrange the beets in the baking dish. Pour in the water. Cover tightly.

3   Bake for about 45 minutes, until the beets are fork-tender.

4   Meanwhile, melt the butter in a small saucepan over medium heat. Add the shallot and sauté until softened, 2 to 3 minutes. Stir in the flour to form a smooth paste. Add the milk and wine and bring just to a boil. The sauce will thicken. Remove from the heat and season with salt, pepper, and nutmeg.

5   Pour the sauce over the beets. Return to the oven and bake, uncovered, for about 10 minutes, until the sauce is bubbling and golden around the edges. Serve hot.

 ## Variation: Baked Root Vegetables in Béchamel

Béchamel is a lovely topping for other roasted root vegetables, too. Just follow this recipe, substituting 1 pound of any other root vegetable for the beets.

Harvard Beets

Serves 4–6

This "old-school" recipe may or may not have originated with a Harvard (or Yale) student. It is a classic way to prepare beets — in a sweet-and-sour sauce, enhanced with orange. If it doesn't seem likely that the recipe was invented by a student, you may think it more credible that the recipe originated in a tavern in England by the name of Harwood, with "Harvard" being a mispronunciation of the name. Either way, the beets are glisteningly beautiful with a tasty glaze.

2	pounds beets, unpeeled
½	cup sugar
1	tablespoon cornstarch
½	teaspoon salt
¼	teaspoon whole allspice berries or 2 whole cloves
⅔	cup artisanal apple cider vinegar or dry white wine
1	tablespoon butter
1	tablespoon orange marmalade

1   Cover the beets with water in a saucepan. Bring to a boil and boil gently until the beets are tender, 30 to 60 minutes, depending on their size. Drain, let cool, and cut into matchsticks, slices, or wedges.

2   Combine the sugar, cornstarch, salt, allspice, and vinegar in a medium saucepan. Cook over medium heat, stirring, until the liquid thickens and becomes clear. Add the beets, remove from the heat, and let stand for at least 30 and up to 60 minutes.

3   To serve, remove the allspice berries, add the butter and marmalade, and reheat.

Kitchen Note: *The quality of the vinegar does make a difference in this dish. If you don't have artisanal, unfiltered apple cider vinegar, it is best to make the dish with wine.*

Basic Roasted Brussels Sprouts

Serves 4

It cannot be said too often: roasting is the very best way to prepare Brussels sprouts. It is the only method that does not risk bringing out the cabbagey flavors so many people object to when faced with over-cooked steamed or boiled Brussels sprouts. When you roast Brussels sprouts, if you overcook them, the outer leaves will char, creating a sweet and crunchy texture that is actually quite wonderful.

1–1½	pounds Brussels sprouts, trimmed and halved, or quartered if large
2	tablespoons extra-virgin olive oil
	Coarse sea salt or kosher salt

1 Preheat the oven to 425°F. Lightly oil a half sheet pan (preferred) or large shallow roasting pan.

2 Mound the Brussels sprouts on the sheet pan, drizzle the oil over them, and toss gently to coat. Arrange the sprouts in a single uncrowded layer.

3 Roast for about 15 minutes, shaking the pan occasionally for even cooking, until the sprouts are tender and lightly browned.

4 Transfer the sprouts to a serving bowl and sprinkle with salt. Serve immediately.

Kitchen Note: *For even cooking, it is important that the sprouts all be roughly the same size. That often means that some will be halved and some will be quartered. Size is more important than shape in this instance.*

Crunchy Roasted Brussels Sprouts

Serves 4

Roasting is my favorite way to prepare Brussels sprouts because it brings out their sweet flavors. Adding shallots and garlic adds more sweetness and flavor, and the pumpkin seeds add a delicious crunch. Whether you consider yourself a fan of the unruly sprout or not, you may find yourself loving this dish.

1½ pounds Brussels sprouts, trimmed and halved, or quartered if large	¼ cup pumpkin seeds
2 shallots, diced	3 tablespoons extra-virgin olive oil
4 garlic cloves, minced	Coarse sea salt or kosher salt

1 Preheat the oven to 425°F. Lightly oil a large sheet pan (preferred) or large shallow roasting baking pan.

2 Mound the Brussels sprouts, shallots, garlic, and pumpkin seeds on the sheet pan, drizzle the oil over them, and toss gently to coat. Spread in a single uncrowded layer.

3 Roast for about 15 minutes, shaking the pan occasionally for even cooking, until the sprouts are tender and lightly browned.

4 Transfer the mixture to a serving bowl and sprinkle with the salt. Serve immediately.

Toasted Seed Snacks

1. Wash pumpkin or squash seeds and discard any fibers. Arrange in a single layer on a baking sheet and allow to dry overnight.

2. Preheat the oven to 250°F.

3. Drizzle the seeds with oil and toss to coat. Spread the seeds on the baking sheet. Salt generously. Bake about 45 minutes, until browned and crunchy.

4. Crack the seeds, discard the shells, and enjoy the seed kernels within.

Cornmeal-Crisped Brussels Sprouts

Serves 4

Another way to dress up roasted Brussels is with cornmeal and shallots. Both the flavor and the texture are enhanced to crispy new heights.

2	tablespoons extra-virgin olive oil
1½	pounds Brussels sprouts, trimmed and halved, or quartered if large
½	cup coarse-grain cornmeal
1	large shallot, minced
1	teaspoon salt
½	teaspoon freshly ground black pepper

1 Preheat the oven to 425°F. Generously oil a half sheet pan (preferred) or large shallow roasting pan.

2 In a large bowl, drizzle the oil over the Brussels sprouts and toss gently to coat. In a separate small bowl, combine the cornmeal, shallot, salt, and pepper; pour over the sprouts and toss again to coat. Arrange the sprouts in a single uncrowded layer on the sheet pan.

3 Roast for about 20 minutes, shaking the pan occasionally for even cooking, until the sprouts are tender and lightly browned.

4 Transfer the sprouts to a serving bowl and serve immediately.

Garlic-Crumbed Roasted Brussels Sprouts

Serves 4

A garlic-crumb topping works with many vegetables, including Brussels sprouts. It is a simple way to dress up an everyday dish.

1-1½ pounds Brussels sprouts, trimmed and halved, or quartered if large
2 tablespoons extra-virgin olive oil
4 tablespoons butter, melted
2 garlic cloves, minced
1 cup fresh breadcrumbs
½ cup grated Parmesan cheese
   Salt and freshly ground black pepper

1 Preheat the oven to 425°F. Lightly oil a half sheet pan (preferred) or large shallow roasting pan.

2 Mound the Brussels sprouts on the sheet pan, drizzle the oil over them, and toss gently to coat. Arrange the sprouts in a single uncrowded layer.

3 Roast for about 15 minutes, shaking the pan occasionally for even cooking, until the sprouts are tender and lightly browned.

4 Meanwhile, combine the butter, garlic, breadcrumbs, and cheese in a small bowl; season with salt and pepper.

5 Sprinkle the breadcrumb mixture over the Brussels sprouts, return to the oven, and roast for about 8 minutes longer, until the breadcrumbs are golden. Serve hot.

Pan-Seared Brussels Sprouts

Serves 4

Achieving a good sear on the Brussels sprouts is the secret to cooking them, whether you are sautéing on top of the stove or roasting in the oven. This recipe is a fine alternative when you don't want to roast. Don't crowd the Brussels sprouts in the pan; if you wish to cook more, choose a skillet larger than 12 inches in diameter or cook in batches.

3	tablespoons extra-virgin olive oil
4	garlic cloves, minced
½–1	teaspoon crushed red pepper flakes
1½	pounds Brussels sprouts, trimmed and halved, or quartered if large
	Coarse sea salt or kosher salt

1   Heat the oil in a large skillet over medium heat. Add the garlic and red pepper flakes and simmer until fragrant, about 1 minute. Pour off most of the oil, setting it aside, to leave a thin film of oil on the bottom of the skillet.

2   Increase the heat to high and add the Brussels sprouts; sprinkle with salt and cook, stirring occasionally, until browned and crisp on all sides, about 6 minutes.

3   Add the reserved oil to the pan, toss the sprouts to coat, and sauté for 1 minute. Cover and steam until the Brussels sprouts are tender crisp, 3 to 5 minutes longer. Taste for salt and add more if desired. Serve immediately.

Cream-Braised Brussels Sprouts

Serves 4

This is a luxurious way of cooking Brussels sprouts, perhaps not for every day (or even every week), but the cream does have a wonderful way of taming the often unruly (read: sulfurous) flavor of Brussels sprouts. Don't underestimate the power of the salt and balsamic vinegar for bringing the flavors together; taste and adjust as needed.

3	tablespoons extra-virgin olive oil
1½	pounds Brussels sprouts, trimmed and halved, or quartered if large
1	large or 2 small shallots, finely diced
1	cup heavy whipping cream
	Salt and freshly ground black pepper
1	tablespoon balsamic vinegar, or more to taste

1   Heat the oil in a large skillet or Dutch oven over medium-high heat. Add the Brussels sprouts and shallot and sauté, stirring occasionally, until the sprouts are browned in spots, about 5 minutes.

2   Pour in the cream, season generously with salt and pepper, stir to mix, and cover. Reduce the heat to low and simmer, stirring occasionally, until the sprouts are tender enough to be pierced easily with the tip of a paring knife, 30 to 35 minutes.

3   Stir in the vinegar. Taste and add more salt and vinegar if needed. Simmer, uncovered, for 1 to 2 minutes to marry the flavors. Serve immediately.

Bacon-Sautéed Brussels Sprouts

Serves 4

It doesn't take much bacon to alter the flavor profile of Brussels sprouts. This classic recipe is a favorite in many Brussels sprouts–growing regions, including Great Britain.

4 strips thick-cut bacon, diced

1 shallot, diced

1½ pounds Brussels sprouts, trimmed and halved, or quartered if large

Freshly ground black pepper

1 Bring a large pot of salted water to a boil.

2 Meanwhile, cook the bacon in a large skillet over medium heat until it begins to release its fat, about 3 minutes. Add the shallot and continue to sauté until the bacon is crisp, 2 to 3 minutes longer. Drain off all the fat.

3 Add the Brussels sprouts to the boiling water and blanch until tender, 4 to 7 minutes; do not overcook. Drain well.

4 Add the Brussels sprouts to the skillet and cook over medium heat, gently tossing the sprouts until they have taken on the flavor of the bacon left in the pan, about 2 minutes. Season with pepper and serve hot.

Lemony Brussels Sprouts

Serves 4-6

Thinly slicing the Brussels sprouts produces a beautiful confetti mixture of colors from dark green to white. Properly cooked, the sprouts are light and crispy, but do watch your timing carefully. Overcooking, which can happen easily when the sprouts are in such small pieces, turns this dish drab olive green and cabbagey.

1½	pounds Brussels sprouts
2	tablespoons extra-virgin olive oil
1	shallot, minced
1	garlic clove, minced
1	teaspoon finely grated lemon zest
3	tablespoons lemon juice
2	teaspoons sugar
¼	cup white wine
	Salt and freshly ground black pepper

1   Cut the stem ends from the Brussels sprouts and remove any blemished leaves. Halve each sprout lengthwise and very thinly slice each half or run through a food processor.

2   Heat the oil in a large skillet or wok over high heat. Stir in the Brussels sprouts, shallot, garlic, lemon zest, lemon juice, and sugar. Sauté, stirring constantly, until the mixture is slightly limp and well blended.

3   Add the wine and sauté, stirring constantly, until the sprouts are brightly colored and lightly softened but still crunchy, 3 to 4 minutes.

4   Reduce the heat to low, season with salt and pepper, and cook for 1 minute longer. Serve hot.

Discovering the Apple in Apple Cider Vinegar

One taste is all you will need for proof that an artisanal, never-pasteurized cider vinegar tastes superior to supermarket cider vinegar, which tastes like, well, vinegar: sharp and sour. Artisanal, unpasteurized cider vinegar is redolent of apples. Its flavor and aroma is complex and fruity. Its ability to bring life to collard greens, kale, cabbage salads, and roasted vegetable salads is unparalleled.

I discovered the flavor difference when I was writing a piece about Vermont doctor DeForest Clinton Jarvis, who made a name for himself promoting apple cider vinegar mixed with honey as a cure for whatever ailed you: arthritis, infection, indigestion. He also claimed it would guard against osteoporosis, lower cholesterol, prevent cancer, maintain memory, and protect the mind from aging. Oh, and it also makes an excellent additive to dairy-cow feed.

While I am not interested in drinking the vinegar cure, I do swear by artisanal apple cider vinegar. I used to think old Vermonters were incomprehensible with their switchel and shrub (which is made from fresh berries, honey, apple cider vinegar, and water). Who drinks anything made with vinegar and calls it good? But now that I've tasted the real stuff, I wonder how I was ever duped into thinking that mass-produced supermarket vinegar bears any resemblance to the real thing.

Hot Slaw

Serves 6

When I was researching an article on artisanal apple cider vinegar, I spoke with vinegar maker Joanne Lidell, who shared this recipe with me. Lidell and her partner, Robert Machin, make Honest-to-Goodness Apple Cider Vinegar at Gingerbrook Farm in South Washington, Vermont. This slaw is terrific when fresh and hot, and surprisingly good left over and cold. Lidell recommended varying the flavor by adding a shredded carrot, chopped red bell pepper, or minced garlic. The caraway seeds are my idea.

¼ cup extra-virgin olive oil
½ head green or savoy cabbage, thinly sliced or shredded
¼ cup artisanal apple cider vinegar
1 tablespoon caraway seeds
Salt and freshly ground black pepper

1 Heat the oil in a large skillet over medium-high heat. Add the cabbage and toss until well coated with oil. Add the vinegar and continue to toss until the cabbage is wilted, 5 to 8 minutes.

2 Stir in the caraway seeds and season generously with salt and pepper. Serve immediately.

Kitchen Note: *With so few ingredients, the quality of the vinegar really matters here. If you substitute ordinary supermarket cider vinegar, you will be disappointed with the results.*

🌿 Stir-Fried Cabbage in Brown Sauce

Serves 4-6

Chinese restaurants often offer "broccoli in brown sauce." This is a variation on the theme, made with cabbage instead.

½ cup dried shiitake mushrooms	1 tablespoon cornstarch
3 tablespoons oyster sauce	2 tablespoons peanut, sunflower, or canola oil
2 tablespoons soy sauce	4 garlic cloves, minced
1 tablespoon Chinese rice wine or dry sherry	1 (1-inch) piece fresh ginger, peeled and minced
1 teaspoon Asian sesame oil	1 head Chinese cabbage, trimmed and sliced
1 teaspoon sugar	

1   Soak the mushrooms in room-temperature water to cover for at least 4 hours. Drain, reserving the soaking water, and slice.

2   To make the sauce, combine 6 tablespoons of the mushroom soaking water with the oyster sauce, soy sauce, wine, sesame oil, sugar, and cornstarch. Mix well and set aside.

3   Heat the peanut oil in a large wok over high heat. Add the garlic and ginger and sauté just until fragrant, about 30 seconds. Add the cabbage and mushrooms and stir-fry until the cabbage is barely tender, about 3 minutes.

4   Mix the sauce to thoroughly distribute the cornstarch, then add it to the wok. Toss lightly until the sauce is heated through and thickened, about 2 minutes. Serve immediately.

Kitchen Note: *If you don't have the time for a cold-water soak for the mushrooms (it results in the best texture), use boiling water instead of room-temperature water, and soak them for 10 minutes.*

🌿 Variation: Vegetarian Stir-Fried Cabbage in Brown Sauce

For a strictly vegetarian dish, substitute vegetarian oyster sauce, mock oyster sauce, or stir-fry sauce for the oyster sauce; these are vegetarian versions of the original.

East-Meets-West Braised Red Cabbage

Serves 6

The combination of bacon and maple syrup from the West and soy sauce and five-spice powder from the East is magical. Slow cooking the cabbage renders it soft and silky. When the main course is rather bland — anything from mac 'n' cheese to baked chicken or pork — this makes the perfect complement.

4	ounces thick-cut bacon, cut lengthwise into ½-inch-wide strips
1	onion, thinly sliced
2	garlic cloves, minced
1	(½-inch) piece fresh ginger, peeled and minced
1	medium head red cabbage (1½–1¾ pounds), quartered and thinly sliced
¼	cup apple cider vinegar
¼	cup soy sauce
3	tablespoons pure maple syrup
½	teaspoon Chinese five-spice powder

1   Fry the bacon in a large skillet or Dutch oven over medium heat until it renders its fat and begins to become crisp, about 5 minutes. Remove the bacon with a slotted spoon and set aside on paper towels to drain. Pour off all but 2 tablespoons of the bacon fat.

2   Add the onion to the fat remaining in the pan and sauté until limp, about 2 minutes. Stir in the garlic and ginger and sauté just until fragrant, about 20 seconds. Increase the heat to medium-high and add the cabbage, a few handfuls at a time. When all the cabbage is in the skillet, sauté, stirring frequently, until the strands begin to wilt and have a moist gleam, about 6 minutes.

3   Add the vinegar, soy sauce, maple syrup, five-spice powder, and reserved bacon to the pan. Mix well and bring to a boil.

4   Cover the pan, reduce the heat to low, and cook at a gentle simmer, stirring every 20 minutes, until the cabbage is tender and deeply fragrant, 40 to 60 minutes. Serve warm or at room temperature.

Baked Carrots and Fennel in Béchamel

Serves 4

Tarragon is an herb that is classically matched with carrots for good reason. Its slight anise flavor complements the sweetness of the carrots. For fewer dishes to wash, use a baking dish that can be brought directly to the table to serve.

4 large carrots, peeled and thinly sliced	3 tablespoons all-purpose flour
3 tablespoons butter	1 cup milk
1 fennel bulb, trimmed and thinly sliced	¼ cup dry white wine
1 shallot, minced	½ teaspoon dried tarragon
	Salt and freshly ground black pepper

1 Preheat the oven to 425°F. Butter a 1½-quart baking dish.

2 Steam the carrots over boiling water until tender, 7 to 10 minutes. Transfer the carrots to the baking dish.

3 Meanwhile, melt the butter in a small saucepan over medium heat. Add the fennel and shallot and sauté until softened, 2 to 3 minutes. Stir in the flour to form a smooth paste. Add the milk and wine and bring just to a boil. The sauce will thicken. Remove from the heat, add the tarragon, and season with salt and pepper.

4 Pour the sauce over the carrots. Bake, uncovered, for about 10 minutes, until the sauce is bubbling and golden around the edges. Serve hot.

Variation: Baked Root Vegetables and Fennel in Béchamel

This recipe works well with other types of root vegetables. Just substitute 1 pound of any root vegetable for the carrots.

Sautéed Greens with Apple Cider Vinegar

Serves 4

There is a classic preparation of greens in Italy made with sweet-sour flavors (*agrodolce*), usually raisins or currants for the sweet and red wine vinegar for the sour. It occurred to me that a New England–based version of the same dish would use apples for the sweet and apple cider vinegar for the sour. It's a fantastic dish — but it is essential that you use an artisanal unpasteurized apple cider vinegar. Supermarket apple cider vinegar is sharp and without nuance, while the artisanal version is perfumed by apples and so flavorful that you can almost drink it from the bottle. Sunflower oil, which is increasingly available in the Northeast, makes it a totally "locavore" recipe for New Englanders.

2   tablespoons extra-virgin olive oil or sunflower oil
1   large shallot, diced
1½ pounds greens (cabbage, collard greens, or kale; about 18 cups lightly packed; remove and discard any tough stems)
    Salt and freshly ground black pepper
1   large apple, with peel, cored and shredded
3   tablespoons apple cider vinegar, or to taste

1   Heat the oil in a large skillet or Dutch oven over medium-high heat. Add the shallot and sauté until softened, about 3 minutes. Add the greens, toss to coat in the oil, and season with salt and pepper. Cover and let steam until wilted, 3 to 5 minutes.

2   Add the apple, toss again, cover, and cook until the greens are tender, 2 to 10 minutes longer, depending on the green. Drizzle with the vinegar, adjust the seasoning, and serve hot.

Kitchen Notes: *Cabbage should be chopped or sliced; other greens can be left whole or chopped, though tough stems should be discarded. Collard greens take longer to cook than other greens.*

Braised Celery Root Gratin

Serves 4-6

Slowly cooking celery root coaxes extra flavor from this humble root.
This is a fine dish to serve alongside any roast.

3	tablespoons butter, cut into bits
1	shallot, minced
2	large celery roots, peeled and cut into ¼-inch slices
1½	tablespoons lemon juice
2	teaspoons sugar
¾	cup chicken broth or vegetable broth (pages 126-27)
⅔	cup dried breadcrumbs
⅓	cup lightly packed grated Gruyère cheese (about 1½ ounces)

1   Melt the butter in a large saucepan over medium heat. Add the shallot and sauté until limp, about 3 minutes. Add the celery root, lemon juice, sugar, and broth. Bring to a boil, then reduce the heat and simmer, covered, turning the celery root slices occasionally, until the vegetables are very tender, 40 to 45 minutes.

2   Preheat the broiler. Stir together the breadcrumbs and Gruyère. Butter a large gratin dish.

3   Transfer the vegetables and their cooking liquid to the prepared dish. Sprinkle the breadcrumb mixture evenly over the vegetables. Broil about 4 inches from the heat until the cheese is melted and the crumbs are browned, 2 to 3 minutes. Serve hot.

Garlic-Crumbed Greens

Serves 4

It's interesting how little it takes to dress up a mess o' greens.

> 8 cups chopped kale, collards, or mustard greens (remove and discard tough stems)
> 3 tablespoons butter or extra-virgin olive oil
> 3 garlic cloves, minced
> ¼ teaspoon crushed red pepper flakes (optional)
> 1 cup fresh breadcrumbs
> Salt and freshly ground black pepper

1 Bring a large pot of salted water to a boil. Add the greens and cook until tender, about 5 minutes for kale and mustard greens or 10 to 15 minutes for collards. Drain well and plunge into ice water to stop the cooking. Drain again.

2 Melt the butter in a large skillet over medium-high heat. Add the garlic and red pepper flakes, if using, and sauté until softened and fragrant, about 2 minutes. Add the breadcrumbs and continue to sauté until golden and toasted, about 5 minutes.

3 Stir in the greens, season with salt and pepper, and cook until heated through, about 5 minutes. Serve hot.

Kitchen Note: *The higher the quality of breadcrumbs, the better the dish. Try to use an artisan or homemade bread and make your own crumbs. It is easy to do in a food processor or with a box grater.*

Parmesan Greens

Serves 4

Another simple way to dress up greens. The pine nuts add crunch while the Parmesan adds rich flavor.

> 8 cups chopped kale, collards, or mustard greens (remove and discard tough stems)
> 3 tablespoons butter or extra-virgin olive oil
> 2 garlic cloves, minced
> ¼ cup pine nuts
>   Salt and freshly ground black pepper
> ¼ cup freshly shaved or grated Parmesan cheese

1   Bring a large pot of salted water to a boil. Add the greens and cook until tender, about 5 minutes for kale and mustard greens or 10 to 15 minutes for collards. Drain well and plunge into ice water to stop the cooking. Drain again.

2   Melt the butter in a large skillet over medium-high heat. Add the garlic and sauté until softened and fragrant, about 2 minutes. Add the pine nuts and continue to sauté until golden and toasted, about 3 minutes.

3   Stir in the greens, season with salt and pepper, and cook until heated through, about 5 minutes. Remove from the heat and sprinkle the cheese over the greens; cover with a lid and let the cheese melt, about 1 minute. Serve hot.

Chinese Steamed Greens

Serves 4

It doesn't get any simpler than this, and preparing greens this way is simply perfect. It is terrific with kale, especially Lacinato kale, and most Chinese greens, including baby bok choy, Chinese broccoli, and napa cabbage. It is also an excellent method for preparing regular broccoli and broccoli rabe.

1½–2 pounds greens (napa or Chinese cabbage, bok choy, kale, or mustard greens; remove and discard tough stems)
   Soy sauce
   Asian sesame sauce

1 Fill a saucepan with a couple of inches of water and bring to a boil. Steam the greens in a steaming basket over the boiling water until tender, about 5 minutes.

2 Arrange the greens on a platter. Drizzle generously with soy sauce and sparingly with sesame oil. Serve hot.

Kitchen Note: *For an extremely simple one-dish meal, steam cubed silken tofu and place on the greens before drizzling with soy sauce and sesame oil. Serve over rice.*

Sichuan-Style Stir-Fried Greens

Serves 4

A few Chinese ingredients give this easy stir-fry unusual flavor. Sichuan peppercorns are actually the berry of the prickly ash tree. They can be found at Asian groceries, perhaps under the name anise pepper, Chinese pepper, fagara, flower pepper, or sansho. Chinese black vinegar has a distinctive flavor, closer to balsamic vinegar than to regular rice vinegar. You can use any Asian green in this recipe, or use a mix of greens.

2	tablespoons peanut, sunflower, or canola oil
4	small dried chilis or ½ teaspoon crushed red pepper flakes
2	teaspoons Sichuan peppercorns
2	garlic cloves, minced
1½	pounds bok choy, napa or Chinese cabbage, kale, or other Chinese greens, trimmed and sliced into 1-inch pieces (about 18 cups lightly packed; remove and discard any tough stems)
½	teaspoon sugar
1	tablespoon Asian sesame oil
	Salt
	Chinese black vinegar

1   Heat the peanut oil in a large wok over high heat. Add the chilis, peppercorns, and garlic, and sauté just until fragrant, about 30 seconds. Add the greens and stir-fry until wilted, about 3 minutes. Cover and let steam until tender, 1 to 3 minutes, depending on the greens and your preferences.

2   Add the sugar, sesame oil, and salt to taste. Toss to mix. Drizzle with vinegar and serve immediately.

Kitchen Note: *If you don't have Chinese black vinegar on hand, you can come reasonably close to it with a mixture of one part soy sauce, one part Worestershire sauce, and one part rice vinegar.*

Sautéed Collard Greens

Serves 4

Most collard-green recipes call for very slow cooking of the greens. This recipe speeds up the process, and the result is delicious.

2 pounds collard greens, cut into 1-inch ribbons (about 24 cups lightly packed; remove and discard tough stems)

3 tablespoons extra-virgin olive oil

2 garlic cloves, minced

1 shallot, minced

Salt and freshly ground black pepper

2 teaspoons apple cider vinegar (artisanal apple cider vinegar is recommended), or to taste

1 Bring a large pot of salted water to a boil. Add the collards to the boiling water and cook until the leaves are tender, about 15 minutes.

2 Drain in a colander, pressing out the excess liquid with the back of a spoon.

3 Heat the oil in a large skillet over medium-high heat. Add the garlic, shallot, and collards, and sauté until the collards are heated through and the garlic and shallot are transparent, about 4 minutes. Season with salt and pepper and drizzle with the vinegar. Serve hot.

Crispy Kale Chips

Serves 1–4

Potato chips, be gone! Roasted kale is so delicious that you never need to turn to them again for a hit of crisp and salt. My son introduced me to this delicacy, but he learned to make it in a cast-iron frying pan over a hot wood fire outdoors. It took me a while to figure out this version, which is faster, more suited to the average lifestyle, and so good it will make kale lovers out of the most picky eaters. This is more appropriate as a snack or hors d'oeuvre than a side dish because of the high volume of the pieces.

1   bunch curly kale, chopped into 1-inch pieces (remove and discard tough stems)

2   tablespoons extra-virgin olive oil, plus more as needed

Coarse sea salt or kosher salt

1   Preheat the oven to 425°F.

2   Measure the kale and transfer it to a large bowl. For every 4 cups firmly packed leaves, add 1 tablespoon oil. Mix well with your hands to make sure the leaves are evenly coated. Spread in a single layer on a large sheet pan.

3   Roast for about 10 minutes, until the curly tips of the leaves are darkened and the interior of the leaves are a bright green. The leaves should be mostly crunchy but not blackened. Toss with salt and serve.

Kitchen Note: *Although any salt can be used to add the appropriate flavor, salt in larger flakes is more pleasing in texture.*

Winter is the time of promise because there is so little to do — or because you can now and then permit yourself the luxury of thinking so.

— Stanley Crawford

Crisp Roasted Jerusalem Artichokes

Serves 4

Roasting brings out the natural sweet flavor of these often under-appreciated tubers. This is probably the very best way to prepare them. Peeling is optional, but I prefer it. If you decide to peel, buy a bit extra (2 pounds should do it), use a sharp paring knife, and don't worry about paring away the small, hard-to-peel knobs.

1–2	pounds Jerusalem artichokes
2	tablespoons extra-virgin olive oil or any nut oil
	Coarse sea salt or kosher salt and freshly ground black pepper

1 Preheat the oven to 500°F. Lightly oil a half sheet pan (preferred) or large shallow roasting pan.

2 Peel the artichokes or scrub them well. Cut into 1-inch pieces. Mound on the sheet pan, drizzle with the oil, and toss gently to coat. Arrange in a single layer on the pan.

3 Roast for about 15 minutes, shaking the pan occasionally for even cooking, until the vegetables are tender and well browned. Shake the pan more frequently toward the end of the roasting time, as they will go from well browned to burned rather quickly. Sprinkle with salt and pepper and serve at once.

Oven-Braised Leeks

Serves 4

As a member of the Onion family, leeks are prized for their delicate flavor and their affinity for cream and potatoes. But they are far too infrequently served on their own as the delicious vegetable they are.

8	small to medium leeks, trimmed, tender white and pale green parts only
2	tablespoons extra-virgin olive oil
1	cup chicken broth or vegetable broth (pages 126–27)
	Coarse sea salt or kosher salt and freshly ground black pepper
	Balsamic vinegar

1 Preheat the oven to 425°F. Lightly oil a 9- by 13-inch baking dish.

2 Brush the leeks with the oil and arrange in a single layer in the prepared dish.

3 Roast for about 20 minutes, shaking the pan occasionally for even cooking. Add the broth, return to the oven, and braise for 10 minutes.

4 Transfer the leeks and their cooking liquid to a serving platter and sprinkle with salt and pepper. Drizzle with balsamic vinegar. Serve at once or at room temperature.

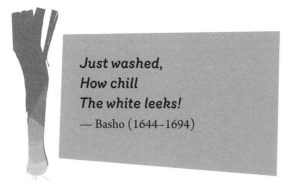

Just washed,
How chill
The white leeks!
— Basho (1644–1694)

Braised Balsamic-Glazed Parsnips and Pears

Serves 4–6

Pears do well in savory dishes, as this recipe illustrates.

4   parsnips (about 1 pound), peeled and thinly
      sliced on the diagonal
2   firm pears, peeled, cored, and sliced
½   cup vegetable broth, chicken broth, or turkey broth
      (pages 126–27)
¼   cup extra-virgin olive oil
¼   cup balsamic vinegar
      Salt and freshly ground black pepper

1   Combine the parsnips, pears, broth, oil, and vinegar in a large, nonreactive skillet or
     Dutch oven. Season with salt and pepper. Bring to a boil.

2   Reduce the heat and simmer, stirring occasionally, until the parsnips are tender crisp,
     20 to 30 minutes. The parsnips and pears will absorb the liquid and become glazed.
     Serve hot.

Kitchen Note: *Any firm pear will work here. Anjou pears are particularly recommended.*

Honey-Balsamic Roasted Parsnips

Serves 4

If parsnips are a vegetable you haven't fully appreciated, try roasting them. Even better, try roasting them with this delicious honey and balsamic vinegar glaze. The sweetly nutty flavor of roasted parsnips is perfectly complemented by the sweet-tart glaze.

4 parsnips (about 1 pound), peeled and cut into matchsticks	2 tablespoons balsamic vinegar
1 onion, halved and slivered (sliced vertically)	1 tablespoon honey
2 tablespoons extra-virgin olive oil	2 garlic cloves, minced
Salt and freshly ground black pepper	1 teaspoon crushed dried rosemary

1 Preheat the oven to 425°F. Lightly oil a half sheet pan (preferred) or large shallow roasting pan.

2 Mound the parsnips and onion on the prepared pan. Drizzle with the oil, season with salt and pepper, and toss gently to coat. Spread in a single layer. Roast for 15 minutes, until the parsnips are mostly tender.

3 Meanwhile, combine the vinegar, honey, garlic, and rosemary in a small bowl. Remove the vegetables from the oven. Drizzle the honey mixture over the vegetables and toss to coat evenly. Roast for 10 to 15 minutes longer, until vegetables are browned in spots and completely tender. Taste and adjust the seasoning before serving.

Variation: Honey-Balsamic Roasted Carrots

Substitute carrots for the parsnips or roast a mixture of the two vegetables.

Neeps and Tatties

Serves 4

Mashed potatoes and turnips (or rutabagas) is a classic combination, especially popular in the American South. But the Scottish name for the dish — "neeps and tatties" — sounds wonderfully exotic yet homey. This is a down-home dish, perfect with a warming wintry stew. Neeps and tatties is the traditional accompaniment to haggis (sheep's stomach stuffed with organ meats and oatmeal), but that is another story.

1	**large rutabaga (about 1 pound), peeled and cut into ½-inch cubes**
2	**russet (baking) potatoes (about 1 pound), peeled and cut into chunks**
4	**tablespoons butter**
4-6	**tablespoons whole milk or half-and-half**
	Salt and freshly ground black pepper

1 Cover the rutabaga and potatoes with cold water in a saucepan and generously salt the water. Bring to a boil and boil until the vegetables are very tender, 10 to 12 minutes.

2 Meanwhile, melt the butter in 4 tablespoons milk. Keep warm.

3 Drain the vegetables. Return them to the pan and cook over high heat, shaking the pan until any excess liquid is evaporated, about 30 seconds. Remove the pan from the heat and add the butter mixture to the potato mixture. Mash the vegetables with a potato masher until smooth and beat with a wooden spoon until fluffy. Add the remaining milk if needed for a smooth and creamy texture. Season with salt and pepper. Serve hot.

Smashed Potatoes with Root Vegetables

Serves 4

Colorful roasted root vegetables are blended with ordinary mashed potatoes to make a pretty terrific dish. Make sure at least some of the root vegetables (carrots, red or golden beets, rutabagas) are other than white (celery root, parsnips, salsify, turnips) or you will lose half the appeal of this dish. Serve it any time you would serve ordinary mashed potatoes.

6	cups peeled and cubed mixed root vegetables (beets, carrots, celery root, parsnips, rutabaga, salsify, and/or turnips)
2	tablespoons extra-virgin olive oil
3–4	medium russet (baking) potatoes, peeled and cut into chunks
4	garlic cloves, peeled
⅓	cup milk or cream, plus more as needed
2	tablespoons butter
	Salt and freshly ground black pepper

1 Preheat the oven to 450°F. Lightly oil a large sheet pan (preferred) or large shallow roasting pan.

2 Mound the mixed root vegetables on the sheet pan, drizzle the oil over them, and toss gently to coat. Spread in a single layer. Roast for about 25 minutes, stirring occasionally, until tender and lightly browned.

3 Meanwhile, combine the potatoes and garlic in a medium saucepan and cover with cold salted water. Bring the water to a boil and boil until the potatoes are very tender, about 20 minutes.

4 Heat the milk and butter in a small saucepan over low heat and keep warm.

5 Drain the potatoes and garlic, return to the saucepan, add the milk mixture, and mash until smooth. Add the root vegetables and mash briefly, until about half the vegetables are broken down but not puréed. Season with salt and pepper, adding more milk if the mixture seems dry. Serve hot.

Samosas

Makes 18

Indian samosas are traditionally made with a flaky pastry and fried. In this easier version, the potatoes are encased in store-bought puff pastry and baked. If you happen to have about 1½ cups leftover mashed potatoes, you can use that instead of cooking the potatoes from scratch.

¾ pound (1 large or 2–3 small) thin-skinned potatoes	1 tablespoon cumin seeds
¼ cup sunflower or canola oil	1 cup frozen green peas, thawed
1 onion, finely chopped	3 tablespoons chopped fresh cilantro (optional)
2 garlic cloves, minced	Salt and freshly ground black pepper
1½ inch piece fresh ginger, peeled and finely minced	1 (17-ounce) package frozen puff pastry, defrosted
¼ cup chopped fresh or canned green chilis	1 egg, lightly beaten
2 teaspoons garam masala	Chutney, such as Major Grey's, for serving

1   To make the filling, cover the potatoes with water in a saucepan. Bring to a boil, and boil until tender, about 15 minutes. Let cool, then peel and cut into ¼-inch dice.

2   Heat the oil in a wok or large skillet over medium heat. Add the onion and sauté until slightly colored, about 5 minutes. Add the garlic, ginger, chilis, garam masala, and cumin, and sauté until fragrant, about 1 minute. Add the potatoes and stir until well coated with the spices. Add the peas and the cilantro, if using. Season with salt and pepper. Sauté over low heat until the flavors have blended, about 5 minutes.

3   Preheat the oven to 400°F. Line a large baking sheet with parchment paper.

4   Lightly dust a work surface with flour. Roll out one sheet of the puff pastry to a 12-inch square, about ⅛ inch thick. Using a pizza cutter or a knife, cut the dough into nine equal squares.

5   Place a tablespoon of the potato mixture in the corner of a square. Lift the opposite diagonal corner over to seal the triangular package, pinching the edges together. Continue in the same manner for the rest of the squares. Repeat with the remaining pastry sheet and filling. Arrange the samosas on the baking sheet, spacing them about 1 inch apart. Brush the tops of the samosas with the beaten egg.

6   Bake for 18 to 20 minutes, until puffed and golden brown. Serve warm with chutney.

Kitchen Note: *Samosas are traditionally served as a snack or hors d'oeuvre, but they easily make a vegetarian main dish.*

Potato Knishes

Makes 27

What samosas are to Indians, knishes are to Jews. New York City delis are famous for their knishes (pronounced kuh-NISH-es), which is the Yiddish word for "cakes." These baked or fried pastries can be made into bite-size appetizers (as they are here) or sandwich-size side dishes. They can be filled with cabbage, meat, or cheese, but kasha and mashed potato are the most common fillings. Chicken fat is the preferred medium for sautéing the onions that flavor the filling, but any cooking oil works just fine.

1½	pounds russet (baking) potatoes, peeled and cut into chunks	1	large onion, diced
4	tablespoons butter		Salt and freshly ground black pepper
¼	cup chicken fat or any vegetable oil	1½	(17-ounce) packages puff pastry, thawed
			Spicy mustard, for serving

1 Lightly oil a half sheet pan.

2 Cover the potatoes with cold salted water in a saucepan. Bring to a boil and boil until tender when pierced with a fork, about 15 minutes. Drain well and return to the saucepan; add the butter.

3 Meanwhile, melt the chicken fat in a medium skillet over medium heat. Add the onion and sauté until golden and soft, about 10 minutes. Scrape the onion into the potatoes and mash well. Season generously with salt and pepper.

4 Remove the pastry sheets from the refrigerator one at a time (chilled pastry is easier to work with). Cut each sheet into nine equal squares. Stretch each square to form a much larger square about 1/16 inch thick. Drop a rounded tablespoon of the filling in the center of each square. Fold over two opposite sides of the dough, then fold over the two ends to form a neat square parcel. Place seam-side down on the prepared sheet pan. Repeat until all the pastry and filling are used. Transfer the formed knishes to the freezer while you preheat the oven to 400°F.

5 Bake the knishes for about 20 minutes (30 minutes if completely frozen), until golden brown. Serve warm with spicy mustard.

Kitchen Notes: *These snacks freeze beautifully, so don't worry if this recipe makes more than you need. Freeze extras, unbaked or baked. Baked leftovers can be covered and stored in the refrigerator. Reheat, uncovered, in a 350°F oven for about 20 minutes.*

Buttermilk Mashed Potatoes

Serves 4

When you want to cut down on the fat but still retain a rich flavor, butter-milk should do the trick. These mashed potatoes are light on the butter and heavy on the creamy goodness. Peeling is optional, but not at all necessary when you use a thin-skinned potato. Likewise the garlic is optional; I always add garlic to my mashed potatoes because it adds a buttery note.

1½	pounds thin-skinned potatoes (Yukon Golds are recommended), cut into 2-inch chunks
2	garlic cloves, peeled (optional)
1	cup buttermilk
1	tablespoon butter
	Salt and freshly ground black pepper

1 Cover the potatoes and the garlic, if using, with cold salted water in a saucepan. Bring to a boil and boil gently until the potatoes are tender when pierced with a fork, about 15 minutes. Reserve about ½ cup of the cooking liquid, and then drain.

2 Return the potatoes to the pan. Cook, uncovered, over low heat for 2 to 3 minutes, stirring occasionally, to let the potatoes dry out a little (too much moisture will dilute their flavor).

3 Mash the potatoes with a potato masher or beat with a hand mixer. Beat in the buttermilk and butter until thoroughly incorporated. If the potatoes seem dry, add a little of the reserved cooking liquid. Season with salt and pepper. Serve at once, or keep the potatoes warm, covered, in a double boiler over hot water for up to 1 hour.

Kitchen Note: *It is fine to use russet or baking potatoes for this recipe, but peel the potatoes before cooking.*

🍃 Potato-Stuffed Pierogi

Makes about 36

Winter is a good time to vanquish a fear of dough, and delicious pierogi are a great place to start. These potato-stuffed (or sauerkraut-stuffed) dumplings are found throughout eastern Europe and may be served as a snack, appetizer, side dish, or main dish. The recipe calls for "about 1 pound" baking potatoes, which is 1 large potato, more or less. Go less rather than more; you don't use much filling in each pierogi. Yes, you can use leftover mashed potatoes; you'll need about 1½ cups.

About 1 pound russet (baking) potatoes, peeled and cut into chunks	Salt and freshly ground black pepper
2 garlic cloves, peeled	2¾ cups all-purpose flour, plus more for dusting
4 tablespoons butter, plus more as needed for frying	1 egg, lightly beaten
1 shallot, minced	1 cup sour cream, plus more for serving
½ cup shredded cheddar cheese (2 ounces)	2 tablespoons water, as needed

1   To make the filling, combine the potatoes and garlic in a saucepan and cover with salted water. Bring to a boil and boil until the potatoes are completely tender, 12 to 15 minutes. Drain and transfer to a medium bowl. Mash with 2 tablespoons of the butter. Stir in the shallot and cheese; season with salt and pepper.

2   To make the dough, combine the flour and 1 teaspoon salt in a large bowl. Make a well in the center of the flour; add the egg and sour cream and stir into the flour. Continue stirring until the dough forms a ragged mass. If you can't gather all the flour into the dough ball, add the water, 1 tablespoon at a time, and continue working the dough into a ball.

3   Transfer the dough to a work surface lightly dusted with flour. Knead until a smooth dough forms. (Kneading helps develop the gluten, which will enable you to stretch the dough without tearing, so don't skimp on this step.) Cut the dough into quarters, wrap each in plastic, and refrigerate for 30 minutes.

4   On a floured work surface, form each quarter of dough into a log. Cut the log into nine equal pieces. Using a small Asian rolling pin (see Kitchen Note), roll out each piece into a 3-inch circle. Place 1 tablespoon of potato filling slightly off center on

each circle. Moisten the edge of the dough, fold the dough over the filling, and press the edges firmly to seal. Repeat with the remaining dough and filling.

5 Bring a large pot of water to a boil. Boil the pieorgi in three batches for 5 to 7 minutes each, until the dough is cooked through. Scoop out each batch with a slotted spoon, drain well, and set aside.

6 Just before serving, melt the remaining 2 tablespoons butter in a large skillet. Add enough pieorgi to fit in a single layer and fry over medium heat until crisp and browned. Remove and keep warm. Repeat with the remaining pierogi, using more butter as needed. Serve hot, accompanied by sour cream.

Kitchen Note: *Asian rolling pins are nothing more than 2-inch dowels cut about 6 inches long. They are easier to use with small pieces of dough than Western rolling pins.*

Potato Galette

Serves 4–6

This is a simple but elegant way to prepare potatoes. A galette is a rustic cake.

3 tablespoons butter
3 tablespoons extra-virgin olive oil
1 shallot, minced
1 teaspoon chopped dried rosemary
2 pounds russet (baking) potatoes, peeled and very thinly sliced
Salt and freshly ground pepper

Kitchen Note: *The potatoes must be evenly and thinly sliced to cook through. A food processor or mandoline does a great job if your knife skills aren't up to the task.*

1 Preheat the oven to 400°F. Lightly oil a 10-inch tart pan.

2 Melt the butter with the oil. Stir in the shallot and rosemary. Pour over the potatoes in a large bowl and toss to coat. Season generously with salt and pepper. Transfer the potatoes to the tart pan and compress to form an even cake. The potatoes on top should lie flat.

3 Bake for about 40 minutes, until the top layer of potatoes is golden and crisp and the potatoes are cooked through. Serve hot, sliced into wedges.

Mashed Potatoes with Greens

Serves 6

Mashed potatoes with greens is an inevitable combination. In Ireland, it is called colcannon, the green is cabbage, and the flavor is carried by generous helpings of cream and butter. In Italy, the green may be kale or dandelion greens, and the flavor is carried with olive oil. Either way, it is a terrific way to serve mashed potatoes.

2	pounds russet (baking) potatoes, peeled and cut into large pieces
2–4	garlic cloves, peeled
1	large bunch kale or collards (remove and discard tough stems)
4–5	tablespoons extra-virgin olive oil, plus more as needed
	Salt and freshly ground black pepper
¼	cup dried breadcrumbs

1   Combine the potatoes and two garlic cloves in a large pot of salted water. Bring to a boil and boil gently until completely tender, 15 to 25 minutes. Lift the potatoes and garlic out of the pot with a slotted spoon and transfer to a bowl.

2   Add the greens to the potato cooking water and boil over high heat until tender, about 4 minutes for kale or 10 to 15 minutes for collards. Drain well, pressing out any excess water.

3   Mash the potatoes with a potato masher, adding 3 to 4 tablespoons of the oil to moisten.

4   Preheat the broiler.

5   Transfer the greens to a cutting board and chop; stir into the mashed potatoes. Add additional oil to taste. Season generously with salt and pepper.

6   Transfer the mixture to a baking dish and top with the breadcrumbs. If you are a garlic lover, mince the remaining two garlic cloves and sprinkle over the breadcrumbs. Drizzle with 1 tablespoon oil. Broil until the breadcrumbs are golden, about 2 minutes. Serve hot.

Kitchen Note: *Homemade breadcrumbs are always better than store-bought. To make dried breadcrumbs, bake slices of fresh bread in a 300°F oven for 10 to 15 minutes, turning once, until dry. Then break into pieces and grind into crumbs in a food processor.*

Rosemary Roasted Potatoes

Serves 4

A basic potato preparation that goes with everything. I prefer it to hash browns or home fries with my Sunday morning eggs — less fuss.

> 2 **pounds thin-skinned potatoes, cut into bite-size chunks**
> 2 **shallots, minced**
> 2 **teaspoons dried rosemary or thyme**
> ¼ **cup extra-virgin olive oil**
> **Coarse sea salt or kosher salt and freshly ground black pepper**

1 Preheat the oven to 400°F. Lightly oil a half sheet pan (preferred) or large shallow roasting pan.

2 Mound the potatoes, shallots, and herbs on the sheet pan. Drizzle with the oil, season with salt and pepper, and toss gently to coat. Arrange in a single layer.

3 Roast for 45 to 60 minutes, turning occasionally for even cooking, until the potatoes are tender when pierced with a fork and browned. Serve hot.

Kitchen Note: *If you happen to have duck or goose fat on hand, you can melt it and use it instead of the olive oil. The potatoes will be transformed from delicious to sublime.*

I do not believe that you have to spend a lot of money to eat well: it is hard to beat a plain old baked potato.

— Laurie Colwin (1944–1992)

Roasted Spiced Potatoes

Serves 4

Roasted potatoes are welcome at any meal, but spicy roasted potatoes can make an otherwise plain meal seem exciting.

¼	cup sunflower or canola oil
1	teaspoon salt
1	teaspoon curry powder
1	teaspoon ground cumin
1	teaspoon onion powder
¼	teaspoon freshly ground black pepper
¼	teaspoon Chinese five-spice powder
¼	teaspoon ground ginger
⅛	teaspoon ground cayenne pepper
2	pounds thin-skinned potatoes, cut into 1-inch cubes

1 Preheat the oven to 425°F. Lightly oil a half sheet pan (preferred) or large shallow roasting pan.

2 Combine the oil with the salt, curry powder, cumin, onion powder, black pepper, five-spice powder, ginger, and cayenne in a large bowl. Mix well. Add the potatoes and toss to coat. Spread the potatoes in a single layer on the sheet pan.

3 Roast for 35 to 40 minutes, turning occasionally for even cooking, until the potatoes are tender when pierced with a fork and browned. Serve hot.

Kitchen Note: *The potatoes are cut into smaller cubes than in the previous recipe, to increase the surface area for more spicy goodness and to reduce the baking time so the spices don't scorch.*

Saffron Potatoes

Serves 4–6

Braising in saffron-scented water adds great flavor. A yellow potato like Yukon Gold picks up the yellow coloring nicely, but any thin-skinned potato can be used.

3	tablespoons extra-virgin olive oil
2	pounds (6 medium) thin-skinned potatoes, peeled and cut into ½-inch cubes
1	shallot, minced
¼	cup dry white wine
1½	cups water
1	teaspoon salt
	Pinch of saffron threads
3	tablespoons butter, cut into pieces

1   Heat the oil in a large saucepan over medium-high heat. Add the potatoes and shallot and sauté until the shallot is translucent, 3 to 4 minutes.

2   Add the wine, water, salt, and saffron, and bring to a boil. Simmer for about 10 minutes, until the potatoes are tender. Do not overcook or the potatoes will turn to mush. Drain well.

3   Return the potatoes to the pan. Add the butter and stir until melted. Serve hot.

Kitchen Note: *A garnish of chopped parsley is lovely with this dish.*

Garnishing with Green

There isn't a lot of green in winter vegetables, with the exception of kale and collard greens. Many dishes just beg for a garnish of parsley. If you have some on hand — growing in your garden or in a box on the windowsill — use it freely.

If you can't keep some plants going through the winter, consider chopping a few bunches from your summer planting, putting it in a ziplock bag, and storing it in the freezer. Use as needed.

Potatoes with Dill and Sour Cream

Serves 6

If you love to slather a baked potato with butter and sour cream, consider this alternative. While not exactly a low-fat dish, it does make a little butter and sour cream go further, with rich-tasting results.

3 tablespoons butter
2 pounds (6 medium) thin-skinned potatoes, peeled and cut into ½-inch cubes
1 onion, diced
2 garlic cloves, minced
¼ cup dry white wine
1¾ cups water
1 teaspoon salt
¼ teaspoon black pepper
1 cup sour cream
1 tablespoon dried dill

1 Heat the butter in a large saucepan over medium-high heat. Add the potatoes, onion, and garlic, and sauté until the onion is translucent, 3 to 4 minutes.

2 Add the wine, water, salt, and pepper, and bring to a boil. Simmer until the potatoes are tender, about 10 minutes. Drain and transfer the potatoes to a heated serving bowl.

3 Add the sour cream and toss gently until well combined. Sprinkle with the dill. Serve immediately.

Kitchen Note: *The easiest way to warm a serving bowl is to fill it with hot tap water and let it sit for a few minutes, then drain and wipe dry. Most hot dishes are enhanced by being served in warmed bowls.*

Hasselback Potatoes

Serves 4

Created and named in a Stockholm restaurant, these dressed-up roasted potatoes are sometimes called "hedgehog" potatoes because of their appearance. The goal is a potato that is crispy on the outside and creamy inside, like a roasted potato, and that looks terrific.

4	russet (baking) potatoes
¼	cup freshly grated Parmesan cheese
⅓	cup fresh breadcrumbs
3	tablespoons extra-virgin olive oil
2	garlic cloves, minced
1	teaspoon crushed dried rosemary
1	teaspoon paprika
1	teaspoon salt

1   Preheat the oven to 450°F. Oil a shallow baking dish just large enough to hold the potatoes without crowding them.

2   Peel the potatoes and place on a cutting board. Cut a narrow slice from the bottom of each potato to help the potato lie flat and not roll. Place a wooden chopstick on each side of the potato lengthwise. Slice each potato crosswise down the length of the potato, making the cuts ¼ inch apart, and cutting down vertically. The chopsticks will prevent the knife from cutting entirely through the potato.

3   Combine the Parmesan, breadcrumbs, 1 tablespoon of the oil, garlic, rosemary, paprika, and salt in a small bowl and mix well. Brush the potatoes with the remaining 2 tablespoons oil and pat the breadcrumb mixture on top of each potato. Transfer the potatoes to the prepared baking dish and cover the dish with aluminum foil.

4   Bake for 45 minutes. Remove the foil and bake 15 to 30 minutes longer, until the potatoes are crisp on the outside and tender within. Serve hot.

Two-Potato Latkes

Serves 4–6

Hannukah is the world's first and only holiday dedicated to fuel efficiency. It marks the miracle of a tank of oil fueling a light for eight days instead of the expected one day. Fried potato pancakes, or latkes, are the traditional food for this holiday. Although it is usually made with white potatoes only, in a bid for diversity I offer it here with a mixture of white and sweet potatoes. The white potatoes can be left unpeeled if the skin is thin.

2 pounds white potatoes, peeled if necessary	2 teaspoons salt
1 pound sweet potatoes, peeled	¼ teaspoon freshly ground black pepper
1 large onion	Sunflower or canola oil, for frying
2 eggs, lightly beaten	Applesauce, for serving
¼ cup all-purpose flour	Sour cream, for serving

1 Coarsely grate the white potatoes, sweet potatoes, and onions by hand or in a food processor.

2 Transfer the potato mixture to a large bowl filled with acidulated water (1 tablespoon lemon juice or vinegar added to 4 cups water). Swish around with your hands for 1 minute and drain well. Place a clean kitchen towel on the counter. Mound the potatoes on the towel and pat dry. This step will keep the potatoes from turning pink and then gray as they are exposed to air.

3 Transfer the potato mixture to a food processor and pulse until the mixture is finely chopped but not puréed.

4 Transfer the potato mixture to a large mixing bowl and add the eggs, flour, salt, and pepper; mix well.

5 Preheat the oven to 200°F.

6 Heat ½ inch of oil in a frying pan over medium-high heat. Drop the potato mixture, ¼ cup at a time, into the pan and fry until golden on the bottom, 3 to 4 minutes. Turn and fry on the other side until golden, 3 to 4 minutes. Drain on paper towels.

7 Keep the latkes warm in the oven while cooking the remaining batter, but serve as soon as possible. Pass the applesauce and sour cream at the table.

Potato-Carrot Tart

Serves 4–6

Slice your potatoes thin and even for best results. This is a simple dish to put together, but quite tasty and attractive.

- 1 large russet (baking) potato (about 12 ounces), peeled and very thinly sliced
- 2 tablespoons butter, melted
- 1 teaspoon dried thyme
- ½ teaspoon Dijon mustard
- ½ teaspoon salt
- ¼ teaspoon freshly ground black pepper
- 2 tablespoons extra-virgin olive oil
- 1 onion, halved and thinly sliced
- 1 carrot, peeled and shredded
- ½ cup shredded Swiss, Gruyère, or cheddar cheese (2 ounces)

1 Preheat the oven to 400°F. Lightly oil a 10-inch tart pan or pie pan.

2 Combine the potato, butter, thyme, mustard, salt, and pepper in a bowl. Toss gently to coat. Press into the bottom and up the sides of the tart pan to form a tart shell. Bake for 20 minutes.

3 While the tart shell bakes, heat the oil in a medium skillet over medium heat. Add the onion and carrot and sauté until the onion is limp and well colored, about 10 minutes.

4 When the tart shell comes out of the oven, top with the onion mixture, spreading evenly. Sprinkle with the cheese. Return to the oven to bake until the cheese is melted and golden, 10 to 15 minutes.

5 Let cool for at least 5 minutes. Serve warm or at room temperature, sliced into wedges.

Twice-Baked Stuffed Potatoes

Serves 4

There's a reason that stuffed baked potatoes are so popular: They are incredibly tasty and satisfying. They are also incredibly convenient. Bake the potatoes in advance, and fill and stuff later.

4   large russet (baking) potatoes, about 1 pound each
    Vegetable oil
8   strips bacon
1   cup sour cream
4   tablespoons butter, softened
1   cup lightly packed grated cheddar cheese (4 ounces)
1   shallot, minced

1   Preheat the oven to 400°F. Scrub the potatoes under running water. Poke each potato in several places with the tines of a fork and rub the potatoes all over with a little oil. Bake for 1 to 1¼ hours, until the potatoes give a little when pressed.

2   Meanwhile, cook the bacon in a skillet over medium heat until crisp, 8 to 10 minutes. Drain on paper towels. Let cool. Crumble.

3   Reduce the oven temperature to 350°F. Allow the potatoes to cool enough to be handled. Remove a slice lengthwise from the top of each potato. Use a spoon to scoop out the insides to form a potato "boat," leaving a shell about ¼ inch thick.

4   Combine the potato flesh, sour cream, and butter in a large bowl. Mash with a potato masher, then beat with a wooden spoon until fairly smooth and creamy. Mix in ¾ cup of the cheese, the bacon, and the shallot. Spoon the filling into the potato shells, mounding up the filling. Sprinkle the remaining cheese over the top.

5   Place the potatoes in a baking dish and bake until the potatoes are heated through and the cheese is melted, 15 to 20 minutes.

Variation: Vegetarian Twice-Baked Potatoes

Omit the bacon. Increase the number of shallots to two. If you have it on hand, mix 1 teaspoon pimenton (smoked paprika) into the potato filling.

Hot German Potato Salad with Sauerkraut

Serves 4–6

Although called a salad because it is dressed with oil and vinegar, German potato salad is usually served as a warm side dish. The sauerkraut adds a healthy dose of fiber and flavor.

> 1 cup sauerkraut, homemade (page 84) or store-bought (choose the refrigerated type, not the canned type), drained
>
> 2 pounds thin-skinned potatoes, scrubbed, halved, and cut into ¼-inch slices
>
> 4 ounces bacon, diced
>
> 1 shallot, minced
>
> 5 tablespoons apple cider vinegar, plus more to taste
>
> 2 tablespoons extra-virgin olive oil
>
> 1 tablespoon brown sugar
>
> Salt and freshly ground black pepper

1 Taste the sauerkraut and rinse with warm water if it is very salty. Drain well.

2 Cover the potatoes with salted water in a medium saucepan. Bring to a boil, then reduce the heat and simmer until the potatoes are tender, 5 to 10 minutes. Reserve ¼ cup of the cooking liquid, then drain. Transfer the potatoes to a large mixing bowl and keep warm.

3 Cook the bacon in a medium skillet over medium heat until brown and crisp, about 4 minutes. Remove the bacon with a slotted spoon and transfer to the bowl with the potatoes. Drain off all but 2 tablespoons of the bacon grease.

4 Add the shallot to the skillet and cook over medium heat until slightly softened, about 3 minutes. Stir in the vinegar, oil, and brown sugar. Bring to a boil. Pour the mixture over the potatoes and toss to coat. Add the sauerkraut. Taste and season with more vinegar, salt, if needed (both the bacon and sauerkraut may be salty), and pepper. Add some or all of the reserved potato cooking water if the mixture seems dry (it may not need any). Serve immediately.

Spicy Sweet-Potato Oven Fries

Serves 4

The devil is in the details when it comes to making sweet-potato oven fries. The potatoes must be cut to a uniform thickness, or they will cook unevenly. The pan must not be too crowded, or the potatoes will steam and never brown. The pan must not be too empty, or the potatoes will burn. The touch of sugar in the recipe encourages browning and should not be omitted. The mix of spices is, however, just a suggestion and can be varied at will. The sweet-potato fries will not become as crisp as oven fries made with white potatoes, nor will they brown uniformly. But they are entirely delicious. The lemon aioli makes the perfect accompaniment.

4	medium sweet potatoes, peeled and cut into ¼-inch sticks
¼	cup sunflower or canola oil
1	tablespoon chili powder
1	tablespoon sugar
1	teaspoon onion powder
1	teaspoon salt
½	teaspoon ground cumin
¼	teaspoon freshly ground black pepper
¼	teaspoon ground allspice or cinnamon
	Coarse sea salt or kosher salt (optional)
	Lemon Aioli (page 181)

1   Preheat the oven to 500°F, with the rack in the lower third of the oven. Generously oil a half sheet pan (preferred) or large shallow roasting pan.

2   Combine the oil, chili powder, sugar, onion powder, salt, cumin, black pepper, and allspice in a large bowl and mix well. Add the potatoes and toss to coat. Arrange the potatoes in a single layer on the prepared pan.

3   Roast in the lower third of the oven for 30 to 35 minutes, turning once or twice and shaking the pan for even cooking, until the potatoes are well colored. (The timing will depend on how closely spaced the potatoes are on the pan.)

4   Briefly drain the fries on paper towels to blot excess oil. Taste and sprinkle with coarse salt, if desired. Serve hot, with aioli on the side.

Kitchen Note: *If you have the choice, Garnet is a good sweet potato cultivar for roasting because it holds its shape well.*

Lemon Aioli

Makes 1 cup

A dangerously delicious sauce, aioli is basically homemade mayonnaise with garlic added. In this case, both garlic and lemon are added to make the perfect accompaniment for sweet potato fries. Lemon aioli is a great dip for a plate of any raw or roasted vegetables. It is also perfect dolloped on poached or grilled salmon — or any fish, for that matter.

4   garlic cloves
1   teaspoon Dijon mustard
    Zest and juice of 1 lemon
2   egg yolks
1   cup canola or sunflower oil
    Salt and white pepper

1   Mince the garlic in a food processor. Add the mustard and lemon zest and juice and process to combine. Add the egg yolks and process until smooth.

2   With the motor running, slowly drizzle in the oil in a steady stream until a thick, creamy sauce forms. Season with salt and white pepper. Keep refrigerated until you are ready to serve.

Kitchen Note: *Dishes containing raw eggs should never be served to infants, the elderly, or people with compromised immune systems because of the risk of salmonella. If you wish to avoid the raw eggs, either purchase pasteurized eggs or start with 1 cup mayonnaise and season with the garlic, lemon juice and zest, salt, and white pepper.*

Mashed Sweet Potatoes

Serves 4

Although you can make mashed sweet potatoes exactly as you make mashed white potatoes, braising the sweet potatoes in butter first creates a richer flavor and smoother texture.

> 4 tablespoons butter
>
> 2 tablespoons light cream, half-and-half, or whole milk
>
> 1 tablespoon brown sugar
>
> 1 teaspoon salt
>
> 2 pounds sweet potatoes, peeled, quartered lengthwise, and sliced
>
> Freshly ground black pepper

1 Combine the butter, cream, brown sugar, salt, and sweet potatoes in a saucepan over low heat. Cover and cook, stirring occasionally, until the potatoes are quite tender and fall apart as you stir, about 35 minutes.

2 Remove the pan from the heat and mash the potatoes with a potato masher. Whip with a whisk or spoon. Add pepper, taste, and adjust the seasonings. Serve hot.

Kitchen Notes: *Pure maple syrup or honey can replace the brown sugar. If you have the choice, Jewel is a good sweet potato cultivar for mashing.*

Maple-Candied Sweet Potatoes

Serves 6

Candied sweet potatoes is a controversial dish — people either love it or hate it. Where the candied sweet potatoes of my youth went wrong was starting with canned yams. Where other recipes go wrong is using corn syrup, a neutral sweetener that does nothing for flavor. Where this recipe goes right, I think, is using maple syrup tempered with lemon juice, bourbon, and salt and pepper. The result is simply yummy — sweet, but not cloyingly so, and deeply flavorful.

1	cup maple syrup
4	tablespoons butter
	Juice of ½ lemon
1	teaspoon salt
½	teaspoon black pepper
¼–⅓	cup bourbon or dark rum
3	pounds sweet potatoes, peeled and cut into large chunks

1   Preheat the oven to 375°F. Butter a 9- by 13-inch nonstick baking pan all the way to the top of its sides. If you don't have a nonstick baking pan and you hate scrubbing pans, you can line yours with aluminum foil.

2   Combine the maple syrup, butter, lemon juice, salt, and pepper, and heat until the butter is melted. Stir in bourbon to taste.

3   Combine the syrup and the sweet potatoes in the prepared pan and turn to coat.

4   Bake in the middle of the oven for about 1¼ hours, basting occasionally, until the potatoes are completely tender. After 1 hour, check frequently to avoid burning the sugars in the syrup. Serve hot.

Cider-Braised Sweet Potatoes with Apples

Serves 6

The sweet potatoes get a double punch of apple, with cider providing the braising liquid and sliced apples adding additional color, texture, and flavor. Onions and rosemary provide a savory balance.

3   tablespoons butter
1   tablespoon sunflower or canola oil
1   onion, sliced
3   large sweet potatoes, peeled, halved if large, and cut into 1-inch slices
1   tablespoon crushed dried rosemary
1   cup apple cider
    Salt and freshly ground black pepper
2   large apples, peeled, cored, and cut into 1-inch wedges

1   Melt the butter in the oil in a Dutch oven over medium heat. Add the onion and sweet potatoes and sauté until the onion is limp, about 3 minutes. Add the rosemary and cider. Season with salt and pepper.

2   Bring to a simmer and cook for 15 minutes.

3   Stir in the apples and cook until the potatoes are tender, 15 minutes longer. Serve hot.

Southern-Style Mashed Rutabagas or Turnips

Serves 4

A little bit of sugar and some bacon go a long way to making any vegetable irresistible. If you find yourself resisting root vegetables, consider this recipe — it works for all manner of roots, my favorite being rutabagas or a combination of rutabagas and turnips.

3	ounces salt pork, bacon, or pancetta, diced
2	cups water
2½	pounds rutabagas and/or turnips, peeled and cut into 1-inch cubes
	Sugar
	Salt and freshly ground black pepper
2	tablespoons butter

1   Combine the salt pork and water in a large saucepan and bring to a boil.

2   Add the vegetables, a generous pinch of sugar, and a pinch each of salt and pepper. Cover, return to a boil, and boil gently until the vegetables are completely tender, about 45 minutes.

3   Drain the vegetables, reserving the cooking water. Add the butter and mash until smooth, adding a little cooking water as needed to obtain a fairly smooth purée. Taste and adjust the seasoning with additional sugar, salt, and pepper; serve hot.

 Sautéed Turnips

Serves 4-6

Cooking takes the raw, biting edge off turnips, so it is important to cook them until they are very tender, especially if you are unsure whether you enjoy turnips. These are best cooked in a very large skillet, with enough room to brown the turnips. For best results if you don't have a large skillet, work in two batches.

2-3 tablespoons extra-virgin olive oil
2 pounds turnips (2 large), peeled and cut into matchsticks
Salt and freshly ground black pepper

1 Pour enough oil into a very large skillet to generously coat the bottom of the pan. Heat over medium-high heat. Add the turnips and sauté, turning and tossing the turnips frequently, until well browned and tender, 10 to 20 minutes, depending on how crowded the turnips are in the pan.

2 Season with salt and pepper and serve hot.

Rutabaga Chips

Serves 4-6

Rutabagas wouldn't get such a bad rap if they were prepared as chips more often. This is a great introductory recipe. Then, once a person concedes that rutabagas are terrific, you can slip rutabagas into all sorts of dishes. If you want to elevate rutabaga chips (or any vegetable chip) to high art, try frying the chips in duck fat saved from a roasted duck and stored in the refrigerator.

1 large (or 2-3 small) rutabaga
Sunflower oil, extra-virgin olive oil, or duck fat
Coarse sea salt or kosher salt

1 Preheat the oven to 300°F. Line a large baking sheet with paper towels.

2 Peel the rutabaga and slice very thin. A food processor or mandoline does a good job of keeping the slices thin and consistent, which is what you want. If the rutabaga slices bead up with water, pat them dry with paper or clean kitchen towels.

3 Heat about ½ inch of oil in a large skillet over medium-high heat. When the oil is hot but not yet smoking, slip only enough rutabaga slices into the oil so they will cook without touching. Fry until lightly browned on the edges and more deeply golden in the middle, turning once, 3 to 4 minutes per batch. Drain on paper towels. Keep warm in the oven. Repeat with the remaining rutabaga slices.

4 Blot excess oil with additional towels as needed. Sprinkle with salt and serve warm.

Rutabaga Squares

Serves 8–10

The rutabaga lies somewhat disguised in this tasty cross between a bread and a gratin. A food processor makes grating the rutabaga quite easy.

1½ cups all-purpose flour	1 rutabaga, peeled and shredded (about 4 cups)
½ cup cornmeal	1 onion, diced
1 tablespoon baking powder	1 cup lightly packed grated cheddar cheese (4 ounces)
2 teaspoons salt	
1 teaspoon dried thyme	3 eggs, beaten
1 teaspoon dried sage	½ cup sunflower or canola oil
½ teaspoon freshly ground black pepper or lemon pepper	½ cup milk

1 Preheat the oven to 350°F. Butter a 9- by 13-inch baking dish.

2 In a medium bowl, stir together the flour, cornmeal, baking powder, salt, thyme, sage, and pepper. Add the rutabaga, onion, and cheese. Mix well with a fork, breaking up any clumps. In a small bowl, whisk together the eggs, oil, and milk; pour into the rutabaga mixture and mix well. Spread evenly in the baking dish.

3 Bake for 40 to 45 minutes, until golden and a knife inserted in the center comes out clean.

4 Let cool on a wire rack for 5 minutes. Cut into squares and serve warm or at room temperature.

Butter-Braised Salsify

Serves 4–6

The delicate flavor of salsify is wonderfully enhanced by butter, salt, and pepper. This simple recipe is the best way to introduce yourself to the delicious flavor of this underappreciated root vegetable.

1½ pounds salsify
  3 tablespoons butter
     Salt and freshly ground black pepper

1 Peel the salsify and cut into 1-inch pieces. Immediately put into a bowl of acidulated water (1 tablespoon white vinegar added to 4 cups water) to prevent browning.

2 Melt the butter in a large skillet over medium-high heat. When the butter foams, drain the salsify and add it to the skillet. Sauté for 5 minutes, until the salsify is well coated with butter and partly tender. Season with salt and pepper.

3 Cover and braise until fully tender, 5 to 10 minutes longer. Serve hot.

Salsify Mash

Serves 4

This is another simple recipe that will enable you to experience the flavor of salsify, which is a cross between globe and Jerusalem artichokes.

1½–2 pounds salsify
    2 tablespoons butter
       Salt and freshly ground black pepper

Kitchen Note: *The recipe is called a "mash," not a purée, for a reason. Do not give in to the temptation to purée the cooked roots in a food processor. They will exude a gummy substance that is unbelievably hard to clean off.*

1 Peel the salsify and cut into 3-inch pieces. Immediately put into a bowl of acidulated water (1 tablespoon white vinegar added to 4 cups water) to prevent browning.

2 Bring a pot of salted water to a boil. Drain the salsify and add to the boiling water. Boil until the roots are very tender, 15 to 20 minutes.

3 Drain the salsify and transfer to a bowl. Add the butter. Mash with a fork or potato masher. Season with salt and pepper. Serve hot.

● Salsify Fritters

Serves 4

"Classic" recipes for salsify are rare and hard to uncover. This is one of the few. It is a gem. Handle the fritters carefully. They are very delicate and fall apart easily.

1½	pounds salsify
2	tablespoons butter
	Salt and freshly ground black pepper
	Extra-virgin olive oil, sunflower oil, or canola oil, for frying
1½	cups fresh breadcrumbs or panko (Japanese-style breadcrumbs)

1 Peel the salsify and cut into 3-inch pieces. Immediately put into a bowl of acidulated water (1 tablespoon white vinegar added to 4 cups water) to prevent browning.

2 Bring a pot of salted water to a boil. Drain the salsify and add to the boiling water. Boil until the roots are very tender, 15 to 20 minutes.

3 Drain the salsify and transfer to a bowl. Add the butter. Mash with a fork or potato masher. Season with salt and pepper.

4 Pour about ¼ inch of oil into a large skillet and heat over medium-high heat. Pour the breadcrumbs into a shallow bowl. Scoop up about ¼ cup of the salsify mash and compress well with your hands to form into a patty. Dredge in the breadcrumbs to completely cover. Carefully slip into the pan. Continue until the pan is filled, but do not crowd the pan. Fry on both sides until browned, 3 to 4 minutes. Transfer to paper towels to drain. Repeat with the remaining salsify mash. Serve hot.

Gratin of Turnips and Rutabagas

Serves 4-6

All vegetables benefit from the "au gratin" treatment — baking them in a creamy cheese sauce and topping them with crispy breadcrumbs. Feel free to substitute other root vegetables in this delicious casserole, or use only turnips or only rutabagas. The thinner you can slice the vegetables, the briefer the baking time.

4	tablespoons butter
1	onion, halved and thinly sliced
¼	cup all-purpose flour
2	cups milk
2	cups lightly packed grated Gruyère or cheddar cheese (8 ounces)
	Salt and freshly ground pepper
3-4	turnips, peeled and sliced paper thin (about 3 cups)
1	small rutabaga, peeled and sliced paper thin (about 3 cups)
½	cup fresh breadcrumbs

1   Preheat the oven to 350°F. Lightly butter or oil a 2-quart baking dish.

2   Melt the butter in a medium saucepan over medium heat. Add the onion and sauté until translucent, about 3 minutes. Stir in the flour to make a smooth paste. Cook for 2 minutes. Gradually whisk in the milk and cook until thickened, 4 to 5 minutes. Stir in 1½ cups of the cheese and remove from the heat. Season with salt and pepper. Keep warm.

3   Spread a little of the cheese sauce in the prepared baking dish. Layer the turnip and rutabaga slices in the dish. Cover with the remaining sauce.

4   Mix the breadcrumbs and remaining ½ cup cheese in a small bowl. Sprinkle on top of the mixture in the baking dish.

5   Bake for 40 to 60 minutes, until the vegetables are fork-tender. Serve hot.

Turnip Puff

Serves 4

Not all root-vegetable dishes are rustic, as this elegant casserole proves. Turnip doubters may be converted with this light dish. You can also prepare it with rutabagas in place of the turnips.

4	cups peeled and cubed turnip (about 2 pounds)
4	tablespoons butter
2	garlic cloves, minced
1	onion, finely chopped
	Salt and freshly ground black pepper
2	eggs, separated
½	cup fresh breadcrumbs

1 Cover the turnips with salted water in a medium saucepan. Bring to a boil and boil until tender, 10 to 15 minutes. Drain well.

2 Preheat the oven to 350°F. Butter a 1-quart casserole dish.

3 Combine the turnips, 3 tablespoons of the butter, the garlic, and the onion in a medium bowl. Mash well, but do not purée; it will not be completely smooth. Season to taste with salt and pepper. Add the egg yolks and beat until smooth.

4 Beat the egg whites in a clean bowl until stiff peaks form. Fold one-third of the egg whites into the turnip mixture to lighten it. Carefully fold in the remaining egg whites. Spoon the turnip mixture into the prepared baking dish and sprinkle with the breadcrumbs. Dot with the remaining 1 tablespoon butter.

5 Bake for about 40 minutes, until the top is golden. Serve hot.

Spicy Turnip Stir-Fry

Serves 4–6

A very quick way to prepare turnips is to make a stir-fry. Be sure the turnips are cut into fine matchsticks for the quickest cooking and best appearance. The black bean sauce, which gives this stir-fry its distinctive flavor, is made from fermented soybeans. It is available wherever Chinese foods are sold.

SAUCE

- 2 garlic cloves, minced
- 1 (½-inch) piece fresh ginger, peeled and minced
- ¼ cup soy sauce
- 1 tablespoon rice vinegar
- 1 tablespoon Asian sesame oil
- 1 tablespoon Chinese black bean sauce
- 1 tablespoon Chinese chili paste with garlic
- 2 teaspoons sugar

VEGETABLES

- 2 tablespoons peanut or sunflower oil
- 3 large turnips, peeled and cut into matchsticks
- ¼ cup chopped fresh cilantro (optional)

Hot cooked white rice, for serving

1 To make the sauce, mix together the garlic, ginger, soy sauce, vinegar, sesame oil, black bean sauce, chili paste, and sugar. Set aside.

2 Heat the oil in a wok or skillet over high heat. Add the turnips and stir-fry until just barely tender, about 3 minutes.

3 Add the sauce and toss to coat. Cover and let steam until the turnips are tender, about 2 minutes. Stir in the cilantro, if using. Serve hot, with rice.

Kitchen Note: *The cilantro adds both flavor and color. If you don't have the fresh herb on hand, consider adding some color in the form of frozen peas added with the sauce or carrots cut in matchsticks added with the turnips.*

❧ Stuffed Sweet Dumplings

Serves 4

Sweet dumpling and buttercup winter squashes are ideal for stuffing because of their size and ability to sit firmly in a baking dish. Both are teacup shaped and about 4 inches in diameter. The ivory-colored skin of the sweet dumpling has the same orange and green markings of a delicata squash, and the flesh is similarly yellow-orange in color and sweet tasting. Most stuffing recipes emphasize the sweetness of winter squash; this stuffing is both sweet and savory.

4	sweet dumpling or buttercup squashes, halved and seeded
3	tablespoons butter
2	leeks, trimmed and thinly sliced
2	large apples, peeled, cored, and chopped
½	cup slivered almonds
½	cup firmly packed brown sugar
1	cup lightly packed grated cheddar cheese (4 ounces)
	Salt and freshly ground black pepper

1   Preheat the oven to 350°F.

2   Place the squashes skin-side up in a baking pan just large enough to hold them. Add about 1 inch of water.

3   Bake for 40 minutes, then remove from the oven.

4   Meanwhile, melt the butter in a medium skillet over medium heat. Add the leeks, apples, and almonds, and sauté until the leeks are tender, about 4 minutes. Scrape the mixture into a bowl and add the brown sugar and cheese. Season with salt and pepper. Divide the mixture evenly among the partially cooked squashes.

5   Return the squashes to the oven and bake for 30 minutes, or until they are tender when the flesh is pierced with a fork.

Kitchen Note: *You can substitute two acorn squashes for the sweet dumplings. If you do, divide them into quarters instead of halves.*

Apple-Braised Delicata Squash

Serves 4–6

All winter squashes combine well with apples, so feel free to substitute other squashes in this recipe. I am fond of delicata squash in particular because its skin is edible; this makes preparation quite easy.

> 2 **tablespoons butter**
> 2 **large delicata squashes, seeded and sliced into ½-inch rounds**
> 1 **shallot, diced**
> 2 **cups apple cider or juice**
> 1 **teaspoon chopped fresh or dried rosemary**
> **Salt and freshly ground black pepper**

1 Melt the butter in a large skillet or Dutch oven over medium heat. Add the squash and shallot and sauté, coating in the butter, for about 1 minute. Add the cider and rosemary. Bring to a boil, then reduce the heat and simmer, covered, until the squash is fork-tender, about 20 minutes.

2 Remove the cover, increase the heat to high, and cook until the liquid is reduced to a syrupy glaze, 2 to 3 minutes. Season with salt and pepper and serve hot.

❧ Baked Winter Squash

Serves 4

Just about every winter squash can be prepared this way. How much butter and sweetener to use is up to you — but if you are serving to people who are ambivalent about this high-nutrition vegetable, use a generous hand.

> 1–4   **hard-shelled winter squashes, such as acorn, buttercup, golden nugget, Hubbard, red kuri, sweet dumpling, or turban**
> **Butter (optional)**
> **Salt and freshly ground black pepper (optional)**
> **Brown sugar, honey, or maple syrup (optional)**

1   Preheat the oven to 400°F.

2   Cut the squash into halves if small, or into quarters or serving-size pieces if large. Remove and discard the seeds and fibers. Place skin-side up in a baking dish and add about 1 inch of water to the dish.

3   Bake for 45 to 60 minutes, until tender when pierced with a fork.

4   Drain off the water. Turn the pieces flesh-side up, brush with butter, and sprinkle with salt and pepper, if using. Sprinkle with brown sugar or drizzle with honey or maple syrup, if using. Bake for 10 minutes longer. Serve hot.

Baked Spaghetti Squash

Serves 4-6

Spaghetti squash is less aggressively sweet than most of the other winter squashes. Its oddball stringy texture makes it fun to eat, though I don't think it is a good substitute for pasta.

1	large spaghetti squash (about 3 pounds)
4	tablespoons butter
4	garlic cloves, minced
	Salt and freshly ground black pepper

1   Preheat the oven to 350°F.

2   Cut the squash in half lengthwise. Scoop out and discard the seeds. Place skin-side up in a baking dish and add about 1 inch of water to the dish.

3   Bake for about 40 minutes, until the skin begins to give. Let cool slightly.

4   Melt the butter in a small saucepan over low heat. Add the garlic and cook, stirring, until the garlic is fragrant, about 2 minutes.

5   Using a large fork, scoop the squash out of its skin, pulling it into strands. Transfer to a serving bowl. Add the garlic butter and toss to coat. Season with salt and pepper. Toss again and serve.

Whipped Winter Squash

Serves 4-6

A generous hand with the butter and sweetener makes winter squash come alive with flavor. Whipping makes the texture velvety smooth. This is a deliciously simple way to serve winter squash. The best squashes for this treatment are the ones that are least fibrous, but you can use what you have on hand.

1	large winter squash (buttercup, butternut, red kuri, or baby blue Hubbard squashes are recommended)
4-6	tablespoons butter
4-6	tablespoons maple syrup or honey
3-4	tablespoons whole milk, half-and-half, or light cream
	Salt and freshly ground black pepper

1 Preheat the oven to 400°F.

2 Cut the squash into halves if small, or into quarters if large. Remove and discard the seeds and fibers. Place skin-side up in a baking dish and add about 1 inch of water to the dish.

3 Bake for 60 to 90 minutes, depending on the size of the pieces, until completely tender when pierced with a fork.

4 Drain off the water. Turn the pieces flesh-side up and allow to cool until they can be easily handled. Scrape the flesh from the skins into a mixing bowl. Add the butter and mash or beat until smooth. Beat in the maple syrup and milk. Season with salt and pepper.

5 If desired, reheat in a microwave or in the top of a double boiler set over boiling water. Serve hot.

Kitchen Note: *If you can afford the extra fat and calories, making this with cream or half-and-half adds an exquisite richness.*

🍃 Kathleen Pemble's Winter Squash

Serves 6

Once a month, I serve dinner to performers who come to the Ripton Community Coffee House. Sometimes I try out recipes on them, and Kathleen was a willing veggie eater. I mentioned that I had made a chocolate chip–pumpkin loaf to sell at the coffeehouse and Kathleen asked, "What kind of a person thinks to combine chocolate and pumpkin?" What kind, indeed? Someone, I explained, who had tapped out all the likely combinations of winter squash recipes in two previous books, *Serving Up the Harvest* and *The Classic Zucchini Cookbook* (which contains lots of winter squash recipes). Kathleen then shared this recipe. I've changed the spicing a bit, but the recipe and method are essentially hers — and it is as lovely as her music.

1 large butternut squash (about 2 pounds)	1 teaspoon onion powder
¼ cup sunflower or canola oil	½ teaspoon ground cumin
1 tablespoon sugar	¼ teaspoon ground allspice
1 teaspoon salt	¼ teaspoon freshly ground black pepper
1 teaspoon ground cinnamon	¼ teaspoon cayenne pepper

1   Preheat the oven to 300°F. Lightly oil a half sheet pan (preferred) or large shallow roasting pan.

2   Peel the squash and slice in half lengthwise. Remove and discard the seeds and fibers. Cut the halves into ¼-inch-thick slices.

3   Combine the oil, sugar, salt, cinnamon, onion powder, cumin, allspice, black pepper, and cayenne in a large bowl and mix well. Add the squash and toss gently to coat. Arrange the squash slices in a single layer on the prepared pan.

4   Bake for about 2 hours, until the squash is completely tender. It is best served hot but can be served warm.

Kitchen Note: *Any winter squash can be used here, but butternut is recommended because it is easy to peel.*

Winter Squash with Caramelized Apples

Serves 4-6

Hands down, this is my favorite winter squash recipe. I can't imagine anyone not liking this appealing combination of apples and squash. Generously seasoning with salt and pepper is essential. Because it is such a crowd pleaser, and because it can be made in advance and reheated, it makes a perfect side dish for the Thanksgiving table.

1 **large buttercup, butternut, or red kuri squash, or ½ small baby blue Hubbard squash**
4 **tablespoons butter**
2 **large apples, peeled, cored, and chopped**
¼ **cup firmly packed brown sugar**
½ **teaspoon ground cinnamon**
¼ **teaspoon freshly grated nutmeg**
Salt and freshly ground black pepper

1 Preheat the oven to 400°F.

2 Cut the squash into halves if small, or into quarters if large. Remove and discard the seeds and fibers. Place skin-side up in a baking dish and add about 1 inch of water to the dish.

3 Bake for 60 to 90 minutes, depending on the size of the pieces, until completely tender when pierced with a fork.

4 Meanwhile, melt the butter in a large skillet over medium heat. Add the apples, brown sugar, cinnamon, and nutmeg. Sauté until the brown sugar is dissolved and the apples are tender and coated in the sugar syrup, about 5 minutes. Set aside.

5 When the squash is done, drain off the water. Turn the pieces flesh-side up, and allow to cool until they can be handled easily. Scrape the flesh from the skins into a mixing bowl and discard the skins. Mash or beat until smooth.

6 Fold in the apples and their syrup. Season generously with salt and pepper.

7 If desired, reheat in a microwave or in the top of a double boiler set over boiling water. Serve hot.

If summer is the time for salads and quickly made dishes, then winter is the time for soups, slow-simmered stews, and rib-sticking beans. Dried beans are especially sustaining and are very easy, and generally inexpensive, to make. A few simple rules apply:

- Never add acidic ingredients, such as tomatoes, to beans before they are fully cooked or they will never become completely tender.
- If your beans are becoming too dry, add boiling hot (not cold) water, or the skins will toughen.
- Add salt late in the cooking process; otherwise, as the water reduces, the dish may become too salty.
- Add flavor to beans as they cook with onions, garlic, dried herbs, and chilis, fresh or dried.
- The age of the beans is a factor in cooking times. The fresher the beans, the shorter the cooking time.

Vegetarians take note: chipotles do an excellent job of adding flavor to beans instead of the traditional meats. Chipotles are smoke-dried jalapeños. They can be purchased dried, or canned in a vinegar sauce, called adobo sauce. Liquid smoke is another ingredient that adds the smoke flavoring without the bacon.

5

Beans, Rice, and Grains

RECIPE LIST FOR
BEANS, RICE, AND GRAINS

Black Beans in Chipotle Sauce

Cajun-Spiced Black Beans and Sausage

Black Bean, Sweet Potato, and Chorizo Stew

Chili Beans

Sunday Supper Baked Beans

New England Baked Beans

Spicy-Sweet Barbecued Beans

Refried Pinto Beans

Curried Dahl

Mujdhara

Lentils and Greens

Curried Lentil-Stuffed Delicata Squash

Golden Carrot Risotto

White Bean Stew with Smoked Turkey

Winter-Vegetable Nori Rolls

Southern-Style Rice with Collard Greens

Leek Risotto

Risotto with Butternut Squash

Lemony Barley-Carrot Pilaf

Kasha Varnishkes

Carrot Spoon Bread

Vegetarian dishes are marked with this symbol:

Black Beans in Chipotle Sauce

Serves 4–6

There's a lot of flavor packed into these smoky, rich, vegetarian beans — and a fair amount of heat. You can serve it with sour cream to tame the flames if you wish. The beans are delicious served as a side dish or main course, on top of rice, or inside a burrito.

2	cups dried black beans, soaked overnight and drained
6	cups water
1	large onion, diced
2	bay leaves
1½	cups unseasoned tomato sauce or purée, or 1 (15-ounce) can
2	chipotles canned in adobo sauce, minced
2	tablespoons adobo sauce (from the can of chilis)
4	garlic cloves, minced
2	tablespoons apple cider vinegar
	Salt and freshly ground pepper

1   Combine the beans, water, onion, and bay leaves in a large saucepan. Bring to a boil, then reduce the heat and simmer, partially covered, until the beans are completely tender but not mushy, 1 to 2 hours.

2   Check the water level in the saucepan. The beans should be just barely covered by water. If there is more water than a slight covering, drain off the excess water and reserve. Remove the bay leaves. Add the tomato sauce, chipotles, adobo sauce, garlic, and vinegar. Season with salt and pepper.

3   Simmer until the liquid is reduced to a saucy consistency and the flavors have blended, about 30 minutes. Add some of the reserved cooking liquid if the beans become dry. Taste and adjust the seasoning. Serve hot.

Cajun-Spiced Black Beans and Sausage

Serves 6

If I were making this dish in the summer, I would swap out the celery root for the more traditional celery and include a green bell pepper in the sauté along with the onion. Without these vegetables — the "holy trinity" of Cajun cooking — the dish isn't really a Cajun dish. On the other hand, it is tasty and delicious with just the ingredients on hand in the winter.

2 tablespoons extra-virgin olive oil

1 large onion, diced

1 celery root, peeled and diced

3 garlic cloves, minced

2 cups dried black beans, soaked overnight and drained

8 cups water

2 bay leaves

1 tablespoon dried thyme

8 ounces andouille or other smoked pork sausage, cut into ½-inch lengths

2 tablespoons Louisiana-style hot pepper sauce, like Frank's or Crystal, plus more as needed

Salt and freshly ground black pepper

Cayenne pepper

Hot cooked white rice, for serving

2 scallions, white and tender green parts, chopped (optional), for garnish

1　Heat the oil in a large saucepan over medium-high heat. Add the onion and celery root and sauté until the vegetables are soft, 4 to 5 minutes. Add the garlic and sauté until fragrant, about 30 seconds. Add the beans, water, bay leaves, and thyme. Bring to a boil, then reduce the heat to just a simmer and cook, uncovered and stirring occasionally, until the skin on the beans is tender and the beans are soft, 1 to 2 hours.

2　Add the sausage and continue to cook, stirring occasionally, until the beans are soft and creamy, about 1 hour longer. Remove the bay leaves. Stir in the hot sauce. Season with salt, black pepper, and cayenne.

3　Serve the beans and sausage over the white rice, garnished with scallions. Pass the hot sauce at the table.

Black Bean, Sweet Potato, and Chorizo Stew

Serves 6

Combining two superfoods in a stew — beans and sweet potatoes — makes a delectable, healthful dish. The sausage can be omitted for a vegetarian version. If you can't find Mexican chorizo, which is a fresh sausage, substitute spicy Italian sausage.

2 cups dried black beans, soaked overnight and drained	8 ounces Mexican chorizo, casing removed and meat crumbled
6 cups water	1½ cups diced tomatoes with juice, or 1 (15-ounce) can
1 onion, diced	Salt and freshly ground black pepper
2 tablespoons chili powder	
1 tablespoon cumin seeds	Warmed corn tortillas or hot white rice, for serving
2 small to medium sweet potatoes, peeled and diced	
1 tablespoon extra-virgin olive oil	

1 Combine the beans, water, onion, chili powder, and cumin in a large saucepan. Bring to a boil, then reduce the heat and simmer, partially covered, until the beans are completely tender, 1 to 2 hours.

2 Cover the sweet potatoes with salted water in a medium saucepan. Bring to a boil and boil until the potatoes are just tender, about 5 minutes. Drain.

3 Heat the oil in a large saucepan over medium heat. Add the sausage and sauté until browned, about 5 minutes.

4 Add the sweet potatoes, sausage, and tomatoes to the beans. Season with salt and pepper. Bring just to a boil, then reduce the heat and simmer for 10 minutes. Taste and adjust the seasoning. Serve at once, accompanied by warm corn tortillas or spooned over rice.

Variation: Quick Black Bean, Sweet Potato, and Chorizo Stew

Omit the cooked beans and water. Rinse and drain three 15-ounce cans of cooked black beans. Heat the beans with 1 cup chicken broth or vegetable broth (pages 126–27), the chili powder, and the cumin seed. Cook the sweet potato as above. Sauté the onion with the sausage. Combine the ingredients and cook as above.

🍃 Chili Beans

Serves 4

These wonderful beans in a slightly spicy tomato sauce can serve as the basis for a simple meal of rice and beans or beans and cornbread. Or you can use these beans to make burritos, enchiladas, or tacos. They are a great dish to have in your repertoire. I add a little salt pork to most of my bean recipes — it adds an incomparable depth of flavor. You can skip the meat altogether for a vegetarian version, or you can substitute bacon, if you prefer.

2	cups dried kidney beans, soaked overnight and drained
6	cups water
1	large onion, diced
2	chipotles canned in adobo sauce or 2 dried chipotles
4	garlic cloves, minced
¼	pound salt pork (optional)
1½	cups unseasoned tomato sauce or purée, or 1 (15-ounce) can
1	tablespoon sugar
	Salt and freshly ground pepper

1   Combine the beans, water, onion, chipotles, garlic, and salt pork, if using, in a large saucepan. Bring to a boil, then reduce the heat and simmer, partially covered, until the beans are completely tender but not mushy, 1 to 2 hours.

2   Check the water level in the saucepan. The beans should be just barely covered by water. If there is more water than a slight covering, drain off the excess water and reserve. Remove the chiles and salt pork. Mince the chiles and return them to the pot. Separate the meat from the fat of the salt pork. Shred the meat and return it to the pot, discarding the fat and skin. Add the tomato sauce and sugar.

3   Simmer until the liquid is reduced to a saucy consistency and the flavors have blended, about 30 minutes. Add some of the reserved cooking liquid if the beans become dry. Season with salt and pepper. Serve hot.

Sunday Supper Baked Beans

Serves 6

The two-stage cooking process (boiling and then baking the beans) is necessary to achieve a perfect texture. Once the beans come in contact with the acidic flavorings (ketchup, coffee, and so on), the skins will soften no further, so they must be cooked to tenderness first. This is a fairly classic baked bean recipe, tweaked a little for greater flavor. In the vegetarian version, chipotles replace the bacon for a touch of smoky flavor.

2	cups dried navy or pea beans, soaked overnight and drained
8	cups water
1	large onion, halved and thinly sliced
½	cup pure maple syrup or firmly packed brown sugar
½	cup ketchup
½	cup brewed coffee
2	tablespoons soy sauce
1	tablespoon yellow ballpark mustard
2	teaspoons ground ginger
4	ounces thick-cut bacon, diced

1 Combine the beans with the water in a large saucepan. Bring to a boil, then reduce the heat and simmer, partially covered, until just tender, 1 to 1½ hours. Skim off any foam that rises to the top of the pot.

2 Transfer the beans and their cooking water to a bean pot or covered casserole dish. Add the onion, maple syrup, ketchup, coffee, soy sauce, mustard, ginger, and bacon, and mix well.

3 Cover and bake at 300°F (no need to preheat) for about 3 hours. Check occasionally and add hot water if necessary to keep the beans moist. On the other hand, if the beans seem too soupy, remove the cover during the last 30 minutes. Serve hot.

Variation: Vegetarian Baked Beans

Omit the bacon. Add 2 tablespoons chopped chipotles canned in adobo sauce and proceed as above.

New England Baked Beans

Serves 6

The Puritans who settled in New England were prohibited from cooking on the Sabbath, which began at sundown on Saturday and lasted until sundown on Sunday. Baked beans were popular because the beans could be cooked on Saturday and served cold or reheated for breakfast or lunch the next day. Molasses and salt pork define the flavor of classic New England baked beans. In the vegetarian version, liquid smoke replaces the salt pork.

2 cups dried navy or pea beans, soaked overnight and drained

8 cups water

1 large onion, halved and thinly sliced

¼ cup firmly packed brown sugar

½ cup dark unsulfured molasses

½ cup brewed coffee

2 tablespoons coarse-grain mustard

4 ounces salt pork, diced

Salt and freshly ground black pepper

1 Combine the beans with the water in a large saucepan. Bring to a boil, then reduce the heat and simmer, partially covered, until just tender, 1 to 1½ hours. Skim off any foam that rises to the top of the pot.

2 Transfer the beans and their cooking water to a bean pot or covered casserole dish. Add the onion, brown sugar, molasses, coffee, mustard, salt pork, 1 teaspoon salt, and ½ teaspoon pepper; mix well.

3 Cover and bake at 300°F (no need to preheat) for about 3 hours. Check occasionally and add hot water if necessary to keep the beans moist. On the other hand, if the beans seem too soupy, remove the cover during the last 30 minutes. Taste and adjust the seasoning as needed. Serve hot.

Variation: Vegetarian New England Baked Beans

Omit the bacon. Add 1 tablespoon liquid smoke in step 2 and proceed as above.

● Spicy-Sweet Barbecued Beans

Serves 4–6

Smoky, sweet, and hot, these beans are a terrific vegetarian baked bean, great to serve with coleslaw and cornbread, or as a vegetarian alternative to pulled pork.

2	cups dried pinto or kidney beans, soaked overnight and drained
6	cups water
1	onion, thinly sliced
4	garlic cloves, minced
1½	cups unseasoned tomato sauce, or 1 (15-ounce) can
⅓	cup firmly packed brown sugar
2	tablespoons minced chipotle canned in adobo sauce
2	tablespoons soy sauce

1 Combine the beans with the water in a large saucepan. Bring to a boil, then reduce the heat slightly and boil gently, covered, for 1 to 1½ hours, until the beans are completely tender. Do not undercook; the beans will not soften once they are combined with the tomato sauce.

2 Preheat the oven to 300°F.

3 Using a slotted spoon, transfer the beans to a bean pot or covered casserole dish. Add the onion, garlic, tomato purée, brown sugar, chipotles, and soy sauce.

4 Cover and bake for 2 to 3 hours, until the sauce is a nice thick consistency. If necessary, uncover during the last 30 minutes to reduce the cooking liquid. Serve hot.

Variation: Quick Spicy Sweet Barbecued Beans

Substitute three 15-ounce cans of pinto or red kidney beans, drained and rinsed, for the dried beans and water. Begin with step 3.

Refried Pinto Beans

Serves 6-8

Although decent (not great) refried beans are available in cans, home-made is always better (and less expensive), as this recipe amply proves. It is very important to cook the beans until they are meltingly tender — a state that would be overcooked for most other recipes.

> 2 cups dried pinto, kidney, black, or red beans, soaked overnight and drained
> 8 cups water
> 3 tablespoons safflower, sunflower, or extra-virgin olive oil
> 3 garlic cloves, minced
> 1 small onion, minced
> 1 teaspoon chili powder
> 1 teaspoon ground cumin
> ¼ cup minced chipotle canned in adobo sauce, or 1 (4-ounce) can chopped roasted chilis, drained
> Salt and freshly ground black pepper

1 Combine the beans with the water in a large saucepan. Bring to a boil, then reduce the heat and simmer, partially covered, until the beans are very, very tender, 1½ to 2 hours.

2 Heat the oil in a large skillet over medium heat. Add the garlic, onion, chili powder, and cumin, and sauté until the onion is soft and fragrant, about 5 minutes. Using a slotted spoon, transfer the beans to the skillet, adding about ½ cup of the cooking liquid at the same time. Mash the beans with the back of your spoon or a potato masher, adding more cooking liquid as needed to achieve a creamy consistency. Keep stirring until creamy. Stir in the chipotles and season to taste with salt and pepper. Serve warm.

Kitchen Note: *The recipe makes enough refried beans to fill about eight large burritos, allowing about ½ cup of refried beans per tortilla, but why stop there? Refried beans can be layered with corn tortillas, salsa, and cheese to make a "Mexican lasagna"; mixed with cheese and heated to make a dip for corn chips; used as a nacho topping, a thickener for chili, a side dish . . .*

Curried Dahl

Serves 4–6

Whenever I make a curry and I'm not sure the dish will stretch far enough, or if my guests include vegetarians, I fall back on this simple dish. It can be made with red lentils or yellow split peas, also known as channa dahl.

2 cups red lentils or yellow split peas
6 cups water
1 teaspoon salt, plus more as needed
3 tablespoons safflower, peanut, sunflower, or canola oil
1 large onion, halved and thinly sliced
4 garlic cloves, minced
1 (1-inch) piece fresh ginger, peeled and minced
1 tablespoon cumin seeds
Hot cooked rice, for serving

1 Combine the lentils, water, and salt in a medium saucepan. Bring to a boil, then reduce the heat and boil gently, covered, until the lentils are completely tender, 30 to 40 minutes.

2 Meanwhile, heat the oil in a small skillet over medium heat. Add the onion, garlic, ginger, and cumin, and sauté until the onion is golden, about 10 minutes. Keep warm.

3 Stir the onion mixture into the lentils and continue stirring until the lentils are creamy. If the mixture is too loose, increase the heat and boil until the mixture thickens to a pleasing texture. The lentils are done when they have the consistency of creamed corn. Taste and add salt if needed. Serve hot with rice.

Kitchen Note: *This dish is mildly spiced. To add heat, season with cayenne pepper.*

Mujdhara

Serves 4

A Syrian rice-and-lentil classic, this dish has as many variations as it has spellings, including mjudra, mujadra, and mejadra. Among Jewish communities in the Middle East, the dish is sometimes nicknamed "Esau's favorite," after the Biblical story in which Esau sold his birthright for a "mess of pottage." It is *that* good.

1	cup dried green or brown lentils, rinsed
1	teaspoon salt, plus more as needed
1½	cups brown rice
3	tablespoons extra-virgin olive oil
3	large onions, halved and thinly sliced
4	garlic cloves, minced
1¼	cups buttermilk
	Freshly ground black pepper

1   In a medium saucepan, cover the lentils with water by about 3 inches and add ½ teaspoon salt. Bring to a boil, then reduce the heat and boil gently, partially covered, until the lentils are tender but still hold their shape, about 25 minutes. Drain and rinse the lentils with hot water.

2   Meanwhile, combine the rice, ½ teaspoon salt, and 3¼ cups water. Bring to a boil, then reduce the heat and simmer, covered, until the rice is tender and the water absorbed, about 30 minutes.

3   While the rice and lentils cook, heat the oil over medium-low heat in a large saucepan. Add the onions and garlic and cook, stirring frequently, until golden, about 10 minutes.

4   Add the cooked lentils and rice to the onions. Add the buttermilk to moisten and bind the mixture. Season to taste with salt and pepper. Serve warm or at room temperature.

Variation: Wheat-Berry Mujdhara

For an interesting variation, substitute cooked wheat berries for the rice.

Lentils and Greens

Serves 4

For a simple, healthful, easily put together vegetarian main dish, serve these flavorful lentils over brown rice. Be sure the lentils are fully cooked before adding the tomatoes.

2 tablespoons sunflower, peanut, or canola oil	4 cups water
1 onion, halved and thinly sliced	1 teaspoon salt, plus more as needed
2 garlic cloves, minced	6 cups chopped collards or kale leaves (remove and discard tough stems)
1 (1-inch) piece fresh ginger, peeled and minced	1½ cups diced tomatoes with juice, or 1 (15-ounce) can
1 tablespoon cumin seeds	Freshly ground black pepper
1 teaspoon fenugreek seeds	
1 cup red or brown lentils	

1   Heat the oil in a large saucepan over medium-high heat. Add the onion, garlic, ginger, cumin, and fenugreek. Sauté until softened, about 3 minutes.

2   Add the lentils, water, and salt. Bring to a boil, then reduce the heat and simmer, covered, until the lentils are tender, 25 to 30 minutes. Add the collards and tomatoes. Mix well and simmer, covered, until the collards are tender, about 20 minutes, stirring occasionally.

3   Remove from the heat, season with salt and pepper, and serve.

Musical Vegetables

Beans, beans, the musical fruit
The more you eat, the more you toot.

That's a tired rhyme, appreciated only by third-graders and those whose mentality is stuck at third grade. It's time we developed a fuller, more sophisticated approach to musical vegetables. Visit www.vegetableorchestra.org to see how you can make real music from vegetables. Not surprisingly, winter vegetables — carrots, celery root, turnips, winter squash, and pumpkins — figure prominently.

Curried Lentil-Stuffed Delicata Squash

Serves 4

The long, narrow shape of delicata squashes makes them the perfect vehicles for stuffing. Just slice horizontally to create two canoes or boats from each squash.

1 cup channa dhal, or yellow split peas

7 cups water

1 teaspoon salt

2 large delicata squashes (about 8 ounces each)

3 tablespoons sunflower, peanut, or canola oil

2 medium onions, thinly sliced

2 garlic cloves, minced

1 tablespoon cumin seeds

1 teaspoon curry powder

½ cup buttermilk

Hot cooked rice, for serving

1 Preheat the oven to 400°F.

2 Combine the lentils, water, and salt in a medium saucepan. Bring to a boil, then reduce the heat and simmer, partially covered, until the lentils are tender but still hold their shape, about 25 minutes.

3 Meanwhile, slice the squashes in half horizontally. Remove and discard the seeds and fiber. Place skin-side up in a baking dish and add 1 inch of water to the dish. Bake for about 30 minutes, until the squashes are partly tender.

4 While the squashes are baking, heat the oil in a medium skillet over medium heat. Add the onions, garlic, cumin, and curry powder, and sauté gently until the onions are golden and tender, about 10 minutes.

5 Drain the lentils and return to the pan. Stir the onion mixture and buttermilk into the lentils and cook over low heat, stirring, until the lentils are creamy, about 5 minutes.

6 Drain the water from the baking dish that holds the squashes. Turn the squashes flesh-side up and fill with the lentil mixture. Return to the oven and bake for 20 minutes, until the squashes are completely tender. Serve hot, accompanied by the rice.

Kitchen Notes: *The filling is delicious without the squash and can be served over rice. Also, sweet dumpling squashes can be substituted for the delicata squashes; allow one per serving.*

Golden Carrot Risotto

Serves 4-6

Saffron gives this risotto its golden color while carrots add flavor, texture, and nutrition. This is a lovely dish.

5½	cups vegetable broth or chicken broth (pages 126–27)
½	cup dry white wine
¼	teaspoon crushed saffron
2	tablespoons extra-virgin olive oil
2	shallots, minced
3	garlic cloves, minced
1½	cups Arborio rice
2	carrots, peeled and shredded
1	cup freshly grated Parmesan cheese
2	tablespoons butter
	Salt and freshly ground black pepper

1. Heat the broth, wine, and saffron to a simmer in a medium saucepan.

2. Heat the oil in a large skillet over medium heat. Add the shallots, garlic, and rice, and toss to coat with the oil. Sauté until the rice appears toasted, 3 to 5 minutes.

3. Add 1 cup of the simmering broth to the rice. Stir until the liquid is mostly absorbed. Continue adding more broth, 1 cup at a time, cooking and stirring as the liquid is absorbed. Add the carrots with the last cup of broth and continue cooking and stirring until the liquid is absorbed and the rice is tender and creamy. The total cooking time will be 18 to 35 minutes. You may not need all of the broth; taste the rice before adding the final cup.

4. Stir in ½ cup of the cheese and the butter. Season with salt and pepper. Serve hot, passing the remaining ½ cup cheese at the table.

Kitchen Note: *Risotto is very easy to prepare as long as you give it your attention and add the broth slowly. Use a neutral-tasting broth for best results.*

White Bean Stew with Smoked Turkey

Serves 6–8

A very simplified, healthful variation on cassoulet, this scrumptious white bean stew is made with root vegetables and smoked turkey, which stands in for the duck legs, sausage, and goose fat of a classic cassoulet. Although far lower in fat than the original (and requiring far less labor), this is a luscious way to enjoy beans. Serve with French bread and a rustic red wine.

2	smoked turkey legs or 1 thigh, scored with a knife
6	cups unsalted chicken broth (page 127) or water
4	cups water
¼	teaspoon black pepper
2	bay leaves
¼	cup extra-virgin olive oil
1	onion, diced
1	celery root, peeled and diced
1	carrot, peeled and diced
6	garlic cloves, minced
1	tablespoon dried sage
1	pound dried white beans, such as navy or Great Northern, soaked overnight and drained
2	tablespoons tomato paste
	Salt and freshly ground black pepper
¾	cup dried breadcrumbs
1	tablespoon dried thyme

1   Combine the turkey, broth, water, pepper, and bay leaves in a large soup pot. Bring to a boil, then reduce the heat and simmer, covered, until the turkey is tender and falling off the bone, 1½ to 2 hours. Remove the turkey and set aside until cool enough to handle. Discard the bay leaves. Measure the broth; if you have less than 6 cups, add water to bring the volume up to 6 cups.

2   Heat 2 tablespoons of the oil in a large Dutch oven over medium-high heat. Add the onion, celery root, and carrot, and cook, stirring, until the vegetables are softened, about 5 minutes. Add the garlic and sage and cook for 1 minute. Add the beans and the reserved stock. Return to a boil, then reduce the heat and simmer, partially covered, until the beans are tender but still firm enough to hold their shape, 1½ to 2 hours. The beans should be moist but not soupy.

3   Remove the turkey meat from the bones and discard the bones and skin. Chop the meat and stir it into the beans. Stir in the tomato paste and season with salt and pepper; it may not need any salt.

4   Preheat the oven to 375°F.

5   Sprinkle the breadcrumbs evenly over the beans, sprinkle the thyme over the crumbs, and drizzle with the remaining 2 tablespoons oil.

6   Bake for 25 to 30 minutes, or until the topping is golden brown and the beans are bubbly around the edges. Serve hot.

Winter-Vegetable Nori Rolls

Makes 48 to 56 pieces

Ever since sushi hit these shores, the California roll, a vegetarian nori roll made with vinegared rice, avocado, and cucumbers, has been popular. When those summer vegetables aren't in season, other vegetables can be used to great effect. Nori is available wherever Asian foods are sold, including most supermarkets. To serve these nori rolls as a main course, accompany them with Onion-Miso Soup (page 113) and Wilted-Kale Salad (page 70).

3	cups short-grain white rice
3¾	cups water
3	tablespoons mirin (Japanese sweet rice wine)
⅔	cup rice vinegar
2½	tablespoons sugar
2½	teaspoons salt
6–7	toasted dried nori seaweed sheets (each about 8 inches square)
1	tablespoon wasabi powder mixed with 1 tablespoon water
½	cup pickled ginger
1	(3-inch) piece daikon radish or 1 small turnip, peeled and very finely julienned
1	carrot, peeled and very finely julienned
1	cup very thinly sliced red cabbage
	Soy sauce, for dipping

1   To prepare the rice, combine the rice, water, and mirin in a medium saucepan. Bring to a boil, then reduce the heat and simmer, covered, until the rice is tender and the water absorbed, 12 to 15 minutes.

2   Combine the vinegar, sugar, and salt in a small saucepan and bring to a boil. Remove from the heat and keep warm.

3   Transfer the cooked rice to a shallow bowl or baking pan. Gradually pour the hot vinegar mixture over the rice and toss with a spoon or rice paddle until the rice is cooled to the touch and appears glossy.

4   To assemble the rolls, set out a bamboo rolling mat or clean kitchen towel. Set a small bowl of water nearby to moisten your fingertips. Place a sheet of nori on the bamboo mat. With moistened fingertips, spread about 1 cup of rice in an even layer over the nori, leaving empty about 1 inch at the top edge of the sheet. Spread about ½ teaspoon of wasabi paste in a line across the bottom of the rice. Top the wasabi with a layer of ginger. Arrange a few pieces each of the daikon, carrot, and cabbage in a straight line over the rice. Brush the top edge of the seaweed with warm water. Using the bamboo rolling mat as a guide, roll the seaweed into a tight cylinder, starting with the edge closest to you. Press on the moistened seaweed flap to seal the roll and set aside, seam-side down, while you repeat with the remaining ingredients, making six or seven rolls in all.

5   To serve, trim away the ragged ends of each roll. Then cut each roll into tidy 1-inch slices. Serve with soy sauce for dipping.

Southern-Style Rice with Collard Greens

Serves 4–6

Here's a quick one-pot supper for a busy weeknight. Kale can replace the collard greens if you are so inclined. Do not forget to pass the hot sauce at the table. It adds a necessary vinegary zing that brings the dish together.

2	tablespoons extra-virgin olive oil
1	medium onion, diced
2	cups long-grain rice
2	cups diced ham
1	pound collard greens, chopped into bite-size pieces (about 12 cups lightly packed; remove and discard tough stems)
3½	cups water
	Salt and freshly ground black pepper
	Louisiana-style hot pepper sauce, such as Frank's or Crystal

1 Heat the oil in a large Dutch oven over medium heat. Add the onion and sauté until the onion is translucent, about 3 minutes. Add the rice and continue to sauté until the rice appears dry and toasted, 3 to 5 minutes longer. Stir in the ham, collard greens, and water. Cover and bring to a boil, then reduce the heat to low and simmer very gently until the liquid is absorbed, about 15 minutes.

2 Fluff the rice with a fork. Taste and season with salt and pepper. Replace the lid and set the rice aside for 5 minutes.

3 Fluff the rice with a fork and serve hot, passing the hot sauce at the table.

Kitchen Note: *To "fluff" rice is to toss the rice with a fork so it is not compacted.*

Leek Risotto

Serves 4-6

This outstanding risotto stands well on its own (serving four), or it makes a delicious base for chicken marsala or other gravy-rich dish (in which case it serves six).

5½   cups vegetable broth or chicken broth (pages 126-27)
½   cup dry white wine
2   tablespoons butter
2   tablespoons extra-virgin olive oil
2-3   leeks, trimmed and sliced
1½   cups Arborio rice
1   cup freshly grated Parmesan cheese
    Salt and freshly ground black pepper

1   Heat the broth and wine to a simmer in a medium saucepan.

2   Melt the butter in the oil in a large skillet over medium heat. Add the leeks and sauté until wilted, 3 to 5 minutes. Add the rice and sauté until the rice appears toasted, 5 minutes.

3   Add 1 cup of the simmering broth to the rice. Stir until the liquid is mostly absorbed. Continue adding more broth, 1 cup at a time, cooking and stirring until the liquid is absorbed and the rice is tender and creamy. The total cooking time will be 18 to 35 minutes. You may not need all of the broth; taste the rice before adding the final cup.

4   Stir in the cheese. Season to taste with salt and pepper. Serve hot.

Risotto with Butternut Squash

Serves 4

A delicious one-dish meal, in which the squash cooks alongside the rice. If you are making this with vegetable broth, be sure it doesn't taste strongly of tomatoes or carrots (which many do). Water would be a better choice if your broth isn't mildly flavored.

¾ cup white wine	1½ cups Arborio rice
5¼ cups water, neutral-tasting vegetable broth or chicken broth (pages 126–27), or a combination	1 teaspoon salt, plus more as needed
	1 small to medium butternut squash, peeled and diced (about 4 cups)
3 tablespoons extra-virgin olive oil	½ cup freshly grated Parmesan cheese
2 shallots, finely diced	
2 garlic cloves, minced	2 tablespoons butter
1 teaspoon dried sage or thyme	Freshly ground black pepper

1 Heat the wine and water to a simmer in a medium saucepan.

2 Heat the oil in a large nonstick skillet over medium heat. Add the shallots, garlic, and sage, and sauté until the shallot softens and appears transparent, about 3 minutes. Add the rice and salt and toss to coat with the oil. Sauté for 3 to 5 minutes, until the rice appears toasted. Stir in the squash.

3 Add ½ cup of the simmering wine mixture to the rice. Stir until the liquid is mostly absorbed. Continue adding more liquid, ½ cup at a time, cooking and stirring until the liquid is absorbed and the rice is tender and creamy. The total cooking time will be 18 to 35 minutes. You may not need all of the broth; taste the rice before adding the final cup.

4 Vigorously stir in the Parmesan and butter. Season with pepper and additional salt, if needed. Serve hot.

Kitchen Note: *Make sure the butternut squash is diced small (¼- to ⅓-inch pieces) so that it is fully tender by the time the rice is cooked. It also looks more appealing this way.*

Lemony Barley-Carrot Pilaf

Serves 6

The carrots retain their crunch when added at the end of the cooking process, and they look like little jewels. Barley is an underutilized grain, perhaps because it takes about 45 minutes to cook. But winter is all about slow cooking, isn't it?

2 tablespoons extra-virgin olive oil
1 medium onion, diced
1 cup pearl barley
3 cups vegetable broth or chicken broth (pages 126–27)
2 carrots, peeled and finely diced
1 teaspoon finely grated lemon zest
1 tablespoon lemon juice
1 garlic clove, minced
Salt and freshly ground black pepper

1 Heat the oil in a large saucepan over medium heat. Add the onion and sauté until softened, 2 to 3 minutes. Add the barley and stir for 1 minute. Add the broth and bring to a boil, then reduce the heat and simmer, covered, until the barley has absorbed most of the liquid, about 30 minutes.

2 Sprinkle the carrots over the barley but do not stir. Continue cooking until the barley has absorbed all the liquid and the grains are tender, about 15 minutes.

3 Fluff with a fork, mixing in the carrots. Add the lemon zest, lemon juice, and garlic. Season with salt and pepper; mix gently. Serve hot.

Kasha Varnishkes

Serves 4

Immigrants from eastern Europe, like my grandparents, brought kasha to this country. *Kasha* means "cereal" in Russian, but in this country it generally means buckwheat groats and a cooked dish made from buckwheat groats. Although buckwheat looks and cooks like a grain, it is actually part of buckwheat's fruiting seed. To make kasha, the seed's husk is dried and split so that the inner kernel, called the groat, can be extracted. The groats are then roasted until they become dark; this step turns buckwheat groats into kasha. Buckwheat was indispensible to the peasants of eastern Europe because it can grow in poor soil and difficult weather. It has an earthy flavor unlike any grain.

1 cup small bowtie pasta	1 onion, diced
1 cup roasted whole buckwheat groats or medium-grind kasha	2 cups boiling water or chicken broth (page 127)
1 egg, lightly beaten	Salt and freshly ground black pepper
2 tablespoons extra-virgin olive oil	

1   Bring a large pot of salted water to a boil. Cook the bowties in the boiling water until done. Drain, rinse under lukewarm running water, and set aside.

2   Combine the buckwheat groats and egg in a bowl and mix well.

3   Heat a large nonstick skillet over medium heat. Add the buckwheat mixture and cook, stirring constantly, until the grains are dry and separated, about 3 minutes. Scrape the mixture out of the skillet and set aside.

4   Return the skillet to medium-high heat. Add the oil and onion and sauté until the onion begins to color, about 5 minutes. Stir in the buckwheat mixture. Slowly add the boiling water and season with salt and pepper. Reduce the heat, cover, and cook over very low heat, without stirring, until the water has been completely absorbed and the grains are tender, 15 to 25 minutes.

5   Stir in the bowties. Wipe the pot lid dry, cover, and let stand for 5 minutes. Then fluff with a fork, season generously with salt and pepper, and serve.

Kitchen Note: *Mushrooms sautéed with the onion make a nice addition.*

Carrot Spoon Bread

Serves 6–8

Spoon bread, a classic Southern side dish made with cornmeal, is more like a pudding or soufflé than a bread. It's so soft that it can be served and eaten with a spoon. Like a soufflé, it is best served immediately after it is baked.

2 cups milk
2 medium carrots, peeled and shredded
1 shallot, finely chopped
⅓ cup yellow cornmeal
1 tablespoon butter
1 teaspoon salt, plus more for seasoning
    Freshly ground black pepper
1 cup lightly packed grated sharp cheddar cheese (4 ounces)
1 pinch dried tarragon
4 eggs, separated

1 Preheat the oven to 400°F. Butter a 2-quart soufflé dish or 9- by 13-inch baking dish.

2 Combine the milk, carrots, shallot, cornmeal, butter, salt, and pepper to taste in a medium saucepan over medium-high heat. Bring to a boil, then reduce the heat and simmer, stirring, until the mixture is thickened, 3 to 4 minutes. Remove from the heat; stir in the cheese and tarragon. Let cool until just warm to the touch, about 15 minutes.

3 Stir in the egg yolks until well blended.

4 In a clean mixing bowl, beat the egg whites with a pinch of salt until soft peaks form. Stir one-third of the whites into the cornmeal mixture, then gently fold in the remaining whites with a rubber spatula. Pour into the prepared dish.

5 Place the dish in the oven and lower the temperature to 375°F. Bake for 25 to 30 minutes, until the top is browned and the center is barely set. Serve immediately.

6

Vegetarian Main Dishes

There was a time when vegetarian main dishes were endured by meat eaters (or not), but these dishes weren't expected to bring pleasure to the committed omnivore. Those days are gone. Who doesn't enjoy a delicious combination of vegetables with pasta, in a pie shell, or on a pizza? And that's just for starters.

Eggs are often overlooked as a dinner ingredient in America. But combined with potatoes, eggs make a hearty main-dish frittata. They are also delicious and comforting on a bed of roasted root vegetables.

Greens are an obvious choice to combine with pasta, but root vegetables are also great with pasta, and shredded root vegetables can cook in the same time that it takes to heat the water for the pasta.

Scattered in the previous chapters are plenty of recipes that also make wonderful vegetarian main dishes. So don't forget the soups, salads, and rice-and-bean dishes when planning your menus.

RECIPE LIST FOR
VEGETARIAN MAIN DISHES

Potato-Leek Frittata

Sweet-Potato and Goat Cheese Frittata

Rumbledethump

Vermont Sugarmaker's Supper

Mashed Potatoes with Caramelized
  Winter Vegetables

Savory Winter-Vegetable Bread Pudding

Vegetarian Egg Rolls

Vegetarian Lo Mein with Spicy Tofu

Japanese-Style Greens with Tofu

Pasta Inverno

Mushroom Lo Mein

Pasta with Tomato-Braised Root
  Vegetables

Cheesy Mac with Root Vegetables

Shredded Root-Vegetable Linguine

Fettuccine with Caramelized Cabbage,
  White Beans, and Goat Cheese

Pasta with Kale and Chickpeas

Kale-Ricotta Cannelloni

Tortellini with Kale

Vegetable Couscous

White Lasagna with Leeks and Butternut
  Squash

Caramelized Cabbage and Onion Tart

Winter-Vegetable Pie

Kale-Feta Pie

Kale Pizza

Frizzled-Kale Pizza

Leek and Goat Cheese Pizza

Apple, Leek, and Cheddar Quiche

African Sweet-Potato Stew

Basic Pizza Dough

Basic Pie Pastry

Vegetarian dishes are marked with this symbol:

Potato-Leek Frittata

Serves 6–8

Everyone should have a good frittata or two in their repertoire because they're something you can whip up with kitchen staples, most everyone enjoys them, and they are delicious hot or at room temperature. I like to serve this frittata with salsa or chutney on the side when I serve it hot, but I love it plain at room temperature. It can even be served as finger food at room temperature, cut into tiny squares. You'll need a skillet that can go from stovetop to oven. If you have a nonstick skillet, it should be easy to slide the frittata onto a serving plate, but it is fine to serve the frittata right out of the skillet.

3	tablespoons extra-virgin olive oil
1½	pounds thin-skinned potatoes, peeled or scrubbed and shredded
2	medium leeks, trimmed and thinly sliced
8	eggs
¼	cup milk
	Salt and freshly ground black pepper
1	cup lightly packed grated cheddar cheese (4 ounces)

1   Preheat the oven to 400°F.

2   Heat the oil in a large ovenproof nonstick or cast-iron skillet over medium-high heat. Add the potatoes and leeks and sauté until the vegetables are tender, 6 to 7 minutes. Taste to make sure the potatoes are fully cooked. If needed, sauté for a few minutes longer.

3   Meanwhile, beat the eggs with the milk. Season with salt and pepper. Pour the eggs into the skillet over the cooked vegetables and cook for 1 minute. Then, using a spatula, raise the cooked egg off the bottom of the pan, allowing any still-liquid egg to run onto the bottom of the skillet.

4   When the eggs are set, sprinkle the top with the cheese and transfer to the oven. Bake for about 12 minutes, until the top is deep golden brown.

5   Let stand for at least 5 minutes. Cut into wedges and serve hot or at room temperature.

Sweet-Potato and Goat Cheese Frittata

Serves 6–8

The harmonious combination of sage and goat cheese allows you to experience the savory side of sweet potatoes. Like the potato-leek frittata (page 229), this dish can be served hot or at room temperature. In this case, I slightly prefer it hot.

3	tablespoons extra-virgin olive oil
2	large sweet potatoes, peeled and shredded
1	onion, shredded
2	garlic cloves, minced
8	eggs
¼	cup milk
1½	teaspoons dried sage
½	teaspoon salt
¼	teaspoon freshly ground black pepper
4	ounces soft fresh goat cheese (chèvre), crumbled

1 Preheat the oven to 400°F.

2 Heat the oil in a large ovenproof nonstick or cast-iron skillet over medium-high heat. Add the sweet potatoes, onion, and garlic, and sauté until the vegetables are tender, 6 to 7 minutes. Taste to make sure the sweet potatoes are fully cooked. If needed, sauté for a few minutes longer.

3 Meanwhile, beat the eggs with the milk. Stir in the sage, salt, and pepper. Pour the eggs into the skillet over the cooked vegetables and cook for 1 minute. Then, using a spatula, raise the cooked egg off the bottom of the pan, allowing any still-liquid egg to run onto the bottom of the skillet.

4 When the eggs are set, sprinkle the top with the cheese and transfer to the oven. Bake for 10 to 15 minutes, until the top is browned.

5 Let stand for at least 5 minutes. Cut into wedges and serve hot or at room temperature.

Rumbledethump

Serves 6

Who could resist a recipe so whimsically named? This is the Scottish variation on colcannon, made with the addition of cheese. It makes a hearty main dish.

2	pounds russet (baking) potatoes, peeled and cut into chunks
4	tablespoons butter
½	head green or savoy cabbage, finely shredded or sliced
1	large onion, halved and thinly sliced
1½	cups lightly packed grated cheddar cheese (6 ounces)
	Salt and freshly ground black pepper

1 Preheat the oven to 400°F.

2 Cover the potatoes with salted water in a saucepan. Bring to a boil, then reduce the heat and boil gently, covered, until completely tender, 15 to 25 minutes. Drain and mash.

3 Meanwhile, melt the butter in a large skillet over medium-high heat. Add the cabbage and onion and sauté until they wilt, 20 to 25 minutes.

4 Add two-thirds of the cheese and all of the cabbage mixture to the potatoes. Season with salt and pepper.

5 Transfer the mixture to a casserole dish. Level the top and sprinkle with the remaining cheese. Bake for about 15 minutes, until the cheese is melted and the top is golden. Serve immediately.

Vermont Sugarmaker's Supper

Serves 4

Sugaring season (when Vermonters tap maple trees and boil the sap to make maple syrup) comes at the end of the winter, when nighttime temperatures are still below freezing but daytime temperatures can climb into the 40s. It is also a time when folks who once got by without grocery stores were eating the last of the stored vegetables from the root cellar. I don't know for a fact that anyone ever ate this dish, but it is a delicious combination of flavors.

VEGETABLES

4 cups peeled and diced mixed root vegetables (beets, carrots, celery root, parsnips, rutabagas, salsify, and/or turnips) or winter squashes

2-4 thin-skinned potatoes, diced

1 whole garlic head, cloves separated and peeled

4 shallots, halved if large

2 tablespoons extra-virgin olive oil

2 teaspoons crushed dried rosemary

Salt and freshly ground black pepper

Maple syrup

EGGS

8 eggs

2 tablespoons milk

Salt and freshly ground black pepper

2 tablespoons butter

FOR SERVING

Whole-wheat or white toast

1   Preheat the oven to 450°F. Lightly oil a half sheet pan (preferred) or large shallow roasting pan.

2   Mound the root vegetables, potatoes, garlic, and shallots on the sheet pan. Drizzle the oil over them and sprinkle with the rosemary, salt, and pepper; toss well. Arrange in a shallow (preferably single) layer.

3   Roast the vegetables for 35 to 40 minutes, stirring or shaking the pan occasionally for even cooking, until tender and lightly browned.

4   When the vegetables are almost done, prepare the eggs. Crack the eggs into a bowl. Beat with the milk. Season with salt and pepper.

5   When the vegetables are done, drizzle with the maple syrup and keep warm.

6   Melt the butter in a medium skillet over medium heat. When the butter foams, add the eggs and immediately reduce the heat to low. With a wooden spoon or heatproof spatula, push the eggs gently as they set, folding and stirring them into soft curds. Continue to cook until the eggs are just set, 2 to 5 minutes.

7   To serve, divide the vegetables among four serving plates. Top with the eggs. Serve immediately, passing maple syrup and toast on the side.

Burdock Root

Burdock, a noxious weed, has a surprisingly edible taproot. It is used in folk medicine in China, is popular in Japan and Hawai'i, and is eaten in copious quantities by followers of macrobiotic diets. You can often find it today in natural-foods stores and Asian markets.

To prepare burdock root, peel away the brown skin and drop in acidulated water (1 tablespoon vinegar or lemon juice added to 4 cups water) for a brief bath to prevent browning. Then add to salads, soups, stews, and stir-fries. A popular Japanese dish is kinpira gobo: julienned or shredded burdock root and carrot, braised with soy sauce, sugar, mirin and/or sake, and sesame oil.

Mashed Potatoes with Caramelized Winter Vegetables

Serves 4

Colcannon, the Irish dish that matches up mashed potatoes with cabbage and leeks, can be played with. In this version, the mashed potatoes are upgraded with cabbage, onions, and carrots. This hearty dish makes a wonderful main-dish supper, but it can also be served as an accompaniment to quiche, meatloaf, or another rustic meat dish. It is important to cook the vegetables slowly to coax out all their sweetness.

3	tablespoons extra-virgin olive oil
1	small head green or savoy cabbage, shredded (6–8 cups)
2	onions, halved and thinly sliced
2	carrots, peeled and shredded
2	pounds russet (baking) potatoes, peeled and cut into large pieces
3	tablespoons butter
¾	cup milk or cream, warmed
	Salt and freshly ground black pepper

1 Heat the oil in a large skillet over medium heat. Add the cabbage and onions and sauté, stirring frequently, until very tender and sweet, about 25 minutes. Stir in the carrots and sauté for 5 minutes longer.

2 Meanwhile, cover the potatoes with salted water in a saucepan. Bring to a boil, then reduce the heat and boil gently, covered, until completely tender, 15 to 25 minutes.

3 Drain the potatoes well. Mash the potatoes with a potato masher, press through a ricer, or whip in a standing mixer until they are fluffy. Beat in the butter and milk.

4 Fold the cabbage mixture into the potatoes. Season generously with salt and pepper. Serve hot.

❧ Savory Winter-Vegetable Bread Pudding

Serves 8–12

You can serve this dish as either a vegetarian main dish or a side dish, filling the role of both starch and vegetable. It is tasty and colorful.

1 beet, peeled and diced	4 eggs
1 carrot, peeled and diced	3 cups milk
1 celery root, peeled and diced	1 teaspoon crushed dried rosemary or sage
1 parsnip, peeled and diced	
1 turnip, peeled and diced	1 teaspoon dried thyme
1 onion, diced	1 (1-pound) loaf firm white bread, cut into ½-inch cubes (about 12 cups)
2 tablespoons extra-virgin olive oil or sunflower oil	
Salt and freshly ground black pepper	2 cups lightly packed grated cheddar cheese (8 ounces)

1   Preheat the oven to 425°F. Lightly oil a large sheet pan (preferred) or large shallow roasting pan. Butter a 9- by 13-inch baking pan.

2   Mound the beet, carrot, celery root, parsnip, turnip, and onion on the sheet pan. Drizzle the oil over them, season with salt and pepper, and toss to coat. Arrange in a single layer on the pan. Roast for about 45 minutes, stirring and shaking the pan for even cooking, until the vegetables are tender and lightly browned.

3   In a large bowl, whisk the eggs, milk, rosemary, and thyme. Add the bread cubes and let soak for 5 minutes.

4   Add the vegetables and cheese to the bread-cube mixture and gently toss to mix. Season generously with salt and pepper and mix well. Pack the mixture into the prepared baking pan.

5   Bake for 45 to 55 minutes, until the top is crusty brown and a knife inserted in the center comes out clean. If the pudding begins to look dark before it's finished, cover with foil. Serve warm.

Kitchen Note: *Stick with white bread to avoid making the dish too heavy, and be sure to cut the bread cubes and vegetables to about the same size.*

🍃 Vegetarian Egg Rolls

Serves 6–10

Maybe it is time to get over your fear of frying. Deep-frying is surprisingly easy, and egg rolls are a fabulous way to enjoy cabbage and carrots. Although they're not a traditional main dish, with all the effort required, why not make these egg rolls a meal?

1 medium head green cabbage, shredded or very thinly sliced (about 10 cups)	4 scallions, finely chopped
	2 garlic cloves, minced
1 tablespoon salt	1 (1-inch) piece fresh ginger, peeled and minced
1 tablespoon Asian sesame oil	
1 tablespoon peanut or sunflower oil	Canola or other vegetable oil, for deep-frying
6 ounces shiitake mushrooms, thinly sliced (remove and discard the stems)	1 egg white
	1 (1-pound) package egg roll wrappers (about 20)
1 tablespoon soy sauce	
1 carrot, peeled and shredded	Hot mustard and Thai sweet chili sauce or Chinese plum sauce, to serve
1 cup bean sprouts	

1 Combine the cabbage and salt in a medium bowl. Mix well and set aside until the cabbage is limp and wilted, at least 30 minutes. Rinse under cold running water and drain well. The cabbage should taste a little salty. If it is very salty, rinse again.

2 Heat a small wok or skillet over high heat. Add the sesame oil and peanut oil and heat until shimmering. Add the mushrooms and soy sauce and stir-fry until the mushrooms are tender, 4 to 5 minutes.

3 Combine the cabbage, mushrooms, carrot, bean sprouts, scallions, garlic, and ginger in a large bowl. Mix well.

4 Begin heating 2 to 3 inches of the canola oil in a wok, tall saucepan, or deep-fat fryer over medium heat. Put the egg white in a bowl. Dust a work surface and a baking sheet with cornstarch.

5 To fill the egg rolls, place an egg roll wrapper on the work surface with one corner pointing toward you. Mound 2 heaping tablespoons (about ¼ cup) of filling in the center of the wrapper. Bring the corner of the wrapper closest to you up over the filling and tuck under the filling, making a log shape. Bring in the two side corners. Apply egg white with your fingers or a pastry brush to the last corner of the wrapper and finish rolling up the egg roll, sealing it closed. Transfer the roll, seam-side down, to the prepared baking sheet. Continue filling and rolling until all the filling is used. If an egg roll wrapper rips, roll it in a second wrapper.

6 When all the egg rolls are made, use a deep-frying thermometer to test whether the oil has reached 365°F. Or drop a cube of bread into the oil; if the oil bubbles around the bread and the cube browns uniformly in 60 seconds, the oil is at the right temperature. Slide three egg rolls into the hot oil and fry until golden all over, about 3 minutes. Remove with tongs and let drain in a colander or on a wire rack, turning frequently. Meanwhile, continue frying in batches of three until all the egg rolls are fried.

7 Serve hot, passing hot mustard and sweet chili sauce on the side.

Kitchen Notes: *I usually have a second package of egg roll wrappers on hand in case of rips. On the other hand, if you end up with extra filling, you can always stir-fry it and serve it over rice. The oil can be recycled by passing it through a coffee filter into a glass jar.*

The Great Rutabaga Curl

The Ithaca Winter Farmers' Market used to be sparsely attended. Maybe it was the cold weather; the building protected shoppers from the rain and snow and sleet, but the cold was unrelenting. Back then, eating locally produced foods was not the guiding principle of many shoppers, and so the market languished. One Saturday morning in the late 1990s, in a moment of frost-induced hilarity, vendors began lobbing their wares down the main aisle of the long market building. Potatoes, cinnamon rolls, cabbages, loaves of bread, and even frozen chickens were heaved with abandon in this impromptu outburst. It occurred to at least one of the vendors that a more organized event involving pitching vegetables might draw in more shoppers.

Steve Sierigk, the self-proclaimed High Commissioner of the International Rutabaga Curling Championship, developed rules, and the World Championship Rutabaga Curl was begun, always held on the last Saturday before Christmas at the Ithaca Farmers' Market.

The event draws huge crowds, but the field is limited to 30 youngsters for the Turnip Toss and 100 adults for the Rutabaga Curl. So far, the rest of the world hasn't joined in the championship competition. But it is only a matter of time.

Vegetarian Lo Mein with Spicy Tofu

Serves 4–6

Stir-fried tofu tends to fall apart, but baking the tofu allows it to retain its shape and absorb all the wonderful flavors of the marinade. If you like, just make the baked tofu and enjoy it as a snack. But it is particularly delicious in this vegetarian lo mein.

TOFU

3	tablespoons soy sauce
1½	tablespoons toasted sesame oil
2	tablespoons Chinese rice wine, dry sherry, or rice wine
2	teaspoons sugar
2	garlic cloves, minced
1	teaspoon Chinese chili paste with garlic
1	pound extra-firm tofu

NOODLES AND VEGETABLES

1	pound Chinese wheat noodles or thin spaghetti
2	tablespoons peanut, sunflower, or canola oil
2	carrots, peeled and cut into matchsticks
¼	head green or savoy cabbage, or ½ head napa or Chinese cabbage, very thinly sliced
1	(4-inch) piece daikon radish or 1 small turnip, peeled and cut into matchsticks
3–4	garlic cloves, minced
1	(1-inch) piece fresh ginger, peeled and minced
	Soy sauce, as needed
¼	cup Chinese mock oyster sauce or stir-fry sauce

1   Preheat the oven to 350°F.

2   To prepare the tofu, combine the soy sauce, sesame oil, Chinese rice wine, sugar, garlic, and chili paste in an 8-inch square glass baking dish and mix to blend. Wrap the tofu in paper towels and squeeze to get rid of excess moisture. Cut the tofu into bite-size cubes and add to the baking dish. With a rubber spatula, very carefully toss the tofu in the mixture until well coated. Spread the tofu in a single layer.

3   Roast for about 60 minutes, turning the tofu cubes every 15 minutes, until the marinade has been mostly absorbed.

4   Bring a large pot of salted water to a boil. Add the noodles and boil until al dente. Drain well.

5   Heat a large wok or frying pan over high heat. When the pan is hot, add the oil. When the oil is hot, add the carrots and stir-fry until just barely tender, about 3 minutes. Add the cabbage, daikon, garlic, and ginger to the wok and stir-fry until the cabbage is wilted, about 3 minutes. At any point, add a little soy sauce to encourage the vegetables to steam if they don't seem to be cooking.

6   Add the tofu and any remaining marinade to the wok, along with the noodles. Pour the mock oyster sauce over the noodles and toss until well coated and the tofu and vegetables are mixed into the noodles.

7   Taste and add additional soy sauce, if needed. Serve hot.

Kitchen Note: *Stir-fry sauce and mock oyster sauce are vegetarian versions of Chinese oyster sauce, which contains "oyster extractives," whatever that is. The sauce is what gives Chinese lo mein and fried rice its distinctive flavor. It can be found wherever Chinese foods are sold.*

Japanese-Style Greens with Tofu

Serves 4

Although any winter green would work here, this is particularly wonderful with kale. Serve with rice or other Asian-style dishes. It can be served hot or at room temperature.

2	pounds greens (green, savoy, napa, or Chinese cabbage; collard greens; kale or mustard greens), coarsely chopped (remove and discard tough stems)
3	tablespoons soy sauce
1½	tablespoons Asian sesame oil
1½	tablespoons Chinese black vinegar
1	pound silken tofu, cut into 1-inch cubes
1–2	tablespoons hulled or black sesame seeds

1   Fill a large saucepan with a couple inches of water and bring to a boil. Steam the greens in a large steaming basket over the boiling water until tender, about 5 minutes.

2   Mix the soy sauce, sesame oil, and vinegar in a small bowl.

3   Arrange the greens on a platter and top with the tofu. Drizzle with the soy sauce mixture and garnish with the sesame seeds. Serve hot or at room temperature.

Kitchen Note: *If you don't have Chinese black vinegar on hand, you can come reasonably close to it with a mixture of 1 part soy sauce, 1 part Worcestershire sauce, and 1 part rice vinegar. Otherwise, omit the vinegar.*

🌰 Pasta Inverno

Serves 6

The dish *pasta primavera* ("springtime pasta") has come to mean pasta in a cream sauce with vegetables — any vegetables, and often an unseasonal mixture. *Inverno* means "winter," so this is pasta for winter, with a mixture of winter vegetables in a delicious cream sauce. In the mix of root vegetables, turnips, celery root, parsnips, and salsify will disappear in the white sauce, which may or may not be a good thing, depending on your point of view. Choose those vegetables to carry the wintry white theme; choose carrots, golden beets, rutabagas, and/or winter squash to make the dish more colorful.

4	tablespoons butter
4	cups peeled and shredded or very finely julienned mixed root vegetables (carrots, celery root, golden beets, parsnips, rutabagas, salsify, and/or turnips) or winter squashes
6	garlic cloves, minced
1	shallot, minced
½	cup dry white wine
2	cups light cream or half-and-half
	Salt and freshly ground black pepper
1	pound angel hair pasta
½	cup freshly grated Parmesan cheese, plus more to serve

1   Begin heating a large pot of salted water to a boil for the pasta.

2   Meanwhile, melt the butter in a large Dutch oven over medium heat. Add the root vegetables, garlic, and shallot, and sauté until the vegetables are limp, about 8 minutes. Add the wine and cream. Simmer until the vegetables are tender, about 5 minutes. Reduce the heat to keep warm and season with salt and pepper.

3   Cook the pasta in the boiling water until al dente. Reserve about 1 cup of the cooking water, and then drain.

4   Toss the pasta with the sauce until well coated, and then transfer to a serving dish. Add the Parmesan and toss, adding some of the reserved cooking water if the mixture appears dry. Serve at once, passing additional Parmesan at the table.

 Mushroom Lo Mein

Serves 4-6

Eggs provide the protein in this vegetarian lo mein, while the mushrooms contribute a hearty focus.

3	eggs
1	teaspoon Asian sesame oil
¼	teaspoon salt
8	ounces shiitake mushrooms, sliced (remove and discard the stems)
3-4	garlic cloves, minced
1	(1-inch) piece fresh ginger, peeled and minced
2	tablespoons soy sauce, plus more as needed
1	tablespoon sugar
1	tablespoon Chinese rice wine or dry sherry
1	pound Chinese wheat noodles or thin spaghetti
¼	cup peanut or other vegetable oil, plus more as needed
2	carrots, peeled and cut into matchsticks
¼	head green or savoy cabbage, or ½ head napa or Chinese cabbage, very thinly sliced
1	(4-inch) piece daikon radish or 1 small turnip, peeled and cut into matchsticks
¼	cup Chinese mock oyster sauce or stir-fry sauce

1   Begin heating a large pot of salted water to a boil for the noodles.

2   Beat together the eggs, sesame oil, and salt in a small bowl. Set aside.

3   Combine the mushrooms, garlic, ginger, soy sauce, sugar, and rice wine in a small bowl. Mix well and set aside.

4   Cook the noodles in the boiling water until al dente. Drain well.

5   Heat a large wok or frying pan over high heat. When the pan is hot, add 1 tablespoon of the peanut oil and heat for 30 seconds. Pour in the egg mixture. As the bottom sets, push the edges in toward the middle to allow the liquid egg to run to the outside to cook. Continue pushing in the edges until the top has almost no more liquid egg. Flip the egg and cook just until dry, about 30 seconds. Remove the egg cake to a cutting board. Slice into matchsticks.

6   Add 1 tablespoon of the peanut oil to the wok. When the oil is very hot, add the mushrooms and marinade and stir-fry until the mushrooms are cooked through, about 5 minutes. Scrape the mushrooms and juices back into the bowl.

7   Heat the remaining 2 tablespoons peanut oil in the wok. Add the carrots and stir-fry until just barely tender, 3 minutes. Add the cabbage and daikon to the wok and stir-fry until wilted, about 3 minutes. At any point, add a little soy sauce to encourage the vegetables to steam if they don't seem to be cooking.

8   Return the mushroom mixture and eggs to the wok and add the noodles. Add the mock oyster sauce and toss until the noodles are well coated and the mushrooms and vegetables are all mixed into the noodles.

9   Taste and add additional soy sauce, if needed. Serve hot.

Kitchen Note: *Pickled ginger can be substituted for fresh ginger in most stir-fries. Figure that 1 tablespoon minced pickled ginger is equivalent to a 1-inch piece of fresh ginger, peeled and minced.*

Pasta with Tomato-Braised Root Vegetables

Serves 4–6

It's very important to finely chop the vegetables — using a food processor makes it easy. The root vegetables add a richness and heartiness to the sauce that is quite surprising.

¼	cup extra-virgin olive oil
1	carrot or parsnip, peeled and finely chopped
1	celery root, peeled and finely chopped
1	onion, finely chopped
1	rutabaga, peeled and finely chopped
1½	cups vegetable broth (page 126) or water
1	cup medium-bodied red wine
1	(6-ounce) can tomato paste
1½	cups diced tomatoes with juice, or 1 (15-ounce) can
1	whole garlic head, cloves separated and peeled
2	bay leaves
1	tablespoon mixed dried Italian herbs
	Salt and freshly ground black pepper
1	pound rigatoni or other short pasta
1	cup freshly grated Parmesan cheese, plus more for serving

1   Heat the oil in a Dutch oven over medium-high heat. Add the carrot, celery root, onion, and rutabaga, and sauté until the vegetables are a little softened, about 5 minutes.

2   Add the broth, stirring to loosen any browned bits. Stir in the wine, tomato paste, tomatoes, garlic, bay leaves, and Italian herbs. Season with salt and pepper.

3   Cover and simmer, stirring occasionally, until the sauce is cooked down and the vegetables are completely soft, about 2 hours. Mash the garlic cloves into the sauce (if they don't mash easily, the sauce should cook longer).

4   Bring a large pot of salted water to a boil. Add the pasta and boil until al dente. Drain well.

5   Combine the pasta with the sauce and mix well. Stir in the Parmesan. Taste and adjust the seasonings. Serve hot, passing the extra cheese at the table.

 ## Variation: Polenta with Tomato-Braised Root Vegetables

Polenta is a wonderful alternative to pasta. Prepare the sauce, through step 3, as above. About an hour before you are ready to serve, bring 5 cups salted water to a boil in a large saucepan. Stir 1 cup stone-ground cornmeal into 1½ cups cold water to make a smooth paste. Pour into the boiling water, reduce the heat, and cook at a low boil, stirring frequently, for about 30 minutes, until the polenta begins to pull away from the sides of the pan. Reduce the heat to low and add 4 tablespoons butter and 1 cup Parmesan cheese, stirring until melted. Add ½ to 1 cup milk, a little at a time, until the polenta is a creamy, pleasing consistency. To serve, mound the polenta in each pasta bowl and spoon the sauce on top. Serve hot, passing the extra cheese at the table.

Cheesy Mac with Root Vegetables

Serves 6

I have always regarded macaroni and cheese as an opportunity to sneak vegetables into a one-dish favorite. It turns out that any vegetable that works well under a blanket of cheese, as in a gratin (think cauliflower gratin, rutabaga gratin, et cetera), complements macaroni and cheese. In this dish, any of the root vegetables you happen to have in the house will work well, though turnips and rutabagas are my personal favorites. If you have a pasta pot with a colander insert, you can easily cook the vegetables in the same boiling water as the macaroni.

1 pound elbow macaroni

4 cups peeled and diced mixed root vegetables (carrots, celery root, golden beets, parsnips, rutabagas, salsify, and/or turnips) or winter squashes

6 tablespoons butter

1 shallot, minced

2 garlic cloves, minced (optional)

6 tablespoons all-purpose unbleached flour

3 cups milk

2 cups lightly packed grated sharp cheddar cheese (8 ounces)

Salt and freshly ground black pepper

⅓ cup dried breadcrumbs

1   Preheat the oven to 350°F. Lightly butter a large casserole dish.

2   Bring two large pots of salted water to a boil. Add the macaroni to one pot and cook until al dente. Drain well. Transfer to the casserole dish.

3   In the second pot of boiling water, cook the vegetables until fork-tender, about 10 minutes; the vegetables should still hold their shape. Drain well. Transfer to the casserole dish.

4   To make the cheese sauce, melt the butter in a medium saucepan over medium heat. Add the shallot and garlic, if using, and sauté until limp, about 3 minutes. Stir in the flour to form a smooth paste. Stir in the milk and bring to a boil, stirring to prevent lumps. When the sauce thickens, add the cheese, stirring until melted. Remove from the heat and season with salt and pepper.

5   Stir the sauce into the macaroni and vegetables. Taste and adjust the seasonings. Sprinkle the breadcrumbs over the top.

6   Bake for about 30 minutes, until the sauce is bubbly and the breadcrumbs are browned. Serve hot.

Kitchen Note: *You can vary the vegetables as you please. A sliced leek or one-quarter of a yellow onion can replace the shallot. If you have only carrots on hand, you can simply grate a couple of them and add them to the cheese sauce with the milk. Or you can add 2 cups shredded root vegetables (any type) to the cheese sauce and add 2 cups frozen vegetables (any type) to the pasta, 1 to 3 minutes before the pasta will be done.*

Shredded Root-Vegetable Linguine

Serves 4

Shredded root vegetables cook very quickly, so the sauce for this pasta is made in the time it takes to heat the water. If you include golden beets in your root vegetable mix, the dish turns a lovely saffron color; with red beets, everything is dyed pink — startling but delicious nonetheless.

¼ cup extra-virgin olive oil

4 cups peeled and shredded mixed root vegetables (beets, carrots, celery root, parsnips, rutabagas, salsify, and/or turnips)

1 leek, trimmed and thinly sliced

4 garlic cloves, minced

1 cup vegetable broth or chicken broth (pages 126–27)

½ cup dry white wine

  Salt and freshly ground black pepper

1 pound linguine

4 tablespoons butter, diced

1 Begin heating a large pot of salted water to a boil for the linguine.

2 Meanwhile, heat the oil in a large Dutch oven over medium heat. Add the root vegetables, leek, and garlic, and sauté until the vegetables are limp, about 8 minutes. Add the broth and wine. Bring to a boil, then reduce the heat and simmer until the vegetables are tender, about 5 minutes. Reduce the heat to keep warm and season with salt and pepper.

3 Cook the linguine in the boiling water until al dente. Reserve about 1 cup of the cooking water, and then drain.

4 Toss the linguine with the butter until well coated and transfer to a serving dish. Add the vegetable mixture and toss to combine, adding some of the reserved cooking water if the mixture appears dry. Serve at once.

Variation: Root Vegetable Scampi over Linguine

Add 1 pound peeled and deveined shrimp with the broth and wine in step 2.

Fettuccine with Caramelized Cabbage, White Beans, and Goat Cheese

Serves 6

A medley of intriguing flavors blend in this quickly made one-dish vegetarian meal. The goat cheese melts and makes a simple but exquisite sauce.

2 tablespoons extra-virgin olive oil
1 small head green or savoy cabbage, thinly sliced (6–8 cups)
1 onion, thinly sliced
1½ cups cooked white beans, or 1 (15-ounce) can, rinsed and drained
⅓ cup dry white wine
1 teaspoon dried sage or thyme
  Salt and freshly ground black pepper
1 pound fettuccine or pappardelle noodles
2 garlic cloves, minced
8 ounces soft fresh goat cheese (chèvre), crumbled

1   Begin heating a large pot of salted water to a boil for the pasta.

2   Heat the oil in a large saucepan over medium heat. Add the cabbage and onion and sauté until the cabbage is completely wilted and the onion is golden, about 25 minutes. Stir in the white beans and wine. Add the sage and season with salt and pepper.

3   Cook the pasta in the boiling water until just al dente. Reserve about 1 cup of the cooking water, and then drain.

4   Return the pasta to the pot. Add the garlic and goat cheese. Pour in half the reserved cooking water and toss to form a creamy sauce. Add more cooking water if the mixture seems dry. Add the cabbage mixture and toss to mix. Season generously with salt and pepper. Serve at once.

Pasta with Kale and Chickpeas

Serves 6

In no time at all you can have dinner on the table — a hearty one-dish vegetarian pasta meal. This dish is outstanding in flavor, nutrition, and ease of preparation. Other greens and other beans can be substituted for the ones recommended here.

1	pound orecchiette or medium shells
3	tablespoons extra-virgin olive oil
4	garlic cloves, minced
1	shallot, minced
8	ounces kale, cut into thin ribbons (about 6 cups lightly packed; remove and discard tough stems)
1	tablespoon dry white wine
	Salt and freshly ground black pepper
1	pound ricotta cheese
½	cup freshly grated Parmesan cheese
1½	cups cooked chickpeas, or 1 (15-ounce) can, rinsed and drained

1   Bring a large pot of salted water to a boil. Cook the pasta in the boiling water until just al dente. Reserve about ½ cup of the cooking water, and then drain. Return the pasta to the pot and keep warm.

2   Heat the oil in a large skillet over medium heat. Add the garlic, shallot, and kale, and sauté until the kale is completely wilted, about 3 minutes. Stir in the wine, cover, and steam until the kale is tender, about 3 minutes. Season with salt and pepper.

3   Add the ricotta and Parmesan to the pasta in the pot. Pour in half the reserved cooking water and toss to form a creamy sauce. Add more water if the mixture seems dry. Add the chickpeas and the kale mixture and toss to combine. Season generously with salt and pepper. Serve at once.

Kale-Ricotta Cannelloni

Serves 4 or 5

When it comes to baked filled pasta, I don't think I will ever bother with dried manicotti or shells again. Using egg roll wrappers (of all things!) is so much easier than using dried pasta, which must be cooked before it is filled, is hard to handle, and loses its shape. Egg roll wrappers are made simply of flour, water, and eggs, just as fresh pasta is, and they make the assembly easy and the presentation lovely.

6 cups chopped kale (remove and discard tough stems)	⅛ teaspoon ground nutmeg
	Salt and pepper
3 garlic cloves	10 egg roll wrappers (each 6 inches square)
1 shallot	
1 (15-ounce) container part-skim ricotta cheese	2 cups grated mozzarella cheese
	3 cups well-seasoned tomato sauce, or 2 (15-ounce) cans
½ cup freshly grated Parmesan cheese	
2 eggs	

1 Bring a large pot of salted water to a boil. Add the kale and blanch until wilted and bright green, about 3 minutes. Drain and plunge into a bowl of ice water to stop the cooking. Drain again, squeezing out the excess liquid.

2 Preheat the oven to 425°F. Lightly oil a large roasting pan or casserole (if necessary, use one 9- by 13-inch pan and one 9-inch square pan).

3 To make the filling, finely chop the garlic and shallot in a food processor. Add the kale, ricotta, Parmesan, eggs, and nutmeg, and season with salt and pepper. Pulse until very finely chopped.

4 To assemble the dish, mound a scant ½ cup of the filling evenly along one side of each egg roll wrapper. Roll each wrapper to enclose the filling. Set the rolled cannelloni, seam down and slightly apart, in the prepared roasting pan. Cover the cannelloni with the mozzarella cheese. Spoon the sauce over and around the cannelloni.

5 Bake, uncovered, for 20 to 25 minutes, until the sauce bubbles, the cannelloni are hot in the center, and the wrappers are tender. Serve hot.

Kitchen Note: *Obviously, if you can find sheets of fresh pasta, use those instead of egg roll wrappers. Fresh pasta is sometimes found in the refrigerated case of Italian delis and specialty food stores.*

🌿 Tortellini with Kale

Serves 4

Fresh tortellini can be found refrigerated in most supermarkets. It is a good product to have on hand for quick suppers, like this one.

1½   pounds kale, cut into ribbons (about 18 cups lightly packed; remove and discard tough stems)

1   (20-ounce) package fresh cheese-filled tortellini

2   tablespoons butter

2   tablespoons extra-virgin olive oil

2   garlic cloves, minced

1   shallot, minced

    Pinch of crushed red pepper flakes

2   tablespoons balsamic vinegar, or more to taste

1   cup freshly grated Parmesan cheese, plus more for serving

---

1   Bring a large pot of salted water to a boil. Add the kale and boil just until tender, about 3 minutes. Remove from the pot with tongs or a slotted spoon and drain in a colander.

2   Bring the water back to a boil. Add the tortellini to the boiling water and boil gently until the tortellini are cooked through and rise to the surface, about 8 minutes, or according to the package directions. Reserve ½ cup of the pasta cooking water. Drain the tortellini over the kale in the colander.

3   Melt the butter in the oil in the pasta pot. Add the garlic, shallot, and red pepper flakes, and sauté until fragrant, about 1 minute. Add the pasta, kale, and vinegar, and sauté until heated through, about 3 minutes longer.

4   Pour the pasta mixture into a large serving bowl or platter. Sprinkle with half the Parmesan and toss. Taste and add more vinegar if desired. Sprinkle the remaining Parmesan on top and serve.

Kitchen Note: *I don't recommend substituting dried tortellini for fresh; the filling is quite inferior.*

Vegetable Couscous

Serves 4–6

Slow-simmered vegetables scented with cumin and cinnamon atop a mound of couscous: this dish is guaranteed to provoke wanderlust. If you have access to fresh herbs, mint or cilantro will bring all the flavors together in a most harmonious manner.

2 tablespoons extra-virgin olive oil	1½ cups cooked chickpeas, or 1 (15-ounce) can, rinsed and drained
1 large onion, diced	
½ small head green or savoy cabbage, thinly sliced	4 garlic cloves, minced
2 carrots, peeled and thinly sliced	1½ teaspoons ground cumin
1 small rutabaga or medium turnip, peeled and diced	½ teaspoon ground cinnamon
	Salt and freshly ground black pepper
1 quart peeled whole or diced tomatoes with juice, or 1 (28-ounce) can	1½ cups couscous
	3 cups boiling water
¼ cup tomato paste	3 tablespoons chopped fresh mint or cilantro or both (optional)
1½ cups water	

1   Heat the oil in a large saucepan over medium-high heat. Add the onion, cabbage, carrots, and rutabaga, and sauté until the vegetables are slightly tender, about 5 minutes. Add the tomatoes, tomato paste, water, chickpeas, garlic, cumin, and cinnamon. Simmer until the vegetables are meltingly tender, about 1 hour. Season with salt and pepper. Let simmer while you prepare the couscous.

2   Pour the boiling water over the couscous in a large bowl. Cover and let steam for about 10 minutes, until all the liquid is absorbed. Fluff with a fork.

3   Stir the fresh herbs into the vegetables, if using. Taste and adjust the seasoning.

4   To serve, mound the couscous onto a large platter or into individual serving bowls. With a spoon, make a depression in the center of the mound. Spoon the vegetable mixture on top. Serve hot.

White Lasagna with Leeks and Butternut Squash

Serves 6–9

Lasagna is a festive dish, and everyone loves it. Make yours special with a white sauce and roasted vegetables. It is a perfect make-ahead dish for a big gathering.

LASAGNA

- 1 butternut squash (about 1½ pounds), peeled and cut into ⅓-inch cubes
- 2 leeks, trimmed and thinly sliced
- 3 tablespoons extra-virgin olive oil
  Salt and freshly ground black pepper
- 12 no-boil lasagna noodles or 1 pound fresh pasta sheets
- 2 cups freshly grated Parmesan cheese

BÉCHAMEL SAUCE

- 6 tablespoons butter
- 3 garlic cloves, minced
- 6 tablespoons all-purpose flour
- 3¾ cups milk
- ½ cup dry white wine
- 1 teaspoon dried sage
  Salt and freshly ground black pepper

Winter squashes are the forgotten vegetables. Almost no vegetable is as easy to grow or keep. With fertile soil, full sun and ample water, vines take off. And after plants become established, they're so carefree, it's easy to forget them until fall when their rediscovery makes the harvest that much sweeter.

— Andy Tomolonis

1 Preheat the oven to 425°F. Lightly oil a half sheet pan (preferred) or a large shallow roasting pan.

2 Mound the squash and leeks on the sheet pan. Drizzle the oil over them, sprinkle with salt and pepper, and toss gently to coat. Arrange in a shallow (preferably single) layer.

3 Roast the vegetables for 25 to 35 minutes, stirring or shaking the pan occasionally for even cooking, until lightly browned and tender.

4 Meanwhile, make the sauce. Melt the butter in a saucepan over medium heat. Add the garlic and sauté until fragrant, about 2 minutes. Whisk in the flour to make a smooth paste. Cook, whisking constantly, for 1 minute. Add the milk and whisk until smooth. Bring to a slow boil and stir in the wine and sage. Season with salt and pepper. Remove from the heat.

5 When the vegetables are done, remove from the oven and reduce the oven temperature to 350°F.

6 To assemble the lasagna, spread about ½ cup of the béchamel in a 9- by 13-inch baking dish. Arrange three of the lasagna noodles on top. Pour about ½ cup of the sauce evenly over the noodles. Spread about one-third of the roasted vegetables evenly over the sauce. Sprinkle about one-quarter of the Parmesan on top. Repeat the layers two more times. Top with the remaining three lasagna noodles. Spread the remaining sauce on top and sprinkle with the remaining Parmesan. Cover with foil.

7 Bake the lasagna for 30 minutes. Remove the foil and bake for 10 to 15 minutes longer, until hot and bubbly.

8 Let the lasagna stand for 5 minutes before cutting into serving pieces. Serve hot or warm.

Caramelized Cabbage and Onion Tart

Serves 6

This simple tart is elegant and rustic at the same time. Because it is best at room temperature, it makes a perfect offering for a potluck or a buffet.

2	tablespoons extra-virgin olive oil
½	head green or savoy cabbage, thinly sliced
1	onion, thinly sliced
1	teaspoon dried thyme
	Salt and freshly ground black pepper
1	cup lightly packed grated cheddar cheese (4 ounces)
1	(9-inch) prebaked single-crust pie shell (page 265)
2	eggs
1	cup milk

1 Heat the oil in a large saucepan over medium heat. Add the cabbage and onion and sauté until the cabbage is completely wilted and the onion is golden, about 25 minutes. Add the thyme and season with salt and pepper.

2 Preheat the oven to 375°F.

3 Sprinkle half the cheese into the pie shell. Arrange a layer of the vegetables on top of the cheese.

4 Beat the eggs and milk together and pour over the vegetables. Sprinkle the remaining cheese on top.

5 Bake for 30 to 35 minutes, until puffed and browned. Let stand to set for at least 10 minutes. Serve warm or at room temperature.

Winter-Vegetable Pie

Serves 4–6

My earliest explorations into vegetarian cooking were guided by Anna Thomas's *Vegetarian Epicure*, first published in 1972. The book contained a recipe for "Russian Vegetable Pie," which was the inspiration for this recipe.

3 tablespoons extra-virgin olive oil
3 cups thinly sliced green or savoy cabbage
1 onion, thinly sliced
1 carrot, peeled and shredded
1 teaspoon dried dill
   Salt and freshly ground black pepper
   Pastry for a 9-inch double-crust pie (page 265)
1 cooked beet, thinly sliced
6 ounces soft fresh goat cheese (chèvre), at room temperature

1 Heat the oil in a large saucepan over medium heat. Add the cabbage and onion and sauté until the cabbage is completely wilted and the onion is golden, about 25 minutes. Stir in the shredded carrot. Add the dill and season with salt and pepper.

2 Preheat the oven to 400°F.

3 Fit the bottom crust into a 10-inch pie pan. Arrange the beet slices over the crust in concentric circles. Crumble half the goat cheese over the beets. Spoon in the cabbage mixture and top with the remaining goat cheese. Fit the top crust over the pie and fold together the overhanging dough. Crimp the edges with a fork to seal and prick several holes in the top.

4 Bake for 15 minutes, then decrease the oven temperature to 350°F and bake for 30 to 35 minutes longer, until browned. Let stand for at least 10 minutes. Serve warm or at room temperature.

Kitchen Notes: *If you are madly in love with goat cheese, you can increase the quantity to 8 ounces. The beets can be omitted, if desired.*

Kale-Feta Pie

Serves 6

What do you get when you make spanakopita with kale instead of spinach? A delicious pie! A topping of sesame seeds makes it particularly attractive.

6 cups chopped kale (remove and discard tough stems)	3 eggs
1 onion, peeled and quartered	Salt and freshly ground black pepper
2 garlic cloves	½ cup (1 stick) butter, melted
3 tablespoons all-purpose flour	1 (1-pound) package phyllo dough, thawed
1 pound cottage cheese	2 tablespoons sesame seeds
8 ounces feta cheese, crumbled	

1 Bring a large pot of salted water to a boil. Add the kale and blanch until wilted and bright green, about 3 minutes. Drain and plunge into a bowl of ice water to stop the cooking. Drain again, squeezing out the excess liquid.

2 Preheat the oven to 375°F.

3 Combine the onion and garlic in a food processor and process until finely chopped. Add the kale and process until finely chopped. Add the flour, cottage cheese, feta, and eggs, and season with salt and pepper. Process until well mixed.

4 With a pastry brush, spread some of the melted butter along the bottom and sides of a 9- by 13-inch baking dish. Place a sheet of phyllo in the pan, allowing the excess to hang over the edges. Brush with butter. Layer four more sheets of phyllo on top, brushing each piece with butter. Cover with half the kale filling. Cover with five more sheets of phyllo, brushing each sheet with melted butter. Cover with the remaining filling. Fold any overhanging phyllo over the filling. Cover the top with the remaining sheets of phyllo, brushing each with melted butter. Sprinkle the sesame seeds over the top. With a sharp serrated knife, slice through the pastry to make six or twelve equal squares.

5 Bake for about 45 minutes, until the pastry is golden. Serve hot or warm.

Kitchen Note: *Slicing through the sheets of phyllo before the pie is baked makes it possible to serve the dish in tidy squares.*

 Kale Pizza

Serves 4

Take a regular cheese pizza and add a layer of yummy, nutrient-rich kale, and this is what results.

½ recipe Basic Pizza Dough (page 264)
2 tablespoons extra-virgin olive oil, plus more for brushing
2 cups sliced kale (remove and discard tough stems)
   Salt and freshly ground black pepper
1 cup well-seasoned tomato sauce
2 garlic cloves, minced
2 cups grated mozzarella cheese (8 ounces)
½ cup freshly grated Parmesan cheese

1 Prepare the pizza dough and set aside in a warm, draft-free place to rise until doubled in bulk, about 1 hour.

2 Preheat the oven to 500°F.

3 Heat the oil in a large skillet over medium-high heat. Add the kale, season with salt and pepper, and sauté until limp, about 3 minutes. Cover and let steam until just barely tender, 1 to 2 minutes; do not overcook. Set aside.

4 Lightly oil a 10-inch or 12-inch round pizza pan or a 12- by 15-inch baking sheet. Stretch the dough to fit the pan. Brush the dough with a little oil and spread the tomato sauce over it. Distribute the kale over the sauce. Sprinkle with the garlic, the mozzarella, and the Parmesan, in that order.

5 Bake the pizza on the bottom shelf of the oven for about 12 minutes, until the cheese is melted and the crust is golden brown. Slice and serve warm.

Kitchen Notes: *The recipe is easily doubled. Who doesn't enjoy a slice of cold (or reheated) pizza on the second day? If you happen to have a pizza stone, by all means use it. Bake the pizza on the preheated stone instead of on the oiled pan.*

Frizzled-Kale Pizza

Serves 4

For this pizza the kale is roasted, which gives it a crunchy texture. It is both surprising and wonderful on pizza.

½ recipe Basic Pizza Dough (page 264)
2 tablespoons extra-virgin olive oil, plus more for brushing
4 cups sliced kale (remove and discard tough stems)
   Salt and freshly ground black pepper
1 cup well-seasoned tomato sauce
2 cups grated mozzarella cheese (8 ounces)
½ cup freshly grated Parmesan cheese

1 Prepare the pizza dough and set aside in a warm, draft-free place to rise until doubled in bulk, about 1 hour.

2 Preheat the oven to 425°F.

3 Drizzle the oil over the kale in a large bowl. Mix with your hands until the kale is well coated. Spread in a single layer on a large baking sheet. Roast until the kale is browned and crisp, about 10 minutes. Remove from the oven and season with salt. Increase the oven temperature to 500°F.

4 Lightly oil a 10-inch or 12-inch round pizza pan or a 12- by 15-inch baking sheet. Stretch the dough to fit the pan. Brush the dough with a little oil and spread the tomato sauce over it. Distribute the mozzarella and Parmesan evenly over the pizza.

5 Bake the pizza on the bottom shelf of the oven for about 5 minutes, until the cheese is melted and the crust is beginning to color. Sprinkle the roasted kale over the pizza, return to the oven, and bake for 5 minutes longer, until the crust is firm and golden brown. Slice and serve warm.

Kitchen Notes: *The recipe is easily doubled, but the kale will have to be made in two batches. Also, the crisp kale will lose its frizzle if covered and refrigerated, so leftovers are not particularly appealing.*

Leek and Goat Cheese Pizza

Serves 4

This "white" pizza has spectacular flavor from the combination of leeks and goat cheese and a sprinkling of sun-dried tomato.

½   recipe Basic Pizza Dough (page 264)
2   tablespoons extra-virgin olive oil, plus more for brushing
3   leeks, trimmed and thinly sliced
2   garlic cloves, minced
    Salt and freshly ground black pepper
1   tablespoon finely chopped sun-dried tomatoes
6   ounces soft fresh goat cheese (chèvre), crumbled

1   Prepare the pizza dough and set aside in a warm, draft-free place to rise until doubled in bulk, about 1 hour.

2   Preheat the oven to 500°F.

3   Heat the oil in a large skillet over medium-high heat. Add the leeks and garlic and sauté until tender, about 5 minutes. Set aside.

4   Lightly oil a 10-inch or 12-inch round pizza pan or a 12- by 15-inch baking sheet. Stretch the dough to fit the pan. Brush the dough with a little oil. Scatter the leek mixture over the pizza dough. Sprinkle with sun-dried tomatoes and then the goat cheese.

5   Bake the pizza on the bottom shelf of the oven for about 12 minutes, until the crust is golden brown. Slice and serve warm.

Kitchen Notes: *This recipe is easily doubled. Feta cheese or ricotta salata can replace the goat cheese, if you prefer. If you happen to have a pizza stone, by all means use it. Bake the pizza on the preheated stone instead of on the oiled pan.*

Apple, Leek, and Cheddar Quiche

Serves 4–6

This is a delicious quiche, good for brunch, lunch, or supper. It is fantastic when made with a smoked cheddar.

> **Pastry for a 9-inch or 10-inch
>   single-crust pie (page 265)**
> 3 **tablespoons butter**
> 1 **large leek, trimmed and thinly sliced**
> 1 **large apple, peeled, cored, and chopped**
> 2 **tablespoons all-purpose flour**
> ½ **teaspoon dried thyme**
> 1 **cup firmly packed grated smoked cheddar
>   or sharp cheddar cheese (4 ounces)**
> 3 **eggs**
>   **Milk or cream**
>   **Salt and freshly ground black pepper**

1 Preheat the oven to 375°F.

2 Roll out and fit the pastry into a 9- or 10-inch pie pan. Fold the overhang under and flute the edges of the dough.

3 Melt the butter in a large skillet over medium heat. Add the leek and sauté until limp, about 3 minutes. Add the apple and sauté until the leeks are tender, about 3 minutes. Stir in the flour and thyme.

4 Sprinkle ½ cup of the cheese into the pie shell. Layer the leek mixture on top of the cheese. Cover with the remaining cheese.

5 Beat the eggs in a glass measuring cup. Add enough milk to make 1½ cups. Season with salt and pepper. Pour over the pie filling.

6 Bake for 30 to 35 minutes, until puffed and browned. Let stand for at least 10 minutes. Serve warm or at room temperature.

African Sweet-Potato Stew

Serves 6

Peanuts, which originated in South America, were introduced to sub-Saharan Africa by Spanish or Portuguese traders in the 1500s. Peanuts and peanut butter are used widely as flavorings in African soups and stews. Sweet potatoes, peanuts, and chickpeas provide tremendous flavor and nutrition in this all-vegetable stew.

2	tablespoons extra-virgin olive oil
1	onion, diced
4	garlic cloves, minced
1	(1-inch) piece fresh ginger, peeled and minced
1	teaspoon cumin seeds
½	teaspoon crushed red pepper flakes
3	cups water
2	large sweet potatoes, peeled and diced
4–6	cups chopped collard greens (remove and discard tough stems)
1½	cups cooked chickpeas, or 1 (15-ounce) can, rinsed and drained
1½	cups diced tomatoes with juice, or 1 (15-ounce) can
1	cup roasted peanuts
3	tablespoons natural (unsweetened) peanut butter, chunky or smooth
	Salt and freshly ground black pepper
	Hot cooked rice, for serving
	Hot sauce, for serving

1   Heat the oil in a large saucepan over medium-high heat. Add the onion, garlic, ginger, cumin, and red pepper flakes, and sauté until the onion is softened, about 3 minutes.

2   Add the water, sweet potatoes, collards, chickpeas, tomatoes, and peanuts. Bring to a boil, then reduce the heat and simmer, covered, until the sweet potatoes are tender, 15 to 20 minutes.

3   Stir in the peanut butter. Season with salt and pepper and serve over rice, passing hot sauce at the table.

Kitchen Note: *Since you will season the stew to taste with salt and pepper at the end of cooking, it doesn't matter whether the peanuts have been salted or not.*

Basic Pizza Dough

Makes two 10- to 12-inch round or two 12- by 15-inch rectangular pizza crusts

3¾–4 cups all-purpose unbleached flour
1 tablespoon salt
1½ cups warm (110°–115°F) water
1 (¼-ounce) packet, or 2¼ teaspoons active dry yeast
3 tablespoons extra-virgin olive oil, plus more for greasing

1 In a food processor fitted with a dough hook or in a large bowl, combine 3¾ cups of the flour and the salt. Measure the warm water into a glass measuring cup, add the yeast, and stir until foamy. Stir in the 3 tablespoons oil.

2 With the motor running, pour the water mixture into the food processor and process until the dough forms into a ball. Continue processing for 1 minute to knead the dough. Alternatively, add the yeast mixture to the dough and stir until the dough comes together in a ball. Transfer to a lightly floured surface and knead until the dough is springy and elastic, about 5 minutes. The dough should be firm and just slightly sticky, not dry.

3 Grease a bowl with oil and place the dough ball in the bowl, turning the dough to coat it with the oil. Cover and let rise in a warm, draft-free place until doubled in bulk, about 1 hour.

4 Divide the dough into two balls. Brush two baking sheets or pizza pans with oil. Stretch the dough to fit each pan. The dough is now ready for topping with sauce and vegetables.

🌰 Basic Pie Pastry

Makes one double or two single 9-inch or 10-inch piecrusts

> 2 cups all-purpose unbleached flour
> 1 teaspoon salt
> 2/3 cup butter or vegetable shortening
> 6-7 tablespoons cold water

▶ Stir together the flour and salt. Cut the butter into the flour with a pastry blender or two knives until the mixture resembles coarse crumbs. Sprinkle the water over the flour mixture and stir together. Press the mixture into two disks, wrap each in plastic wrap, and refrigerate for 30 minutes.

TO MAKE A SINGLE-CRUST PIE: On a lightly floured surface, roll out one ball of dough, working from the center out in all directions until you have a 12-inch round. Fold the dough in half and ease into the pie pan, with the fold in the center. Unfold the dough and trim it to overhang the edge of the pie pan by about 1 inch. Fill the pie shell as directed in the recipe.

TO MAKE A DOUBLE-CRUST PIE: Roll out one ball of dough as directed for the single-crust pie. Roll out the remaining piece of dough in the same manner, but make it into a slightly larger circle. Fold the dough in half, place on top of the filling, and unfold. Trim the dough to 1 inch beyond the edge of the pie pan. Fold the extra pastry under the bottom crust. Crimp the edges. Prick holes in the top in several places to allow steam to escape. Bake as directed.

TO MAKE A PREBAKED SINGLE-CRUST PIE SHELL: Preheat the oven to 450°F. Roll out one ball of dough as directed for the single-crust pie, and set it in the pie pan as directed. Trim and crimp the edges. Prick the dough with a fork, covering the surface with tiny holes. Bake for 10 to 15 minutes, until golden. Cool on a wire rack. Fill the pie shell as directed in the recipe.

7

Main Dishes with Fish and Seafood

When thinking about the somewhat limited vegetable-seafood combinations of winter, it helps to think of coastal communities that endure harsh winters, such as the maritime provinces of Canada and the New England coast. Cooks from these regions made a virtue of creamy mixtures of seafood and potatoes, both simmered in chowders and baked in pies. I restricted myself to just two recipes in this tradition (Creamy Fish Pie, on page 276, and Clam Pot Pie, on page 282), but the possibilities are endless.

My favorite recipe in this chapter is Seafood Boil (page 280), a traditional Southern recipe that combines finfish, shellfish, potatoes, carrots, and celery and is meant to be eaten casually. It is hardly a stretch to replace the celery with celery root — and incredibly delicious. The same Lemon Aïoli (page 181) that tastes sublime with roasted vegetables is also perfect with fish, so it makes sense to roast salmon alongside roasted vegetables — another favorite recipe.

The recipes gathered here are mostly very quick to make and offer delicious, easy one-dish meals.

RECIPE LIST FOR
MAIN DISHES WITH FISH AND SEAFOOD

Oven-Roasted Salmon and Vegetables
  with Lemon Aioli

Mustard-Molasses Roasted Salmon and
  Vegetables

Saffron Fish Stew

Pan-Seared Tuna with Potatoes and
  Anchovy-Shallot Vinaigrette

Winter Fish Tacos

Thai Coconut Curry with Shrimp

Creamy Fish Pie

Mediterranean Fish on a Bed of Rice and
  Leeks

Shrimp and Kale Sauté

Seafood Boil

Moules Marinière with Leeks

Clam Pot Pie

Shrimp Egg Rolls

Thai Sweet-Chili Shrimp Rolls

Salsify Scampi on Linguine

Vegetarian dishes are marked with this symbol:

Oven-Roasted Salmon and Vegetables with Lemon Aioli

Serves 4

Poseidon meets Persephone in this delightful combination, and the lemon aioli brings it all together harmoniously.

- 6 cups peeled and diced mixed root vegetables (beets, carrots, celery root, parsnips, rutabagas, salsify, and/or turnips), white or sweet potatoes, and/or winter squashes
- 4 shallots, halved if large
- 2 tablespoons extra-virgin olive oil
  Salt and freshly ground black pepper
- 4 (1-inch-thick) salmon steaks
- 1 lemon, cut into large wedges
  Lemon Aioli (page 181)
- 1 teaspoon dried dill

1 Preheat the oven to 450°F. Lightly oil a half sheet pan (preferred) or large shallow roasting pan.

2 Mound the diced vegetables and shallots on the prepared pan. Drizzle the oil over them, sprinkle with salt and pepper, and toss gently to coat. Spread in a single layer in the pan.

3 Roast for 20 to 25 minutes, stirring or shaking the pan occasionally for even cooking, until the vegetables are lightly browned and tender.

4 Push the vegetables to the side of the pan to make room for the salmon. Arrange the salmon in a single layer in the pan. Roast for 10 to 12 minutes longer, until the salmon is just cooked through.

5 Arrange the fish, vegetables, and lemon wedges on serving plates. Top the fish with a dollop of aioli. Sprinkle the dill over the fish and vegetables. Pass additional aioli on the side.

Kitchen Note: *Aioli is a homemade mayonnaise made bright with flavor by the addition of garlic. Homemade mayonnaise is made with raw eggs. If you wish to avoid the raw eggs, combine 1 cup mayonnaise with 6 to 8 finely minced garlic cloves, the finely grated zest and juice of 1 lemon, and 1 tablespoon extra-virgin olive oil. Add salt and white pepper to taste and let sit for about 30 minutes to allow the flavors to develop.*

Mustard-Molasses Roasted Salmon and Vegetables

Serves 4

The haunting combination of mustard and molasses is perfect for both sweet root vegetables and full-flavored fish, such as salmon.

VEGETABLES AND SALMON

6 cups peeled and diced mixed root vegetables (beets, carrots, celery root, parsnips rutabagas, salsify, and/or turnips), white or sweet potatoes, and/or winter squashes

2 tablespoons extra-virgin olive oil

Salt and freshly ground black pepper

4 (1-inch-thick) salmon steaks

MUSTARD-MOLASSES SAUCE

⅓ cup Dijon mustard

⅓ cup dark molasses

2 tablespoons dry sherry or marsala wine

2 garlic cloves, minced

1 Preheat the oven to 450°F. Lightly oil a half sheet pan (preferred) or large shallow roasting pan.

2 Mound the vegetables on the sheet pan. Drizzle the oil over them, sprinkle with salt and pepper, and toss gently to coat. Spread in a single layer in the pan.

3 Roast for 20 to 25 minutes, stirring or shaking the pan occasionally for even cooking, until the vegetables are lightly browned and tender.

4 Meanwhile, prepare the sauce. Combine the mustard, molasses, sherry, and garlic in a small bowl. Mix well.

5 Drizzle half the sauce over the vegetables and toss to coat. Push the vegetables to the side of the pan to make room for the salmon. Brush each salmon steak with the sauce and arrange in a single layer on the pan. Roast for 10 to 12 minutes, until the salmon is just cooked through and the vegetables are glazed.

6 Arrange the fish and vegetables on serving plates. Top each fish steak with a dollop of the remaining sauce. Pass additional sauce on the side.

Saffron Fish Stew

Serves 4

Is it a chowder or a stew? You could call it either, but with the big chunks of fish, it is definitely a filling dish. The milk gives it a creamy consistency, while cream makes it richer; both are optional if you prefer to go dairy-free. Serve with a fresh, crusty bread for dipping.

3	cups chicken broth or neutral-tasting vegetable broth (pages 126–27)
½	cup dry white wine
¼	teaspoon saffron threads
2	tablespoons sunflower or canola oil or butter
2	leeks, trimmed and sliced
1½	pounds thin-skinned potatoes, peeled and diced
2	carrots, peeled and diced
½	cup milk or cream (optional)
1½	pounds thick white-fleshed fish fillets, such as Pacific cod, cut into chunks
	Salt and freshly ground black pepper

1 Combine the broth, wine, and saffron in a small saucepan. Bring to a boil, then let simmer while you prepare the vegetables.

2 Heat the oil in a large saucepan over medium-high heat. Add the leeks and sauté until limp, about 3 minutes. Add the potatoes, carrots, and broth. Bring to a boil, then reduce the heat and simmer until the potatoes and carrots are completely tender, about 40 minutes.

3 Stir in the milk, if using, breaking up some of the potatoes with the spoon to thicken the liquid. Add the fish, cover, and let cook until tender, about 10 minutes. Stir the stew, breaking the fish into bite-size bites. Season with salt and pepper. Serve hot.

Pan-Seared Tuna with Potatoes and Anchovy-Shallot Vinaigrette

Serves 4

Any meaty fish would work in this delicious and quickly made dish, including salmon and swordfish. Add a salad and dinner is made.

VINAIGRETTE

½ cup chicken broth or neutral-tasting vegetable broth (pages 126–27)

3 anchovy fillets

2 shallots, chopped

2 garlic cloves, chopped

¼ cup red wine vinegar

¼ cup extra-virgin olive oil, plus more for frying

Salt and freshly ground black pepper

TUNA AND POTATOES

2 pounds thin-skinned potatoes, sliced (halved first if large; peeling is not necessary)

2 tablespoons extra-virgin olive oil

4 (1-inch-thick) tuna steaks

4 teaspoons capers and/or ¼ cup caperberries, for garnish

1   To make the vinaigrette, combine the broth, anchovies, shallots, garlic, and vinegar in a blender. Blend until almost smooth. With the motor running, slowly drizzle in the oil and blend until fully incorporated. Season with salt and pepper and set aside.

2   Cover the potatoes by 1 inch with cold salted water in a large saucepan. Bring to a simmer over medium-high heat and simmer until the potatoes are tender, about 10 minutes; do not overcook. Drain well.

3   Heat the oil in a large skillet over medium-high heat. Add the tuna and sear on both sides, 1 to 2 minutes per side, depending on how rare you like your tuna. Remove the tuna from the pan and keep warm.

4   Add the vinaigrette to the skillet and bring to a boil, stirring to scrape up any browned bits. Add the potatoes to the skillet and gently toss to coat.

5   Spoon the potatoes with the vinaigrette onto serving plates and top with the tuna. Spoon a little vinaigrette over the tuna and garnish with capers and/or caperberries. Serve at once.

Kitchen Note: *Don't overcook tuna! It is best when seared on the outside and still pink on the inside, like a rare steak.*

Winter Fish Tacos

Serves 6

Pickled red onions and thinly sliced cabbage are the traditional vegetable garnishes for fish tacos. In winter, I cook the fish in a skillet rather than on the grill, a concession to the season. In summer, I would probably add cilantro to the marinade and sour cream sauce, but the dish is just fine without it. Fresh corn tortillas are the preferred wrap, but flour wrappers do fine, especially where fresh corn tortillas aren't available.

PICKLED RED ONION

- 1 small red onion, halved lengthwise and thinly sliced
- ½ cup rice vinegar
  Juice of 1 lime
- 2 teaspoons sugar
- 1 teaspoon salt
  Dash of hot pepper sauce

SOUR CREAM SAUCE

- 1 cup sour cream
- ½ cup mayonnaise
- 2 tablespoons lime juice
- 1 teaspoon (packed) finely grated lime zest
  Pinch of salt
  Dash of hot sauce

FISH AND MARINADE

- 3 tablespoons extra-virgin olive oil
- 2 tablespoons lime juice
- 1½ pounds mahimahi or other white fish fillet

TORTILLAS AND GARNISHES

- 18 small flour or corn tortillas
- 2 cups shredded green or savoy cabbage
  Salsa

1 To make the pickled onion, combine all the ingredients in a small nonreactive saucepan and bring to a boil. Remove from the heat, transfer to a serving bowl, and let cool.

2 To prepare the fish, combine the oil and lime juice in a large, shallow glass baking dish. Add the fish and turn to coat. Set aside and let marinate for 15 minutes.

3 To prepare the sauce, combine all the ingredients in a small bowl and stir until well combined. Set aside.

4 Preheat a large skillet over medium-high heat. Transfer the fish from the marinade to the hot pan, skin-side down. Cook the fish for 4 minutes on the first side, flip, and drizzle with the marinade. Cook on the second side for 3 to 5 minutes, depending on the thickness of the fish. Let rest for a few minutes, then flake the fish with a fork.

5 To warm the tortillas, stack them between damp paper towels and microwave for about 60 seconds.

6 Serve the warm tortillas, fish, pickled onions, sour cream sauce, cabbage, and salsa in separate bowls and allow the diners to assemble their own tacos.

Thai Coconut Curry with Shrimp

Serves 4

In Thai restaurants, you'll find this dish made with summer vegetables — zucchini, green beans, snow peas, cherry tomatoes — but the surprising thing is how well root vegetables pair with the coconut curry sauce. Rutabagas are particularly recommended.

4 cups peeled and diced mixed root vegetables (carrots, celery root, golden beets, parsnips, rutabagas, salsify, and/or turnips) or winter squashes

1 tablespoon sunflower or canola oil

1 (1-inch) piece fresh ginger, peeled and minced

4 garlic cloves, minced

2 teaspoons Thai green curry paste

1 (11-ounce) can coconut milk

½ cup chicken broth or vegetable broth (pages 126–27)

1 stalk lemongrass, smashed with a knife

2 tablespoons lime juice

2 tablespoons Asian fish sauce

Cayenne pepper

1 pound shrimp, peeled and deveined

1 (15-ounce) can baby corn, drained

2 tablespoons chopped fresh cilantro (optional)

1 tablespoon torn fresh basil leaves (optional)

Hot cooked rice, for serving

1 lime, cut into wedges, for serving

1 Cover the vegetables with generously salted water in a medium saucepan. Bring to a boil and boil until the vegetables are fork-tender, about 10 minutes. The vegetables should still hold their shape. Drain well.

2 Heat the oil in a large saucepan over medium heat. Add the ginger, garlic, and curry paste, and sauté until fragrant, about 1 minute. Add the coconut milk, broth, lemongrass, lime juice, and fish sauce. Bring to a simmer and simmer for 10 minutes. Taste and season with cayenne pepper (it may not need any).

3 Add the shrimp, root vegetables, and baby corn, and simmer until the shrimp are cooked through, 8 to 10 minutes. Remove from the heat and discard the lemongrass. Add the fresh herbs, if using. Taste again and adjust the seasoning.

4 Serve hot, spooned over the rice, with the lime wedges on the side.

Creamy Fish Pie

Serves 4–6

Think New England–style fish chowder in solid form, and you have some idea of the flavor of this fabulous fish dish — or potentially fabulous dish. Everything hinges on the absolute freshness of the fish. While any white fish will work, choose first the freshest fillet, then the thickest one you can find. Made with a thick fillet of fresh cod, this simple dish is exquisite, with the fresh cod adding a sweetness that is almost lobsterlike. Fish pies goes back centuries in British cooking; this dish is a Good Friday tradition.

2½	cups milk
6	whole peppercorns
2	bay leaves
2	pounds cod or other white-fleshed fish fillets, cut into large chunks
1	large onion, halved and sliced
2	pounds russet (baking) potatoes, peeled and cut into chunks
6	tablespoons butter
	Salt and freshly ground black pepper
3	tablespoons all-purpose flour
1	large carrot, peeled and shredded
½	cup lightly packed grated cheddar cheese (2 ounces; optional)

1 Lightly butter a deep ovenproof casserole dish, 9 to 10 inches in diameter.

2 Combine the milk, peppercorns, and bay leaves in a saucepan over medium heat. Bring to a simmer.

3 Layer the fish and onion in the baking dish and pour the warm milk mixture over the fish. Allow to stand for 15 minutes.

4 Meanwhile, cover the potatoes with salted water in a saucepan. Bring to a boil and boil under tender, about 15 minutes. Drain and set aside.

5 While the potatoes cook, remove the fish and onions from the baking dish and set aside on a plate. Strain the milk through a fine sieve, reserving all the liquid. Return the fish and onions to the baking dish.

6 Preheat the oven to 400°F.

7 Return the potatoes to the saucepan, mash with 3 tablespoons of the butter, and season with salt and pepper. Place the pan over low heat and beat the potatoes with a wooden spoon until smooth, 2 to 3 minutes. Set aside.

8 Melt the remaining 3 tablespoons butter in a large saucepan, stir in the flour to make a smooth paste, and cook for 1 minute. Gradually stir in the reserved milk to form a white sauce. Add the carrot and season with salt and pepper. Cook gently, stirring frequently, for 3 minutes. Remove from the heat.

9 Pour the white sauce over the fish in the baking dish. Spoon or pipe the mashed potato over the top of the fish mixture, and sprinkle with grated cheese, if using.

10 Bake for 30 to 40 minutes, until golden brown and bubbling. Serve hot.

Kitchen Note: *Pacific cod is considered sustainably fished.*

> **Fish, to taste right, must swim three times — in water, in butter, and in wine.**
> — Polish proverb

Mediterranean Fish on a Bed of Rice and Leeks

Serves 4

The leeks provide a moist background for the delicately flavored fish, with bursts of flavor provided by the lemons, olives, and caperberries. Capers are the immature buds of the caper bush; caperberries are the fruit. They are oblong green fruits, about the size of a grape, and are milder in flavor than caper buds. If you can't find caperberries, substitute capers.

1 cup long-grain white rice	Freshly ground black pepper
1¾ cups cold water	2 lemons
Salt	½ cup pitted Niçoise or other cured olives
¼ cup extra-virgin olive oil	½ cup caperberries, sliced, or 1 tablespoon capers
2–3 large leeks, trimmed and sliced	½ cup dry white wine
2 garlic cloves, minced	
1½ pounds white-fleshed fish fillets	

1 Combine the rice, water, and ¼ teaspoon salt in a saucepan. Bring to a boil, then reduce and boil gently, covered, until the liquid has been absorbed and the rice is tender, 12 to 15 minutes. Fluff the rice with a fork and set aside.

2 Preheat the oven to 425°F. Lightly oil a 9- by 13-inch baking dish or large casserole dish.

3 Heat 2 tablespoons of the oil in a large skillet over medium-high heat. Add the leeks and sauté until slightly tender, about 3 minutes. Add the garlic and sauté for 1 minute longer. Set aside.

4 Wash and pat dry the fish. Season the fish on both sides with salt and pepper. Slice 1 lemon very thinly. Juice the other lemon.

5 Transfer the rice to the baking dish. Top with the leek mixture. Arrange the fish in a single layer on top. (If the fish pieces overlap, you may have to add a few minutes to the baking time.) Arrange the lemon slices on top of the fish. Sprinkle with the olives and caperberries. Pour in the lemon juice, wine, and remaining oil.

6 Bake for 10 to 15 minutes, until the fish flakes easily with a fork. Serve hot.

Kitchen Note: *The wine in the dish should be the same as the one you drink with this luxurious one-pot dish. A crisp Sauvignon Blanc is lovely here.*

Shrimp and Kale Sauté

Serves 4–6

Lacinato kale is especially nice in this dish because it is more tender than the curly or Scotch kale. Whichever kale you use, be sure to slice it into very fine ribbons — not more than ¼ inch thick — because you want the kale to cook in the same amount of time as the shrimp. This is a fast dish to pull together and just fine as a special-occasion meal.

⅓ cup extra-virgin olive oil	¾ cup chicken broth or vegetable broth (pages 126–27)
1 large shallot, minced	¼ cup dry white wine
4 garlic cloves, minced	Salt and freshly ground black pepper
½ teaspoon crushed red pepper flakes	1–2 tablespoons high-quality balsamic vinegar
1½ pounds shrimp, peeled and deveined	Hot cooked rice, for serving
10 cups thinly sliced kale (preferably Lacinato; remove and discard tough stems)	

1 Heat the oil in a large Dutch oven over medium heat. Add the shallot, garlic, and red pepper flakes, and sauté until fragrant, about 2 minutes. Stir in the shrimp and kale and sauté for 2 minutes, stirring to evenly mix. Cover and let steam until the shrimp are firm and the kale is tender, about 4 minutes.

2 Stir in the broth and wine and cook for 2 minutes longer. Season with salt and pepper. Drizzle with the vinegar. Serve immediately over rice.

Kitchen Note: *If you prefer, you can skip the rice and serve with a good crusty loaf of French or Italian bread.*

Seafood Boil

Serves 6

I took a very traditional recipe, swapped celery root for celery, added carrots, and voilà! A recipe with winter vegetables. The onions and celery root taste delicious here, and once when I admonished my kids to be sure to eat some of the vegetables, my son Sam replied, "Who could object to vegetables that taste like seafood?" You will need a stockpot that holds at least 3 gallons.

4	quarts water
¼	cup coarse sea salt or kosher salt
¼	cup Old Bay or Zatarain seafood seasoning
1½	pounds thin-skinned potatoes, cut into chunks
3	carrots, peeled and cut into 2-inch lengths
1	large celery root, peeled and cut into chunks
2	onions, quartered
8	ounces smoked sausage (andouille is recommended), cut into 2-inch lengths
4-5	pounds shell-on fresh or frozen shrimp, fresh clams or mussels, and/or any other fresh shellfish (crabs, crawfish, et cetera)
	Melted butter, for serving
1-2	lemons, cut into wedges, for serving
	Cocktail sauce, for serving

1   Combine the water, salt, and seafood seasoning in a large pot and bring to a boil. Add the potatoes, carrots, and celery root. Cover, bring back to a boil, and boil for 10 minutes.

2   Add the onions and sausage and boil for 5 minutes.

3   Add the seafood. Boil until all the mollusk shells open, about 5 minutes longer. Discard any clams and mussels that have not opened. Ladle into bowls, capturing some of the broth, and serve hot, passing the butter, lemon wedges, and cocktail sauce at the table.

Kitchen Note: *Although you can buy cocktail sauce, it is easy to mix it up in your kitchen, making just enough for one meal. Start with ¾ cup ketchup and add 2 tablespoons prepared horseradish. Taste. Add more horseradish if you like. You can also add 1 to 2 tablespoons of lemon or lime juice. And that's about it.*

Moules Marinière with Leeks

Serves 4

Years ago, traveling in France with my soon-to-be husband and choosing restaurants from the *France on $5 a Day* guidebook, we fell in love with moules marinière (mussels in white wine). A good thing, too, because it was usually the least expensive option on the prix fixe menus. I've added leeks and canned tomatoes to the traditional broth to make it more of a main dish. This *must* be served with French bread to mop up the broth.

4	pounds mussels in their shells
2	tablespoons extra-virgin olive oil
3	leeks, trimmed and sliced
4	garlic cloves, minced
1½	cups white wine
1½	cups diced tomatoes with juice, or 1 (15-ounce) can
	Salt and freshly ground black pepper

1 Scrub the mussels under cold running water, pulling off any beards hanging from the shells. Discard any mussels that do not close if tapped on a counter. Also discard those with broken shells. Set the cleaned mussels aside.

2 Heat the oil in a large pan over medium heat. Add the leeks and garlic and sauté until fragrant, about 3 minutes.

3 Increase the heat, add the white wine and tomatoes, and let simmer for 10 minutes to allow the flavors to blend. Season with salt and pepper.

4 Add the mussels. Cover the pan and steam for about 7 minutes, shaking the pan occasionally to ensure even cooking. Check to see if the mussels have opened. If not, cover and let cook for 1 to 2 minutes longer, until all the shells are open. Remove from the heat and discard any mussels that have not opened.

5 Ladle the broth and mussels into bowls and serve.

Kitchen Note: *A good fishmonger will inspect each mussel and discard any dead ones. If the supermarket sells bagged mussels, you may want to buy extra because inevitably some will have broken shells and need to be discarded.*

Clam Pot Pie

Serves 6

Swanson made famous the chicken pot pie and, to a far lesser extent, the tuna pie. But, in fact, seafood pies are an Atlantic seaboard classic, from Hudson Bay all the way down coastal New England. The fish may change from cod to clams and the topping from short crust to biscuit, but the basic goodness of seafood, potatoes, and carrots in a creamy sauce remains unchanged.

FILLING

- 1   pound thin-skinned potatoes, peeled and diced
- 1   carrot, peeled and diced
- 1   large celery root, peeled and diced
- 2   cups chopped fresh clams, or 2 (6.5-ounce) cans chopped clams
- 2   (8-ounce) bottles clam juice
- 6   tablespoons butter
- 1   shallot or ½ small onion, diced
- 6   tablespoons all-purpose flour
- ½   cup dry white wine
- 1   teaspoon dried thyme
-     Salt and freshly ground black pepper

BISCUIT TOPPING

- 3   cups all-purpose flour
- 2   tablespoons baking powder
- 1½ teaspoons salt
- ⅔   cup butter, cut into small pieces
- 1   cup buttermilk

1 Cover the potatoes with salted water in a medium saucepan and bring to a boil. When the potatoes come to a boil, add the carrot and celery root, cover, and cook until the vegetables are just tender, 5 to 8 minutes. Drain.

2 Drain the clams, reserving the juice in a large glass measuring cup. Add the clam juice. You should have 3 cups. Add water if needed to make up the difference.

3 Melt the butter in a large saucepan over medium heat. Add the shallot and sauté until softened, about 3 minutes. Sprinkle in the flour and stir until all the flour is absorbed into the butter. Whisk in the 3 cups clam juice and the wine and cook, stirring, until thickened and smooth. Stir in the drained vegetables and thyme. Taste and adjust the seasoning; be cautious with the salt and generous with the pepper. Bring to a boil. Keep hot while you prepare the biscuit topping.

4 Preheat the oven to 400°F. Set out a 9- by 13-inch baking dish.

5 Combine the flour, baking powder, and salt in a food processor. Add the butter and process until the mixture resembles coarse crumbs. Add the buttermilk and process to make a soft dough. Knead a few times on a lightly floured work surface. Pat out the dough to a thickness of about ½ inch. Cut into 3-inch rounds. By gathering the scraps and patting out again, you should get 12 biscuits.

6 Stir the clams into the vegetable mixture and pour into the baking dish. Arrange the dough rounds on top.

7 Bake for about 20 minutes, until the biscuits are golden and the clam mixture is bubbling. Let stand for a few minutes before serving.

Shrimp Egg Rolls

Makes 20 to 24 egg rolls

The variable in this recipe is the size of the cabbage and the number of egg roll wrappers required. Buy extra egg roll wrappers to allow you to double-wrap your egg rolls if the wrappers tear. Extra egg rolls can be partially cooked and then frozen. Before serving frozen egg rolls, fry them again. Store extra egg roll wrappers in the refrigerator, well wrapped, for up to a week. If you don't want to make more egg rolls, use the wrappers as pasta.

1	pound shrimp, peeled, deveined, and coarsely chopped
2	tablespoons soy sauce
2	tablespoons Chinese rice wine or dry sherry
4	garlic cloves, minced
1	(1-inch) piece fresh ginger, peeled and minced
2	teaspoons cornstarch
1	teaspoon sugar
	Sunflower, canola, or other vegetable oil, for deep-frying
1	small head green cabbage, finely shredded or very thinly sliced (6–8 cups)
1	carrot, peeled and shredded
1	teaspoon salt
1	teaspoon Asian sesame oil
	Freshly ground black pepper
1	egg white
	Cornstarch, for dusting
2	(1-pound) packages egg roll wrappers
	Thai sweet chili sauce or Chinese plum sauce, for serving
2–3	tablespoons Colman's dry mustard powder, mixed with enough water to make a smooth paste, for serving

1   Combine the shrimp, soy sauce, wine, garlic, ginger, cornstarch, and sugar in a medium bowl. Mix well and set aside to marinate for at least 10 minutes, or up to 1 hour.

2   Heat a large wok over high heat. Add 2 tablespoons of oil and heat until shimmering. Add the shrimp mixture and stir-fry until the shrimp are pink and firm, 4 to 5 minutes. Add the cabbage and carrot and stir-fry until limp, about 3 minutes. Stir in the salt and sesame oil and season with pepper. Remove from the heat and transfer to a colander set over a bowl or plate.

3   Begin heating 2 to 3 inches of oil for deep-frying in a wok, tall saucepan, or deep-fat fryer over medium heat. Put the egg white in a bowl. Dust a work surface and a baking sheet with cornstarch.

4   To fill the egg rolls, place an egg roll wrapper on the work surface with one corner pointing toward you. Mound 2 heaping tablespoons (about ¼ cup) of filling in the center of the wrapper. Bring the corner of the wrapper closest to you up over the filling and tuck under the filling, making a log shape. Bring in the two side corners. Apply egg white with your fingers or a pastry brush to the last corner of the wrapper, and finish rolling up the egg roll, sealing it closed. Transfer the roll, seam-side down, to the prepared baking sheet. Continue filling and rolling until all the filling is used. If an egg roll wrapper tears, roll it in a second wrapper.

5   When all the egg rolls are made, use a deep-frying thermometer to test whether the oil has reached 365°F. Or drop a cube of bread into the oil; if the oil bubbles around the bread and the cube browns uniformly in 60 seconds, the oil is at the right temperature. Slide three to five egg rolls into the hot oil and fry until golden all over, about 3 minutes. Remove with tongs, and let drain in a colander or on a wire rack, turning frequently. Meanwhile, continue frying the remaining egg rolls in batches.

6   Serve hot, passing the sweet chili sauce and mustard on the side.

Thai Sweet-Chili Shrimp Rolls

Serves 4–6

Rice-paper rolls also make beautiful party food, so consider serving this as an appetizer at your next dinner party. (They aren't recommended as finger food, unless you fill and roll them to be quite thin and cut them into bite-size pieces, because they tend to fall apart.) It may take a couple of tries to learn how to handle the rice paper, but once you get the hang of it, it's easy to use. The exotic ingredients — cellophane noodles, Thai sweet chili sauce, and rice-paper sheets — can be found wherever Asian foods are sold.

8 ounces large shrimp (about 15)	2 cups shredded napa or Chinese cabbage
1 (2-ounce) package cellophane noodles	¼ cup Thai sweet chili sauce, plus more to serve
1 cup peeled and shredded carrot	12 (8- to 9-inch) round rice-paper sheets
1 cup shredded daikon radish	

1   Bring a small saucepan of water to a boil. Add the shrimp and cook until pink and firm, 3 to 5 minutes. Drain and rinse under cold water to stop the cooking process. Peel, devein, and slice in half lengthwise. Set aside.

2   Cover the cellophane noodles with hot water in a large bowl. Let stand until softened, 20 to 30 minutes. Drain. Cut into 3-inch lengths; set aside.

3   Combine the carrot, daikon, and cabbage in a bowl. Add the sweet chili sauce and toss to coat.

4   Fill a large bowl with warm water. Cover a work surface with a clean cloth. Set 1 rice-paper sheet in the water and turn until it begins to soften, about 30 seconds (the sheet will still be stiff in a few spots). Transfer to the towel. Arrange about 2 tablespoons of cellophane noodles in a line across the lower third of the sheet, leaving a 1-inch border on the edge closest to you. Arrange about ¼ cup of the vegetable mixture on top of the noodles and top with a line of shrimp. Fold the bottom of the rice sheet over the filling, then fold in the ends and roll into a tight cylinder. Transfer the roll, seam-side down, to a cutting board. Repeat the steps to form 12 rolls. Cut each roll in half and arrange on a platter with a bowl of sweet chili sauce alongside.

Kitchen Note: *The rolls can be made up to 6 hours ahead and kept in the refrigerator. Cover with a damp paper towel and plastic wrap.*

Salsify Scampi on Linguine

Serves 4

With a name like oyster plant, salsify is natural to combine with seafood, as in this recipe of garlicky shrimp and pasta.

1½ pounds salsify
1 teaspoon salt
1 pound linguine
⅓ cup extra-virgin olive oil
1 shallot, minced
4 garlic cloves, minced
1½ pounds shrimp, peeled and deveined
¼ cup dry white wine
¾ cup chicken broth or vegetable broth (pages 126–27)
2 tablespoons minced fresh parsley (optional)
Salt and freshly ground black pepper

1 Peel the salsify and cut into 1-inch pieces. Immediately place in a saucepan of acidulated water (1 tablespoon white vinegar added to 4 cups water). Add the salt. Bring to a boil and boil until partly tender, about 5 minutes. Drain well.

2 Bring a large pot of salted water to a boil for the linguine. Cook the linguine until just al dente. Drain and keep warm.

3 Meanwhile, heat the oil in a large skillet or Dutch oven over medium heat. Add the shallot and garlic and sauté until fragrant, about 2 minutes. Add the shrimp and salsify and sauté until the shrimp are firm and the salsify is tender, about 5 minutes.

4 Stir the wine, broth, and parsley into the shrimp and cook for another 2 minutes. Season with salt and pepper. Serve over the linguine.

8

Main Dishes with Poultry

We eat more chicken than ever, for good reasons. It is healthful, quickly cooked, and extremely versatile. For busy weeknights, you'll find in this chapter several stir-fries and sautés, quickly made, especially if the vegetables are shredded or very thinly sliced. For more leisurely cooking, there are roasts and braises, with root vegetables basted in the juices of the cooking bird.

This chapter starts with chicken recipes that use lots of different vegetables, then moves on to chicken recipes with specific individual vegetables. It concludes with a few turkey and duck recipes.

We don't eat much duck. It is expensive compared to chicken and turkey and has the bad reputation of being fatty. But it is the fat that makes the duck such a prize. Try basting roasting potatoes and root vegetables with duck fat for a sublime taste treat. You will probably find yourself cooking more ducks in the future.

RECISE LIST FOR
MAIN DISHES WITH POULTRY

Roasted Chicken with Root Vegetables

Balsamic Chicken with Vegetables

Chicken and Rice with Winter
   Vegetables

Chicken Stew with Root Vegetables

Chicken in Red Wine with Root
   Vegetables

Chicken Pot Pie with Sweet-Potato
   Biscuits

Chicken Paella

Chicken and Barley Pilaf with Winter
   Vegetables

Rigatoni with Tomato-Braised Chicken
   and Root Vegetables

Chicken Sauté with Brussels Sprouts

Chicken and Brussels Sprouts Stir-Fry

Spicy Black Bean Brussels Sprouts and
   Chicken Stir-Fry

Chicken and Chinese Cabbage Stir-Fry

Orzo with Kale, Chicken, and Feta
   Cheese

Lemon-Braised Chicken with Turnips

Red-Cooked Chicken with Turnips

Sunshine Turkey

Braised Turkey Breast with Winter
   Vegetables

Braised Turkey on a Bed of Kale

Roasted and Braised Duck with
   Sauerkraut and Root Vegetables

Roasted Stuffed Duck with Roasted
   Vegetables

Vegetarian dishes are marked with this symbol:

Roasted Chicken with Root Vegetables

Serves 4-6

Root vegetables bathed in drippings from a roasting bird are exceptionally tasty. Mashed potatoes are the obvious accompaniment.

1 whole roasting chicken (3½-5 pounds), neck and giblets removed

1 whole garlic head, cloves separated and peeled

2 teaspoons crushed dried rosemary or sage

8 cups peeled and cubed mixed root vegetables (beets, carrots, celery root, parsnips, rutabagas, salsify, and/or turnips)

1-2 onions, cut into wedges

2 tablespoons sunflower, canola, or extra-virgin olive oil

Salt and freshly ground black pepper

3 cups chicken broth (page 127)

3 tablespoons all-purpose flour

2 tablespoons water or dry white wine

1   Preheat the oven to 350°F.

2   Rinse the chicken under cold running water and pat dry. Set in a large roasting pan. (The pan must be large enough to hold the vegetables in a single layer surrounding the chicken.) Insert a few garlic cloves and 1 teaspoon of the rosemary in the cavity of the chicken.

3   Combine the root vegetables and onions in a large bowl. Add the remaining garlic cloves to the vegetables, along with the remaining 1 teaspoon rosemary. Add the oil, season with salt and pepper, and toss to coat. Arrange the vegetables in a single layer around the chicken.

4   Roast for 1½ to 2 hours (20 to 25 minutes per pound), until the juices run clear from the chicken, a leg moves easily, and an instant-read thermometer inserted into the thickest part of the thigh reads 165°F. Stir the vegetables once or twice during the roasting to promote even cooking and to baste the vegetables.

5   Transfer the chicken to a serving platter and keep warm under a tent of foil. Spoon the vegetables into a serving bowl and cover to keep warm.

6   To make a gravy, place the roasting pan over one or two burners on medium-high heat. Add the broth and stir to deglaze the pan, bringing the broth to a boil. In a small bowl, combine the flour and water, mixing until completely smooth; stir into the boiling pan juices. Taste and add salt and pepper, if needed.

7   Carve the chicken and serve with the gravy, passing the vegetables separately.

Balsamic Chicken with Vegetables

Serves 4

Here's a simple one-dish meal of roasted chicken, vegetables, and potatoes. Although perfect for a busy midweek meal, it makes a fine dinner for company when served with red wine and crusty French bread.

8	bone-in chicken thighs
6	shallots, peeled and halved if large
1	whole garlic head, cloves separated (peeling is optional)
1¼	pounds russet (baking) potatoes, peeled and cut into wedges
1	rutabaga, peeled and cut into 1-inch cubes
2	parsnips, peeled and sliced
2	carrots, peeled and sliced
1	tablespoon dried rosemary
	Salt and freshly ground black pepper
6	tablespoons extra-virgin olive oil
3	tablespoons balsamic vinegar

1 Preheat the oven to 400°F.

2 Remove any fat from the chicken. Rinse and pat dry. Combine the chicken, shallots, garlic, potatoes, rutabaga, parsnips, and carrots in a large roasting pan. Add the rosemary and season with salt and pepper. Whisk together the oil and vinegar, pour over the chicken and vegetables, and toss to coat well. Arrange the chicken skin-side up, tucked among the vegetables in a single layer.

3 Roast for 45 to 55 minutes, until the vegetables are tender and the chicken is cooked through.

4 Transfer the chicken and vegetables (leaving behind the fat that has accumulated) to a heated platter and serve hot.

Kitchen Note: *Chicken is done when the juices run clear (not pink) when the chicken is pierced with a knife.*

Chicken and Rice with Winter Vegetables

Serves 6

Chicken and rice is one of those great combinations that shows up in many different styles. This crowd-pleasing one-dish pilaf combines the starring ingredient with leeks, carrots, and turnips.

12	bone-in chicken thighs (4–5 pounds)	3	garlic cloves, minced
	Salt and freshly ground black pepper	2	cups long-grain white rice
2	tablespoons extra-virgin olive oil	2½	cups chicken broth (page 127)
1	large leek, trimmed and sliced	½	cup dry sherry
1	carrot, peeled and diced	2	teaspoons dried thyme
2	turnips or 1 small rutabaga, peeled and diced	2	bay leaves

1   Preheat the oven to 400°F. Set out a large roasting pan.

2   Remove any fat from the chicken. Rinse and pat dry. Season the chicken with salt and pepper. Heat the oil in a large skillet over medium-high heat. Add enough chicken pieces to fit in the skillet in a single layer, and brown, turning several times, 5 to 10 minutes. Remove the chicken from the skillet and keep warm. Repeat with the remaining chicken pieces.

3   Pour off all but 2 tablespoons of the fat from the skillet. Lower the heat to medium. Add the leek, carrot, turnips, and garlic, and sauté until the vegetables have softened, about 5 minutes. Use a slotted spoon to transfer the vegetables to the roasting pan.

4   Add the rice to the skillet and sauté until the rice appears opaque and white and smells toasted, 3 to 5 minutes. Scrape the rice into the roasting pan. Add the broth, sherry, thyme, and bay leaves. Mix well. Arrange the chicken on top of the rice mixture. Cover with aluminum foil.

5   Bake for 60 minutes. Fluff the rice. Taste and adjust the seasoning. Serve hot.

Chicken Stew with Root Vegetables

Serves 6

When meat is cooked on the bone, the flesh is juicier and more flavorful, and the chicken in this stew is no exception. Use a good heavy cleaver, if you have one, to chop the chicken parts into easily served pieces. You have your choice of root vegetables, but it is a good idea to include carrots or a yellow-fleshed rutabaga for a touch of color. Serve with crusty bread for mopping up the gravy. Or for a more rustic presentation, serve on a bed of barley.

4–5	pounds chicken, in parts or whole
⅔	cup all-purpose unbleached flour
1	tablespoon dried dill, plus more for garnish
	Salt and freshly ground black pepper
¼	cup extra-virgin olive oil
1	onion, halved and thinly sliced
4	garlic cloves, minced
2	cups chicken broth (page 127)
1	cup white wine
1	pound rutabagas or turnips, peeled and cut into ½-inch cubes
1	pound carrots or parsnips, peeled and cut into ½-inch cubes
1	pound celery root, peeled and cut into ½-inch cubes

1   Cut the chicken into small pieces with a cleaver. (Cut the breast into quarters and the thighs into halves.) Remove any fat, rinse, and pat dry. Combine the flour and dill in a medium bowl. Season generously with salt and pepper. Dredge the chicken pieces in the flour until well coated.

2   Heat 3 tablespoons of the oil in a large Dutch oven over medium-high heat. Lift the chicken pieces out of the flour, shaking off the excess, and add a single layer of chicken to the pan. Cook in batches; do not crowd the pan. Let the chicken brown, turning as needed, 5 to 10 minutes per batch. Set aside. Reserve any excess flour.

3   Add the remaining 1 tablespoon oil, onion, and garlic to the Dutch oven and sauté until the onion is soft, about 3 minutes. Add the broth and wine. Stir to scrape up any browned bits from the bottom of the pan. Bring to a boil, then reduce the heat to a slow simmer. Return the chicken to the pan. Partially cover the pan and let simmer for 15 minutes.

4   Add the rutabagas, carrots, and celery root to the pan and let simmer until the vegetables and chicken are tender, about 1 hour.

5   Use a slotted spoon to transfer the chicken and vegetables to a bowl; keep warm. Pour the pan juices into a tall, narrow container and let stand for 15 minutes. The fat will rise to the top; skim it off. Return the juices to the pan and bring to a boil. If the pan juices are too thin (the consistency of heavy cream is ideal), combine 2 tablespoons of the reserved seasoned flour with 2 tablespoons of water and stir to make a smooth paste. Add to the pan juices and let boil until thickened. Taste and add salt and pepper as needed.

6   Return the chicken and vegetables to the pan and heat through. Serve hot, garnished with additional dill.

Kitchen Note: *There are several different ways to remove the fat from pan drippings, including using a bulb baster to suck up the fats that rise to the surface. You can also use large flat kitchen spoons to skim along the top where the liquid fat is floating. My favorite utensil to use is a called a fat separator. It is a narrow, clear pitcher with a spout rising from the lower part of the pitcher. The fat rises to the top, but you pour from the bottom, leaving the fat behind.*

Chicken in Red Wine with Root Vegetables

Serves 4–6

I make a variation of this dish throughout the year, varying the vegetables and the seasoning. The chicken, red wine, and tomatoes remain the same. Any red wine that you would care to sip with dinner works in the recipe. I recommend a medium-bodied red, such as a Pinot Noir or Merlot.

1	whole chicken or 3½ pounds chicken parts
½	cup all-purpose flour
2	teaspoons dried thyme
	Salt and freshly ground black pepper
3	tablespoons extra-virgin olive oil
1	onion, halved and thinly sliced
3	cups peeled and cubed mixed root vegetables (carrots, celery root, golden beets, parsnips, rutabaga, salsify, and/or turnips)
1½	cups diced tomatoes with juice, or 1 (15-ounce) can
1	cup dry red wine
1	whole garlic head, cloves separated and peeled
2	bay leaves

1   Cut the chicken into small serving pieces (cut the breast into quarters and the thighs into halves). Remove any fat, rinse, and pat dry. Combine the flour and 1 teaspoon of the thyme in a shallow bowl. Season with salt and pepper. Dredge the chicken pieces in the flour until well coated.

2   Heat the oil in a Dutch oven over medium-high heat. Lift the chicken pieces out of the flour, shaking off the excess, and add a single layer of chicken to the pan. Cook in batches; do not crowd the pan. Let the chicken brown, turning as needed, 5 to 10 minutes per batch. Adjust the temperature as needed to allow the chicken to brown but not scorch. (For the best presentation, make sure the chicken is well browned.) Transfer the browned chicken to a bowl or plate and keep warm.

3   In the oil remaining in the pan, sauté the onion and root vegetables over medium-high heat until the vegetables are a little softened, 3 to 5 minutes.

4   Return the chicken to the pan. Add the tomatoes, wine, garlic, bay leaves, and the remaining 1 teaspoon thyme. Cover and simmer, turning the chicken every 15 minutes or so, until the chicken is cooked through and the vegetables are tender, 45 to 60 minutes.

5   Remove the chicken and vegetables from the sauce with a slotted spoon; keep warm. Let the fat rise to the surface of the pan juices and remove by skimming. Remove the bay leaves. Return the chicken and vegetables to the pan. Taste and adjust the seasonings. Serve hot.

Kitchen Note: *Leftovers, should there be any, can be made into soup by taking the chicken off the bone and adding chicken broth.*

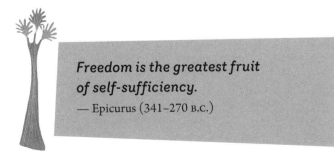

Freedom is the greatest fruit of self-sufficiency.
— Epicurus (341–270 B.C.)

Chicken Pot Pie with Sweet-Potato Biscuits

Serves 6

Chicken pot pie is a dish I make year-round, varying the vegetables as the seasons suggest. This is my fall/winter version, filled with yummy root vegetables. If you prefer, different root vegetables, such as parsnips and carrots, can be used, though I do think this is one of the best uses for celery root. The sweet potato biscuit topping is a colorful variation on the traditional white-flour biscuit topping.

FILLING

3	pounds chicken pieces (dark meat preferred)
8–10	cups water
2	onions, quartered
2	garlic cloves
1	teaspoon dill seeds
1	teaspoon black peppercorns
1	medium rutabaga or turnip, peeled and diced
1	large celery root, peeled and diced
6	tablespoons extra-virgin olive oil
1	leek, trimmed and sliced
6	tablespoons all-purpose flour
½	cup dry white wine
1	teaspoon dried thyme
	Salt and freshly ground black pepper

TOPPING

2⅓	cups all-purpose flour
1	tablespoon brown sugar
2	tablespoons baking powder
1½	teaspoons salt
⅔	cup (1 stick plus 3 tablespoons) butter, cut into small pieces
1¼	cups cooked mashed sweet potatoes, chilled
¼	cup buttermilk

1   Combine the chicken and water in a large pot. Add the onion, garlic, dill seeds, and peppercorns. Bring to a boil, then reduce the heat and simmer, uncovered, until the chicken is tender, 1 to 2 hours. Turn off the heat and let the chicken cool in the cooking liquid.

2   Cover the rutabaga and celery root with salted water in a saucepan. Bring to a boil and boil until just tender, 5 to 8 minutes. Drain.

3   When the chicken is cool enough to handle, remove from the broth. Discard the skin and bones. Chop the meat into bite-size pieces.

4   Strain the broth and discard the solids. Skim off any fat that rises to the top. Reserve 3 cups broth for the pot pie and refrigerate or freeze the remainder to use in soups, stews, or pilafs.

5   Heat the oil in a large saucepan over medium heat. Add the leek and sauté until softened, about 3 minutes. Sprinkle in the flour and stir until absorbed into the oil. Whisk in the 3 cups reserved broth and the wine and stir until thickened and smooth. Stir in the chicken, rutabagas, celery root, and thyme. Taste and adjust the seasoning with salt and pepper. Bring to a boil. Keep hot while you prepare the biscuits.

6   Preheat the oven to 400°F. Set out a 9- by 13-inch baking pan.

7   Combine the flour, brown sugar, baking powder, and salt in a food processor. Add the butter and process until the mixture resembles coarse crumbs. Add the sweet potatoes and buttermilk and process to make a soft dough.

8   Pour the hot chicken mixture into the baking pan. Spoon the dough on top of the chicken mixture in 12 mounds. Bake for about 30 minutes, until the biscuits are golden and the chicken mixture is bubbling. Let stand for a few minutes before serving.

Variation: Chicken Pot Pie with Biscuit Topping

To make a regular biscuit topping, omit the sweet potato and brown sugar. Increase the flour to 3 cups and the buttermilk to 1 cup. This dough will be stiff enough to roll out to a ½-inch thickness and cut into twelve 3-inch biscuits. Arrange the dough circles on the chicken mixture and bake at 425°F for 20 to 25 minutes.

Chicken Paella

Serves 6

There are hundreds, perhaps thousands, of versions of the classic Spanish dish, paella. So why not one featuring winter vegetables? This is a festive dish, perfect for a special occasion, and one that takes very little time to prepare.

¼ teaspoon crushed saffron threads
4 cups chicken broth (page 127)
1 pound boneless skinless chicken thighs, cut into bite-size pieces.
2 tablespoons extra-virgin olive oil
1 leek, trimmed and thinly sliced
1 carrot, peeled and finely chopped
1 celery root, peeled and finely chopped
2 cups short-grain white rice
1 pound shrimp, peeled and deveined
4 ounces Spanish chorizo, diced
1 cup frozen green peas
Salt and freshly ground black pepper

1 Toast the saffron in a dry skillet over medium heat until fragrant, 2 to 3 minutes. Combine with the broth and set aside. Remove any fat from the chicken, rinse, and pat dry.

2 Heat the oil in a large skillet or Dutch oven over medium-high heat. Add the chicken and brown on both sides, about 6 minutes. Remove from the skillet and set aside.

3 Add the leek, carrot, and celery root to the skillet, lower the heat to medium, and sauté until softened, about 3 minutes. Add the rice and sauté until the rice appears opaque and smells toasted, 3 to 5 minutes.

4 Return the chicken to the skillet, add the broth mixture, and stir well. Bring to a boil, then reduce the heat and boil gently, stirring occasionally, until the liquid is mostly absorbed and the rice is tender, about 15 minutes.

5 Fluff the rice with a fork. Carefully stir in the shrimp, chorizo, and peas. Season with salt and pepper. Cover and cook over low heat until the shrimp are cooked through, about 10 minutes longer. Serve hot.

Chicken and Barley Pilaf with Winter Vegetables

Serves 6

A pilaf made with barley instead of rice is rustic, hearty, and better for you. This dish is simply delicious.

12	bone-in chicken thighs (4–5 pounds)
	Salt and freshly ground black pepper
2	tablespoons extra-virgin olive oil
1	onion, diced
4	cups peeled and diced mixed root vegetables (carrots, celery root, golden beets, parsnips, rutabagas, salsify, and/or turnips) or winter squashes
3	garlic cloves, minced
2	cups pearl barley
3½	cups chicken broth (page 127)
½	cup dry red wine
2	teaspoons crushed dried sage

1   Preheat the oven to 400°F. Set out a large roasting pan.

2   Remove any fat from the chicken, rinse, and pat dry. Season the chicken with salt and pepper. Heat the oil in a large skillet over medium-high heat. Add enough chicken pieces to fit in the skillet in a single layer, and brown, turning several times, 5 to 10 minutes. Remove the chicken from the skillet and keep warm. Repeat with the remaining chicken pieces.

3   Pour off all but 2 tablespoons of the fat from the skillet. Lower the heat to medium. Add the onion, diced vegetables, and garlic, and sauté until vegetables have softened, about 5 minutes. Use a slotted spoon to transfer the vegetables to the roasting pan.

4   Add the barley to the skillet and sauté for 3 to 5 minutes, until the barley smells toasted and the skillet is dry. Scrape the barley into the roasting pan. Add the broth, wine, and sage to the roasting pan. Mix well. Arrange the chicken on top of the barley mixture. Cover with aluminum foil.

5   Bake for 60 minutes. Fluff the barley with a fork. Taste and adjust the seasoning. Serve hot.

Rigatoni with Tomato-Braised Chicken and Root Vegetables

Serves 6–8

The root vegetables virtually disappear in this thick, slow-cooked ragù, but they contribute richness and flavor.

4 boneless, skinless chicken thighs, cut into 1-inch cubes	1 cup medium-bodied red wine
Salt and freshly ground black pepper	1 (6-ounce) can tomato paste
2 tablespoons extra-virgin olive oil	1 whole garlic head, cloves separated and peeled
1 carrot, peeled and finely diced	2 bay leaves
1 celery root, peeled and finely diced	1 tablespoon mixed dried Italian herbs
1 onion, finely diced	1 pound rigatoni
1 parsnip, peeled and finely diced	1 cup freshly grated Parmesan cheese, plus more for serving
1½ cups chicken broth (page 127)	

1 Remove any fat from the chicken, rinse, and pat dry. Season the chicken with salt and pepper. Heat the oil in a Dutch oven over medium-high heat. Add the chicken and brown, turning as needed, 5 to 10 minutes. Remove the browned chicken from the pan with a slotted spoon and keep warm.

2 Add the carrot, celery root, onion, and parsnip to the pan and sauté until the vegetables are a little softened, about 5 minutes. Add the broth, stirring to loosen any browned bits. Bring to a boil, then reduce the heat to a simmer.

3 Return the chicken to the pan, and stir in the wine, tomato paste, garlic, Italian herbs, and bay leaves. Cover and simmer, stirring occasionally, until the chicken is completely tender and falling apart and the vegetables are soft, 2 to 2½ hours.

4 Bring a large pot of salted water to a boil. Cook the rigatoni in the boiling water until al dente. Drain well.

5 Combine the pasta with the sauce and mix well. Stir in the Parmesan. Taste and adjust the seasoning. Serve hot, passing the extra Parmesan at the table.

Chicken Sauté with Brussels Sprouts

Serves 4

Here's a quick dish to make on a busy night. By pounding the chicken breasts until they are very thin, you guarantee a quick cooking time. And what better way to release a little aggression after a rough day at the office than a few minutes of whacking on something that will only taste better for it?

4	boneless, skinless chicken breast halves
	Salt and freshly ground black pepper
½	cup all-purpose flour
¼	cup extra-virgin olive oil
2	pounds Brussels sprouts, trimmed and quartered
2	large carrots, peeled and julienned
2	large shallots, minced
½	cup chicken broth (page 127)
4	teaspoons white balsamic vinegar

1   Remove any fat from the chicken, rinse, and pat dry. Using a meat mallet, pound the chicken breast halves between sheets of plastic wrap to ½-inch thickness. Sprinkle the chicken with salt and pepper. Dredge the chicken in the flour until lightly coated.

2   Heat 2 tablespoons of the oil in a large nonstick skillet over medium-high heat. Add the chicken and fry until cooked through, about 3 minutes per side. If the chicken will not fit in a single layer in the skillet, fry in two batches. Transfer the chicken to a plate and tent with foil.

3   Add the remaining 2 tablespoons oil to the same skillet and heat through. Add the Brussels sprouts, carrots, and shallots, and sauté until partly tender, about 4 minutes. Add the broth, stirring to scrape up any browned bits on the bottom of the pan, and continue cooking until the vegetables are completely tender, 2 to 4 minutes longer. Add the vinegar; toss to coat. Season with salt and pepper.

4   Divide the vegetables among four plates. Top with the chicken and serve.

Kitchen Note: *If you don't have a meat mallet, try pounding the chicken with a heavy skillet. It really works!*

Chicken and Brussels Sprouts Stir-Fry

Serves 4–6

Brussels sprouts are a natural for stir-fries; they blend well with all the usual stir-fry flavorings.

1 pound boneless, skinless chicken breast, cut into matchsticks	2 garlic cloves, minced
4 ounces shiitake mushrooms, sliced (remove and discard the stems)	3 tablespoons peanut, sunflower, or canola oil
¼ cup soy sauce	1½ pounds Brussels sprouts, trimmed and halved, or quartered if large
3 tablespoons Chinese rice wine or dry sherry	1 (7-ounce) can water chestnuts, rinsed and drained
3 tablespoons oyster sauce	1 tablespoon cornstarch dissolved in 2 tablespoons water
1 tablespoon sugar	Hot cooked rice, for serving
1 (1-inch) piece fresh ginger, peeled and minced	

1   Combine the chicken and mushrooms in a medium bowl with 2 tablespoons of the soy sauce, 2 tablespoons of the rice wine, and the oyster sauce, sugar, ginger, and garlic. Set aside to marinate for at least 20 minutes or cover and refrigerate for up to 2 hours.

2   Heat a large wok over high heat. Add 1 tablespoon of the oil and swirl in the hot wok. Add the chicken and mushroom mixture and stir-fry until the chicken is cooked through, 5 to 8 minutes. Scrape the mixture from the wok and keep warm.

3   Wipe out the wok. Heat the remaining 2 tablespoons oil in the wok. Add the Brussels sprouts and stir-fry for about 2 minutes, until lightly seared. Add the remaining 2 tablespoons soy sauce and 1 tablespoon rice wine, tossing to mix. Cover and steam until the Brussels sprouts are barely tender, about 3 minutes.

4   Return the chicken mixture and sauce to the wok, along with the water chestnuts. Stir-fry for 2 minutes longer to finish cooking the Brussels sprouts and heat everything through. Add the cornstarch mixture and cook until the sauce thickens, about 1 minute. Serve at once over hot rice.

Kitchen Note: *Cutting chicken into matchsticks is easiest if the chicken is partially frozen, so put it in the freezer an hour or so before you begin cooking.*

Spicy Black Bean Brussels Sprouts and Chicken Stir-Fry

Serves 4

All of the ingredients in this spicy stir-fry are readily found wherever Chinese foods are sold. It is a vibrantly flavored way to enjoy Brussels sprouts.

1 pound boneless, skinless chicken breasts, cut into matchsticks	1 teaspoon sugar
1 (1½-inch) piece fresh ginger, peeled and minced	1 teaspoon Asian sesame oil
3 garlic cloves, minced	3 tablespoons peanut, sunflower, or canola oil
3 tablespoons soy sauce	1 onion, halved and sliced lengthwise
2 tablespoons Chinese rice wine or dry sherry	1 carrot, peeled and cut into matchsticks
2 tablespoons Chinese black bean sauce	1½ pounds Brussels sprouts, trimmed and halved, or quartered if large
2 teaspoons Chinese chili paste with garlic	1 cup chicken broth (page 127)
	2 tablespoons cornstarch
	Hot cooked rice, for serving

1   Combine the chicken, ginger, garlic, 2 tablespoons of the soy sauce, rice wine, black bean sauce, chili paste, sugar, and sesame oil in a medium bowl.

2   Heat a large wok or deep skillet over high heat. Add 1 tablespoon of the peanut oil and swirl in the hot wok. Add the chicken mixture and stir-fry until the chicken is cooked through, 5 to 8 minutes. Scrape the mixture out of the wok and into a medium bowl; keep warm.

3   Wipe out the wok. Heat another 1 tablespoon of the peanut oil in the wok. Add the onion and carrot and stir-fry until just tender, about 3 minutes. Transfer to the bowl with the chicken.

4   Heat the remaining 1 tablespoon oil in the wok. Add the Brussels sprouts and stir-fry until slightly softened, about 3 minutes. Add the remaining 1 tablespoon soy sauce and ½ cup of the chicken broth. Cover and steam until the Brussels sprouts are barely tender, about 3 minutes.

5   Return the chicken and vegetables to the wok and stir-fry for 1 minute to heat through. Stir the cornstarch into the remaining ½ cup chicken broth and add to the wok. Stir-fry until the sauce thickens and coats the Brussels sprouts, about 2 minutes longer. Serve at once over hot rice.

Chicken and Chinese Cabbage Stir-Fry

Serves 4-6

I confess to an impossible fondness for the chicken chow mein of my youth. This recipe is an unabashed attempt to re-create it. Feel free to add those delicious little crispy noodles if you share my nostalgia.

CHICKEN AND MARINADE

- 2 boneless, skinless chicken breast halves
- 4 garlic cloves, minced
- 1 (½-inch) piece fresh ginger, peeled and minced
- 3 tablespoons Chinese rice wine or dry sherry
- 2 teaspoons Asian sesame oil
- 1 teaspoon salt
- 1 teaspoon sugar
- 2 tablespoons cornstarch

VEGETABLES

- 3 tablespoons peanut, sunflower, or canola oil
- 1 onion, halved and very thinly slivered (sliced vertically)
- 8 cups sliced Chinese cabbage, napa cabbage, bok choy, or a combination
- 1 tablespoon soy sauce
- 2 cups mung bean sprouts
- 1 (2-inch) piece daikon radish, peeled and thinly sliced
- 2 cups chicken broth (page 127)
- 2 tablespoons cornstarch dissolved in 2 tablespoons water
  Hot cooked white rice, for serving

1 Turn each chicken breast half on its side and cut into very thin slices. Cut the slices into bite-size pieces. Combine the chicken, garlic, ginger, wine, sesame oil, salt, and sugar in a medium bowl. Toss to coat. Add the cornstarch and mix well. Set aside to marinate for at least 20 minutes or cover and refrigerate for up to 2 hours.

2 Heat a large wok over high heat. Add 2 tablespoons of the peanut oil and swirl in the hot wok. Add the chicken mixture and stir-fry until the chicken is cooked through, about 5 minutes. Scrape the chicken out of the wok and keep warm.

3 Wipe out the wok. Heat the remaining 1 tablespoon peanut oil in the wok over high heat. Add the onion and stir-fry until limp, about 2 minutes. Add the cabbage and soy sauce and stir-fry until the cabbage is barely tender, about 4 minutes. Add the bean sprouts and daikon and stir-fry for 1 minute.

4 Return the chicken to the wok, along with the broth. Stir-fry for 2 minutes longer to heat everything through. Add the cornstarch mixture and cook until the sauce thickens, about 2 minutes. Serve at once over hot rice.

Kitchen Note: *The way the chicken is cut is key to the recipe. It's easiest to cut into thin slices if it's partially frozen, so put it in the freezer an hour or so before you begin cooking. Cut into thin horizontal slices, as if you were carving slices from the breast of the whole bird. Then cut the slices into bite-size squares.*

One cannot think well, love well, sleep well, if one has not dined well.
— Virginia Woolf (1882–1941)

Orzo with Kale, Chicken, and Feta Cheese

Serves 6–8

I am often left with cooked chicken when I make chicken broth; it goes into the freezer in small batches for use in other recipes, such as this one. If you don't have cooked chicken on hand, you can substitute 1 pound of shrimp, peeled and deveined, or just omit it. Either way, this is a simple one-dish baked pasta meal that packs plenty of flavor.

8	cups lightly packed chopped kale (remove and discard tough stems)
1	pound orzo (rice-shaped pasta)
2	tablespoons extra-virgin olive oil
2	shallots, minced
2	garlic cloves, minced
1½	cups diced tomatoes with juice, or 1 (15-ounce) can
½	cup dry white wine
½	teaspoon crushed red pepper flakes
	Salt and freshly ground black pepper
2	cups shredded cooked chicken
12	ounces feta cheese, crumbled

1　Bring a large pot of salted water to a boil. Add the kale and cook until limp but still bright green, about 3 minutes. Remove the kale from the water with tongs or a slotted spoon and drain in a colander.

2　Return the water to a boil. Add the orzo and cook until just done. Drain well.

3　Preheat the oven to 400°F. Lightly oil a 9- by 13-inch glass baking dish. Transfer the orzo and kale to the baking dish.

4　Heat the oil in a large skillet over medium-high heat. Add the shallots and garlic and sauté until limp, about 2 minutes. Add the tomatoes with juice, wine, and red pepper flakes. Simmer, uncovered, until the sauce is somewhat reduced, stirring occasionally, about 3 minutes. Season with salt and pepper.

5　Add the tomato sauce to the orzo mixture, along with the chicken and half the feta. Mix well. Top with the remaining feta.

6　Bake for about 30 minutes, until the casserole is heated through. Serve hot.

Lemon-Braised Chicken with Turnips

Serves 4

A combination of lemon, capers, and olives makes a rich-flavored braise for the chicken, which is fully complemented by the turnips. Serve with rice or mashed potatoes to round out the meal.

8 bone-in chicken thighs	1 cup chicken broth (page 127)
½ cup all-purpose flour	½ cup dry white wine
Salt and freshly ground black pepper	1 lemon, very thinly sliced
2 tablespoons extra-virgin olive oil	2 tablespoons brined capers
2 shallots, thinly sliced	½ cup green olives, such as Picholine
2 garlic cloves, minced	4 turnips or 1 rutabaga, peeled and sliced

1 Remove any fat from the chicken, rinse, and pat dry. Season the flour with salt and pepper in a shallow bowl. Dredge the chicken in the flour.

2 Heat the oil in a large Dutch oven over medium-high heat. Add the chicken in a single layer and brown on both sides, about 8 minutes, turning once. You may have to do this in two batches.

3 Transfer the chicken to a plate. Add the shallots to the Dutch oven and sauté until softened, about 2 minutes. Add the garlic, broth, and wine, and bring to a boil, stirring to scrape up any browned bits stuck to the bottom of the pan.

4 Return the chicken to the pan and place a lemon slice on each piece. Add the capers, olives, and turnips. Reduce the heat to low and simmer, covered, until the chicken is cooked through and tender, about 1 hour.

5 There will be a layer of fat on top of the liquid; skim it off. With a slotted spoon, transfer the chicken and vegetables to a bowl and keep warm. Pour the cooking liquid into a tall, narrow container and let stand for 15 minutes. The fat will rise to the top; skim it off.

6 Return the liquid to the pan along with the chicken and vegetables. Taste and adjust the seasoning. Cook just long enough to heat through. Serve hot.

Kitchen Note: *You can add caperberries to the cooking liquid in addition to, or instead of, the capers.*

Red-Cooked Chicken with Turnips

Serves 4-6

Chicken simmered in a soy-sauce-based liquid with spices is a style of cooking that is popular throughout China. When I worked in a Chinese restaurant, the chef would make this dish for the staff about once a week, and we ate it gratefully. He called it "hacked chicken," which always struck me as an incongruous name for such a comforting dish. Turnips added to the cooking liquid absorb the flavorful liquid, making it even more wonderful.

4	cups water
1	cup soy sauce
½	cup Chinese rice wine or sake
⅓	cup brown sugar
1	tablespoon Chinese five-spice powder
6	garlic cloves
6	thin slices fresh ginger
1	cinnamon stick or tangerine peel
4-5	pounds chicken, in parts or whole
4-6	turnips, peeled and cut into 1-inch cubes
	Asian sesame oil
	Hot cooked rice, for serving

1   Combine the water, soy sauce, rice wine, brown sugar, five-spice powder, garlic, ginger, and cinnamon stick in a large Dutch oven. Bring to a boil, then reduce the heat to low and simmer for 20 minutes.

2   While the liquid simmers, remove any fat from and rinse the chicken. Transfer the chicken to the red cooking liquid (breast-side down if using a whole chicken) and simmer for about 1 hour.

3   Add the turnips. Continue simmering for 30 minutes, turning the chicken occasionally.

4   Turn off the heat and let the chicken and vegetables cool in the liquid for 15 minutes.

5   Remove the chicken and vegetables from the cooking liquid and set aside. Preheat the oven to 400°F.

6   Cut the chicken into small pieces, cutting through the bone. Arrange in a single layer, skin-side up, on a baking sheet. Scatter the turnips among the chicken pieces. Brush the chicken with sesame oil and drizzle the vegetables with a little more oil. Place in the hot oven for 10 minutes to crisp the chicken skin.

7   Meanwhile, skim the fat from the cooking liquid, strain out the solids, and return the liquid to the Dutch oven. Bring to a boil.

8   To serve, place the chicken and vegetables on a platter and spoon a little cooking liquid over them. Pour the rest of the cooking liquid into a pitcher. Spoon the rice into individual bowls, passing the chicken, vegetables, and cooking liquid at the table.

Kitchen Note: *If you prefer, you can omit the turnips and serve the chicken with a stir-fry of vegetables. In that case, the cooking liquid can be strained, frozen, and reused, with additional water and fresh spices added as needed.*

Sunshine Turkey

Serves 4

Orange marmalade creates sunny flavors in a delicious dish that combines turkey breast cutlets with a nutrient-rich blend of orange-colored vegetables. This is a great dish for a busy weekend night if you use a food processor to grate the veggies.

> 3 tablespoons extra-virgin olive oil
> 4 turkey breast cutlets (about 1 pound)
>   Salt and freshly ground black pepper
> 4 cups peeled and shredded mixed carrots,
>   golden beets, and/or winter squashes
> 1 leek, trimmed and thinly sliced
> ½ cup chicken broth (page 127)
> ½ cup orange marmalade
> 3 tablespoons dry white wine

1 Heat the oil in a large skillet over medium-high heat. Season the cutlets with salt and pepper on each side, add to the skillet, and pan-fry until cooked through, about 5 minutes per side. Remove the cutlets from the pan and keep warm.

2 Add the shredded vegetables and leek to the skillet and sauté until tender, 8 to 10 minutes.

3 Stir in the chicken broth, orange marmalade, and wine. Bring to a boil. Season with salt and pepper.

4 Serve the turkey cutlets with the vegetables mounded on top and the pan juices poured over all.

Kitchen Note: *If you happen to have any leftovers, they make excellent sandwiches — just slap the turkey and some of the veggies in a hard roll and enjoy!*

Only in dreams are carrots as big as bears.
— Yiddish proverb

Braised Turkey Breast with Winter Vegetables

Serves 6

White meat tends to dry out when roasted on a whole bird, but cooking it separately ensures that it will be moist and perfect. This easy dish can be the centerpiece of a holiday meal.

1	bone-in turkey breast (5–6 pounds)
2	tablespoons extra-virgin olive oil
1	shallot, finely chopped
2	garlic cloves, minced
1	cup chicken broth (page 127)
½	cup white wine
2	teaspoons mixed dried herbs
1	bay leaf
	Paprika
6	cups peeled and diced mixed root vegetables (beets, carrots, celery root, parsnips, rutabagas, salsify, and/or turnips), white and sweet potatoes, and/or winter squashes

1   Preheat the oven to 325°F.

2   With a pair of poultry shears, cut though the ribs on either side of the turkey backbone and remove the backbone. Turn the turkey breast-side up, place the palm of your hand over the breastbone, and press hard to flatten it.

3   Heat the oil in a large Dutch oven over medium-high heat. Add the turkey and brown on all sides, about 4 minutes per side. Remove the turkey from the pan. Add the shallot and garlic and sauté until fragrant and slightly translucent, 1 to 2 minutes. Return the turkey to the pan with the broth, wine, herbs, and bay leaf. Sprinkle the turkey generously with paprika. Cover the pan and bake for 1½ hours.

4   Add the vegetables to the pan. Replace the cover and cook for about 45 minutes longer, until the vegetables are tender and a meat thermometer inserted in the thickest part of the breast registers 170° to 175°F.

5   Let stand for 10 to 15 minutes. Carve the turkey into slices and transfer to a platter. Spoon the vegetables into a serving bowl. Serve hot.

Braised Turkey on a Bed of Kale

Serves 4

Braising is an excellent way to coax the most flavor from turkey, particularly for parts that tend to dry out when roasting. The kale takes on delicious flavor from the turkey-braising liquid. The presentation of this dish is lovely; serve with a crusty French bread for sopping up the gravy.

2	tablespoons extra-virgin olive oil
4	turkey drumsticks
	Salt and freshly ground black pepper
1	large onion, diced
1	cup chicken broth (page 127)
½	cup dry white or red wine
1½	cups diced tomatoes with juice, or 1 (15-ounce) can
2	teaspoons mixed Italian herbs
4	garlic cloves, minced
12	cups lightly packed chopped kale (remove and discard tough stems)

1   Preheat the oven to 300°F.

2   Heat the oil in a large Dutch oven over medium-high heat. Add the drumsticks in a single layer and brown on all sides, seasoning with salt and pepper as they cook, about 5 minutes per side. You may have to do this in batches. Transfer the turkey to a plate.

3   Add the onion to the pan and sauté until softened, about 3 minutes. Pour the broth and wine into the pan, scraping up the browned bits. Bring to a boil, stirring. Add the tomatoes with their juice, herbs, and garlic. Return the turkey to the pan and cover.

4   Bake for 1½ to 2 hours, until the drumsticks are very tender (a fork inserted into the meaty part will meet with little resistance on its way in or out).

5   Remove the turkey from the pan and keep warm. Skim the fat from the cooking liquid, then bring to a boil. Add the kale, cover, and cook, stirring occasionally, until the kale is tender, 4 to 6 minutes.

6   To serve, make a bed of the kale, vegetables, and cooking juices in individual shallow bowls. Place a drumstick on top of each and serve hot.

Roasted and Braised Duck with Sauerkraut and Root Vegetables

Serves 4

This recipe solves two problems: keeping the duck meat moist while still producing crisp skin and imbuing the vegetables with flavor — great flavor, in fact. If you think root vegetables are delicious, then try them roasted in duck fat (heavenly!).

1 whole duck (4–5 pounds)	4 shallots, peeled and halved
Salt and freshly ground black pepper	1 quart sauerkraut (2 pounds), homemade (page 84) or store-bought (choose the refrigerated type, not the canned type), drained
3 potatoes, peeled and cut into 1-inch cubes	
3–4 cups peeled and cubed mixed root vegetables (carrots, celery root, golden beets, parsnips, rutabagas, salsify, and/or turnips)	½ cup dry white wine
	2 bay leaves

1   Preheat the oven to 375°F.

2   To prepare the duck, remove the giblets and neck from the body cavity and set aside (reserve the liver for another use). Discard any fat that can be readily removed. Wash the duck, pat dry, and place in a large roasting pan. Prick the duck all over with a fork (very important) to help release the fat and sprinkle with salt and pepper.

3   Roast for 45 minutes. Remove from the oven and scatter the potatoes and vegetables around the duck, turning them so they are well coated with the rendered duck fat. Return to the oven and roast for another 45 minutes, checking occasionally to make sure the duck is browning. (If the duck is barely browning, increase the heat by 50 degrees; if it seems to be browning too quickly, reduce the heat slightly.)

4   Meanwhile, taste the sauerkraut and rinse with warm water if it is very salty. Drain well.

5   Remove the duck from the oven and reduce the oven temperature to 300°F. Pour off all but a few tablespoons of the fat from the roasting pan (save for your next batch of roasted root vegetables). Scatter the sauerkraut around the duck, moisten it with the wine, and tuck the bay leaves in. Return to the oven and roast for about 30 minutes longer, until the duck is tender. Carve and serve with the sauerkraut and vegetables.

Roasted Stuffed Duck with Roasted Vegetables

Serves 3 or 4

I thought plain roasted Brussels sprouts couldn't get any better until I had them in this dish, where they are basted by duck fat as they cook. Wow.

DUCK AND VEGETABLES

- 1　whole duck (4–5 pounds)
- 2　tablespoons butter, melted
- 1　pound Brussels sprouts
- 2　carrots, peeled and cut into 1-inch pieces

STUFFING

- 2　tablespoons butter
- 1　onion, finely diced
- 1　tablespoons dried sage
- 1　teaspoon salt
- 2　cups fresh breadcrumbs
- 1　egg, lightly beaten
- 1　tablespoon Dijon mustard
- 　 Freshly ground black pepper

GRAVY

- 1　tablespoon sunflower or canola oil
- 1　onion, coarsely chopped
- 3　garlic cloves, coarsely chopped
- 1　teaspoon dried thyme
- 1　bay leaf
- ½　teaspoon peppercorns
- 4　cups water
- 2　tablespoons cornstarch dissolved in 3 tablespoon cold water
- 　 Salt and freshly ground black pepper

1   Preheat the oven to 400°F.

2   To prepare the duck, remove the giblets and neck from the body cavity and set aside (reserve the liver for another use). Discard any fat that can be readily removed. Wash the duck and pat dry. Use a fork to pierce the skin all over (very important) to help release the fat.

3   To make the stuffing, melt the butter in a large skillet over medium heat. Add the onion and sauté until translucent, about 5 minutes. Remove the pan from the heat and add the sage, salt, breadcrumbs, egg, mustard, and a few grinds of pepper. Mix well.

4   Put the stuffing inside the cavity of the duck. Close up the flaps of the cavity, securing them with toothpicks. Brush the duck with melted butter. Transfer the duck, breast-side down, onto a rack, and set the rack in a roasting pan. Add a little water to the bottom of the pan to prevent burning. Roast for 15 minutes, then lower the heat to 350°F and roast for 30 minutes longer.

5   Meanwhile, begin to make the gravy by preparing duck stock. Chop the duck neck into pieces with a meat cleaver. Combine the neck pieces and oil in a saucepan over medium heat. When some of the duck fat has melted, add the onion, garlic, thyme, bay leaf, and peppercorns, and sauté over medium heat until the vegetables and neck are well browned, about 20 minutes. Add the water and bring slowly to a boil, skimming off any scum that forms. Lower the heat and simmer gently, skimming again from time to time.

6   After roasting for 45 minutes, turn the duck breast-side up. Add the Brussels sprouts and carrots to the roasting pan, turning to coat in the pan juices, and continue roasting for 60 to 70 minutes longer, stirring the vegetables occasionally, until the duck is well browned and the juices run clear.

7   When the duck is almost done, strain the duck stock through a fine sieve to remove the solids. Push down hard with the back of a spoon to extract as much juice as possible. Discard the solids. In a clean saucepan, bring the stock to a boil, stirring occasionally. When the stock has reduced by a third, add the cornstarch mixture and continue to cook until thickened. Season with salt and pepper.

8   Let the duck rest for 15 minutes, then carve. Serve with the vegetables, stuffing, and gravy on the side.

9
Main Dishes with Meat

As fall moves into winter, the outdoor grill gets stowed away and the back of the stove is engaged in slowly simmering stews. The recipes in this chapter utilize tough cuts of meat that melt into tenderness with slow braises, as well as leaner cuts that are perfect for stir-fries. There are also a few recipes for sausage, since it pairs so well with kale and sauerkraut.

Even if you don't eat much red meat, don't ignore this chapter, because some of the recipes can be made with chicken. Also, many of the sausage recipes can be made with chicken and turkey sausage.

The chapter begins with beef recipes, then moves on to lamb recipes, and ends with pork and sausage. There are many classic, old-fashioned favorites represented here, and some very good eating.

RECILE LIST FOR
MAIN DISHES WITH MEAT

Winter-Vegetable Beef Stew

Pot Roast with Root Vegetables

Mustard-Braised Short Ribs with
   Root Vegetables

Reuben Pie

New England Boiled Dinner

Braised Beef Rigatoni

Lamb Stew with Root Vegetables

Stuffed Cabbage Rolls

Shepherd's Pie

Lamb and Leek Flatbread

Spicy Meat Lo Mein

Five-Spice Pork and Cabbage Stir-Fry

Stir-Fried Pork with Hearty Greens

Roast Pork with Sauerkraut and
   Vegetables

Choucroute Garnie

Oven-Braised Sausage and Vegetables

Sausage with Kale and White Beans

Pasta with Kale and Sausage

Ravioli with Smoky Greens

Pasta with Kale, Sausage, and Tomatoes

Braised Kale on Toast

Vegetarian dishes are marked with this symbol:

Winter-Vegetable Beef Stew

Serves 6

I've never met a man who didn't love beef stew — it's one of those dishes to employ when you want to go straight to a man's proverbial heart.

⅔ cup unbleached all-purpose flour

1 tablespoon dried thyme

1 teaspoon dried oregano

Salt and freshly ground black pepper

2 pounds stew beef (chuck or round), cut into bite-size pieces

¼ cup extra-virgin olive oil

1 large onion, thinly sliced

1½ cups beef broth (page 125)

2 cups diced tomatoes with juice, or 1 (15-ounce) can

1 cup red wine

2 garlic cloves, minced

1½ pounds thin-skinned potatoes, peeled and cut into 1-inch cubes

1 pound carrots, peeled and cut into 1-inch cubes

1 pound parsnips, peeled and cut into 1-inch cubes

1 pound rutabagas or turnips, peeled and cut into 1-inch cubes

1 Combine the flour, 1 teaspoon of the thyme, and the oregano in a shallow bowl. Season generously with salt and pepper. Add the beef and toss to coat.

2 Heat 3 tablespoons of the oil over medium heat in a large saucepan or Dutch oven. Lift the beef pieces out of the flour, shaking off the excess, and add a single layer of meat to the pan. Do not crowd the pan. Cook, turning as needed, until browned, about 5 minutes. Remove the meat as it browns and set aside. Continue browning the remaining meat.

3 Add the remaining 1 tablespoon oil and the onion to the pan and sauté until the onion is soft, about 3 minutes. Add the broth, tomatoes, wine, and garlic, and the remaining 2 teaspoons thyme. Stir to scrape up any browned bits from the bottom of the pan. Bring to a boil, then reduce the heat to a slow simmer. Return the meat to the pan. Partially cover the pan and simmer until the meat is tender, about 2 hours.

4 Add the potatoes, carrots, parsnips, and rutabagas to the pan and simmer until the vegetables are tender, about 1 hour.

5 Taste and season with salt and pepper. Serve hot.

Pot Roast with Root Vegetables

Serves 4–6

Low and slow is the secret to pot roast, an easy dish to prepare if you allow enough time. It is excellent on the second day, so feel free to make it in advance. Vary the root vegetables cooked in the gravy according to what you have on hand. I'm not a huge fan of parsnips, but I think they are particularly good prepared this way. Mashed potatoes makes the perfect accompaniment.

4	garlic cloves, minced
2	teaspoons chopped dried rosemary leaves
2	teaspoons dried thyme
2	teaspoons salt, plus more as needed
1	teaspoon freshly ground black pepper, plus more as needed
1	brisket, beef chuck, or beef rump roast (3–5 pounds)
2	tablespoons extra-virgin olive, sunflower, or canola oil
1	onion, finely chopped
1½	cups diced tomatoes with juice, or 1 (15-ounce) can
½	cup dry red wine
2	bay leaves
2–3	carrots, peeled and thickly sliced
1	small rutabaga, peeled and thickly sliced
2	parsnips, peeled and cut into 1-inch cubes
2	turnips, peeled and cut into 1-inch cubes
	About 1 cup beef broth (page 125)
2	tablespoons all-purpose unbleached flour
3	tablespoons water

1   Mix the garlic, rosemary, thyme, salt, and pepper in a small bowl. Rub the mixture all over the meat and let stand for 15 to 20 minutes.

2   Preheat the oven to 275°F.

3   Heat the oil in a large Dutch oven over medium-high heat. Add the meat and brown on all sides until dark and crusty, about 20 minutes.

4   Remove the meat from the pan. Pour off all but 2 tablespoons of the fat. Add the onion and sauté until softened, about 3 minutes. Add the tomatoes, wine, and bay leaves, and bring to a boil, stirring up any browned bits from the bottom of the pan. Return the meat to the pan and cover.

5   Roast in the oven for 2 to 3 hours, turning the meat every half hour, until the meat is tender. The timing varies, depending on the cut and shape of the roast. You can tell the meat is tender when a fork pierces the meat without much resistance. Add the carrots, rutabaga, parsnips, and turnips, and continue to roast about 1 hour longer, until the vegetables are tender and the meat is almost falling-apart tender.

6   Transfer the meat and vegetables to a platter and cover to keep warm. To make gravy, pour the pan juices into a tall glass measure. Discard the bay leaves and skim off any fat from the surface. Add enough beef broth to make 2 cups of liquid. Return to the pan and bring to a boil. Make a paste of the flour and water. Stir in the flour paste and boil until the liquid in the pan is thickened.

7   Slice the meat and serve with the vegetables and gravy.

Never bolt your door with a boiled carrot.
— Irish proverb

Mustard-Braised Short Ribs with Root Vegetables

Serves 4 or 5

Short ribs benefit from the low-slow cooking that fills the house with an aroma promising a hearty meal after a long day of cold-weather activities. Like pot roast, it is excellent on the second day and can be made ahead. Risotto, polenta, barley, and mashed potatoes all make excellent accompaniments.

2	tablespoon extra-virgin olive oil		2	tablespoons whole-grain mustard
3–4	pounds beef short ribs		1	tablespoon dried thyme
	Salt and freshly ground black pepper		1	tablespoon dried rosemary
2	large onions, diced		4	cups peeled and diced mixed root vegetables (carrots, celery root, golden beets, parsnips, rutabagas, salsify, and/or turnips)
½	cup beef broth or chicken broth (pages 125–27)			
½	cup red wine		1	whole garlic head, cloves separated and peeled

1   Heat the oil in a large Dutch oven over medium-high heat. Season the short ribs with salt and pepper. Brown the ribs on all sides, adjusting the heat so the ribs brown well but do not burn.

2   Transfer the ribs to a plate. Preheat the oven to 275°F.

3   Pour off all but 2 tablespoons of the fat from the pan. Reduce the heat to medium and add the onions. Sauté until soft and beginning to turn golden in color, about 10 minutes. Stir in the broth, wine, and mustard, and bring to a boil, scraping up any browned bits. Return the short ribs to the pan, sprinkle the thyme and rosemary over the meat, and cover.

4   Braise in the oven for about 2 hours, until the meat is very tender when pierced with a fork. Add the vegetables and garlic and continue to braise for 45 to 60 minutes longer, until the meat is practically falling off the bone and the vegetables are tender.

5   Pour off the liquid and skim off the fat. Return the liquid to the pan. Taste and adjust the seasoning. Cover and reheat if necessary. Serve hot.

Kitchen Note: *A fat separator is a wonderfully convenient tool. It is a narrow, clear pitcher with a pouring spout that emerges from the bottom. The fat rises to the top, and you pour off the stock from below the fat. I find a quart-size fat separator to be much more useful than a cup-size one.*

Reuben Pie

Serves 4–6

You've heard of Reuben sandwiches, but sandwiches are for lunch. The same ingredients make up this pie, which is good for dinner. In times past, pies were much more popular than sandwiches, for lunch or for dinner.

1½	cups sauerkraut, homemade (page 84) or store-bought (choose the refrigerated type, not the canned type), drained
	Pastry for a 10-inch double-crust pie (page 265)
8	ounces Swiss or Gruyère cheese, thinly sliced
8	ounces corned beef, diced or cut into strips (about 1 cup)
1	small onion, halved and sliced

1 Preheat the oven to 425°F.

2 Taste the sauerkraut and rinse with warm water if it is very salty. Drain well.

3 Prepare the pastry according to the recipe directions. Roll out one piece of dough into a 12-inch round and ease into a 10-inch pie plate. Layer half the cheese in the pie shell. Top with half the corned beef. Layer the sauerkraut on top. Scatter the onion over the sauerkraut, then the remaining corned beef, then the remaining cheese. Roll out the second piece of dough slightly larger than the first and place on the filled pie. Trim the dough ½ inch beyond the edge of the pie plate. Fold the extra under the bottom crust. Crimp the edges. Prick holes in the top to allow steam to escape.

4 Reduce the oven temperature to 375°F. Bake for 35 to 45 minutes, until the top of the pie is golden.

5 Let stand for 10 minutes. Serve hot.

Kitchen Note: *Use either thin-sliced deli corned beef (cut into strips) or about 1 cup of diced leftover homemade corned beef.*

New England Boiled Dinner

Serves 4–6

The original New England boiled dinner was probably made with salt beef, but when was the last time (or the first time) you saw salt beef in the supermarket? Corned beef was an inexpensive replacement, adopted by immigrant Irish cooks in the 1800s. The first printed recipe, which appeared in a 1936 edition of the Fannie Farmer's *Boston Cooking-School Cookbook*, called for rutabagas, potatoes, carrots, and cabbage, as does this version, which cooks the beef in a slow oven for an extra-tender, fuss-free dinner. Substitute other root vegetables as you please. If you are from Newfoundland, you might call this "Jiggs Dinner" and serve it with "pease pudding," which is a purée of yellow split peas.

4–6	pounds corned beef brisket
2	tablespoons mixed pickling spices
3	thin-skinned potatoes, peeled and cut into bite-size pieces
2	small carrots, peeled and cut into bite-size pieces
1	small rutagaba, peeled and cut into bite-size pieces
½	head green cabbage, cut into wedges
	Mustard, for serving
	Prepared horseradish, for serving

1   Preheat the oven to 250°F.

2   Cover the corned beef with water in a large Dutch oven. Add the pickling spices. Cover with a lid.

3   Bake for about 3 hours, until the meat is tender when poked with a fork. Let the meat cool in the cooking liquid for 15 minutes. Transfer the meat to a platter and tent with foil to keep warm.

4   Set the pan on the stovetop and bring to a boil. Add the potatoes, carrots, and rutabaga, and simmer for 20 minutes. Add the cabbage and simmer for 5 to 10 minutes longer, until all the vegetables are tender.

5   Use a slotted spoon to transfer the vegetables to a serving bowl. Cover and keep warm. Return the meat to the cooking liquid to reheat for about 5 minutes.

6   Slice the meat against the grain and serve with the vegetables, passing the mustard and horseradish at the table.

Kitchen Note: *This dish is far more pleasing when the vegetables are cooked separately and care is taken not to overcook the cabbage.*

Horseradish

A handy root to have around, horseradish is notorious for being hard to eradicate once well established in the garden. If you want to have horseradish over the winter, you can dig up some roots after a few frosts but before the ground is frozen and store them in the root cellar with other root vegetables (at 32° to 40°F and 90 to 95 percent humidity). When the ground thaws in spring, roots left over the winter will be in harvest-ready condition.

To use horseradish, peel the roots and grind in a food processor, adding a bit of white vinegar to help with the puréeing and to help preserve the root. Puréed horseradish will keep for several months in the refrigerator, but it loses flavor over time. It can be added to sour cream or mayonnaise to make a delicious dip or spread for sandwiches. It is the traditional condiment for roast beef sandwiches.

Braised Beef Rigatoni

Serves 6-8

A hearty ragù of beef and vegetables makes an outstanding sauce for the pasta. This is a terrific, rib-sticking meal. If you like, replace the pancetta with 2 tablespoons olive oil for a more virtuous dish — virtue being relative, all things considered.

4   ounces pancetta or bacon, diced

1   pound beef chuck steak, cut into 1-inch cubes

1   carrot, peeled and finely diced

1   celery root, peeled and finely diced

1   onion, finely diced

1   parsnip, peeled and finely diced

1   cup beef broth (page 125)

1   cup medium-bodied red wine

1   (6-ounce) can tomato paste

1   whole garlic head, cloves separated and peeled

1   tablespoon mixed dried Italian herbs

2   bay leaves

1   pound rigatoni

1   cup freshly grated Parmesan cheese, plus more for serving

Salt and freshly ground black pepper

1   Heat a Dutch oven over medium-high heat. Add the pancetta and cook until browned, about 8 minutes. Remove the pancetta with a slotted spoon and set aside. Add the beef to the pan and brown, turning as needed, about 10 minutes. Transfer the meat to a bowl or plate and keep warm. Add the carrot, celery root, onion, and parsnip, and sauté until the vegetables are a little softened, about 5 minutes.

2   Add the broth, stirring to loosen any browned bits. Bring to a boil, then reduce the heat and return the beef and pancetta to the pan. Stir in the wine, tomato paste, garlic, Italian herbs, and bay leaves. Cover and simmer, stirring occasionally, until the meat is completely tender and falling apart and the vegetables are soft, about 3 hours. During the final half hour of cooking, break up the meat and vegetables with a spoon to form a thick, chunky sauce.

3   Bring a large pot of salted water to a boil. Cook the rigatoni in the boiling water until al dente. Drain.

4   Combine the pasta with the sauce and mix well. Stir in the Parmesan. Taste and adjust the seasoning. Serve hot, passing extra cheese at the table.

Kitchen Note: *Pancetta is cured, but not smoked, bacon. It is flavorful and usually salty, adding great flavor to sauces. Substitute smoked bacon or 2 tablespoons olive oil if you can't find pancetta.*

Lamb Stew with Root Vegetables

Serves 4–6

Lamb isn't for everyone, though I don't understand why. A lamb stew with a lovely Pinot Noir and a crusty loaf of French bread keeps the cold winds of winter at bay.

4	pounds lamb stew meat with bones (from the neck and shoulder)	3	cups chicken broth or beef broth (pages 125–27)
⅔	cup unbleached all-purpose flour	1	cup red wine
2	tablespoons chopped fresh thyme leaves	2	garlic cloves, minced
	Salt and freshly ground black pepper	1	pound carrots and/or parsnips, peeled and cut into 1-inch cubes
¼	cup sunflower or canola oil	1	pound celery root, peeled and cut into 1-inch cubes
1	large onion, halved and thinly sliced	1	pound rutabagas and/or turnips, peeled and cut into 1-inch cubes

1   Pat the lamb dry. Combine the flour and 1 tablespoon of the thyme in a shallow bowl. Season generously with salt and pepper. Add the lamb and toss to coat.

2   Heat 3 tablespoons of the oil in a large Dutch oven over medium-high heat. Lift the lamb pieces out of the flour, shaking off the excess, and add in a single layer to the pan. Do not overcrowd the pan; you may have to cook in batches. Brown the meat on all sides, 5 to 8 minutes. Remove the meat as it browns and set aside. Continue browning the remaining meat.

3   Add the remaining 1 tablespoon oil and the onion to the pan and sauté until soft, about 3 minutes. Add the broth and wine, scraping up any browned bits from the bottom of the pan. Bring to a boil, then reduce the heat to a slow simmer. Return the meat to the pan. Partially cover the pan and let simmer until the meat is tender, about 2 hours.

4   Add the carrots, celery root, and rutabagas, and simmer until the vegetables are tender, about 1 hour.

5   Taste and adjust the seasoning, as needed. Serve hot.

Kitchen Notes: *Shoulder and neck meat are perfect for the stew, becoming very tender with slow cooking. And cooking meat on the bone tends to result in a more flavorful dish. But it is difficult to eat this stew delicately, so provide large napkins and don't be too dainty.*

Stuffed Cabbage Rolls

Serves 4 or 5

You can call stuffed cabbage golumpkies, golabkis, holupkis, or sarmas. They are pretty ubiquitous in eastern Europe. My mother's version called for gingersnaps in the tomato sauce, which I thought was weird until I read that same version in *The Joy of Cooking*. Actually, I still think it is weird, which is why I came up with my own version. Plan ahead and freeze the cabbage, which avoids the awkward process of blanching the whole head of cabbage to make the leaves pliant.

CABBAGE ROLLS
- 1 medium head green cabbage
- 1 pound ground beef or ground turkey
- 1 cup cooked white or brown rice
- ½ onion, finely chopped
- 2 eggs, beaten
- 2 garlic cloves, minced
- 2 teaspoons salt
- ½ teaspoon freshly ground black pepper

SAUCE
- 2 cups unseasoned tomato sauce or tomato purée
- ½ onion, finely chopped
- ¼–½ cup apple cider vinegar (artisanal cider vinegar is recommended)
- ½ cup firmly packed brown sugar
- 1 teaspoon ground ginger
- Salt and freshly ground black pepper

1   One day before you plan to prepare this dish, remove the core from the cabbage. This is the hardest part. Using a long, thin, sharp knife, cut 2 to 3 inches into the cabbage in a circle about ¼ inch out from the core. Lift out the core, which should leave a hole about 2 inches wide and 2½ inches deep. Transfer the cabbage to the freezer and freeze overnight.

2   The next day, defrost the cabbage at room temperature or in a microwave at 50 percent power. Carefully separate the head into individual leaves. Wash the leaves in cold water. With a small, sharp knife, trim off the tough outer spines and discard them. Set aside the leaves.

3   Combine the ground meat, rice, onion, eggs, garlic, salt, and pepper in a large bowl. Mix until well blended; your hands are the best tool for this. Set aside.

4   In another bowl, thoroughly mix together the tomato sauce, onion, ¼ cup cider vinegar, brown sugar, and ginger. Season with salt and pepper. Add more cider vinegar as needed for a sweet-sour sauce (artisanal cider vinegar is less sharp-tasting than supermarket cider vinegar and works better in this sauce).

5   Spoon about ⅓ cup of the meat mixture onto each cabbage leaf. Fold in the sides and roll up to form a neat parcel. Transfer to a plate or baking sheet. You should have enough filling to make ten rolls.

6   Preheat the oven to 350°F.

7   Chop the remaining cabbage and place in the bottom of a 9- by 13-inch baking dish. Cover with about half the sauce. Arrange the cabbage rolls carefully on top of the sauce and pour in the remainder of the sauce to cover.

8   Cover the casserole and bake for 1 hour. Serve hot.

Kitchen Note: *You'll want to serve this with something to mop up the extra sauce. Mashed potatoes and hearty rye bread are both good choices.*

Shepherd's Pie

Serves 6

Shepherd's pie was first served in England, made from lamb — or mutton — left over from the Sunday roast. This recipe harkens back to the original, with tender lamb chunks floating in a rich gravy alongside tasty root vegetables. This is a dish fit for company, a world apart from the American version made with ground beef and frozen corn.

FILLING

- 2 pounds boneless lamb shoulder or other boneless lamb stew meat, cut into 1-inch cubes
- 1 teaspoon salt
- ¼ teaspoon freshly ground black pepper
- ½ cup all-purpose flour
- 3 tablespoons canola or sunflower oil
- ½ cup dry red wine
- 1 cup beef broth (page 125)
- 2 medium leeks, trimmed and cut into ½-inch slices
- 6 button mushrooms
- 2 carrots, peeled and sliced diagonally
- 2 medium turnips or 1 small rutabaga, peeled and cut into 1-inch cubes
- 4 garlic cloves, minced
- 1 tablespoon dried thyme

TOPPING

- 2½ pounds russet (baking) potatoes
- 2 garlic cloves, peeled (optional)
- 1 cup milk
- 3 tablespoons butter
- Salt and freshly ground black pepper

1   Preheat the oven to 300°F. Pat the lamb dry, place in a small bowl, and sprinkle with the salt and pepper. Add the flour and toss to coat.

2   Heat the oil in a large Dutch oven over medium-high heat. Add half the lamb and cook until well browned on all sides, 5 to 8 minutes. Transfer the browned lamb to a plate with a slotted spoon and repeat with the remaining lamb.

3   Add the wine and bring to a boil over high heat for 1 minute, stirring and scraping up the browned bits from the pan. Add the broth, leeks, mushrooms, carrots, turnips, garlic, and thyme. Return the lamb, along with any juices that have accumulated on the plate, and stir to combine. Season with additional salt and pepper. Reduce the heat to medium-high and bring to a simmer. Cover the Dutch oven with the lid or foil.

4   Set the Dutch oven in the middle of the oven and bake for 1½ to 2 hours, stirring once or twice, until the lamb is tender. Taste and adjust the seasoning.

5   Meanwhile, to make the topping, peel and quarter the potatoes. Cover with cold salted water by 1 inch in a large pot and add the garlic. Bring to a boil and boil, covered, until very tender, 15 to 20 minutes. Drain well.

6   Return the potatoes to the pot and cook over medium heat until the potatoes are dry, about 1 minute. Add the milk and butter and mash the potatoes until smooth. Season with salt and pepper.

7   Preheat the broiler.

8   Transfer the lamb mixture to a 3-quart casserole that can go from oven to tabletop. Spoon the mashed potatoes over the lamb and vegetables and spread evenly. Use a fork to make a decorative pattern in the potatoes. Broil about 3 inches from the heat until the potatoes are golden, about 3 minutes. Serve hot.

Lamb and Leek Flatbread

Serves 4

Think of this as a Greek pizza, and you have some idea of what's to come. The topping is a savory combination of lamb, leeks, and feta cheese. To serve this as an appetizer, make the flatbread on a rectangular baking sheet and cut into small squares. If you have fresh mint on hand, add a few tablespoons of the chopped leaves to the sautéed leek mixture for added flavor.

½ recipe Basic Pizza Dough (page 264)	12 ounces ground lamb
2 tablespoons extra-virgin olive oil, plus more for brushing	1 teaspoon crumbled dried rosemary
	Salt and freshly ground black pepper
2 leeks, trimmed and thinly sliced	5 ounces feta cheese, crumbled
2 garlic cloves, minced	2 tablespoons pine nuts (optional)

1 Prepare the pizza dough and set aside in a warm, draft-free place to rise until doubled in bulk, about 1 hour.

2 Meanwhile, heat the 2 tablespoons oil in a large skillet over medium-high heat. Add the leeks and garlic and sauté until tender, about 5 minutes. Remove from the skillet with a slotted spoon and set aside.

3 Add the lamb to the skillet and sauté until browned, about 8 minutes. Remove from the skillet with a slotted spoon and combine with the leeks. Sprinkle with the rosemary and season generously with salt and pepper.

4 Preheat the oven to 500°F.

5 Lightly oil a 10-inch or 12-inch round pizza pan or a 12- by 15-inch baking sheet. Stretch the dough to fit the pan. Brush the dough with a little olive oil. Scatter the lamb mixture over the pizza dough. Top with the feta and pine nuts, if using.

6 Bake on the bottom shelf of the oven until the crust is golden, about 12 minutes. Slice and serve warm.

Variation: Lamb, Leek, and Potato Cassserole

Replace the pizza dough with Rosemary Roasted Potatoes (page 171). Bake at 350°F for 45 minutes.

Spicy Meat Lo Mein

Serves 4-6

Beef or pork (or even chicken) work equally well in this spicy version of lo mein. This is an "off menu" dish at a local Chinese restaurant. It's called "bastard lo mein" by the kids who work there after school.

1	pound Chinese wheat noodles or thin spaghetti
3-4	garlic cloves, minced
1	(1-inch) piece fresh ginger, peeled and minced
3	tablespoons soy sauce, plus more as needed
1	tablespoon Chinese chili paste with garlic
1	tablespoon Chinese rice wine or dry sherry
1	tablespoon sugar
1	pound boneless pork, beef, or chicken, cut into matchsticks
¼	cup peanut, sunflower, or canola oil, plus more as needed
2	carrots, peeled and cut into matchsticks
¼	head green cabbage or ½ head napa or Chinese cabbage, thinly sliced
1	(4-inch) piece daikon radish or 1 small turnip, peeled and cut into matchsticks
¼	cup Chinese oyster sauce

1   Bring a large pot of salted water to a boil. Add the noodles and boil until al dente. Drain well.

2   Combine the garlic, ginger, soy sauce, chili paste, rice wine, and sugar in a small bowl. Mix well, stir in the pork, and set aside.

3   Heat a large wok or frying pan over high heat. Add 2 tablespoons of the oil and swirl in the hot wok. When the oil is very hot, add the pork mixture and stir-fry until the meat is cooked through, about 5 minutes. (While the meat cooks, wash and dry the bowl.) Scrape the meat and juices back into the bowl.

4   Heat the remaining 2 tablespoons oil in the wok. Add the carrots and stir-fry until just barely tender, about 3 minutes. Add the cabbage and daikon radish and stir-fry until wilted, about 3 minutes. At any point, if the vegetables don't seem to be cooking, add a little soy sauce to encourage them to steam.

5   Return the meat mixture to the wok and add the noodles. Pour in the oyster sauce and toss to coat well and combine all the ingredients.

6   Taste and add additional soy sauce, if needed. Serve hot.

Five-Spice Pork and Cabbage Stir-Fry

Serves 4–6

Shanghai cuisine is bold — sweet and hot — like this simple stir-fry of pork, cabbage, and carrots. The heat of the chili is balanced by the sweetness, but if you don't like your food hot, use a level tablespoon of chili paste rather than a heaping one. The stir-fry is equally delicious made with chicken or beef.

PORK AND MARINADE

- 2 tablespoons Chinese rice wine or dry sherry
- 2 tablespoons soy sauce
- 1 teaspoon Asian sesame oil
- ¼ teaspoon salt
- ¼ teaspoon sugar
- 1 tablespoon cornstarch
- 1 pound boneless pork loin, cut into matchsticks

SAUCE

- ¼ cup soy sauce
- ¼ cup sugar
- 3 tablespoons Chinese rice wine or dry sherry
- 1 heaping tablespoon Chinese chili paste with garlic
- 1 (1½-inch) piece fresh ginger, peeled and minced
- 1 teaspoon Asian sesame oil
- 1 teaspoon Chinese five-spice powder

STIR-FRY

- 3 tablespoons peanut, sunflower, or canola oil
- 2 carrots, peeled and cut into matchsticks
- 8 cups thinly sliced green cabbage or Chinese cabbage

Hot cooked white rice, for serving

1. Combine the rice wine, soy sauce, sesame oil, salt, sugar, and cornstarch in a small bowl. Mix well, stir in the pork, and set aside.

2. To prepare the sauce, combine the soy sauce, sugar, rice wine, chili paste, ginger, sesame oil, and five-spice powder in a small bowl. Set aside.

3. Heat a large wok over high heat. Add 1 tablespoon of the peanut oil and swirl in the hot wok. Add the pork mixture and stir-fry until the pork is cooked through, about 8 minutes. Scrape out of the wok and keep warm.

4. Wipe the wok clean. Heat the remaining 2 tablespoons peanut oil in the wok. Add the carrots and stir-fry until limp, about 2 minutes. Add the cabbage and stir-fry until barely tender, about 4 minutes. Return the pork to the wok. Pour in the sauce. Stir-fry until the cabbage is tender crisp and the sauce is thick, about 3 minutes. Serve at once over hot rice.

Kitchen Note: *Chinese five-spice powder is sold wherever Chinese foods are sold. It is a mixture of equal parts ground cinnamon, cloves, fennel seeds, star anise, and Sichuan peppercorns. It is essential to the flavor of this dish.*

Sowe Carrets in your Gardens, and humbly praise God for them, as for a singular and great blessing.

— Richard Gardiner, *Profitable Instructions for the Manuring, Sowing and Planting of Kitchen Gardens* (1599)

Stir-Fried Pork with Hearty Greens

Serves 4 as a main dish

Kale or mustard greens? Some prefer kale and find mustard greens too spicy or bitter. I love them both and make this stir-fry with whichever green needs using up.

¼ cup soy sauce

3 tablespoons Chinese rice wine or dry sherry

3 tablespoons Chinese oyster sauce

1 tablespoon sugar

1 (1-inch) piece fresh ginger, peeled and minced

2 garlic cloves, minced

1 pound boneless pork tenderloin, cut into matchsticks

2 tablespoons peanut, sunflower, or canola oil

1 pound mustard greens or kale, shredded (about 12 cups lightly packed; remove and discard tough stems)

Hot cooked rice, for serving

1   Combine 2 tablespoons of the soy sauce, 2 tablespoons of the rice wine, the oyster sauce, sugar, ginger, and garlic. Mix well, stir in the pork, and set aside.

2   Heat a large wok over high heat. Add 1 tablespoon of the peanut oil and swirl in the hot wok. Add the pork mixture and stir-fry until the pork is cooked through and no longer pink, about 5 minutes. Remove the pork and sauce from the wok and keep warm.

3   Wipe the wok clean. Heat the remaining 1 tablespoon peanut oil in the wok over high heat. Add the greens and the remaining 2 tablespoons soy sauce and 1 tablespoon rice wine. Stir-fry for 1 minute, then cover and steam until the greens are barely tender, 3 to 5 minutes. Return the pork and sauce to the wok and stir-fry for an additional 2 to 3 minutes to finish cooking the greens. Serve at once over hot rice.

Kitchen Notes: *This stir-fry can be made with cabbage, though I prefer the heartier greens. And chicken or beef can replace the pork.*

Roast Pork with Sauerkraut and Vegetables

Serves 6-8

Don't overcook the pork. Today's lean pork is best roasted until it is medium, not well done. Applesauce is a traditional accompaniment.

1 tablespoon sunflower or canola oil	6 cups peeled and cubed mixed root vegetables (beets, carrots, celery root, parsnips, rutabagas, salsify, and/or turnips), white and sweet potatoes, and/or winter squashes
1 (3- to 5-pound) bone-in pork loin roast	
½ cup chicken broth (page 127)	
4 pounds sauerkraut, homemade (page 84) or store-bought (choose the refrigerated type, not the canned type), drained	1 large onion, halved and slivered (sliced vertically)
	1 large sprig rosemary
	Freshly ground black pepper

1   Preheat the oven to 325°F.

2   Heat the oil in a large skillet over medium-high heat. Add the pork and brown on all sides, about 15 minutes. Transfer the pork to a large roasting pan. Add the broth to the skillet, scraping up any browned bits. Remove from the heat.

3   Taste the sauerkraut and rinse with warm water if it is very salty. Drain well.

4   Add the sauerkraut, root vegetables, onion, and rosemary to the roasting pan. Pour in the broth. Season generously with pepper. Tightly cover the pan with aluminum foil.

5   Roast for 1½ to 2 hours, until the pork registers 145° to 150°F on an instant-read thermometer.

6   Transfer the meat to a warm platter and let rest for 15 minutes. Keep the vegetables warm. Carve the meat and serve with the vegetables.

Vegetables are interesting but lack a sense of purpose when unaccompanied by a good cut of meat.

— Fran Lebowitz

Choucroute Garnie

Serves 6

In Alsace, where French and German cuisine mingle, choucroute garnie is a perfect example of winter peasant food, complexly flavored and deeply satisfying. It is made of sauerkraut braised in white wine and served with an assortment of sausages, ham, and fresh and smoked pork. Boiled potatoes and strong mustard accompany the dish. We can't always find the classic sausages in this country, but the dish is perfect with almost any sausage you might think to use. A slightly fruity Riesling is a good choice for the wine.

12	cups (3 pounds) sauerkraut, homemade (page 84) or store-bought (choose the refrigerated type, not the canned type), drained
4	ounces bacon or salt pork, diced
2–3	carrots, peeled and cut into 1-inch chunks
2	onions, halved and sliced
1	large garlic clove, minced
1	large tart apple, peeled, cored, and chopped
1½	cups chicken broth (page 127)
1	cup white wine
1	bay leaf
6	whole peppercorns
8	juniper berries
	Salt and freshly ground black pepper
1½	pounds assorted smoked and precooked fresh sausages
1	pound smoked boneless pork loin (Canadian bacon), cut into 6 slices, or smoked boneless pork chops
6	thin-skinned potatoes, peeled and quartered
	Dijon mustard, smooth or coarse-grained, for serving

1   Taste the sauerkraut and rinse with warm water if it is very salty. Drain well. Preheat the oven to 325°F.

2   Cook the bacon in a large Dutch oven until lightly browned. Remove with a slotted spoon and set aside. Add the carrots and onions to the pan and sauté until soft, about 3 minutes. Stir in the garlic and apple and sauté for 1 minute. Add the sauerkraut, cooked bacon, broth, wine, bay leaf, peppercorns, and juniper berries. Season with salt, if needed, and pepper. Bring to a simmer and cover.

3   Set the pan in the oven and braise for 1 hour.

4   Add the sausages and pork, burying the meat in the sauerkraut. Taste the sauerkraut and add salt and pepper if needed. Cover the pan, return it to the oven, and braise for 30 minutes longer.

5   Meanwhile, cover the potatoes with salted water in a saucepan. Bring to a boil, then reduce the heat and simmer until just tender, 15 to 20 minutes. Drain and add to the choucroute.

6   Serve the choucroute directly from the pan, or arrange it on a platter, the sauerkraut on the bottom, the meats on top, and the potatoes around. Serve mustard on the side.

Oven-Braised Sausage and Vegetables

Serves 4

When you need a quick burst of flavor, sausage readily fits the bill. The good news is that there are many brands of sausage now available that have quite a healthful profile. Often made of chicken, these new sausages are low in fat and high in flavor. Combined with root vegetables and a loaf of crusty French or hearty whole-grain bread, this dish makes an appealing and quick supper.

- 1 carrot or parsnip, peeled and cut into ¾-inch cubes
- 1 small celery root, peeled and cut into ¾-inch cubes
- 1 medium rutabaga, peeled and cut into ¾-inch cubes
- 1 large beet, peeled and cut into ¾-inch cubes
- 2 medium turnips or Jerusalem artichokes, peeled and cut into ¾-inch cubes
- 1 onion, halved and slivered (sliced vertically)
- 2 tablespoons extra-virgin olive oil
  Salt and freshly ground pepper
- 1 pound precooked sausage, thinly sliced
- 1 whole garlic head, cloves separated, smashed, and peeled
- 1 cup chicken broth, beef broth, or vegetable broth (pages 125–27)
- 1 teaspoon dried thyme

1 Preheat the oven to 450°F. Lightly oil a large shallow roasting pan.

2 Mound the carrot, celery root, rutabaga, beet, turnips, and onion in the prepared pan. Drizzle the oil over them, season with salt and pepper, and toss gently to coat. Arrange in a single layer in the pan.

3 Roast for 15 minutes, stirring or shaking the pan occasionally for even cooking, until the vegetables are partly tender and lightly colored. With a metal spatula, turn and toss the vegetables. Add the sausage and garlic, turning and tossing again. Roast for 10 minutes longer.

4 Turn and toss the vegetables and sausage once more. Pour in the broth and sprinkle with the thyme. Braise in the oven for about 10 minutes, until the broth is mostly absorbed. Taste and adjust the seasoning. Serve hot.

Sausage with Kale and White Beans

Serves 4–6

This hearty dish tastes like it has simmered on the stove for ages but can be produced in less than an hour using canned beans. And if the sausage you choose is low-fat turkey sausage, then the dish is as healthful as it is delicious. Serve with bread for mopping up the tasty juices.

2 tablespoons extra-virgin olive oil, plus more for drizzling

1 pound hot Italian-style sausage (pork or turkey), cut into ½-inch pieces

3 cups cooked cannellini or Great Northern beans, or 2 (15-ounce) cans cannellini beans, rinsed and drained

4 garlic cloves, chopped

2 cups chicken broth (page 127)

1 pound kale, coarsely chopped (about 12 cups lightly packed; remove and discard tough stems)

Salt and freshly ground black pepper

Freshly grated Parmesan cheese, for serving (optional)

1 Heat the oil in a large Dutch oven or saucepan over medium-high heat. Add the sausage and cook until browned, stirring occasionally, about 8 minutes. Add the beans and garlic and cook, stirring occasionally, for 3 minutes.

2 Add the chicken broth and kale. Bring to a boil and stir well, then reduce the heat to medium and cook, covered, until the kale is tender, 15 to 20 minutes.

3 Season with salt and pepper. Serve hot, passing the cheese, if using, at the table.

Pasta with Kale and Sausage

Serves 4

A simple combination of kale and sausage makes a wonderful topping for pasta. If you'd rather use collard greens, blanch the greens for 10 minutes.

3	tablespoons extra-virgin olive oil
1	pound sweet or hot Italian-style sausage (pork or turkey), casings discarded and sausage crumbled
1	pound kale, coarsely chopped (about 12 cups lightly packed; remove and discard tough stems)
1	pound orecchiette, conchiglie, or other cup-shaped pasta
2	garlic cloves, minced
1	shallot, diced
⅔	cup chicken broth (page 127)
½	cup finely grated Parmesan cheese, plus more for serving

1   Begin heating a large pot of salted water to a boil for the kale and linguine.

2   Meanwhile, heat the oil in a large heavy skillet over medium-high heat. Add the sausage and cook until browned, breaking it up with a spoon, 5 to 7 minutes.

3   Blanch the kale in the boiling water, until bright green and slightly tender, about 3 minutes. Remove kale with a large sieve or whatever tool you have handy (a strainer with a handle, a wide flat skimmer, et cetera). Let drain in a colander.

4   Return the water in the pot to a boil. Add the pasta and cook until al dente. Reserve 1 cup of the pasta cooking water, and then drain the pasta.

5   While the pasta cooks, add the garlic and shallot to the sausage in the skillet and sauté over medium-high heat, stirring frequently, until just tender, about 3 minutes. Add the kale and broth, stirring and scraping up any browned bits, and cook until heated through, about 3 minutes. Add the pasta and ½ cup of the reserved cooking water, tossing to combine. Stir in the Parmesan and thin with additional cooking water if desired. Serve immediately.

Kitchen Note: *The pasta shape of choice is one that can be forked up with a few beans, pieces of sausage, and flakes of green. Orecchiette ("little ears") or conchiglie ("conch shells") fit the bill perfectly.*

Ravioli with Smoky Greens

Serves 4

Frozen cheese-filled ravioli is a convenience food I like to have on hand. Combined with hearty greens, it makes a healthful dish that can be prepared in just minutes. It can be made without the bacon if a vegetarian version is preferred.

4   strips bacon, diced
2   garlic cloves, minced
1   pound mustard greens or kale, chopped
        (about 12 cups lightly packed; remove
        and discard tough stems)
    Salt and freshly ground black pepper
1   (30-ounce) package frozen cheese-filled ravioli
½   cup freshly grated Parmesan cheese

1   Begin heating a large pot of salted water to a boil for the ravioli.

2   Meanwhile, cook the bacon in a large Dutch oven over medium-high heat until well browned and crisp. With a slotted spoon, transfer the bacon to paper towels to drain.

3   Add the garlic to the pan and sauté until fragrant, about 30 seconds. Add the greens and continue to sauté until wilted, about 3 minutes. Season with salt and pepper. Add 2 tablespoons water, cover, and steam until tender, about 3 minutes. Keep warm.

4   Add the ravioli to the boiling water and simmer (do not boil) until the ravioli are cooked through and rise to the surface of the water, about 5 minutes. Drain well.

5   With a slotted spoon, transfer the ravioli to the pan with the greens. Sprinkle with half the Parmesan and toss gently. Transfer the ravioli and greens to a serving dish. Sprinkle the remaining Parmesan on top, garnish with the bacon, and serve.

Variation: Vegetarian Ravioli with Greens

Bacon provides the smoky flavor, but an all-vegetarian version can be made by omitting the bacon and using 2 tablespoons of extra-virgin olive oil for sautéing the greens.

Pasta with Kale, Sausage, and Tomatoes

Serves 4-6

This is one of the dishes for which kale and collards can be used inter-changeably, but the sauce needs more time to simmer if collards are used.

2	tablespoons extra-virgin olive oil
1	pound Italian sausage (pork or turkey), casings removed and meat crumbled
1	onion, diced
4	garlic cloves, minced
1	pound kale, mustard greens, or collard greens, chopped (about 12 cups lightly packed; remove and discard tough stems)
1	quart diced tomatoes with juice, or 1 (28-ounce) can
1	cup chicken broth (page 127)
1	teaspoon crushed red pepper flakes (optional)
	Salt and freshly ground black pepper
1	pound short pasta, such as rotini or medium shells
1½	cups freshly grated Parmesan cheese

1 Begin heating a large pot of salted water to a boil for the pasta.

2 Heat the oil in a large saucepan over medium-high heat. Add the sausage, onion, and garlic, and cook, stirring and breaking up the meat with a spoon, until browned, about 8 minutes. Add the greens and sauté until limp, about 2 minutes. Stir in the tomatoes, broth, and red pepper flakes, if using. Bring to a boil, then reduce the heat and simmer until the greens are silky in texture or cooked to your liking, 10 to 30 minutes.

3 Cook the pasta in the boiling water until just barely al dente. Reserve 1 cup of the cooking water, and then drain. Add the pasta to the sauce, mix well, and cook until the pasta is tender, about 1 minute, adding the reserved cooking water if the pasta seems dry.

4 Mix in 1 cup of the Parmesan. Serve immediately, passing the remaining ½ cup Parmesan at the table.

Braised Kale on Toast

Serves 4

Some recipes are so simple, so natural, that it's amazing they aren't already part of your repertoire. That's how I felt when I first read this recipe, which is adapted from *The Zuni Café Cookbook*. Often such simple recipes are examples of the finest rustic European farmhouse recipes and utterly dependent on using top-quality ingredients. So use your best chicken broth and olive oil and your finest rustic bread (the bread can be slightly stale). Don't forget the prosciutto, and don't rush the eggs as they cook. A rough red table wine and Edith Piaf are the perfect accompaniments.

6 tablespoons extra-virgin olive oil	Salt and freshly ground black pepper
1 onion, diced	8 slices rustic white bread
1 pound kale, thinly sliced (about 12 cups lightly packed; remove and discard tough stems)	3-4 garlic cloves, halved
2 large garlic cloves, minced	8 eggs
Pinch of crushed red pepper flakes	2 ounces prosciutto, torn into bite-size bits
3 cups chicken broth (page 127), water, or a combination of the two	

1   Heat 3 tablespoons of the oil in a large saucepan over medium heat. Add the onion and sauté until softened, about 5 minutes. Add the kale, minced garlic, and red pepper flakes, and stir until the kale is fully wilted, 4 to 5 minutes. Add the broth. Bring to a simmer, cover, and continue to simmer until the kale is completely tender, about 20 minutes. Taste and add salt and pepper as needed.

2   Toast the bread in a toaster or under a broiler. Rub both sides of the toast with the halved garlic. Arrange two pieces of toast in the bottom of each of four wide soup bowls.

3   Heat the remaining 3 tablespoons oil in a large skillet over low heat. Crack the eggs into a small bowl or dish (taking care not to break the yolks). Gently slide the eggs into the skillet and cover with a lid. Cook for about 5 minutes, until the egg whites solidify. Do not rush this process! Season with salt and freshly ground black pepper.

4   Mound the kale with some of the broth on the toast in each bowl and top with two fried eggs. Scatter the prosciutto over the dish and serve immediately.

10

Baked Goods and Desserts

The thrifty householder wastes nothing. Apples that are too old to eat out of hand are made into delectable desserts. Yesterday's leftover mashed potatoes are baked into today's dinner rolls, and leftover winter squash is baked into a cake. Maybe hunger — or sheer economic necessity — doesn't drive us anymore, but it has never made sense to waste good food.

Empty calories have never made sense either. Why eat a dessert of no nutritional value when you can get a heaping helping of vitamin A from pumpkin pie? I'm not saying you can get all the vitamins you need from these desserts, but you will definitely get more nutritional bang for your buck when you incorporate fruits and vegetables into all that you bake.

RECIPE LIST FOR
BAKED GOODS AND DESSERTS

Garden Cornbread

Potato Yeast Rolls

Mashed-Potato Biscuits

Applesauce

Applesauce Crumb Cake

Maple-Apple Tea Cake

Pumpkin Waffles

Almond-Squash Quick Bread

*Carrot Cake with Cream Cheese
   Frosting*

Coconut-Pumpkin Pie

Chocolate Chip–Pumpkin Loaf

Marbled Pumpkin Cheesecake

Vegetarian dishes are marked with this symbol: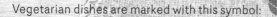

● Garden Cornbread

Makes 9 squares

This recipe falls under the category of "sneaking vegetables into dishes." The winter squash or carrot is barely discernable in this moist cornbread. Leftover cornbread is delicious toasted, buttered, and topped with maple syrup (my personal favorite) or jam for breakfast the next morning.

1 cup all-purpose flour
1 cup stone-ground cornmeal
3 tablespoons sugar
1 tablespoon baking powder
1 teaspoon baking soda
1 teaspoon salt
1 cup buttermilk
2 eggs, lightly beaten
3 tablespoons sunflower or canola oil
1 cup peeled and shredded winter squash or carrot

1 Preheat the oven to 400°F. Lightly oil an 8-inch square baking pan.

2 Combine the flour, cornmeal, sugar, baking powder, baking soda, and salt in a large mixing bowl.

3 In a separate bowl, combine the buttermilk, eggs, oil, and winter squash. Mix well. Pour into the dry ingredients and stir just enough to thoroughly moisten. The batter will be lumpy. Scrape the batter into the prepared pan.

4 Bake for about 25 minutes, until a tester inserted near the center comes out clean. Serve warm.

Kitchen Note: *This is the perfect accompaniment to Chili Beans (page 206).*

Potato Yeast Rolls

Makes 32 rolls

Classic American dinner rolls are sometimes neglected in this age of artisanal European-style breads. Watch these disappear faster than you would expect. I usually make this with leftover mashed potatoes, but if you are starting from scratch, figure that an 8-ounce baking potato, cooked and mashed, will yield about 1 cup.

1	(¼-ounce) package or 2¼ teaspoons active dry yeast	½	cup butter, plus more for brushing, melted
½	cup milk, scalded and cooled to about 115°F	1	cup cold mashed potatoes
2	eggs, at room temperature	1	teaspoon salt
½	cup sugar	4–4½	cups all-purpose flour

1   Sprinkle the yeast over the milk in a small bowl and stir to blend. Let stand for a few minutes until foamy.

2   Combine the eggs, sugar, butter, potatoes, and salt in a food processor and blend well. Add the yeast mixture and pulse to combine. Add 2 cups of the flour and pulse to combine. Add another 1 cup flour and process until fully combined. Continue to add the flour and process until the dough gathers into a soft, slightly sticky ball. You will not need all the flour.

3   Lightly sprinkle a work surface with some of the remaining flour. Knead the dough on the floured work surface until it becomes smooth and slightly soft, adding more flour as necessary. (You may not need all of the flour.) Transfer the dough to a lightly oiled bowl and turn the dough until coated with oil. Set aside to rise in a warm place until doubled in bulk, about 1½ hours.

4   Generously butter two 9-inch round or square cake pans. Transfer the dough to a lightly floured work surface and pat into a rectangle about 16 inches by 8 inches, gently pressing out excess air.

5   Divide the dough into quarters. Cut each of those four sections into eight equal-sized pieces; a pizza wheel or bench scraper works well here. Tuck the edges of the dough under to make round rolls and place them seam-side down in the prepared pans, leaving a little space between rolls. Cover the pans and set aside in a warm place until the rolls rise almost to the rim of the pans and have doubled in size, about 45 minutes.

6   Preheat the oven to 375°F. Position a rack in the middle of the oven.

7   Bake the rolls for about 30 minutes, until they are golden brown and puffy and an instant-read thermometer inserted into the center of the rolls registers 190°F.

8   Remove the rolls from the oven and quickly brush their tops with butter. Cool the rolls in the pans for about 10 minutes. Transfer to a rack in one piece. Cool slightly. Serve warm or at room temperature in one piece or pulled apart as individual rolls.

Kitchen Note: *After the rolls are formed, placed in the pans, and covered, they can be refrigerated overnight. The next day, allow extra time for them to rise before baking, about 1½ hours.*

Mashed-Potato Biscuits

Makes 18 biscuits

This tasty biscuits also can be made with leftover mashed potatoes. Just use 1½ cups mashed potatoes instead of cooking the raw potatoes, and reduce the salt to 1 teaspoon. Like all biscuits, these are best served hot out of the oven.

¾ pound russet (baking) potatoes, peeled and cut into chunks	½ cup (1 stick) butter, chilled and diced
3 cups unbleached all-purpose flour, plus more for dusting	1 egg
2 tablespoons baking powder	½ cup buttermilk
2 teaspoons salt	Milk, for brushing

1   Cover the potatoes with salted water in a small saucepan. Bring to a boil and boil until completely tender, 15 to 20 minutes. Drain well, then mash or run through a potato ricer.

2   Preheat the oven to 450°F.

3   Combine the flour, baking powder, and salt in a food processor and process briefly to mix. Add the butter and pulse until the mixture resembles coarse crumbs. Add the potatoes and egg and process until well blended. Add the buttermilk and process until the mixture comes together in a sticky ball.

4   Transfer the dough to a generously floured work surface and knead until the dough holds its shape. With a rolling pin or by hand, roll or pat to a thickness of about ¾ inch. With a biscuit cutter or water glass, cut into 3-inch rounds and transfer to a baking sheet. Brush the tops of the biscuits with a little milk.

5   Bake for 18 to 22 minutes, until the biscuits are golden. Serve warm.

Applesauce

Makes 4 cups

Every fall when apples are plentiful and bargains are to be had, I make applesauce in quantity. But I also make small amounts with older apples that have gone past their prime. Applesauce makes a wonderful dessert, especially if accompanied by homemade cookies. It also makes a fine side dish with roasted meat. Extra can be frozen. The apples used can be any type at all, peeled or unpeeled. Red skins will result in pink applesauce. Yellow or green skins, or peeling the apples, will make a yellow sauce. If you make applesauce with peeled apples, you can mash the apples by hand to leave a chunky texture. If you leave the skins on the apples, the applesauce must be run through a food mill to get rid of the skins. The advantage of using unpeeled apples is that you can also leave in the cores, pits, and stems — it will all be removed by the food mill. The recipe can be halved, doubled, tripled, or even quadrupled.

2½–3 pounds apples

3 tablespoons light-colored fruit juice, such as apple, white grape, orange, pineapple, or mango, or water

Sweetener, such as white or brown sugar, maple syrup, or honey

1 Either peel, core, and quarter the apples or simply quarter the apples and put them in a large pot. Add the fruit juice.

2 Cover and cook over medium heat, stirring occasionally, until the apples are falling apart and very soft, about 45 minutes.

3 For chunky applesauce with peeled and cored apples, mash the apples with a potato masher until you have achieved the desired consistency. For a smooth applesauce made with unpeeled apples, run the apples and any liquid through a food mill, discarding the skins and pits.

4 Taste and add the sweetener of your choice, if needed. Serve warm or chilled.

Kitchen Note: *For longer-term storage, freeze or process in a boiling-water bath (see the box on facing page).*

Applesauce in Quantity

Apples that you don't really want to eat out of hand (too tart, too soft, too bruised, too many!) can be made into applesauce for enjoying throughout the winter. Applesauce is the perfect accompaniment to many pork and lamb dishes. It can be served as an alternative to vegetables on nights when you are really pressed, or it can be served as dessert in glass bowls — top it with a sprinkling of cinnamon sugar or a drizzle of cream to dress it up.

To preserve the applesauce, plan either to process it in a boiling-water bath or to freeze it. Prepare the recipe on page 354, multiplying the recipe to accommodate the size of your saucepan or the amount of apples you wish to cook. Figure that 15 to 18 pounds of apples will make 6 quarts, which is a canner load.

To freeze applesauce, let the cooked apple-sauce cool to room temperature, then freeze in heavy-duty plastic freezer bags or containers for up to 1 year.

To can applesauce, bring the applesauce to a boil. Fill a boiling-water-bath canner half full with water and bring to a boil. Bring a tea kettle of extra water to a boil as well. Wash the canning jars in hot, soapy water. Prepare the screwbands and lids according to the manufacturer's instructions. (Usually this means placing them in a saucepan of simmering water and removing the saucepan from the heat.)

Pack the hot applesauce into clean, hot jars, leaving ½ inch of headspace. Run a chopstick around the inside of the jars to coax out any trapped air bubbles. Tap the bottom of the jars against the counter to expel more air. Use a clean damp towel to wipe clean the rims of the jars. Set the metal lid of the jars on the rims. Add the screwbands and tighten firmly. Place all of the jars in the canning rack and lower the jars into the boiling-water bath. (If the jars are hot, the water in the boiling-water bath can be boiling.)

When the jars are in the canner, make sure they are covered by at least 2 inches of water. If not, fill with additional boiling water (that's why you heated water in the tea kettle). Place the lid on the canner and begin timing when you see steam coming out of the pot. Process applesauce for 20 minutes.

Remove the jars from the canner using a jar lifter, and place them on a counter lined with a kitchen towel. The jars will seal as they cool. You may hear the ping of the completing seals and see that the top of the lids are depressed. Let the jars cool undisturbed for 24 hours, then label and store. The screwbands can be left in place or removed.

Any jar that doesn't properly seal can be stored in the refrigerator, its contents to be con-sumed within a week or so.

Applesauce Crumb Cake

Serves 12–16

A homey cake that makes good use of the applesauce you stockpiled in the fall, when apples were fresh, local, and abundant. It is perfect for dessert, packing in lunch boxes, or selling by the square at a bake sale.

CRUMB TOPPING		APPLESAUCE CAKE	
½	cup sugar	2½	cups all-purpose flour
⅓	cup all-purpose flour	1	tablespoon baking powder
4	tablespoons butter, at room temperature	1	teaspoon baking soda
1	tablespoon ground cinnamon	1	teaspoon salt
½	teaspoon freshly grated nutmeg	¼	teaspoon ground nutmeg
		½	cup (1 stick) butter, at room temperature
		1	cup sugar
		2	eggs
		2	cups applesauce
		½	cup buttermilk

1   Preheat the oven to 350°F. Butter a 9- by 13-inch baking dish.

2   To make the crumb topping, combine the sugar, flour, butter, cinnamon, and nutmeg in a small bowl. Mix with a fork until the mixture has an uneven pebbly texture. Set aside.

3   Sift together the flour, baking powder, baking soda, salt, and nutmeg.

4   In a large mixing bowl, cream the butter and sugar. Add the eggs one at a time, beating well after each addition. Beat in the applesauce and buttermilk. Beat in the flour mixture until smooth. Transfer the batter to the prepared baking dish. Sprinkle the crumb topping over the batter.

5   Bake for about 50 minutes, until a tester inserted near the center comes out clean. Serve warm or cooled, directly out of the pan.

Maple-Apple Tea Cake

Serves 8–12

The maple syrup is front and forward in this delicious cake, which can be served without frosting or fuss. On the other hand, à la mode doesn't hurt a simple cake like this one.

2½	cups all-purpose flour
1	tablespoon baking powder
½	teaspoon baking soda
½	teaspoon salt
2	apples, peeled, cored, and diced
¾	cup pure maple syrup
¼	cup firmly packed brown sugar
4	tablespoons butter, melted
1	egg, beaten
½	cup sour cream or yogurt
1	teaspoon vanilla extract

1 Preheat the oven to 350°F. Lightly grease a 9- by 5-inch loaf pan and line with parchment paper.

2 Whisk together the flour, baking powder, baking soda, and salt. Add the apples, tossing to coat with the flour.

3 Beat together the maple syrup, brown sugar, butter, egg, sour cream, and vanilla. Stir in the dry ingredients. Scrape the batter into the prepared pan and smooth the top.

4 Bake for about 1 hour 15 minutes, until a toothpick inserted into the center comes out clean.

5 Cool in the pan on a wire rack for 15 minutes. Invert onto the wire rack, remove the paper, and let cool completely.

Kitchen Note: *The easiest way to prepare the apples is to peel them, then thinly slice the apple off the core. Spread the slices out on the cutting board and chop with a chef's knife.*

Pumpkin Waffles

Serves 4-6

The flavor of the pumpkin is rather subtle in these waffles, but the nutritional benefits are substantial, and either pumpkin or winter squash can be used. Pumpkin waffles and sausage are a delicious combination for either breakfast or supper. Don't forget the maple syrup!

2	cups all-purpose flour
1	tablespoon baking powder
1	teaspoon salt
¼	teaspoon freshly grated nutmeg
1¾	cups cooked and puréed pumpkin or winter squash
2	cups milk
¾	cup sunflower or canola oil
4	tablespoons butter, melted
2	eggs, separated
	Pure maple syrup, for serving

1   Preheat a waffle iron. Preheat the oven to 200°F.

2   Combine the flour, baking powder, salt, and nutmeg in a medium bowl. In a separate large bowl, combine the pumpkin, milk, oil, butter, and egg yolks. In another bowl, beat the egg whites until stiff but not dry.

3   Stir the flour mixture into the pumpkin mixture and mix well. Fold in the egg whites.

4   Grease the waffle iron with nonstick spray. Ladle about ⅓ cup batter into each waffle quarter. Cook according to the waffle-iron manufacturer's directions. Hold the cooked waffles in the warm oven until all are made. Serve hot, passing the maple syrup on the side.

❧ Almond-Squash Quick Bread

Serves 8–12

Whenever you find yourself with leftover puréed winter squash or pumpkin (with or without added butter or flavorings), consider making a quick bread. These loaves, more cake than bread, freeze beautifully.

1½	cups all-purpose flour
1½	teaspoons baking soda
1	teaspoon baking powder
1½	teaspoons ground cinnamon
½	teaspoon ground ginger
½	teaspoon freshly grated nutmeg
½	teaspoon salt
½	cup (1 stick) butter, melted and cooled
1¼	cups firmly packed brown sugar
2	eggs
1	cup cooked and puréed winter squash or pumpkin
1	cup flaked almonds

1 Preheat the oven to 350°F. Lightly grease a 9- by 5-inch loaf pan and line with parchment paper.

2 Whisk together the flour, baking soda, baking powder, cinnamon, ginger, nutmeg, and salt in a medium bowl.

3 In a large bowl, whisk the butter and brown sugar until well blended. Beat in the eggs and squash. Stir in the flour mixture. Fold in ¾ cup of the almonds. Scrape the batter into the prepared pan. Sprinkle the top with the remaining almonds.

4 Bake for about 1 hour 15 minutes, until a tester inserted into the center of the cake comes out clean.

5 Transfer to a rack and let cool in the pan for 10 minutes. Invert onto a wire rack, remove the parchment paper, and let cool completely.

Carrot Cake with Cream Cheese Frosting

Serves 12-16

Carrot cakes are often heavy and overspiced, but not this one. The texture is light and the flavor is full but not overpoweringly spicy. It is also very quickly made in a food processor. In fact, this is a very fine cake — my favorite carrot cake ever.

CAKE

- 2 cups all-purpose flour
- 2 teaspoons baking powder
- 1½ teaspoons baking soda
- 1 teaspoon salt
- ½ teaspoon ground cinnamon
- ¼ teaspoon ground allspice
- ¼ teaspoon freshly grated nutmeg
- 3 large carrots, peeled
- 1 cup sunflower or canola oil
- 1¾ cups granulated sugar
- 4 eggs plus 2 egg yolks
- 1 tablespoon finely grated lemon zest
- 2 teaspoons vanilla extract

FROSTING

- ½ cup (1 stick) butter, at room temperature
- 8 ounces cream cheese, at room temperature
- 2½ cups sifted confectioners' sugar

1   Preheat the oven to 350°F. Lightly grease and flour a 9- by 13-inch baking pan.

2   Whisk together the flour, baking powder, baking soda, salt, cinnamon, allspice, and nutmeg in a medium bowl.

3   Shred the carrots in a food processor. Remove and measure 3 cups lightly packed shredded carrots. (If you have more, set aside for a salad. If you have just less than 3 cups, don't worry about it.)

4   Combine the oil and sugar in the food processor (don't bother washing it first) and process until thoroughly combined. Add the eggs and egg yolks, lemon zest, and vanilla, and process until well combined and fluffy. Add the flour mixture and pulse until the batter is smooth and blended. Add the carrots and pulse until blended. Scrape the batter into the prepared pan.

5   Bake for 55 to 60 minutes, until a cake tester inserted in the center of the cake comes out clean. Cool on a wire rack.

6   To make the frosting, beat the butter and cream cheese until creamy and well blended. Gradually add the confectioners' sugar, beating until smooth. Frost the cake in the pan when it is completely cooled.

Coconut-Pumpkin Pie

Serves 6–8

You can look at pumpkin pie as an unalterable Thanksgiving tradition or you can look at it as a well-loved dessert that can be varied at will. This variation is wonderful, and it can be made with either winter squash or pumpkin.

> **Pastry for a 9-inch single-crust pie (page 265)**
> 2 cups cooked and puréed pumpkin or winter squash
> 2 eggs
> 1 cup coconut milk
> ¾ cup firmly packed brown sugar
> 1 teaspoon vanilla extract
> 1 teaspoon ground ginger
> ½ teaspoon salt
> ¼ teaspoon freshly grated nutmeg
> ¼ teaspoon ground allspice
> 1¼ cups unsweetened flaked coconut

1 Preheat the oven to 425°F.

2 Roll out and fit the pastry into a 9-inch pie pan. Fold the overhang under and flute the edges of the dough.

3 To make the filling, combine the pumpkin, eggs, coconut milk, brown sugar, vanilla, ginger, salt, nutmeg, and allspice in a food processor and process until smooth. Add 1 cup of the coconut and pulse just long enough to mix in. Pour the filling into the crust.

4 Bake for 10 minutes, then lower the heat to 350°F and continue to bake for about 40 minutes longer, until the filling is partially set. Sprinkle on the remaining ¼ cup coconut and continue baking about 10 minutes longer, until the filling is mostly set (the center will still be wobbly) and the coconut is toasted.

5 Chill well before serving.

Chocolate Chip– Pumpkin Loaf

Serves 8–12

As my nanny used to say, "Just a spoonful of chocolate helps the winter squash go down . . ." Actually, I didn't have a nanny. And this cake is made with more than a spoonful of chocolate, but you get the idea. This dessert is equally delicious made with a purée of winter squash or pumpkin; use whichever you have on had. The recipe is easily doubled to make two loaves if you are serving a crowd or wish to put one in the freezer.

1⅔ cups all-purpose flour	1⅓ cups sugar
1 teaspoon baking powder	2 eggs
1 teaspoon baking soda	1 cup cooked and puréed pumpkin or winter squash
1 teaspoon ground cinnamon	¼ cup milk
½ teaspoon salt	1 cup mini chocolate morsels
¼ teaspoon freshly grated nutmeg	
⅓ cup sunflower or canola oil	

1 Preheat the oven to 350°F. Grease a 9- by 5-inch loaf pan and line with parchment paper.

2 Whisk together the flour, baking powder, baking soda, cinnamon, salt, and nutmeg in a medium bowl.

3 In a large bowl, combine the oil and sugar and beat until fluffy. Add the eggs one at a time, beating well after each addition. Stir in the pumpkin and milk. Add the flour mixture and stir just to combine. Fold in the chocolate morsels. Spread the batter in the prepared pan.

4 Bake for about 1 hour 15 minutes, until a tester inserted in the center of the loaf comes out clean.

5 Let the bread cool in the pan on a wire rack for about 10 minutes. Invert onto the wire rack, remove the parchment paper, and let cool completely.

Kitchen Note: *Full-size chocolate chips can be substituted for the mini morsels.*

Marbled Pumpkin Cheesecake

Serves 12–16

The marbling is beautiful, the flavor is deep, the texture is creamy. Throw virtue to the wind. The perfect holiday dessert? It just might be.

CRUST

- 1½ cups gingersnap or graham cracker crumbs
- 6 tablespoons butter, melted
- ¼ cup granulated sugar
- 1 teaspoon ground cinnamon

CHEESECAKE

- 1 pound cream cheese, at room temperature
- 1 cup sour cream
- 2 tablespoons Cointreau or Grand Marnier
- 1 cup granulated sugar
- ½ teaspoon freshly grated nutmeg
- 4 eggs plus 2 egg yolks
- 1½ cups cooked and puréed pumpkin or winter squash
- ¼ cup firmly packed brown sugar
- 1 teaspoon ground cinnamon
- ½ teaspoon ground ginger

1   Preheat the oven to 325°F.

2   To make the crust, combine the crumbs, butter, sugar, and cinnamon in a medium bowl. Press the mixture into a 9-inch springform pan, making a 1-inch-high rim around the edge.

3   Bake the crust for 10 minutes. Set aside to cool.

4   To make the filling, combine the cream cheese, sour cream, Cointreau, granulated sugar, and nutmeg in a food processor and process until smooth. Add the whole eggs and pulse just until well blended. Do not overmix.

5   Remove 2 cups of the mixture and set aside. Add the two egg yolks, pumpkin, brown sugar, cinnamon, and ginger to the food processor. Pulse until well blended.

6   Transfer the springform pan to a baking sheet. Pour half of the pumpkin filling onto the crust, then half of the plain filling. Repeat the procedure with the remaining fillings, drizzling the plain so that some of the pumpkin filling is still visible. Gently run a table knife through the batter, drawing first horizontal and then vertical lines 1 inch apart to marble the plain filling into the pumpkin.

7   Bake for about 1 hour 15 minutes, until the center appears set but not firm. Turn off the heat, open the oven door, and allow the cheesecake to cool to room temperature.

8   Gently run a sharp knife around the edge of the pan to loosen. Refrigerate until thoroughly chilled. Remove the sides of the pan and serve.

Metric Conversions

Unless you have finely calibrated measuring equipment, conversions between U.S. and metric measurements will be somewhat inexact. It's important to convert the measurements for all of the ingredients in a recipe to maintain the same proportions as the original.

GENERAL FORMULA FOR METRIC CONVERSION

Ounces to grams	multiply ounces by 28.35
Grams to ounces	multiply grams by 0.035
Pounds to grams	multiply pounds by 453.5
Pounds to kilograms	multiply pounds by 0.45
Cups to liters	multiply cups by 0.24
Fahrenheit to Celsius	subtract 32 from Fahrenheit temperature, multiply by 5, then divide by 9
Celsius to Fahrenheit	multiply Celsius temperature by 9, divide by 5, then add 32

APPROXIMATE EQUIVALENTS BY VOLUME

U.S.	METRIC
1 teaspoon	5 milliliters
1 tablespoon	15 milliliters
¼ cup	60 milliliters
½ cup	120 milliliters
1 cup	230 milliliters
1¼ cups	300 milliliters
1½ cups	360 milliliters
2 cups	460 milliliters
2½ cups	600 milliliters
3 cups	700 milliliters
4 cups (1 quart)	0.95 liter
1.06 quarts	1 liter
4 quarts (1 gallon)	3.8 liters

APPROXIMATE EQUIVALENTS BY WEIGHT

U.S.	METRIC	U.S.	METRIC
¼ ounce	7 grams	0.035 ounce	1 gram
½ ounce	14 grams	1.75 ounces	50 grams
1 ounce	28 grams	3.5 ounces	100 grams
1¼ ounces	35 grams	8.75 ounces	250 grams
1½ ounces	40 grams	1.1 pounds	500 grams
2½ ounces	70 grams	2.2 pounds	1 kilogram
4 ounces	112 grams		
5 ounces	140 grams		
8 ounces	228 grams		
10 ounces	280 grams		
15 ounces	425 grams		
16 ounces (1 pound)	454 grams		

Roasting Vegetables

One of the best ways to prepare root vegetables and winter squashes is to roast them. Roasting brings out so much flavor that salt and pepper is the only seasoning needed. For a change of pace, you can drizzle roasted vegetables with a little high-quality vinegar or pomegranate molasses as well. Before roasting, lightly coat the vegetables with oil and arrange in a single layer on a sheet pan or in a shallow roasting pan. Do not crowd! Stirring or shaking the pan once or twice during roasting will ensure even cooking. The vegetables will diminish considerably in volume as they roast. If your oven allows it, use convection heat, which creates a drier environment for the roasting process.

Roasting Guidelines

VEGETABLE	PREPARATIONS	TIME AND ROASTING TEMPERATURE
Beets	Wrap unpeeled beets in foil; no oil is needed	45 minutes to 1½ hours at 350°F
Belgian endives	Slice in half	25 minutes at 450°F
Brussels sprouts	Slice in half or quarters	15 minutes at 425°F
Cabbage, red and green	Cut into 1-inch strips	20 to 30 minutes at 425°F
Carrots	Cut into matchsticks, small cubes, or slices	30 to 40 minutes at 425°F
Celery root	Cut into matchsticks or small cubes	40 to 45 minutes at 425°F
Garlic	Slice off top of whole head, drizzle with oil, and cover	45 minutes at 425°F
Jerusalem artichokes	Peel and cut into 1-inch pieces	15 minutes at 500°F
Onions	Cut large onions into ¼-inch slices; leave pearl onions whole	20 to 30 minutes at 450°F
Parsnips	Peel and slice into matchsticks or small cubes	25 to 30 minutes at 425°F
Potatoes	Peel, if desired, and cut into wedges	45 to 60 minutes at 425°F
Rutabagas	Peel and cut into small cubes or matchsticks	40 to 45 minutes at 425°F
Salsify	Peel, drop into acidulated water, and then cut into small cubes, slices, or matchsticks	40 to 45 minutes at 425°F
Shallots	Cut into quarters	20 minutes at 425°F
Sweet potatoes	Peel, if desired, and cut into wedges or cubes	20 to 30 minutes at 500°F
Turnips	Peel and cut into small cubes or matchsticks	40 to 45 minutes at 425°F
Winter squash	Peel and cut into wedges, ½-inch slices, or small cubes	30 to 40 minutes at 375°F

Index

A

Acorn squash, 37. *See also* Winter squashes

Baked Winter Squash, 195

African Sweet-Potato Stew, 263

Aioli, Lemon, 181

Almonds

Almond-Squash Quick Bread, 359

Curried Rice Salad with Mango Chutney Dressing, 78–79

Roasted Sweet-Potato Salad with Sesame-Ginger Vinaigrette, 72

Soy-Sesame Cabbage Salad, 59

Stuffed Sweet Dumplings, 193

Apples & apple juice/cider. *See also* Applesauce

Apple-Braised Delicata Squash, 194

Apple, Leek, and Cheddar Quiche, 262

Applesauce, 354–55

Apple-Squash Bisque, 118

Celery Root, Apple, and Walnut Salad, 67

Choucroute Garni, 340–41

Cider-Braised Sweet Potatoes with Apples, 184

Curried Rice Salad with Mango Chutney Dressing, 78–79

Endive and Apple Salad with Candied Nuts and Blue Cheese, 68

Maple-Apple Tea Cake, 357

Stuffed Sweet Dumplings, 193

Winter Squash with Caramelized Apples, 199

Applesauce, 354–55

Applesauce Crumb Cake, 356

Arame

Soba Noodle Salad, 74

Wilted Kale Salad, 70

Asian ingredients, 65

Availability

beets, 25

Brussels sprouts, 4

cabbage, 6

carrots, 26

collard greens, 8

dried beans, 39

garlic, 13

Jerusalem artichokes, 19

kale, 10

leeks, 14–15

mustard greens, 11

onions, 16

parsnips, 28

potatoes, 20

rutabagas, 30

salsify, 31

shallots, 17

sweet potatoes, 21–22

turnips, 34

winter squashes, 36

B

Baby blue Hubbard squash. *See also* Winter squashes

Whipped Winter Squash, 197

Winter Squash with Caramelized Apples, 199

Bacon

Bacon-Sautéed Brussels Sprouts, 144

Choucroute Garni, 340–41

East-Meets-West Braised Red Cabbage, 149

Hot German Potato Salad with Sauerkraut, 179

Ravioli with Smoky Greens, 345

Sunday Supper Baked Beans, 207

Twice-Baked Stuffed Potatoes, 178

Baked Beets in Béchamel, 136

Baked Carrots and Fennel in Béchamel, 150

Baked Root Vegetables and Fennel in Béchamel, 150

Baked Root Vegetables in Béchamel, 136

Baked Spaghetti Squash, 196

Baked Winter Squash, 195

Balsamic vinegar

Balsamic Chicken with Vegetables, 292

Braised Balsamic-Glazed Parsnips and Pears, 161

Honey-Balsamic Roasted Parsnips, 162

Maple-Balsamic Root Vegetables, 132

Banana squash, 37. *See also* Winter squashes

Barley

Barley Vegetable Soup, 95

Chicken and Barley Pilaf with Winter Vegetables, 301

Lemony Barley-Carrot Pilaf, 223

Basic Pie Pastry, 265

Basic Pizza Dough, 264

Basic Roasted Brussels Sprouts, 138

Beans, dried

African Sweet-Potato Stew, 263

basic information, 38–39

Black Beans in Chipotle Sauce, 203

Black Bean, Sweet Potato, and Chorizo Stew, 205

Cajun-Spiced Black Beans and Sausage, 204

Caldo Gallego, 110

Chili Beans, 206

Fettuccine with Caramelized Cabbage, White Beans, and Goat Cheese, 249

New England Baked Beans, 208
Pasta e Fagioli, 94
Pasta with Kale and Chickpeas, 250
Quick Black Bean, Sweet Potato, and Chorizo Stew, 205
Quick Spicy-Sweet Barbecued Beans, 209
Refried Pinto Beans, 210
Sausage with Kale and White Beans, 343
Smoky Black Bean Soup, 122
Smoky Black Bean Soup with Sausage, 122
Spicy-Sweet Barbecued Beans, 209
Sunday Supper Baked Beans, 207
Tuscan White Bean and Kale Soup, 109
Vegetable Couscous, 253
Vegetarian Baked Beans, 207
White Bean and Cabbage Soup, 104
White Bean Stew with Smoked Turkey, 216–17
Winter Minestrone, 93
Beef
    Beef Broth, 125
    Braised Beef Rigatoni, 328
    Italian Wedding Soup, 107
    Mustard-Braised Short Ribs with Root Vegetables, 324
    New England Boiled Dinner, 326–27
    Pot Roast with Root Vegetables, 322–23
    Reuben Pie, 325
    Spicy Meat Lo Mein, 335
    Stuffed Cabbage Rolls, 330–31
    Winter-Vegetable Beef Stew, 321
Beets. *See also* Vegetables
    Baked Beets in Béchamel, 136
    basic information, 24–25

Beet and Napa Cabbage Salad with Goat Cheese, 45
Beets in Sour Cream, 44
Borscht, 99
Braised Turkey Breast with Winter Vegetables, 313
Cheesy Mac with Root Vegetables, 246–47
Chicken and Barley Pilaf with Winter Vegetables, 301
Chicken in Red Wine with Root Vegetables, 296–97
Harvard Beets, 137
Maple-Balsamic Root Vegetables, 132
Maple-Glazed Baked Winter Vegetables, 134
Mustard-Braised Short Ribs with Root Vegetables, 324
Mustard-Molasses Roasted Salmon and Vegetables, 269
Oven-Braised Sausage and Vegetables, 342
Oven-Roasted Salmon and Vegetables with Lemon Aioli, 269
Pasta Inverno, 241
Quick Ginger-Pickled Beets, 83
Roasted and Braised Duck with Sauerkraut and Root Vegetables, 315
Roasted Beet and Potato Salad, 47
Roasted Chicken with Root Vegetables, 291
Roasted Vegetable Salad, 43
Roast Pork with Sauerkraut and Vegetables, 339
Root Vegetable Scampi over Linguine, 248
Sautéed Shredded Vegetables, 131
Savory Winter-Vegetable Bread Pudding, 235

Shredded Root-Vegetable Linguine, 248
Smashed Potatoes with Root Vegetables, 164
Sunshine Turkey, 312
Thai Coconut Curry with Shrimp, 275
Vermont Sugarmaker's Supper, 232–33
Winter-Vegetable Pie, 257
Belgian endive
    basic information, 69
    Endive and Apple Salad with Candied Nuts and Blue Cheese, 68
    Roasted Vegetable Salad, 43
Black beans. *See also* Beans, dried
    Black Beans in Chipotle Sauce, 203
    Black Bean, Sweet Potato, and Chorizo Stew, 205
    Cajun-Spiced Black Beans and Sausage, 204
    Quick Black Bean, Sweet Potato, and Chorizo Stew, 205
    Smoky Black Bean Soup, 122
    Smoky Black Bean Soup with Sausage, 122
Black kale. *See* Kale
Blue cheese, Endive and Apple Salad with Candied Nuts and, 68
Bok choy. *See also* Cabbages
    Chinese Cabbage and Chicken Stir-Fry, 306–7
    Chinese Steamed Greens, 155
    Sichuan-Style Stir-Fried Greens, 156
    Udon with Bok Choy and Tofu, 102
    Vegetarian Udon with Bok Choy and Tofu, 102
Borscht, 99

Braised Balsamic-Glazed Parsnips and Pears, 161
Braised Beef Rigatoni, 328
Braised Celery Root Gratin, 152
Braised Kale on Toast, 347
Braised Turkey Breast with Winter Vegetables, 313
Braised Turkey on a Bed of Kale, 314
Bread and rolls
    Almond-Squash Quick Bread, 359
    Braised Kale on Toast, 347
    Garden Cornbread, 351
    Potato Yeast Rolls, 352–53
    Savory Winter-Vegetable Bread Pudding, 235

Brussels sprouts
    Bacon-Sautéed Brussels Sprouts, 144
    basic information, 4–5
    Basic Roasted Brussels Sprouts, 138
    Brussels Sprouts and Citrus Salad, 49
    Chicken and Brussels Sprouts Stir-Fry, 304
    Chicken Sauté with Brussels Sprouts, 303
    Cornmeal-Crisped Brussels Sprouts, 140
    Cream-Braised Brussels Sprouts, 143
    Crunchy Roasted Brussels Sprouts, 139
    Garlic-Crumbed Roasted Brussels Sprouts, 141
    Lemony Brussels Sprouts, 145
    Pan-Seared Brussels Sprouts, 142
    Roasted Stuffed Duck with Roasted Vegetables, 316–17
    Spicy Black Bean Brussels Sprout and Chicken Stir-Fry, 305
    Wilted Brussels Sprouts Salad, 48

Buckwheat groats
    Kasha Varnishkes, 224
Burdock root, 233
Butter-Braised Salsify, 188
Buttercup squash, 37. *See also* Winter squashes
    Baked Winter Squash, 195
    Stuffed Sweet Dumplings, 193
    Whipped Winter Squash, 197
    Winter Squash with Caramelized Apples, 199
Buttermilk
    Buttermilk Mashed Potatoes, 167
    Garden Cornbread, 351
    Mujdhara, 212
    Wheat-Berry Mujdhara, 212
Butternut squash, 37. *See also* Winter squashes
    Apple-Squash Bisque, 118
    Kathleen Pemble's Winter Squash, 198
    Maple-Glazed Baked Winter Vegetables, 134
    Risotto with Butternut Squash, 222
    Whipped Winter Squash, 197
    White Lasagna with Leeks and Butternut Squash, 254–55
    Wild Rice Salad with Roasted Squash and Fennel, 77
    Winter Squash with Caramelized Apples, 199
Buying
    beets, 25
    Brussels sprouts, 4–5
    cabbage, 6
    carrots, 26
    celery root, 27
    collard greens, 9
    dried beans, 39
    garlic, 13
    Jerusalem artichokes, 19
    kale, 10

    leeks, 15
    mustard greens, 11
    onions, 16
    parsnips, 28–29
    potatoes, 20
    rutabagas, 30
    salsify, 31
    shallots, 17
    sweet potatoes, 22
    turnips, 34
    winter squashes, 36

C

Cabbage
    basic information, 5–7
    Cabbage family, 3–11
    green or savoy
        Cabbage and Tomato Soup, 103
        Caldo Gallego, 110
        Chinese Steamed Greens, 155
        Chipotle-Cabbage Salad, 57
        Classic American Coleslaw, 50
        Creamy Coleslaw, 52
        Creamy Mustard Coleslaw, 51
        Crunchy Dilled Coleslaw, 53
        Festive Fruity Coleslaw, 55
        Fettuccine with Caramelized Cabbage, White Beans, and Goat Cheese, 249
        Five-Spice Pork and Cabbage Stir-Fry, 336–37
        Hot Slaw, 147
        Japanese-Style Greens with Tofu, 240
        Lahanosalata, 58
        Mashed Potatoes with Caramelized Winter Vegetables, 234
        Mushroom Lo Mein, 242–43
        New England Boiled Dinner, 326–27

Rumbledethump, 231

Sauerkraut, 84–85

Sautéed Greens with Apple
  Cider Vinegar, 151

Shrimp Egg Rolls, 284–85

Soy-Sesame Cabbage Salad, 59

Spicy Meat Lo Mein, 335

Stuffed Cabbage Rolls, 330–31

Sweet-Pickle Coleslaw, 54

Thai Sweet-Spicy Cabbage
  Salad, 61

Vegetable Broth, 126

Vegetable Couscous, 253

Vegetarian Cabbage and Tomato
  Soup, 103

Vegetarian Egg Rolls, 236–37

Vegetarian Lo Mein with Spicy
  Tofu, 238–39

White Bean and Cabbage Soup,
  104

Wilted Cabbage Salad, American
  Style, 46

Wilted Cabbage Salad, Italian
  Style, 46

Winter Fish Tacos, 274

Winter Minestrone, 93

Winter Vegetable Pie, 257

Zesty Lemon Coleslaw, 56

napa or Chinese

  Beet and Napa Cabbage Salad
    with Goat Cheese, 45

  Chinese Cabbage and Chicken
    Stir-Fry, 306–7

  Chinese Steamed Greens, 155

  Chinese-Style Chicken Salad, 81

  Chinese Vegetable Pickles, 82

  Five-Spice Pork and Cabbage
    Stir-Fry, 336–37

  Japanese-Style Greens with
    Tofu, 240

  Mushroom Lo Mein, 242–43

  Onion-Miso Soup, 113

Roasted Vegetable Salad, 43

Sichuan-Style Stir-Fried Greens,
  156

Spicy Meat Lo Mein, 335

Stir-Fried Cabbage in Brown
  Sauce, 148

Thai Cabbage Salad, 60

Thai Sweet-Chili Shrimp Rolls,
  286

Vegetarian Lo Mein with Spicy
  Tofu, 238–39

Vegetarian Stir-Fried Cabbage in
  Brown Sauce, 148

red

  Carrot-Mustard Slaw, 56

  Classic American Coleslaw, 50

  Creamy Coleslaw, 52

  Creamy Mustard Coleslaw, 51

  Crunchy Dilled Coleslaw, 53

  East-Meets-West Braised Red
    Cabbage, 149

  Festive Fruity Coleslaw, 55

  Sauerkraut, 84–85

  Sweet-Pickle Coleslaw, 54

  Winter Pasta Salad with Red
    Cabbage and Carrot, 80

  Winter Vegetable Nori Rolls,
    218–19

  Zesty Lemon Coleslaw, 56

Cajun-Spiced Black Beans and
  Sausage, 204

Cakes

  Almond-Squash Quick Bread, 359

  Applesauce Crumb Cake, 356

  Carrot Cake with Cream Cheese
    Frosting, 360

  Chocolate-Chip Pumpkin Loaf,
    362

  Maple-Apple Tea Cake, 357

  Marbled Pumpkin Cheesecake,
    363

Calabaza, 37. *See also* Winter squashes

Caldo Gallego, 110

Caramelized Cabbage and Onion
  Tart, 256

Carrots. *See also* Vegetables

  Baked Carrots and Fennel in
    Béchamel, 150

  Balsamic Chicken with Vegetables,
    292

  Barley Vegetable Soup, 95

  basic information, 26–27

  Beef Broth, 125

  Braised Beef Rigatoni, 328

  Braised Turkey Breast with Winter
    Vegetables, 313

  Carrot Cake with Cream Cheese
    Frosting, 360

  Carrot-Mustard Slaw, 56

  Carrots in Citrus Vinaigrette, 63

  Carrot Spoon Bread, 225

  Cheesy Mac with Root Vegetables,
    246–47

  Chicken and Barley Pilaf with
    Winter Vegetables, 301

  Chicken and Rice with Winter
    Vegetables, 293

  Chicken in Red Wine with Root
    Vegetables, 296–97

  Chicken Noodle Soup, 97

  Chicken Paella, 300

  Chicken Sauté with Brussels
    Sprouts, 303

  Chicken Soup with Rice, 98

  Chicken Stew with Root
    Vegetables, 294–95

  Chinese-Style Chicken Salad, 81

  Chinese Vegetable Pickles, 82

  Chipotle-Cabbage Salad, 57

  Choucroute Garni, 340–41

  Clam Pot Pie, 282–83

  Classic American Coleslaw, 50

  Copper Coins, 62

  Creamy Fish Pie, 276–77

Carrots (continued)
Creamy Mustard Coleslaw, 51
Crunchy Dilled Coleslaw, 53
Curried Potato-Carrot Soup, 114
Curried Rice Salad with Mango
    Chutney Dressing, 78–79
Dilled Potato and Egg Salad, 71
Five-Spice Pork and Cabbage Stir-
    Fry, 336–37
Garden Cornbread, 351
Gingered Purée of Root Vegetables,
    135
Golden Carrot Risotto, 215
Hot-and-Sour Soup, 100–1
Lamb Stew with Root Vegetables,
    329
Leek Soup with Carrots and
    Parsnips, 111
Lemony Barley-Carrot Pilaf, 223
Lentil Salad with Carrots and Goat
    Cheese, 66
Lentil-Vegetable Soup, 96
Maple-Balsamic Root Vegetables,
    132
Maple-Glazed Baked Winter
    Vegetables, 134
Mashed Potatoes with Caramelized
    Winter Vegetables, 234
Miso Noodle Bowl, 112–13
Mushroom Lo Mein, 242–43
Mustard-Braised Short Ribs with
    Root Vegetables, 324
Mustard-Molasses Roasted Salmon
    and Vegetables, 269
New England Boiled Dinner,
    326–27
North African Turnip Salad, 73
Oven-Braised Sausage and
    Vegetables, 342
Oven-Roasted Salmon and
    Vegetables with Lemon Aioli,
    269

Pasta Inverno, 241
Pasta with Tomato-Braised Root
    Vegetables, 244–45
Polenta with Tomato-Braised Root
    Vegetables, 245
Potato-Carrot Tart, 177
Pot Roast with Root Vegetables,
    322–23
Rigatoni with Tomato-Braised
    Chicken and Root Vegetables,
    302
Roasted and Braised Duck
    with Sauerkraut and Root
    Vegetables, 315
Roasted Chicken with Root
    Vegetables, 291
Roasted Stuffed Duck with
    Roasted Vegetables, 316–17
Roasted Vegetable Salad, 43
Roast Pork with Sauerkraut and
    Vegetables, 339
Root Vegetable Scampi over
    Linguine, 248
Saffron Fish Stew, 271
Sautéed Shredded Vegetables, 131
Savory Winter-Vegetable Bread
    Pudding, 235
Seafood Boil, 280
Sesame Noodle Salad, 75
Shepherd's Pie, 332–33
Shredded Root-Vegetable
    Linguine, 248
Shrimp Egg Rolls, 284–85
Smashed Potatoes with Root
    Vegetables, 164
Soba Noodle Salad, 74
Soy-Sesame Cabbage Salad, 59
Spicy Black Bean Brussels Sprout
    and Chicken Stir-Fry, 305
Spicy Meat Lo Mein, 335
Sunshine Turkey, 312
Sweet-Pickle Coleslaw, 54

Thai Cabbage Salad, 60
Thai Coconut Curry with Shrimp,
    275
Thai Sweet-Chili Shrimp Rolls, 286
Thai Sweet-Spicy Cabbage Salad, 61
Turkey Broth, 126–27
Tuscan White Bean and Kale Soup,
    109
Vegetable Broth, 126
Vegetable Couscous, 253
Vegetarian Lo Mein with Spicy
    Tofu, 238–39
Vermont Sugarmaker's Supper,
    232–33
White Bean Stew with Smoked
    Turkey, 216–17
Wilted Kale Salad, 70
Winter Minestrone, 93
Winter Pasta Salad with Red
    Cabbage and Carrot, 80
Winter-Vegetable Beef Stew, 321
Winter Vegetable Nori Rolls,
    218–19
Winter-Vegetable Pie, 257
World Carrot Museum, 62
Cavolo nero. See Kale
Celeriac. See Celery Root
Celery root. See also Vegetables
Barley Vegetable Soup, 95
basic information, 27–28
Beef Broth, 125
Braised Beef Rigatoni, 328
Braised Celery Root Gratin, 152
Braised Turkey Breast with Winter
    Vegetables, 313
Celery Root, Apple, and Walnut
    Salad, 67
Cheesy Mac with Root Vegetables,
    246–47
Chicken and Barley Pilaf with
    Winter Vegetables, 301
Chicken Broth, 127

Chicken in Red Wine with Root
    Vegetables, 296–97
Chicken Noodle Soup, 97
Chicken Paella, 300
Chicken Pot Pie with Biscuit
    Topping, 299
Chicken Pot Pie with Sweet-Potato
    Biscuits, 298–99
Chicken Soup with Rice, 98
Chicken Stew with Root
    Vegetables, 294–95
Clam Pot Pie, 282–83
Creamed Celery Root Soup, 105
Lamb Stew with Root Vegetables,
    329
Lentil-Vegetable Soup, 96
Maple-Glazed Baked Winter
    Vegetables, 134
Mushroom Broth, 124
Mustard-Braised Short Ribs with
    Root Vegetables, 324
Mustard-Molasses Roasted Salmon
    and Vegetables, 269
Oven-Braised Sausage and
    Vegetables, 342
Oven-Roasted Salmon and
    Vegetables with Lemon Aioli,
    269
Pasta Inverno, 241
Pasta with Tomato-Braised Root
    Vegetables, 244–45
Polenta with Tomato-Braised Root
    Vegetables, 245
Rigatoni with Tomato-Braised
    Chicken and Root Vegetables,
    302
Roasted and Braised Duck
    with Sauerkraut and Root
    Vegetables, 315
Roasted Chicken with Root
    Vegetables, 291

Roast Pork with Sauerkraut and
    Vegetables, 339
Root Vegetable Scampi over
    Linguine, 248
Sautéed Shredded Vegetables, 131
Savory Winter-Vegetable Bread
    Pudding, 235
Scallop and Salsify Chowder, 117
Seafood Boil, 280
Shredded Root-Vegetable
    Linguine, 248
Smashed Potatoes with Root
    Vegetables, 164
Thai Coconut Curry with Shrimp,
    275
Turkey Broth, 126–27
Vegetarian Creamed Celery Root
    Soup, 105
Vermont Sugarmaker's Supper,
    232–33
White Bean Stew with Smoked
    Turkey, 216–17
Winter Minestrone, 93
Cellophane noodles
    Chinese-Style Chicken Salad, 81
    Thai Sweet-Chili Shrimp Rolls, 286
Channa dahl
    Curried Lentil-Stuffed Delicata
        Squash, 214
Cheddar cheese
    Apple, Leek, and Cheddar Quiche,
        262
    Caramelized Cabbage and Onion
        Tart, 256
    Carrot Spoon Bread, 225
    Cheesy Mac with Root Vegetables,
        246–47
    Creamy Fish Pie, 276–77
    Gratin of Turnips and Rutabagas,
        190
    Potato-Carrot Tart, 177
    Potato-Leek Frittata, 229

Rumbledethump, 231
Rutabaga Squares, 187
Savory Winter-Vegetable Bread
    Pudding, 235
Stuffed Sweet Dumplings, 193
Twice-Baked Stuffed Potatoes, 178
Vegetarian Twice-Baked Potatoes,
    178
Cheese. See also specific kinds
    Ravioli with Smoky Greens, 345
    Tortellini with Kale, 252
    Vegetarian Ravioli with Greens, 345
    Winter Pasta Salad with Red
        Cabbage and Carrot, 80
Chèvre. See Goat cheese
Chicken
    Balsamic Chicken with Vegetables,
        292
    Chicken and Barley Pilaf with
        Winter Vegetables, 301
    Chicken and Brussels Sprouts Stir-
        Fry, 304
    Chicken and Rice with Winter
        Vegetables, 293
    Chicken Broth, 127
    Chicken in Red Wine with Root
        Vegetables, 296–97
    Chicken Noodle Soup, 97
    Chicken Paella, 300
    Chicken Pot Pie with Biscuit
        Topping, 299
    Chicken Pot Pie with Sweet-Potato
        Biscuits, 298–99
    Chicken Sauté with Brussels
        Sprouts, 303
    Chicken Soup with Rice, 98
    Chicken Stew with Root
        Vegetables, 294–95
    Chinese Cabbage and Chicken
        Stir-Fry, 306–7
    Chinese-Style Chicken Salad, 81

Chicken (*continued*)
Lemon-Braised Chicken with Turnips, 309
Orzo with Kale, Chicken, and Feta Cheese, 308
Red-Cooked Chicken with Turnips, 310–11
Rigatoni with Tomato-Braised Chicken and Root Vegetables, 302
Roasted Chicken with Root Vegetables, 291
Spicy Black Bean Brussels Sprout and Chicken Stir-Fry, 305
Spicy Meat Lo Mein, 335
Chickpeas. *See also* Beans, dried
African Sweet-Potato Stew, 263
Curried Rice Salad with Mango Chutney Dressing, 78–79
Pasta with Kale and Chickpeas, 250
Vegetable Couscous, 253
Chili Beans, 206
Chinese cabbage. *See* Cabbage
Chinese chile paste with garlic, 65
Chinese Steamed Greens, 155
Chinese-Style Chicken Salad, 81
Chinese Vegetable Pickles, 82
Chipotle chiles
Black Beans in Chipotle Sauce, 203
Chili Beans, 206
Chipotle-Cabbage Salad, 57
Quick Spicy-Sweet Barbecued Beans, 209
Refried Pinto Beans, 210
Smoky Black Bean Soup, 122
Smoky Black Bean Soup with Sausage, 122
Spicy-Sweet Barbecued Beans, 209
Vegetarian Baked Beans, 207
Chocolate-Chip Pumpkin Loaf, 362
Choucroute Garni, 340–41

Cider-Braised Sweet Potatoes with Apples, 184
Clams
Clam Pot Pie, 282–83
Seafood Boil, 280
Classic American Coleslaw, 50
Clementines
Brussels Sprouts and Citrus Salad, 49
Festive Fruity Coleslaw, 55
North African Turnip Salad, 73
Coconut & coconut milk
Coconut Curried Winter Squash Soup I, 120
Coconut Curried Winter Squash Soup II, 121
Coconut-Pumpkin Pie, 361
Thai Coconut Curry with Shrimp, 275
Cod. *See also* Fish
Creamy Fish Pie, 276–77
Coleslaw. *See* Salads
Collard greens
African Sweet-Potato Stew, 263
basic information, 8–9
Caldo Gallego, 110
Garlic-Crumbed Greens, 153
Japanese-Style Greens with Tofu, 240
Lentils and Greens, 213
Mashed Potatoes with Greens, 170
Parmesan Greens, 154
Pasta with Kale, Sausage, and Tomatoes, 346
Sautéed Collard Greens, 157
Sautéed Greens with Apple Cider Vinegar, 151
Southern-Style Rice with Collard Greens, 220
Cooking ideas. See also specific vegetables
beets, 25

Brussels sprouts, 5
cabbages, 7
carrots, 26–27
celery root, 28
collard greens, 9
dried beans, 39
garlic, 14
Jerusalem artichokes, 19
kale, 10
leeks, 15
mustard greens, 11
onions, 17
parsnips, 29
potatoes, 20–21
rutabagas, 30
salsify, 32
shallots, 17
sweet potatoes, 22
turnips, 35
winter squashes, 36–37
Copper Coins, 62
Corned beef
New England Boiled Dinner, 326–27
Reuben Pie, 325
Cornmeal
Carrot Spoon Bread, 225
Cornmeal-Crisped Brussels Sprouts, 140
Garden Cornbread, 351
Couscous
Couscous Salad with Kale and Feta, 76
Vegetable Couscous, 253
Cranberries, dried
Festive Fruity Coleslaw, 55
Roasted Sweet-Potato Salad with Sesame-Ginger Vinaigrette, 72
Wild Rice Salad with Roasted Squash and Fennel, 77
Cream-Braised Brussels Sprouts, 143
Creamed Celery Root Soup, 105

Cream of Garlic Soup, 106
Creamy Coleslaw, 52
Creamy Fish Pie, 276–77
Creamy Mustard Coleslaw, 51
Creamy Potato-Leek Soup, 116
Crisp Roasted Jerusalem Artichokes, 159
Crispy Kale Chips, 158
Crunchy Dilled Coleslaw, 53
Crunchy Roasted Brussels Sprouts, 139
Curry
    Coconut Curried Winter Squash Soup I, 120
    Coconut Curried Winter Squash Soup II, 121
    Curried Dahl, 211
    Curried Lentil-Stuffed Delicata Squash, 214
    Curried Potato-Carrot Soup, 114
    Curried Rice Salad with Mango Chutney Dressing, 78–79

D

Daikon radish
    Chinese Cabbage and Chicken Stir-Fry, 306–7
    Chinese-Style Chicken Salad, 81
    Chinese Vegetable Pickles, 82
    Hot-and-Sour Soup, 100–1
    Mushroom Lo Mein, 242–43
    Sesame Noodle Salad, 75
    Soba Noodle Salad, 74
    Spicy Meat Lo Mein, 335
    Thai Sweet-Chili Shrimp Rolls, 286
    Thai Vegetable Salad, 64
    Vegetarian Lo Mein with Spicy Tofu, 238–39
    Winter Vegetable Nori Rolls, 218–19

Delicata squash, 37. See also Winter squashes
    Apple-Braised Delicata Squash, 194
    Curried Lentil-Stuffed Delicata Squash, 214
Desserts
    Applesauce, 354–55
    Applesauce Crumb Cake, 356
    Carrot Cake with Cream Cheese Frosting, 360
    Chocolate-Chip Pumpkin Loaf, 362
    Coconut-Pumpkin Pie, 361
    Maple-Apple Tea Cake, 357
    Marbled Pumpkin Cheesecake, 363
Dilled Potato and Egg Salad, 71
Dinosaur kale. See Kale
Dried beans. See Beans, dried
Duck
    Roasted and Braised Duck with Sauerkraut and Root Vegetables, 315
    Roasted Stuffed Duck with Roasted Vegetables, 316–17

E

East-Meets-West Braised Red Cabbage, 149
Egg noodles
    Chicken Noodle Soup, 97
Egg rolls
    Shrimp Egg Rolls, 284–85
    Vegetarian Egg Rolls, 236–37
Eggs
    Braised Kale on Toast, 347
    Dilled Potato and Egg Salad, 71
    Hot-and-Sour Soup, 100–1
    Lemon Aioli, 181

Mushroom Lo Mein, 242–43
Potato-Leek Frittata, 229
    Sweet-Potato and Goat Cheese Frittata, 230
    Vermont Sugarmaker's Supper, 232–33
Endive. See also Belgian Endive
    Endive and Apple Salad with Candied Nuts and Blue Cheese, 68

F

Fennel
    Baked Carrots and Fennel in Béchamel, 150
    Baked Root Vegetables and Fennel in Béchamel, 150
    Vegetable Broth, 126
    Wild Rice Salad with Roasted Squash and Fennel, 77
Festive Fruity Coleslaw, 55
Feta cheese
    Couscous Salad with Kale and Feta, 76
    Kale-Feta Pie, 258
    Lahanosalata, 58
    Lamb and Leek Flatbread, 334
    Orzo with Kale, Chicken, and Feta Cheese, 308
Fettuccine with Caramelized Cabbage, White Beans, and Goat Cheese, 249
Fish. See also Shellfish
    Creamy Fish Pie, 276–77
    Mediterranean Fish on a Bed of Rice and Leeks, 278
    Mustard-Molasses Roasted Salmon and Vegetables, 270
    Oven-Roasted Salmon and Vegetables with Lemon Aioli, 269

Fish *(continued)*
Pan-Seared Tuna with Potatoes and Anchovy-Shallot Vinaigrette, 272–73
Saffron Fish Stew, 271
Winter Fish Tacos, 274
Five-Spice Pork and Cabbage Stir-Fry, 336–37
Frittatas
Potato-Leek Frittata, 229
Sweet-Potato and Goat Cheese Frittata, 229
Frizzled-Kale Pizza, 260

G

Garlic
Balsamic Chicken with Vegetables, 292
basic information, 12–14
Braised Beef Rigatoni, 328
Chicken in Red Wine with Root Vegetables, 296–97
Cream of Garlic Soup, 106
Garlic-Crumbed Greens, 153
Garlic-Crumbed Roasted Brussels Sprouts, 141
Mustard-Braised Short Ribs with Root Vegetables, 324
Oven-Braised Sausage and Vegetables, 342
Pasta with Tomato-Braised Root Vegetables, 244–45
Polenta with Tomato-Braised Root Vegetables, 245
Potato-Garlic Soup, 115
Rigatoni with Tomato-Braised Chicken and Root Vegetables, 302
Roasted Vegetable Salad, 43

Spaghetti Squash Chowder, 119
Vermont Sugarmaker's Supper, 232–33
Garnishing, 173
Gilfeather turnips, 33
Gingered Purée of Root Vegetables, 135
Goat cheese
Beet and Napa Cabbage Salad with Goat Cheese, 45
Fettuccine with Caramelized Cabbage, White Beans, and Goat Cheese, 249
Leek and Goat Cheese Pizza, 261
Lentil Salad with Carrots and Goat Cheese, 66
Sweet-Potato and Goat Cheese Frittata, 230
Winter-Vegetable Pie, 257
Golden Carrot Risotto, 215
Golden nugget squash. *See also* Winter squashes
Baked Winter Squash, 195
Gratin of Turnips and Rutabagas, 190
Greens, 3–11. *See also specific kinds*
Caldo Gallego, 110
Lentils and Greens, 213
Ravioli with Smoky Greens, 345
Roasted Vegetable Salad, 43
Stir-Fried Pork with Hearty Greens, 338
using interchangeably, 4
Vegetarian Ravioli with Greens, 345
Gruyère cheese
Braised Celery Root Gratin, 152
Gratin of Turnips and Rutabagas, 190
Potato-Carrot Tart, 177
Reuben Pie, 325

H

Ham
Southern-Style Rice with Collard Greens, 220
Harvard Beets, 137
Hasselback Potatoes, 175
Hearty greens. *See* Greens; *specific kinds*
Hoisin sauce, 65
Honey-Balsamic Roasted Parsnips, 162
Horseradish, 327
Hot-and-Sour Soup, 100–1
Hot German Potato Salad with Sauerkraut, 179
Hot Slaw, 147
Hubbard squash, 37–38. See also Baby blue hubbard squash; Winter squashes
Baked Winter Squash, 195

I

Ingredients, Asian, 65
Inulin, 19, 31
Italian Wedding Soup, 107

J

Japanese-Style Greens with Tofu, 240
Jerusalem artichokes. *See also* Tubers
basic information, 18–19
Crisp Roasted Jerusalem Artichokes, 159
Oven-Braised Sausage and Vegetables, 342

K

Kale
basic information, 9–10
Braised Kale on Toast, 347
Braised Turkey on a Bed of Kale, 314
Caldo Gallego, 110
Chicken Noodle Soup, 97
Couscous Salad with Kale and Feta, 76
Crispy Kale Chips, 158
Frizzled-Kale Pizza, 260
Garlic-Crumbed Greens, 153
Italian Wedding Soup, 107
Japanese-Style Greens with Tofu, 240
Kale-Feta Pie, 258
Kale Pizza, 259
Kale-Ricotta Cannelloni, 251
Lentils and Greens, 213
Mashed Potatoes with Greens, 170
Miso Noodle Bowl, 112–13
Orzo with Kale, Chicken, and Feta Cheese, 308
Parmesan Greens, 154
Pasta with Kale and Chickpeas, 250
Pasta with Kale and Sausage, 344
Pasta with Kale, Sausage, and Tomatoes, 346
Portuguese Kale Soup, 108
Ravioli with Smoky Greens, 345
Sausage with Kale and White Beans, 343
Sautéed Greens with Apple Cider Vinegar, 151
Shrimp and Kale Sauté, 279
Sichuan-Style Stir-Fried Greens, 156

Stir-Fried Pork with Hearty Greens, 338
Tortellini with Kale, 252
Tuscan White Bean and Kale Soup, 109
Vegetarian Ravioli with Greens, 345
Wilted Kale Salad, 70
Winter Minestrone, 93
Kasha Varnishkes, 224
Kathleen Pemble's Winter Squash, 198
Kidney beans
Chili Beans, 206
Quick Spicy-Sweet Barbecued Beans, 209
Spicy-Sweet Barbecued Beans, 209
Kohlrabi, 32

L

Lacinato kale. *See also* Kale
Italian Wedding Soup, 107
Shrimp and Kale Sauté, 279
Lahanosalata, 58
Lamb
Lamb and Leek Flatbread, 334
Lamb Stew with Root Vegetables, 329
Shepherd's Pie, 332–33
Leeks
Apple, Leek, and Cheddar Quiche, 262
Apple-Squash Bisque, 118
basic information, 14–15
Beef Broth, 125
Chicken and Rice with Winter Vegetables, 293
Chicken Paella, 300
Chicken Pot Pie with Biscuit Topping, 299

Chicken Pot Pie with Sweet-Potato Biscuits, 298–99
Creamed Celery Root Soup, 105
Creamy Potato-Leek Soup, 116
Hot-and-Sour Soup, 100–1
Lamb and Leek Flatbread, 334
Leek and Goat Cheese Pizza, 261
Leek Risotto, 221
Leek Soup with Carrots and Parsnips, 111
Mediterranean Fish on a Bed of Rice and Leeks, 278
Moules Marinière with Leeks, 281
Mushroom Broth, 124
Oven-Braised Leeks, 160
Potato-Leek Frittata, 229
Root Vegetable Scampi over Linguine, 248
Saffron Fish Stew, 271
Sautéed Shredded Vegetables, 131
Sesame Nooodle Salad, 75
Shepherd's Pie, 332–33
Shredded Root-Vegetable Linguine, 248
Stuffed Sweet Dumplings, 193
Sunshine Turkey, 312
Tomato-Leek Soup, 123
Tomato-Leek Soup with Sausage, 123
Udon with Bok Choy and Tofu, 102
Vegetable Broth, 126
Vegetarian Creamed Celery Root Soup, 105
Vegetarian Udon with Bok Choy and Tofu, 102
White Lasagna with Leeks and Butternut Squash, 254–55
Lemons
Lemon Aioli, 181
Lemon-Braised Chicken with Turnips, 309

Lemons (*continued*)
    Lemony Barley-Carrot Pilaf, 223
    Lemony Brussels Sprouts, 145
    Zesty Lemon Coleslaw, 56
Lentils. *See also* Beans, dried
    Curried Dahl, 211
    Curried Lentil-Stuffed Delicata
        Squash, 214
    Lentil Salad with Carrots and Goat
        Cheese, 66
    Lentils and Greens, 213
    Lentil-Vegetable Soup, 96
    Mujdhara, 212
    Wheat-Berry Mujdhara, 212

M

Mahimahi
    Winter Fish Tacos, 274
Main dishes
    fish and seafood, 267–87
    meat, 319–47
    poultry, 289–317
    vegetarian, 227–65
Maple syrup
    East-Meets-West Braised Red
        Cabbage, 149
    Maple-Apple Tea Cake, 357
    Maple-Balsamic Root Vegetables,
        132
    Maple-Balsamic Vinaigrette, 89
    Maple-Candied Sweet Potatoes,
        183
    Maple-Glazed Baked Winter
        Vegetables, 134
    Maple-Soy Vinaigrette, 89
    Vermont Sugarmaker's Supper,
        232–33
Marbled Pumpkin Cheesecake, 363
Mashed-Potato Biscuits, 353

Mashed Potatoes with Caramelized
    Winter Vegetables, 234
Mashed Potatoes with Greens, 170
Mashed Sweet Potatoes, 182
Measuring
    beets, 25
    Brussel sprouts, 5
    cabbage, 7
    carrots, 27
    celery root, 28
    collard greens, 9
    dried beans, 39
    garlic, 14
    greens, 3–4
    Jerusalem artichokes, 19
    kale, 10
    leek, 15
    mustard greens, 11
    onions, 17
    parsnips, 29
    potatoes, 21
    rutabagas, 30
    salsify, 32
    shallots, 17
    sweet potatoes, 22
    turnips, 35
    winter squash, 37
Meat main dishes, 319–47
Mediterranean Fish on a Bed of Rice
    and Leeks, 278
Metric conversions, 364
Microplane graters, 87
Mirin, 65
Miso, 103
    Miso Noodle Bowl, 112–13
    Onion-Miso Soup, 113
Molasses-Mustard Vinaigrette, 88
Moules Marinière with Leeks, 281
Mozzarella cheese
    Frizzled-Kale Pizza, 260
    Kale Pizza, 259
    Kale-Ricotta Cannelloni, 251

Mujdhara, 212
Mushrooms
    Barley Vegetable Soup, 95
    Chicken and Brussels Sprouts Stir-
        Fry, 304
    Hot-and-Sour Soup, 100–1
    Mushroom Broth, 124
    Mushroom Lo Mein, 242–43
    Onion-Miso Soup, 113
    Shepherd's Pie, 332–33
    Stir-Fried Cabbage in Brown Sauce,
        148
    Udon with Bok Choy and Tofu, 102
    Vegetable Broth, 126
    Vegetarian Egg Rolls, 236–37
    Vegetarian Stir-Fried Cabbage in
        Brown Sauce, 148
    Vegetarian Udon with Bok Choy
        and Tofu, 102
Mussels
    Moules Marinière with Leeks, 281
    Seafood Boil, 280
Mustard-Braised Short Ribs with
    Root Vegetables, 324
Mustard greens
    basic information, 11
    Caldo Gallego, 110
    Chinese Steamed Greens, 155
    Garlic-Crumbed Greens, 153
    Japanese-Style Greens with Tofu,
        240
    Parmesan Greens, 154
    Pasta with Kale, Sausage, and
        Tomatoes, 346
    Ravioli with Smoky Greens, 345
    Stir-Fried Pork with Hearty
        Greens, 338
    Vegetarian Ravioli with Greens,
        345
Mustard-Molasses Roasted Salmon
    and Vegetables, 270

N

Napa cabbage. *See* Cabbage
Navy beans. *See also* Beans, dried;
    White beans
    New England Baked Beans, 208
    Sunday Supper Baked Beans, 207
    Vegetarian Baked Beans, 207
    Vegetarian New England Baked
        Beans, 208
Neeps and Tatties, 163
New England Baked Beans, 208
New England Boiled Dinner, 326–27
Noodles. *See also* Pasta
    cellophane
        Chinese-Style Chicken Salad, 81
        Thai Sweet-Chili Shrimp Rolls,
            286
    egg
        Chicken Noodle Soup, 97
    soba
        Soba Noodle Salad, 74
    udon
        Miso Noodle Bowl, 112–13
        Udon with Bok Choy and Tofu,
            102
        Vegetarian Udon with Bok Choy
            and Tofu, 102
Nori Rolls, Winter Vegetable, 218–19
North African Turnip Salad, 73
Nutrition
    cabbage family, 3
    greens, 3
    root vegetables, 24
Nuts. See also specific kinds
    Endive and Apple Salad with
        Candied Nuts and Blue
        Cheese, 68
    Wild Rice Salad with Roasted
        Squash and Fennel, 77

O

Oil, sunflower, 79
Onions
    basic information, 16–17
    Caramelized Cabbage and Onion
        Tart, 256
    Chinese Cabbage and Chicken
        Stir-Fry, 306–7
    Choucroute Garni, 340–41
    Creamy Fish Pie, 276–77
    Curried Dahl, 211
    Curried Lentil-Stuffed Delicata
        Squash, 214
    Gingered Purée of Root Vegetables,
        135
    Kasha Varnishkes, 224
    Maple-Balsamic Root Vegetables,
        132
    Maple-Glazed Baked Winter
        Vegetables, 134
    Mashed Potatoes with Caramelized
        Winter Vegetables, 234
    Mujdhara, 212
    Mustard-Braised Short Ribs with
        Root Vegetables, 324
    Onion family, basic information,
        12–17
    Onion-Miso Soup, 113
    Oven-Braised Sausage and
        Vegetables, 342
    Pasta with Tomato-Braised Root
        Vegetables, 244–45
    Polenta with Tomato-Braised Root
        Vegetables, 245
    Potato Knishes, 166
    Rigatoni with Tomato-Braised
        Chicken and Root Vegetables,
        302
    Roasted Chicken with Root
        Vegetables, 291

    Roast Pork with Sauerkraut and
        Vegetables, 339
    Rumbledethump, 231
    Savory Winter-Vegetable Bread
        Pudding, 235
    Scallop and Salsify Chowder, 117
    Seafood Boil, 280
    Spicy Black Bean Brussels Sprout
        and Chicken Stir-Fry, 305
    Turkey Broth, 126–27
    Wheat-Berry Mujdhara, 212
    Winter Fish Tacos, 274
    Winter-Vegetable Pie, 257
Orange marmalade
    Sunshine Turkey, 312
Oranges. *See also* Clementines;
        Orange marmalade;
        Tangerines
    Brussels Sprouts and Citrus Salad, 49
    Orange Vinaigrette, 87
Orzo with Kale, Chicken, and Feta
    Cheese, 308
Oven-Braised Leeks, 160
Oven-Braised Sausage and Vegetables,
    342
Oven-Roasted Salmon and Vegetables
    with Lemon Aioli, 269
Oyster sauce, 65

P

Pan-Seared Brussels Sprouts, 142
Pan-Seared Tuna with Potatoes and
        Anchovy-Shallot Vinaigrette,
        272–73
Parmesan cheese
    Braised Beef Rigatoni, 328
    Frizzled-Kale Pizza, 260
    Kale Pizza, 259
    Kale-Ricotta Cannelloni, 251
    Parmesan Greens, 154

Parmesan Cheese (continued)
Pasta Inverno, 241
Pasta with Kale and Chickpeas, 250
Pasta with Kale, Sausage, and
    Tomatoes, 346
Pasta with Tomato-Braised Root
    Vegetables, 244–45
Polenta with Tomato-Braised Root
    Vegetables, 245
Rigatoni with Tomato-Braised
    Chicken and Root Vegetables,
    302
Tortellini with Kale, 252
White Lasagna with Leeks and
    Butternut Squash, 254–55
Parsnips. See also Vegetables
Balsamic Chicken with Vegetables,
    292
basic information, 28–29
Braised Balsamic-Glazed Parsnips
    and Pears, 161
Braised Beef Rigatoni, 328
Braised Turkey Breast with Winter
    Vegetables, 313
Cheesy Mac with Root Vegetables,
    246–47
Chicken and Barley Pilaf with
    Winter Vegetables, 301
Chicken in Red Wine with Root
    Vegetables, 296–97
Chicken Soup with Rice, 98
Chicken Stew with Root
    Vegetables, 294–95
Gingered Purée of Root Vegetables,
    135
Honey-Balsamic Roasted Parsnips,
    162
Lamb Stew with Root Vegetables,
    329
Leek Soup with Carrots and
    Parsnips, 111

Maple-Glazed Baked Winter
    Vegetables, 134
Mustard-Braised Short Ribs with
    Root Vegetables, 324
Mustard-Molasses Roasted Salmon
    and Vegetables, 269
Oven-Braised Sausage and
    Vegetables, 342
Oven-Roasted Salmon and
    Vegetables with Lemon Aioli,
    269
Pasta Inverno, 241
Pasta with Tomato-Braised Root
    Vegetables, 244–45
Polenta with Tomato-Braised Root
    Vegetables, 245
Pot Roast with Root Vegetables,
    322–23
Rigatoni with Tomato-Braised
    Chicken and Root Vegetables,
    302
Roasted and Braised Duck
    with Sauerkraut and Root
    Vegetables, 315
Roasted Chicken with Root
    Vegetables, 291
Roasted Vegetable Salad, 43
Roast Pork with Sauerkraut and
    Vegetables, 339
Root Vegetable Scampi over
    Linguine, 248
Sautéed Shredded Vegetables, 131
Savory Winter-Vegetable Bread
    Pudding, 235
Shredded Root-Vegetable
    Linguine, 248
Smashed Potatoes with Root
    Vegetables, 164
Thai Coconut Curry with Shrimp,
    275
Vermont Sugarmaker's Supper,
    232–33
Winter-Vegetable Beef Stew, 321

Pasta. See also Noodles
Braised Beef Rigatoni, 328
Cheesy Mac with Root Vegetables,
    246–47
Fettuccine with Caramelized
    Cabbage, White Beans, and
    Goat Cheese, 249
Italian Wedding Soup, 107
Kale-Ricotta Cannelloni, 251
Kasha Varnishkes, 224
Mushroom Lo Mein, 242–43
Orzo with Kale, Chicken, and Feta
    Cheese, 308
Pasta e Fagioli, 94
Pasta Inverno, 241
Pasta with Kale and Chickpeas,
    250
Pasta with Kale and Sausage, 344
Pasta with Kale, Sausage, and
    Tomatoes, 346
Pasta with Tomato-Braised Root
    Vegetables, 244–45
Ravioli with Smoky Greens, 345
Rigatoni with Tomato-Braised
    Chicken and Root Vegetables,
    302
Root Vegetable Scampi over
    Linguine, 248
Salsify Scampi on Linguine, 287
Sesame Noodle Salad, 75
Shredded Root-Vegetable
    Linguine, 248
Soba Noodle Salad, 74
Spicy Meat Lo Mein, 335
Vegetarian Lo Mein with Spicy
    Tofu, 238–39
Vegetarian Ravioli with Greens,
    345
White Lasagna with Leeks and
    Butternut Squash, 254–55
Winter Minestrone, 93
Winter Pasta Salad with Red
    Cabbage and Carrot, 80

Pastries, savory
    Potato Knishes, 166
    Samosas, 165
Pea beans. *See also* Beans, dried; Navy
        beans; White beans
    New England Baked Beans, 208
    Sunday Supper Baked Beans, 207
    Vegetarian Baked Beans, 207
    Vegetarian New England Baked
        Beans, 208
Peanuts
    African Sweet-Potato Stew, 263
    Thai Cabbage Salad, 60
    Thai Sweet-Spicy Cabbage Salad,
        61
Pears, Braised Balsamic-Glazed
        Parsnips and, 161
Perogi, Potato-Stuffed, 168–69
Phyllo dough
    Kale-Feta Pie, 258
Pickles
    Chinese Vegetable Pickles, 82
    Crunchy Dilled Coleslaw, 53
    Dilled Potato and Egg Salad, 71
    Quick Ginger-Pickled Beets, 83
    Sauerkraut, 84–85
    Sweet-Pickle Coleslaw, 54
Pies and tarts
    Apple, Leek, and Cheddar Quiche,
        262
    Basic Pie Pastry, 265
    Caramelized Cabbage and Onion
        Tart, 256
    Chicken Pot Pie with Biscuit
        Topping, 299
    Chicken Pot Pie with Sweet-Potato
        Biscuits, 298–99
    Clam Pot Pie, 282–83
    Coconut-Pumpkin Pie, 361
    Creamy Fish Pie, 276–77
    Kale-Feta Pie, 258
    Potato-Carrot Tart, 177

Reuben Pie, 325
    Winter-Vegetable Pie, 257
Pinto beans. *See also* Beans, dried
    Quick Spicy-Sweet Barbecued
        Beans, 209
    Refried Pinto Beans, 210
    Spicy-Sweet Barbecued Beans, 209
Pistachio nuts
    Festive Fruity Coleslaw, 55
Pizza
    Basic Pizza Dough, 264
    Frizzled-Kale Pizza, 260
    Kale Pizza, 259
    Lamb and Leek Flatbread, 334
    Leek and Goat Cheese Pizza, 261
Polenta with Tomato-Braised Root
        Vegetables, 245
Pork
    Choucroute Garni, 340–41
    Five-Spice Pork and Cabbage Stir-
        Fry, 336–37
    Hot-and-Sour Soup, 100–1
    Italian Wedding Soup, 107
    Roast Pork with Sauerkraut and
        Vegetables, 339
    Spicy Meat Lo Mein, 335
    Stir-Fried Pork with Hearty
        Greens, 338
Portuguese Kale Soup, 108
Potatoes. *See also* Tubers
    Balsamic Chicken with Vegetables,
        292
    basic information, 20–21
    Borscht, 99
    Buttermilk Mashed Potatoes, 167
    Caldo Gallego, 110
    Choucroute Garni, 340–41
    Clam Pot Pie, 282–83
    Creamed Celery Root Soup, 105
    Cream of Garlic Soup, 106
    Creamy Fish Pie, 276–77
    Creamy Potato-Leek Soup, 116

Curried Potato-Carrot Soup, 114
Dilled Potato and Egg Salad, 71
Hasselback Potatoes, 175
Hot German Potato Salad with
    Sauerkraut, 179
Mashed-Potato Biscuits, 353
Mashed Potatoes with Caramelized
    Winter Vegetables, 234
Mashed Potatoes with Greens, 170
Mustard-Molasses Roasted Salmon
    and Vegetables, 269
Neeps and Tatties, 163
New England Boiled Dinner,
    326–27
Oven-Roasted Salmon and
    Vegetables with Lemon Aioli,
    269
Pan-Seared Tuna with Potatoes and
    Anchovy-Shallot Vinaigrette,
    272–73
Portuguese Kale Soup, 108
Potato-Carrot Tart, 177
Potatoes with Dill and Sour Cream,
    174
Potato Galette, 169
Potato-Garlic Soup, 115
Potato Knishes, 166
Potato-Leek Frittata, 229
Potato-Stuffed Perogi, 168–69
Potato Yeast Rolls, 352–53
Roasted and Braised Duck
    with Sauerkraut and Root
    Vegetables, 315
Roasted Beet and Potato Salad, 47
Roasted Spiced Potatoes, 172
Roast Pork with Sauerkraut and
    Vegetables, 339
Rosemary Roasted Potatoes, 171
Rumbledethump, 231
Saffron Fish Stew, 271
Saffron Potatoes, 173
Samosas, 165

Potatoes (continued)
  Scallop and Salsify Chowder, 117
  Seafood Boil, 280
  Shepherd's Pie, 332–33
  Smashed Potatoes with Root
    Vegetables, 164
  Spaghetti Squash Chowder, 119
  Twice-Baked Stuffed Potatoes, 178
  Two-Potato Latkes, 176
  Vegetarian Creamed Celery Root
    Soup, 105
  Vegetarian Twice-Baked Potatoes,
    178
  Vermont Sugarmaker's Supper,
    232–33
  White Bean and Cabbage Soup,
    104
  Winter-Vegetable Beef Stew, 321
Pot Roast with Root Vegetables,
  322–23
Poultry main dishes, 289–317
Preparation
  beets, 25
  Brussels sprouts, 5
  cabbage, 6–7
  carrots, 26
  celery root, 28
  collard greens, 9
  dried beans, 39
  garlic, 13–14
  greens, 3
  Jerusalem artichokes, 19
  kale, 10
  leeks, 15
  mustard greens, 11
  onions, 16–17
  parsnips, 29
  potatoes, 20
  rutabagas, 30
  salsify, 32
  shallots, 17
  sweet potatoes, 22

  turnips, 35
  winter squashes, 36
Puff pastry
  Potato Knishes, 166
  Samosas, 165
Pumpkins, 38. See also Winter
  squashes
  Almond-Squash Quick Bread, 359
  Chocolate-Chip Pumpkin Loaf,
    362
  Coconut-Pumpkin Pie, 361
  Marbled Pumpkin Cheesecake,
    363
  Pumpkin Waffles, 358
  seeds, toasting, 139

Quick Black Bean, Sweet Potato, and
  Chorizo Stew, 205
Quick Ginger-Pickled Beets, 83
Quick Spicy-Sweet Barbecued Beans,
  209

Ravioli
  Ravioli with Smoky Greens, 345
  Vegetarian Ravioli with Greens,
    345
Red cabbage. See Cabbages
Red-Cooked Chicken with Turnips,
  310–311
Red kale. See Kale
Red kuri squash, 38. See also Winter
  squashes
  Baked Winter Squash, 195
  Whipped Winter Squash, 197
  Winter Squash with Caramelized
    Apples, 199

Refried Pinto Beans, 210
Reuben Pie, 325
Rice
  Chicken and Rice with Winter
    Vegetables, 293
  Chicken Paella, 300
  Chicken Soup with Rice, 98
  Curried Rice Salad with Mango
    Chutney Dressing, 78–79
  Golden Carrot Risotto, 215
  Leek Risotto, 221
  Mediterranean Fish on a Bed of
    Rice and Leeks, 278
  Mujdhara, 212
  Risotto with Butternut Squash, 222
  Southern-Style Rice with Collard
    Greens, 220
  Stuffed Cabbage Rolls, 330–31
  Winter Vegetable Nori Rolls,
    218–19
Rice wine, 65
Ricotta cheese
  Kale-Ricotta Cannelloni, 251
  Pasta with Kale and Chickpeas, 250
Rigatoni with Tomato-Braised
    Chicken and Root Vegetables,
    302
Risotto with Butternut Squash, 222
Roasted Beet and Potato Salad, 47
Roasted and Braised Duck with
    Sauerkraut and Root
    Vegetables, 315
Roasted Chicken with Root
    Vegetables, 291
Roasted Spiced Potatoes, 172
Roasted Stuffed Duck with Roasted
    Vegetables, 316–17
Roasted Sweet-Potato Salad with
    Sesame-Ginger Vinaigrette, 72
Roasted Vegetable Salad, 43
Roasting vegetables, 364–65
Roast Pork with Sauerkraut and
    Vegetables, 339

Root vegetables. *See also* Vegetables; *specific kinds*
Baked Root Vegetables and Fennel in Béchamel, 150
Baked Root Vegetables in Béchamel, 136
basic information, 23–35
Braised Turkey Breast with Winter Vegetables, 313
Cheesy Mac with Root Vegetables, 246–47
Chicken in Red Wine with Root Vegetables, 296–97
Chicken Stew with Root Vegetables, 294–95
in Europe, viii
Gingered Purée of Root Vegetables, 135
Maple-Balsamic Root Vegetables, 132
Maple-Glazed Baked Winter Vegetables, 134
Mustard-Braised Short Ribs with Root Vegetables, 324
Mustard-Molasses Roasted Salmon and Vegetables, 269
Oven-Roasted Salmon and Vegetables with Lemon Aioli, 269
Pasta Inverno, 241
Pasta with Tomato-Braised Root Vegetables, 244–45
Polenta with Tomato-Braised Root Vegetables, 245
Pot Roast with Root Vegetables, 322–23
Roasted and Braised Duck with Sauerkraut and Root Vegetables, 315
Roasted Chicken with Root Vegetables, 291
roasting, 23

Roast Pork with Sauerkraut and Vegetables, 339
Root Vegetable Scampi over Linguine, 248
Sautéed Shredded Vegetables, 131
Shredded Root-Vegetable Linguine, 248
Smashed Potatoes with Root Vegetables, 164
Thai Coconut Curry with Shrimp, 275
Vermont Sugarmaker's Supper, 232–33
Rosemary Roasted Potatoes, 171
Rumbledethump, 231
Russian kale. *See* Kale
Rutabagas, 133. *See also* Vegetables
Balsamic Chicken with Vegetables, 292
basic information, 29–30
Braised Turkey Breast with Winter Vegetables, 313
Cheesy Mac with Root Vegetables, 246–47
Chicken and Barley Pilaf with Winter Vegetables, 301
Chicken and Rice with Winter Vegetables, 293
Chicken in Red Wine with Root Vegetables, 296–97
Chicken Pot Pie with Biscuit Topping, 299
Chicken Pot Pie with Sweet-Potato Biscuits, 298–99
Chicken Stew with Root Vegetables, 294–95
Gingered Purée of Root Vegetables, 135
Gratin of Turnips and Rutabagas, 190
Lamb Stew with Root Vegetables, 329

Lemon-Braised Chicken with Turnips, 309
Lentil-Vegetable Soup, 96
Maple-Balsamic Root Vegetables, 132
Maple-Glazed Baked Winter Vegetables, 134
Mustard-Braised Short Ribs with Root Vegetables, 324
Mustard-Molasses Roasted Salmon and Vegetables, 269
Neeps and Tatties, 163
New England Boiled Dinner, 326–27
Oven-Braised Sausage and Vegetables, 342
Oven-Roasted Salmon and Vegetables with Lemon Aioli, 269
Pasta Inverno, 241
Pasta with Tomato-Braised Root Vegetables, 244–45
Polenta with Tomato-Braised Root Vegetables, 245
Pot Roast with Root Vegetables, 322–23
Roasted and Braised Duck with Sauerkraut and Root Vegetables, 315
Roasted Chicken with Root Vegetables, 291
Roasted Vegetable Salad, 43
Roast Pork with Sauerkraut and Vegetables, 339
Root Vegetable Scampi over Linguine, 248
Rutabaga Chips, 186–87
Rutabaga Squares, 187
Sautéed Shredded Vegetables, 131
Shepherd's Pie, 332–33
Shredded Root-Vegetable Linguine, 248

Smashed Potatoes with Root
    Vegetables, 164
Southern-Style Mashed Rutabagas
    or Turnips, 185
Thai Coconut Curry with Shrimp,
    275
Vegetable Couscous, 253
Vermont Sugarmaker's Supper,
    232–33
Winter-Vegetable Beef Stew, 321
World Championship Rutabaga
    Curl, 237

∫

Saffron Fish Stew, 271
Saffron Potatoes, 173
Salad dressings
    Maple-Balsamic Vinaigrette, 89
    Maple-Soy Vinaigrette, 89
    Molasses-Mustard Vinaigrette, 88
    Orange Vinaigrette, 87
    Sesame-Ginger Vinaigrette, 88
    Walnut Vinaigrette, 86
Salads, 41–89
    Beet and Napa Cabbage Salad with
        Goat Cheese, 45
    Beets in Sour Cream, 44
    Brussels Sprouts and Citrus Salad,
        49
    Carrot-Mustard Slaw, 56
    Carrots in Citrus Vinaigrette, 63
    Celery Root, Apple, and Walnut
        Salad, 67
    Chipotle-Cabbage Salad, 57
    Classic American Coleslaw, 50
    Copper Coins, 62
    Couscous Salad with Kale and
        Feta, 76
    Creamy Coleslaw, 52
    Creamy Mustard Coleslaw, 51

Crunchy Dilled Coleslaw, 53
Dilled Potato and Egg Salad, 71
Endive and Apple Salad with
    Candied Nuts and Blue
    Cheese, 68
Festive Fruity Coleslaw, 55
Hot German Potato Salad with
    Sauerkraut, 179
Lahanosalata, 58
Lentil Salad with Carrots and Goat
    Cheese, 66
North African Turnip Salad, 73
Roasted Beet and Potato Salad, 47
Roasted Sweet-Potato Salad with
    Sesame-Ginger Vinaigrette, 72
Roasted Vegetable Salad, 43
Sesame Noodle Salad, 75
Soba Noodle Salad, 74
Soy-Sesame Cabbage Salad, 59
Sweet-Pickle Coleslaw, 54
Thai Cabbage Salad, 60
Thai Sweet-Spicy Cabbage Salad,
    61
Thai Vegetable Salad, 64
Wild Rice Salad with Roasted
    Squash and Fennel, 77
Wilted Brussels Sprouts Salad, 48
Wilted Cabbage Salad, American
    Style, 46
Wilted Cabbage Salad, Italian
    Style, 46
Wilted Kale Salad, 70
Winter Pasta Salad with Red
    Cabbage and Carrot, 80
Zesty Lemon Coleslaw, 56
Salmon
    Mustard-Molasses Roasted Salmon
        and Vegetables, 270
    Oven-Roasted Salmon and
        Vegetables with Lemon Aioli,
        269

Salsify. *See also* Vegetables
    basic information, 31–32
    Braised Turkey Breast with Winter
        Vegetables, 313
    Butter-Braised Salsify, 188
    Cheesy Mac with Root Vegetables,
        246–47
    Chicken and Barley Pilaf with
        Winter Vegetables, 301
    Chicken in Red Wine with Root
        Vegetables, 296–97
    Maple-Glazed Baked Winter
        Vegetables, 134
    Mustard-Braised Short Ribs with
        Root Vegetables, 324
    Mustard-Molasses Roasted Salmon
        and Vegetables, 269
    Oven-Roasted Salmon and
        Vegetables with Lemon Aioli,
        269
    Pasta Inverno, 241
    Roasted and Braised Duck
        with Sauerkraut and Root
        Vegetables, 315
    Roasted Chicken with Root
        Vegetables, 291
    Roast Pork with Sauerkraut and
        Vegetables, 339
    Root Vegetable Scampi over
        Linguine, 248
    Salsify Fritters, 189
    Salsify Mash, 188
    Salsify Scampi on Linguine, 287
    Sautéed Shredded Vegetables, 131
    Scallop and Salsify Chowder, 117
    Shredded Root-Vegetable
        Linguine, 248
    Smashed Potatoes with Root
        Vegetables, 164
    Thai Coconut Curry with Shrimp,
        275
    Vermont Sugarmaker's Supper,
        232–33

Salsify Scampi on Linguine, 287
Samosas, 165
Sauerkraut, 84–85
　Choucroute Garni, 340–41
　Hot German Potato Salad with
　　Sauerkraut, 179
　Reuben Pie, 325
　Roasted and Braised Duck
　　with Sauerkraut and Root
　　Vegetables, 315
　Roast Pork with Sauerkraut and
　　Vegetables, 339
Sausage
　Black Bean, Sweet Potato, and
　　Chorizo Stew, 205
　Cabbage and Tomato Soup, 103
　Cajun-Spiced Black Beans and
　　Sausage, 204
　Caldo Gallego, 110
　Chicken Paella, 300
　Choucroute Garni, 340–41
　Oven-Braised Sausage and
　　Vegetables, 342
　Pasta with Kale and Sausage, 344
　Pasta with Kale, Sausage, and
　　Tomatoes, 346
　Portuguese Kale Soup, 108
　Quick Black Bean, Sweet Potato,
　　and Chorizo Stew, 205
　Sausage with Kale and White
　　Beans, 343
　Seafood Boil, 280
　Smoky Black Bean Soup with
　　Sausage, 122
　Tomato-Leek Soup with Sausage,
　　123
　Tuscan White Bean and Kale Soup,
　　109
　White Bean and Cabbage Soup,
　　104
Sautéed Collard Greens, 157
Sautéed Greens with Apple Cider
　Vinegar, 150

Sautéed Shredded Vegetables, 131
Sautéed Turnips, 186
Savory Winter-Vegetable Bread
　Pudding, 235
Savoy cabbage. See Cabbage
Scallop and Salsify Chowder, 117
Scorzonera. See Salsify
Seafood Boil, 280
Sea vegetables (seaweed)
　Soba Noodle Salad, 74
　Wilted Kale Salad, 70
　Winter Vegetable Nori Rolls,
　　218–19
Sesame-Ginger Vinaigrette, 88
Sesame Noodle Salad, 75
Sesame oil, 65
Shallots. See also Onions
　Balsamic Chicken with Vegetables,
　　292
　basic information, 17
　Roasted and Braised Duck
　　with Sauerkraut and Root
　　Vegetables, 315
Shellfish. See also specific kinds
Seafood Boil
Shepherd's Pie, 332–33
Shredded Root-Vegetable Linguine,
　248
Shrimp
　Chicken Paella, 300
　Root Vegetable Scampi over
　　Linguine, 248
　Salsify Scampi on Linguine, 287
　Seafood Boil, 280
　Shrimp and Kale Sauté, 279
　Shrimp Egg Rolls, 284–85
　Thai Coconut Curry with Shrimp,
　　275
　Thai Sweet-Chili Shrimp Rolls, 286
Siberian kale. See Kale
Sichuan-Style Stir-Fried Greens, 156
Smashed Potatoes with Root
　Vegetables, 164

Smoky Black Bean Soup, 122
Smoky Black Bean Soup with Sausage,
　122
Soba Noodle Salad, 74
Soups, 91–127
　Apple-Squash Bisque, 118
　Barley Vegetable Soup, 95
　Beef Broth, 125
　Borscht, 99
　Caldo Gallego, 110
　Chicken Broth, 127
　Chicken Noodle Soup, 97
　Chicken Soup with Rice, 98
　Coconut Curried Winter Squash
　　Soup I, 120
　Coconut Curried Winter Squash
　　Soup II, 121
　Creamed Celery Root Soup, 105
　Cream of Garlic Soup, 106
　Curried Potato-Carrot Soup, 114
　Hot-and-Sour Soup, 100–1
　Italian Wedding Soup, 107
　Leek Soup with Carrots and
　　Parsnips, 111
　Lentil-Vegetable Soup, 96
　Miso Noodle Bowl, 112–13
　Mushroom Broth, 124
　Onion-Miso Soup, 113
　Pasta e Fagioli, 94
　Portuguese Kale Soup, 108
　Potato-Garlic Soup, 115
　Scallop and Salsify Chowder, 117
　Smoky Black Bean Soup, 122
　Smoky Black Bean Soup with
　　Sausage, 122
　Spaghetti Squash Chowder, 119
　Tomato-Leek Soup, 123
　Tomato-Leek Soup with Sausage,
　　123
　Turkey Broth, 126–27
　Tuscan White Bean and Kale Soup,
　　109

Soups *(continued)*
  Udon with Bok Choy and Tofu, 102
  Vegetable Broth, 126
  Vegetarian Cabbage and Tomato Soup, 103
  Vegetarian Creamed Celery Root Soup, 105
  Vegetarian Udon with Bok Choy with Tofu, 102
  White Bean and Cabbage Soup, 104
  Winter Minestrone, 93
Southern-Style Mashed Rutabagas or Turnips, 185
Southern-Style Rice with Collard Greens, 220
Soy sauce, 65
  Maple-Soy Vinaigrette, 89
  Red-Cooked Chicken with Turnips, 310–11
  Soy-Sesame Cabbage Salad, 59
Spaghetti squash, 38. *See also* Winter squashes
  Baked Spaghetti Squash, 196
  Spaghetti Squash Chowder, 119
Spicy Black Bean Brussels Sprout and Chicken Stir-Fry, 305
Spicy Meat Lo Mein, 335
Spicy-Sweet Barbecued Beans, 209
Spicy Sweet-Potato Oven Fries, 180
Spicy Turnip Stir-Fry, 192
Stir-Fried Cabbage in Brown Sauce, 148
Stir-Fried Pork with Hearty Greens, 338
Storage
  alternative methods of, 31
  beets, 25
  Brussels sprouts, 4
  cabbage, 6
  carrots, 26
  celery root, 27

collard greens, 8
dried beans, 39
garlic, 13
Jerusalem artichokes, 19
kale, 10
leeks, 15
mustard greens, 11
onions, 16
parsnips, 28
potatoes, 20
rutabagas, 30
salsify, 31
shallots, 17
sweet potatoes, 22
turnips, 34
winter squashes, 36
Stuffed Cabbage Rolls, 330–31
Stuffed Sweet Dumplings, 193
Sunday Supper Baked Beans, 207
Sunflower oil, 79
Sunflower seeds
  Crunchy Dilled Coleslaw, 53
Sunshine Turkey, 312
Sweet dumpling squash, 38. *See also* Winter squashes
  Baked Winter Squash, 195
  Stuffed Sweet Dumplings, 193
Sweet-Pickle Coleslaw, 54
Sweet potatoes. *See also* Vegetables
  African Sweet-Potato Stew, 263
  basic information, 21–22
  Black Bean, Sweet Potato, and Chorizo Stew, 205
  Chicken Pot Pie with Sweet-Potato Biscuits, 298–99
  Cider-Braised Sweet Potatoes with Apples, 184
  Maple-Candied Sweet Potatoes, 183
  Mashed Sweet Potatoes, 182
  Mustard-Molasses Roasted Salmon and Vegetables, 269

  Oven-Roasted Salmon and Vegetables with Lemon Aioli, 269
  Quick Black Bean, Sweet Potato, and Chorizo Stew, 205
  Roasted Sweet-Potato Salad with Sesame-Ginger Vinaigrette, 72
  Roast Pork with Sauerkraut and Vegetables, 339
  Spicy Sweet-Potato Oven Fries, 180
  Sweet-Potato and Goat Cheese Frittata, 230
  Two-Potato Latke, 176
Swiss cheese
  Potato-Carrot Tart, 177
  Reuben Pie, 325

T

Tangerines
  Brussels Sprouts and Citrus Salad, 49
  Festive Fruity Coleslaw, 55
  North African Turnip Salad, 73
Thai Cabbage Salad, 60
Thai Coconut Curry with Shrimp, 275
Thai Sweet-Chili Shrimp Rolls, 286
Thai Sweet-Spicy Cabbage Salad, 61
Thai Vegetable Salad, 64
Tofu
  Hot-and-Sour Soup, 100–1
  Japanese-Style Greens with Tofu, 240
  Miso Noodle Bowl, 112–13
  Onion-Miso Soup, 113
  Udon with Bok Choy and Tofu, 102
  Vegetarian Lo Mein with Spicy Tofu, 238–39
  Vegetarian Udon with Bok Choy and Tofu, 102

Tomatoes, canned, vii
  African Sweet-Potato Stew, 263
  Black Beans in Chipotle Sauce, 203
  Black Bean, Sweet Potato, and
    Chorizo Stew, 205
  Braised Beef Rigatoni, 328
  Braised Turkey on a Bed of Kale,
    314
  Cabbage and Tomato Soup, 103
  Chili Beans, 206
  Lentils and Greens, 213
  Lentil-Vegetable Soup, 96
  Pasta e Fagioli, 94
  Pasta with Kale, Sausage, and
    Tomatoes, 346
  Pasta with Tomato-Braised Root
    Vegetables, 244–45
  Polenta with Tomato-Braised Root
    Vegetables, 245
  Quick Spicy-Sweet Barbecued
    Beans, 209
  Rigatoni with Tomato-Braised
    Chicken and Root Vegetables,
    302
  Smoky Black Bean Soup, 122
  Smoky Black Bean Soup with
    Sausage, 122
  Spicy-Sweet Barbecued Beans, 209
  Stuffed Cabbage Rolls, 330–31
  Tomato-Leek Soup, 123
  Tomato-Leek Soup with Sausage,
    123
  Vegetable Couscous, 253
  Vegetarian Cabbage and Tomato
    Soup, 103
  Winter Minestrone, 93
  Tomato sauce
  Frizzled-Kale Pizza, 260
  Kale Pizza, 259
  Kale-Ricotta Cannelloni, 251
Tools
  Microplane, 87

Tortellini
  Winter Pasta Salad with Red
    Cabbage and Carrot, 80
  Tortellini with Kale, 252
Tortillas
  Winter Fish Tacos, 274
Tubers, 18–22. See also specific kinds
Tuna, Pan-Seared, with Potatoes and
    Anchovy-Shallot Vinaigrette,
    272–73
Turban squash, 38. See also Winter
    squashes
  Baked Winter Squash, 195
Turkey
  Braised Turkey Breast with Winter
    Vegetables, 313
  Braised Turkey on a Bed of Kale,
    314
  Italian Wedding Soup, 107
  Stuffed Cabbage Rolls, 330–31
  Sunshine Turkey, 312
  Turkey Broth, 126–27
  White Bean Stew with Smoked
    Turkey, 216–17
Turnips. See also Vegetables
  basic information, 34–35
  Braised Turkey Breast with Winter
    Vegetables, 313
  Cheesy Mac with Root Vegetables,
    246–47
  Chicken and Barley Pilaf with
    Winter Vegetables, 301
  Chicken and Rice with Winter
    Vegetables, 293
  Chicken in Red Wine with Root
    Vegetables, 296–97
  Chicken Pot Pie with Biscuit
    Topping, 299
  Chicken Pot Pie with Sweet-Potato
    Biscuits, 298–99
  Chicken Stew with Root
    Vegetables, 294–95

Chinese-Style Chicken Salad, 81
Chinese Vegetable Pickles, 82
Gilfeather variety, 33
Gingered Purée of Root Vegetables,
    135
Gratin of Turnips and Rutabagas,
    190
Hot-and-Sour Soup, 100–1
Lamb Stew with Root Vegetables,
    329
Lemon-Braised Chicken with
    Turnips, 309
Maple-Glazed Baked Winter
    Vegetables, 134
Mushroom Lo Mein, 242–43
Mustard-Braised Short Ribs with
    Root Vegetables, 324
Mustard-Molasses Roasted Salmon
    and Vegetables, 269
North African Turnip Salad, 73
Oven-Braised Sausage and
    Vegetables, 342
Oven-Roasted Salmon and
    Vegetables with Lemon Aioli,
    269
Pasta Inverno, 241
Pot Roast with Root Vegetables,
    322–23
Red-Cooked Chicken with
    Turnips, 310–11
Roasted and Braised Duck
    with Sauerkraut and Root
    Vegetables, 315
Roasted Chicken with Root
    Vegetables, 291
Roast Pork with Sauerkraut and
    Vegetables, 339
Root Vegetable Scampi over
    Linguine, 248
salad variety, 34
Sautéed Shredded Vegetables, 131
Sautéed Turnips, 186

Turnips *(continued)*
Savory Winter-Vegetable Bread
Pudding, 235
Sesame Noodle Salad, 75
Shepherd's Pie, 332–33
Shredded Root-Vegetable
Linguine, 248
Smashed Potatoes with Root
Vegetables, 164
Soba Noodle Salad, 74
Southern-Style Mashed Rutabagas
or Turnips, 185
Spicy Meat Lo Mein, 335
Spicy Turnip Stir-Fry, 192
Thai Coconut Curry with Shrimp,
275
Thai Vegetable Salad, 64
Turnip Puff, 191
Vegetable Couscous, 253
Vegetarian Lo Mein with Spicy
Tofu, 238–39
Vermont Sugarmaker's Supper,
232–33
Winter-Vegetable Beef Stew, 321
Winter Vegetable Nori Rolls,
218–19
Tuscan kale. *See* Kale
Tuscan White Bean and Kale Soup,
109
Twice-Baked Stuffed Potatoes, 178
Two-Potato Latkes, 176

U

Udon noodles
Miso Noodle Bowl, 112–13
Udon with Bok Choy and Tofu,
102
Vegetarian Udon with Bok Choy
and Tofu, 102

V

Varieties
turnips, 33, 34
winter squashes, 37–38
Vegetable. *See also* specific kinds
art from, 44
basic information, 1–39
musical instruments from, 213
roasting, 364–65
side dishes, 128–99
Vegetable Broth, 126
Vegetable Couscous, 253
Vegetarian Baked Beans, 207
Vegetarian Cabbage and Tomato
Soup, 103
Vegetarian Creamed Celery Root
Soup, 105
Vegetarian Egg Rolls, 236–37
Vegetarian Lo Mein with Spicy Tofu,
238–39
Vegetarian main dishes, 227–65
Vegetarian New England Baked
Beans, 208
Vegetarian Ravioli with Greens, 345
Vegetarian Stir-Fried Cabbage in
Brown Sauce, 148
Vegetarian Twice-Baked Potatoes, 178
Vegetarian Udon with Bok Choy with
Tofu, 102
Vermont Sugarmaker's Supper,
232–33
Vinaigrette. *See* Salad dressings
Vinegar
apple cider, 146
Sautéed Greens with Apple
Cider Vinegar, 151
balsamic
Balsamic Chicken with
Vegetables, 292
Braised Balsamic-Glazed
Parsnips and Pears, 161
Honey-Balsamic Roasted
Parsnips, 162
Maple-Balsamic Root
Vegetables, 132

W

Waffles, Pumpkin, 358
Walnuts. *See also* Nuts
Celery Root, Apple, and Walnut
Salad, 67
Walnut Vinaigrette, 86
Wheat-Berry Mujdhara, 212
Whipped Winter Squash, 197
White beans. *See also* Beans, dried;
Navy beans; Pea beans
Caldo Gallego, 110
Fettuccine with Caramelized
Cabbage, White Beans, and
Goat Cheese, 249
Sausage with Kale and White
Beans, 343
Tuscan White Bean and Kale Soup,
109
White Bean and Cabbage Soup,
104
White Bean Stew with Smoked
Turkey, 216–17
Winter Minestrone, 93
White Lasagna with Leeks and
Butternut Squash, 254–55
Wild rice
Chicken Soup with Rice, 98
Wild Rice Salad with Roasted
Squash and Fennel, 77
Wilted Brussels Sprouts Salad, 48
Wilted Cabbage Salad, American
Style, 46

Wilted Cabbage Salad, Italian Style, 46

Wilted Kale Salad, 70

Winter Fish Tacos, 274

Winter Minestrone, 93

Winter Pasta Salad with Red Cabbage and Carrot, 80

Winter squashes

Almond-Squash Quick Bread, 359

Apple-Braised Delicata Squash, 194

Apple-Squash Bisque, 118

Baked Spaghetti Squash, 196

Baked Winter Squash, 195

basic information, 35–38

Braised Turkey Breast with Winter Vegetables, 313

Cheesy Mac with Root Vegetables, 246–47

Chicken and Barley Pilaf with Winter Vegetables, 301

Chocolate-Chip Pumpkin Loaf, 362

Coconut Curried Winter Squash Soup I, 120

Coconut Curried Winter Squash Soup II, 121

Coconut-Pumpkin Pie, 361

Curried Lentil-Stuffed Delicata Squash, 214

Garden Cornbread, 351

Kathleen Pemble's Winter Squash, 198

Maple-Glazed Baked Winter Vegetables, 134

Marbled Pumpkin Cheesecake, 363

Mustard-Molasses Roasted Salmon and Vegetables, 269

Oven-Roasted Salmon and Vegetables with Lemon Aioli, 269

Pasta Inverno, 241

Pumpkin Waffles, 358

Risotto with Butternut Squash, 222

Roast Pork with Sauerkraut and Vegetables, 339

seeds, toasting, 139

Spaghetti Squash Chowder, 119

Stuffed Sweet Dumplings, 193

Sunshine Turkey, 312

Thai Coconut Curry with Shrimp, 275

Vermont Sugarmaker's Supper, 232–33

Whipped Winter Squash, 197

White Lasagna with Leeks and Butternut Squash, 254–55

Winter Squash with Caramelized Apples, 199

Winter-Vegetable Beef Stew, 321

Winter Vegetable Nori Rolls, 218–19

Winter Vegetable Pie, 257

World Carrot Museum, 62

World Championship Rutabaga Curl, 237

Y

Yellow split peas

Curried Dahl, 211

Z

Zesty Lemon Coleslaw, 56

Other Storey Titles
You Will Enjoy

250 Treasured Country Desserts, by Andrea Chesman & Fran Raboff.
A nostalgic collection of more than 250 recipes for home bakers to rely on for all occasions.
416 pages. Paper. ISBN 978-1-60342-152-2.

500 Treasured Country Recipes, by Martha Storey & Friends.
Hundreds of recipes to stock your pantry and put together great meals, each one with country soul.
544 pages. Paper. ISBN 978-1-58017-291-2.

Apple Cookbook, by Olwen Woodier.
More than 140 recipes to put everyone's favorite fruit into tasty new combinations.
192 pages. Paper. ISBN 978-1-58017-389-6.

Maple Syrup Cookbook, by Ken Haedrich.
Recipes both sweet and savory that feature maple syrup and its wonderful earthy, tangy qualities.
144 pages. Paper. ISBN 978-1-58017-404-6.

Pumpkin, by DeeDee Stovel.
A wide-ranging collection of recipes, from soups to desserts and everything in between that use this nutritious orange super food.
224 pages. Paper. ISBN 978-1-58017-594-4.

Root Cellaring, by Mike and Nancy Bubel.
Suitable for city and country folks, with information on harvesting and creating cold storage anywhere — even closets! — plus 50 recipes.
320 pages. Paper. ISBN 978-0-88266-703-4.

Serving Up the Harvest, by Andrea Chesman.
A collection of 175 recipes to bring out the best in garden-fresh vegetables, with 14 master recipes that can accommodate whatever happens to be in your produce basket.
512 pages. Paper. ISBN 978-1-58017-663-7.

These and other books from Storey Publishing are available
wherever quality books are sold or by calling 1-800-441-5700.
Visit us at *www.storey.com*.